The first butterfly of spring,
Orange and purple,
Flits across my path.

A flying flower,
That changes,
The colour of my day.

Michael Bullock——Butterfly

方振宇 主编

每天读点好英文

路过心上的美文

扫一扫 听音频

北京时代华文书局

图书在版编目（CIP）数据

路过心上的美文 / 方振宇主编 .
-- 北京 : 北京时代华文书局 , 2018.1
ISBN 978-7-5699-2078-9

Ⅰ . ①路… Ⅱ . ①方… Ⅲ . ①英语－自学参考资料
Ⅳ . ① H31

中国版本图书馆 CIP 数据核字 (2017) 第 314922 号

路过心上的美文

Luguo Xinshang de Meiwen

主　　编 | 方振宇

出 版 人 | 王训海
选题策划 | 余　玲　高　磊
责任编辑 | 徐敏峰　周海燕
装帧设计 | 程　慧
责任印制 | 刘　银

出版发行 | 北京时代华文书局 http://www.bjsdsj.com.cn
北京市东城区安定门外大街 138 号皇城国际大厦 A 座 8 楼
邮编：100011　电话：010-64267955　64267677
印　　刷 | 固安县京平诚乾印刷有限公司　0316-6170166
（如发现印装质量问题，请与印刷厂联系调换）
开　　本 | 710mm×1000mm　1/16　印　　张 | 23.25　字　　数 | 357 千字
版　　次 | 2018 年 9 月第 1 版　印　　次 | 2019 年 8 月第 2 次印刷
书　　号 | ISBN 978-7-5699-2078-9
定　　价 | 49.80 元

The Lake Isle of Innisfree

I will arise and go now, and go to Innisfree,
And a small cabin build there, of clay and wattles made;
Nine bean-rows will I have there, a hive for the honey-bee,
And live alone in the bee-loud glade.

And I shall have some peace there, for peace comes dropping slow,
Dropping from the veils of the morning to where the cricket sings;
There midnight's all a glimmer, and noon a purple glow,
And evening full of the linnet's wings.

I will arise and go now, for always night and day,
I hear lake water lapping with low sounds by the shore;
While I stand on the roadway, or on the pavements grey,
I hear it in the deep heart's core.

—*William Butler Yeats*

茵湖岛

此刻我将动身前去，去那茵湖岛，
在那儿造一座小屋，由黏土和树枝搭建而成；
种下九垅豆子，为蜜蜂弄个蜂巢，
遗世独立于那片林间空地，耳闻蜂儿的高鸣。

我将在那儿享受安宁，安宁的时光缓缓滴落，
从清晨的帘幕到蟋蟀唱歌的地方；
中午，遍地阳光温暖，子夜，处处星光闪烁，
而黄昏的天地充满朱顶雀的翅膀。

此刻我将动身前去，因为多少个日夜我一直
听到湖水拍岸那喋喋不休的低语；
当我伫立在行车道，或在灰暗的人行道上时，
我听到它的声音回响在我心深处。

——威廉 巴特勒 叶芝

目录

第一篇

善心可依

第二篇

一杯牛奶的温度

第三篇

伴你一生

第四篇

浪漫路曲曲折折

第五篇

莫待花谢时

第六篇

热爱生活

第七篇

谦卑的一课

第八篇

水仙花法则

第九篇

冬日的温暖

第一篇

- 善心可依 -

1 The Apple Tree 苹果树

苹果树与小男孩之间的故事犹如我们与父母之间发生的点滴。正如小男孩习惯了接受苹果树的馈赠，我们也习惯于接受父母所提供的一切，然而又有多少人明白苹果树的悲与喜……

文苑漫步

A long time ago, there was a huge apple tree. A little boy loved to come and played around it every day. He climbed to the tree top, ate the apples, **took a nap** under the shadow... He loved the tree and the tree loved to play with him.

Time went by... the little boy had grown up and he had no longer played around the tree every day. One day, the boy came back to the tree and he looked sad. “Come and play with me,” the tree asked the boy. “I am no longer a kid. I don’t play around trees anymore.” The boy replied, “I want toys. I need money to buy them.” “Sorry, but I don’t have any money... but you can pick all my apples and sell them. So, you will have money.” The boy was so excited. He **grabbed** all

译林畅游

很久以前，有一棵又高又大的苹果树。一个小男孩，天天喜欢到树下来玩耍，他爬上树顶，摘苹果吃，在树阴下打盹……他爱苹果树，苹果树也爱和他一起玩耍。

随着时间的流逝，小男孩长大了，不再天天来玩耍。一天他来到了树下，看起来很悲伤。“来和我玩吧！”树央求男孩。“我不是小孩了，我不会再到树下玩耍了，”男孩答道，“我想要玩具，我需要钱来买。”苹果树说：“很遗憾，我没有钱，不过，你可以把我所有的果子摘下来卖掉，你就有钱买玩具了。”男孩十分激动，他摘下树上所有的苹果，高高兴兴地走了。男

the apples on the tree and left happily. The boy never came back after he picked the apples. The tree was sad.

One day, the boy returned and the tree was so excited. "Come and play with me," the tree said. "I don't have time to play. I have to work for my family. We need a house for **shelter**. Can you help me?" "Sorry, but I don't have a house. But you can **chop off** my branches to build your house." So the boy cut all the branches off the tree and left happily. The tree was glad to see him happy but the boy never came back since then. The tree was again lonely and sad.

One hot summer day, the boy returned and the tree was delighted. "Come and play with me," the tree said. "I am sad and getting old. I want to go sailing to relax myself. Can you give me a boat?" "Use my **trunk** to build your boat. You can sail far away and be happy." So the boy cut the tree trunk to make a boat. He went sailing and never **showed up** for a long time. The tree was happy, but it was not true.

Finally, the boy returned after he left for so many years. "Sorry, my boy. But I don't have anything for you anymore. No more apples for you..." the tree said.

"I don't have teeth to bite," the boy replied.

"No more trunk for you to climb on."

孩摘了苹果后便再没出现。苹果树很伤心。

一天，男孩回来了，树非常激动。"来和我玩吧！"树说。"我没有时间，我要替家里干活，我们需要一幢房子来遮风挡雨，你能帮忙吗？""很遗憾，我没有房子，"苹果树说，"不过你可以砍下我的树枝拿去建房子。"于是男孩砍下所有的树枝，高高兴兴地走了。看到男孩高兴，树很开心。但是，从那之后男孩却杳无踪影，树又孤独伤心起来。

一个炎热的夏天，男孩回来了，树高兴地说："来和我玩吧！"男孩却说："我很伤心，我一天天老去，我要扬帆出海，放松一下，你能给我一艘船吗？""用我的树干去造船吧！你可以航行到很远的地方，并且会很开心的。"于是男孩砍下了树干，造了条船，航海去了，很长时间没有露面。树看似很开心……但并非如此。

许多年后男孩终于回来了，苹果树说："对不起，孩子，我再也没有东西可以给你了。没有苹果可以给你……"

男孩说："我的牙都掉了，吃不了苹果了。"

苹果树又说："没有树干让你爬了。"

"I am too old for that now," the boy said.

"I really can't give you anything... the only thing left is my **dying** roots," the tree said with tears.

"I don't need much now, just a place to rest. I am tired after all these years," the boy replied.

"Good! Old tree roots is the best place to lean on and rest. Come, come sit down with me and rest." The boy sat down and the tree was glad and smiled with tears...

This is a story of everyone. The tree is our parent. When we were young, we loved to play with Mom and Dad... When we grew up, we left them, and only came to them when we need something or when we are in trouble. No matter what, parents will always be there and give everything they could to make you happy. You may think that the boy is cruel to the tree but that's how all of us are treating our parents.

男孩说："现在我老了，爬不上去了。"

"我再也没有什么能给你的了……只剩下将要枯死的老根，"树流着泪说。

男孩说："这么多年过去了，现在我真的感到累了，我什么也不想要，只想找一个能够休息的地方。"

"好啊！老根是最适合靠着休息的，来吧，坐下来和我一起休息吧！"男孩坐下来，苹果树很高兴，流下了喜悦的泪水。

这是一个发生在每一个人身上的故事。这棵树就是我们的父母。小时候，我们喜欢和爸爸妈妈玩……长大后，我们就离开了他们，只在需要什么东西或者遇到麻烦的时候，才回到他们身边。无论如何，父母总是有求必应，为了我们的幸福，无私奉献自己所拥有的一切。你也许觉得那个男孩对树很残忍，然而那确实是我们所有人对待父母的方式。

魅力词汇

take a nap 小睡一会儿，睡午觉

shelter ['ʃeltə] *n.* 避难所

trunk [trʌŋk] *n.* 树干

dying ['daiiŋ] *adj.* 垂死的

grab [græb] *v.*（匆匆地）取或拿

chop off 砍掉

show up 露面

2 We're Raising Children, Not Flowers
我们是在养小孩，而不是在养花

或许在这个世界上很流行的观念就是：事情远比人重要。所以在我们的教育中往往采用严厉的方式来促使孩子达到完美，其实通往完美的途径往往不是这个，看看接下来的几个小故事，或许我们有所启发……

文苑漫步

David, my next-door neighbor, has two young kids aged 5 and 7. One day he was teaching his 7-year-old son Kelly how to push the **lawn mower** around the yard. As he was teaching him how to turn the mower around at the end of the lawn, his wife, Jan, called to ask him a question. As David turned to answer the question, Kelly pushed the lawn mower right through the flower bed at the edge of the lawn — leaving a two-foot wide path **leveled to the ground**!

When David turned back around and saw what had happened, he began to **lose control**. David had put a lot of time and effort into making those flower beds the envy of the neighborhood. As he began to raise his voice to his son, Jan walked

译林畅游

我的邻居David有两个孩子，一个5岁，另一个7岁。一天，David正在庭院里教他7岁的儿子Kelly如何使用割草机。当教到怎样在草坪尽头将割草机掉头时，他的妻子Jan喊他，询问一些事情。当David转过身回答Jan的问题时，Kelly却把割草机从草坪边的花圃上径直推了过去——结果原本美丽的花圃留下了一条两英尺宽的平地小径。

当David转过身，看到所发生的事情时，变得怒不可遏。这个花圃花费了David多少时间和精力才弄成今天这个令邻居们无比羡慕的样子呀！正当他提高嗓门准备训斥Kelly时，Jan快步走到他身边，

quickly over to him, put her hand on his shoulder and said, "David, please, remember... we're raising children, not flowers!"

Jan reminded me how important it is as a parent to remember our **priorities**. Kids and their **self-esteem** are more important than any physical object they might break or destroy. The window **pane shattered** by a baseball, a lamp knocked over by a careless child, or a plate dropped in the kitchen are already broken. The flowers are already dead. We must remember not to add to the destruction by breaking a child's spirit and **deadening** his sense of liveliness.

I was buying a sport coat a few weeks ago and Mark Michaels, the owner of the store, and I were discussing parenting. He told me that while he and his wife and 7-year-old daughter were out for dinner, his daughter knocked over her water glass. After the water was cleaned up without any **recriminating** remarks from her parents, she looked up and said, "You know, I really want to thank you guys for not being like other parents. Most of my friends' parents would have yelled at them and given them a lecture of paying more attention. Thanks for not doing that!"

Once, when I was having dinner with some friends, a similar incident happened.

将手放在他的肩膀上，说："David，别忘了……我们是在养小孩，而不是在养花！"

Jan提醒了我：作为父母记住孰重孰轻有多么重要。孩子以及他们的自尊要比他们可能打破或损坏的任何东西都重要得多。那些曾经被孩子们的棒球砸坏的窗户、不小心碰倒的台灯以及厨房里掉在地上摔碎的碟子都是已经毁坏了的东西。花圃里被割掉的花再也不能复原，我们必须谨记不要再去伤害一个小孩的心灵，降低他们的活跃度，这样只会加重损失。

几个星期前，我去一家服装店买运动衣，跟店主Mark Michaels讨论了一些有关为人父母的问题。他跟我说了这样一件事：他和他的妻子以及他们7岁大的女儿到餐馆里吃晚餐，他的女儿不小心把水杯打翻了。他和妻子并没有责备女儿，而是把水渍擦得干干净净。女儿抬起头看着他们说："你们知道吗，我真的很感谢你们，因为你们没有像其他的父母那样。我很多朋友的父母在发生了这样的事时通常都会对孩子大嚷大叫，教训他们要多加小心，感谢你们没有跟他们一样！"

有一次，我和几位朋友共进晚餐时，同样的事情发生了。他们5

Their 5-year-old son knocked over a glass of milk at the dinner table. When they immediately started in on him, I intentionally knocked my glass over, too. When I started to explain how I still knock things over even at the age of 48, the boy started to **beam** and the parents seemingly got the message and backed off. How easy it is to forget that we are all still learning.

岁的儿子将餐桌上的一杯牛奶弄翻了。朋友夫妇开始齐声责备起他来。这时，我也故意把我的杯子碰翻了。于是我向朋友夫妇解释：我虽然48岁了，也有打翻东西的时候。男孩子愉快地微笑起来。朋友夫妇似乎明白了我的意思，语气也缓和了下来。我们是多么容易忘记我们仍需要不断学习呀！

I recently heard a story about a famous research scientist who had made several very important medical breakthroughs. He was being interviewed by a newspaper reporter who asked him why he thought he was able to be so much more creative than the average person.

最近，我听到了一个关于一位著名科学家的故事。这位科学家在医学领域曾有过几项十分重要的发现和突破。有个报社记者曾经采访过他，询问他为什么认为自己会比一般人更有创造力。

He responded that, in his opinion, it all came from an experience with his mother that occurred when he was about 2 years old. He had been trying to remove a bottle of milk from the refrigerator when he lost his grip on the **slippery** bottle and it fell, spilling all its contents all over the kitchen floor — a **veritable** sea of milk!

他说，在他看来，这一切都与他 2 岁左右时和母亲在一起的一次经历有关。当时他自己尝试着从冰箱里拿一瓶牛奶。可是瓶子太滑了，他没有抓住，牛奶瓶子掉在了地上，牛奶溅满了厨房的地板——看上去简直是一片牛奶的海洋。

When his mother came into the kitchen, instead of **yelling at** him, giving him a lecture or punishing him, she said, "Robert, what a great and wonderful mess you have made! I have rarely seen such a huge puddle of milk. Well, the damage has already been done. Would you like to

他的母亲闻声跑到厨房里来，可并没有对他大叫大嚷，也没有教训或惩罚他，只是说："Robert！你制造的麻烦可真是棒极了！我还从来没有见过这么大的一汪牛奶呢！哎，反正牛奶已经撒了，那么在把它打扫干净之前，你想不想在牛奶

get down and play in the milk for a few minutes before we clean it up?"

Indeed, he did. After a few minutes, his mother said, "You know, Robert, whenever you make a mess like this, eventually you have to clean it up and **restore** everything to its proper order. So, how would you like to do that? We could use a **sponge**, a towel or a **mop**. Which do you prefer?" He chose the sponge and together they cleaned up the **spilled** milk.

His mother then said, "You know, what we have here is a failed experiment in how to effectively carry a big milk bottle with two tiny hands. Let's go out to the back yard and fill the bottle with water and see if you can discover a way to carry it without dropping it." The little boy learned that if he grasped the bottle at the top near the lip with both hands, he could carry it without dropping it. What a wonderful lesson!

This **renowned** scientist then remarked that it was at that moment that he knew he didn't need to be afraid to make mistakes. Instead, he learned that mistakes were just opportunities for learning something new, which is, after all, what scientific experiments are all about. Even if the experiment doesn't work, we usually learn

里玩几分钟呢？"

事实上，他立即在牛奶中玩了起来。几分钟后，母亲对他说道："Robert，你知道吗，无论什么时候，你制造了像今天这样又脏又乱的场面，最后都必须把它打扫干净，并且要把每件东西按原样放好。那么你打算怎么收拾呢？我们可以用海绵、毛巾或者是拖把。你想用哪一种呢？"他选择了海绵。接着，他们就一起将那满地的牛奶打扫干净了。

然后，他的母亲说道："你知道吗，你做的用你的两只小手拿起大牛奶瓶子的试验已经失败了。现在我们到后院去，将瓶子装满水，看看你有没有办法把瓶子拿起来，而不让瓶子掉下去。"小 Robert 很快就发现，只要用双手抓住瓶子顶部靠近瓶嘴的地方，瓶子就不会从手中滑掉。这堂课真是棒极了！

这位著名的科学家补充到，他是从那刻起，懂得不必再害怕犯任何错误，因为他认识到，错误往往是学习新知识的良机。科学实验也是这样，即使实验失败了，我们还是可以从中学到很多有价值的东西。

something valuable from it.

Wouldn't it be great if all parents would respond the way Robert's mother responded to him?

One last story that illustrates the application of this attitude in adult contexts was told on the radio several years back. A young woman was driving home from work when she **snagged** her **fender** on the **bumper** of another car. She was in tears as she explained that it was a new car, only a few days from the showroom. How was she ever going to explain the damaged car to her husband?

The driver of the other car was **sympathetic**, but explained that they must note each other's license numbers and **registration numbers**. As the young woman reached into a large brown envelope to **retrieve** the documents, a piece of paper fell out. In a heavy **masculine scrawl** were these words: "In case of accident... remember, honey, it's you I love, not the car!"

Let's remember that our children's spirits are more important than any material things. When we do, self-esteem and love blossom will grow more beautifully than any bed of flowers ever could.

如果天下的父母都能像Robert的母亲对待Robert那样来教育子女的话，那岂不是太好了吗？

最后，还有一个几年前曾经在收音机里听到的故事，而它对于采用同样的态度处理成人之间的关系有着异曲同工之妙。一天，有个年轻的女子，在下班开车回家的路上与另外一辆车发生了碰撞，结果，她的车挡泥板被撞坏了。她泪流满面地说，这是一辆新车，刚刚从展厅买回来没几天。车撞坏了，她回家后该怎么向丈夫交代呢？

跟她相撞的那辆车的司机满怀同情，但表示他们应该记下彼此的驾驶执照号码和车牌号码。这位年轻女子从棕色的大文件袋中找寻有关文件，一张纸条这时掉了出来。只见上面用男人的厚重笔迹写着：“如果发生事故……请记住，亲爱的，我爱的是你，不是车！”

让我们牢记：孩子的心灵比任何物质的东西都重要！只要我们牢记这一点，那么自尊和爱的花朵就会比花圃中的任何花儿都更加灿烂、美丽！

魅力词汇

lawn mower 割草机
level to the ground
（将堡垒等）夷为平地
lose control 失控
priority [prai'ɔrəti]
n. 优先；优先考虑的事
self-esteem [self ɪ'stiːm] *n.* 自尊
pane [pein] *n.* 窗格；窗格玻璃
shatter ['ʃætə] *v.* 打碎
deaden ['dedən] *v.* 使减弱；使麻木
recriminate [ri'krimineit] *v.* 反责
beam [biːm] *v.* 愉快地微笑
slippery ['slipəri] *adj.* 滑的
veritable ['veritəbl]
adj. 真正的，名副其实的
yell at 对……吼叫
restore [ri'stɔː] *v.* 恢复，还原
sponge [spʌndʒ] *n.* 海绵
mop [mɔp] *n.* 拖把
spill [spil] *v.* 使溢出，使流出
renowned [ri'naund]
adj. 著名的，有声望的
snag [snæg] *v.* 划破
fender ['fendə] *n.*（汽车等的）挡泥板
bumper ['bʌmpə] *n.* 保险杠
sympathetic [ˌsimpə'θetik] *adj.* 同情的
registration number 汽车牌照号码
retrieve [ri'triːv] *v.* 检索
masculine ['mæskjulin]
adj. 男性的；男子气概的
scrawl [skrɔːl] *n.* 潦草的笔迹

温情絮语

East or west, home is best.

东好西好，还是家里最好。

A good mother is worth a hundred schoolmasters.

一个好母亲相当于百个好老师。

3 All You Remember 你所记得的一切

当孩子还是孩子时，你记得他巨大的破坏力； 当孩子不再是孩子，你惊讶于怎么所有一切都那么井然有序。当孩子还是孩子时，你苦恼于生活就是一个接一个的麻烦；当孩子不再是孩子，你苦恼于生活是如此平淡无奇……

文苑漫步

All you remember about your child being an **infant** is the incredible **awe** you felt about the precious miracle you created. You remember having plenty of time to **bestow** all your wisdom and knowledge. You thought your child would take all your advice and make fewer mistakes, and be much smarter than you were. You wished for your child to hurry and grow up.

All you remember about your child being 2 is never using the restroom alone or getting to watch a movie without talking animals. You **recall** afternoons talking on the phone while **crouching** in the bedroom closet, and being convinced your child would be the first **Ivy League** college student to graduate wearing **pullovers** at the ceremony. You remember worrying about the bag of M&M's melting in your pocket

译林畅游

当你的孩子是个婴儿时，你所记得的，是对自己创造出的堪称完美奇迹的作品，感到一种不可思议的敬畏。你记得自己用大量的时间去传授你所有的智慧和知识。你认为你的孩子会接受你所有的忠告而少犯错误，会比孩提时代的你聪明许多。你多希望孩子快快长大。

孩子 2 岁时，你所记得的，是从来都无法独自使用卫生间，和不看一部与动物无关的电影。你记得蜷缩在卧室储衣间跟朋友通电话的那些个下午，深信你的孩子将是第一个身着套头衫出席常春藤名校毕业典礼的大学生。你记得自己担心那袋 M&M's 巧克力糖在衣兜里融化，毁了体面的衣服。你多希望孩子更独立些。

and ruining your good dress. You wished for your child to be more independent.

All you remember about your child being 5 is the first day of school and finally having the house to yourself. You remember joining the **PTA** and being elected president and you left a meeting to use the restroom. You remember being asked “Is Santa real?” and saying “yes” because he had to be for a little bit longer. You remember shaking the sofa **cushions** for **loose change**, so the **toothfairy** could come and take away your child’s first lost tooth. You wished for your child to have all **permanent teeth**.

孩子5岁时，你所记得的，是他上学第一天你终于可以独自占有整个房子了。你记得参加家长教师协会，在离开会议室去洗手间时，你当选为会长。你记得被问及“圣诞老人是真的吗？”你回答“是的”，因为孩子还需要你的肯定回答，尽管不久他就能自己判断了。你记得在沙发垫子下翻腾一通要找出些零钱，这样牙齿仙女就会带走孩子掉的第一颗牙。你多希望孩子的牙都换成了恒牙。

All you remember about your child being 7 is the **carpool** schedule. You learned to apply makeup in two minutes and brush your teeth in the **rearview** mirror because the only time you had to yourself was when you were stopped at red lights. You considered painting your car yellow and posting a “taxi” sign on the lawn next to the garage door. You remember people staring at you, the few times you were out of the car, because you kept **flexing** your foot and making **acceleration** noises. You wished for the day your child would learn how to drive.

孩子7岁时，你所记得的，是合伙用车的时间安排。你学会了在两分钟内化完妆，照着汽车后视镜刷牙，因为你能给自己找出的时间就只有汽车停在红灯前的那一小会儿。你想过把车子漆成黄色，并在车库大门旁的草坪上立一块“出租车”的标志牌。你记得有几次下车后，人们盯着你，因为你不断用脚踩油门加速，制造噪音。你多希望孩子有一天能学会开车。

All you remember about your child being 10 is managing the school fund-raisers. You sold wrapping paper for paint,

孩子10岁时，你所记得的，是怎么组织学校的募捐者。你为油漆兜售包装纸，为购置新家具兜售体

T-shirts for new furniture, and magazine **subscriptions** for shade trees in the school ground. You remember storing a hundred cases of **candy bars** in the garage to sell so the school band could get new uniforms, and how they melted together on an **unseasonably** warm spring afternoon. You wished your child would grow out of playing an instrument.

恤衫，为在学校操场上种植遮阳树劝人订阅各种杂志。你记得你在车库里存放了上百盒糖果等待出售，以便为学校的乐队购置新制服，可是那些糖果竟在一个暖和得过头的春天的下午全都融化在一起了。你多希望孩子长大，不再演奏什么乐器了。

All you remember about your child being 12 is sitting in the stands during baseball practice and hoping your child's team would strike out fast because you had more important things to do at home. The coach didn't understand how busy you were. You wished the baseball season would be over soon.

孩子 12 岁时，你所记得的，是孩子在体育场打棒球练习赛时，你坐在看台上希望他所在的队很快三击不中出局，因为家里还有更重要的事等你去做。教练不明白你到底有多忙。你多希望棒球赛季能尽快结束。

All you remember about your child being 14 is being asked not to stop the car in front of the school in the morning. You had to drive two blocks further and unlock the doors without coming to a complete stop. You remember not getting to kiss your child goodbye or talking to him in front of his friends. You wished your child would be more **mature**.

孩子 14 岁时，你所记得的，是早晨他不让你把汽车停在校门口。你不得不开过两个街区，车还没停稳就赶紧打开车门。你记得没能在他的朋友面前跟他吻别和说话。你多希望孩子能更成熟些。

All you remember about your child being 16 is loud music and **undecipherable lyrics** screamed to a **rhythmic** beat. You wished for your child to grow up and leave home with the **stereo**.

孩子 16 岁时，你所记得的，是吵闹的音乐和以富有节奏的拍子尖声唱出的难以听懂的歌词。你多希望孩子快点长大成人，带着音响离开家吧。

All you remember about your child

孩子 18 岁时，你所记得的，是

being 18 is the day they were born and having all the time in the world.

And, as you walk through your quiet house, you wonder where they went and you wish your child hadn't grown up so fast.

他们出生的那一天，拥有世间所有的时光。

当你在静静的房子里走来走去时，你纳闷他们去哪里了——你多希望孩子别这么快就长大了。

魅力词汇

infant ['infənt] *n.* 婴儿
awe [ɔː] *n.* 敬畏
bestow [bi'stəu] *v.* 授予
recall [ri'kɔːl] *v.* 回想起，记起
crouch [krautʃ] *v.* 蹲伏，蜷伏
Ivy ['aivi] League
常春藤联盟；常春藤名牌大学
pullover ['pulˌəuvə] *n.* 套衫
PTA *abbr.* 家长教师协会（Parent-Teacher Association）
cushion ['kuʃn] *n.* 垫子
loose change 零钱
toothfairy 牙齿仙女
permanent tooth 恒齿，恒牙
carpool ['kaːpuːl] *n.*（轮流用私人汽车为其他成员提供接送的）合伙用车
rearview ['riəvjuː] *n.* 后视镜
flex ['fleks] *v.* 弯曲；折曲
acceleration [əkˌselə'reiʃn] *n.* 加速
subscription [səb'skripʃn] *n.* 订阅
candy bar 单独包装的块状糖
unseasonably [ʌn'siːznəbli]
adv. 不合时宜地
mature [mə'tjuə] *adj.* 成熟的
undecipherable [ˌʌndi'saifərəbl]
adj. 难辨认的
lyric ['lirik] *n.* 歌词
rhythmic ['riðmik] *adj.* 有节奏的
stereo ['steriəu] *n.* 立体音响系统

温情絮语

It is wise father that knows his own child.

了解自己孩子的父亲，是睿智的父亲。

4 A Good Heart to Lean on
善心可依

也许他的表面没有太多可夸耀的，然而他却有一颗善心让我们可以依靠。他就是我的父亲。

文苑漫步

When I was growing up, I was embarrassed to be seen with my father. He was severely **crippled** and very short, and when we would walk together, his hand on my arm for balance, people would stare. I would inwardly **squirm at** the unwanted attention. If he ever noticed or was bothered, he never **let on**.

It was difficult to coordinate our steps — his halting, mine impatient — and because of that, we didn't say much as we went along. But as we started out, he always said, "You set the pace. I will try to **adjust to** you."

Our usual walk was to or from the subway on which he traveled to work. He went to work sick, and despite **nasty** weather. He almost never missed a day, and would make it to the office even if others could not. A matter of pride.

译林畅游

在我成长的过程中，当别人看到我和父亲在一起时，我总是觉得很窘迫。他身材矮小，腿上还有严重的残疾，当我们一起走路时，他总是挽着我的胳膊来保持身体平衡，这时人们总会盯着我们看。这些异样的目光，令我无地自容。可是，即便他注意到我的反应或者他也因此很懊恼，他却从不表露自己的情绪。

我们的步调总是很难协调——他的步子慢慢腾腾，我的步子却焦躁不安——所以走路时，我们很少说话。但每次出门前，他总会说，“你走你的，我想法儿跟上你”。

我们常常往返于从家到他上班乘坐地铁站的那段路上。即使生病或者天气恶劣，父亲也总要坚持上班。他几乎从未请过一天假。即便在别人不去上班的情况下，他也要

When snow or ice was on the ground, it was impossible for him to walk, even with help. At such times my sisters or I would pull him through the streets of Brooklyn, N.Y., on a child's **sleigh** to the subway entrance. Once there, he would cling to the **handrail** until he reached the lower steps that the warmer tunnel air kept free of ice. In Manhattan the subway station was the basement of his office building, and he would not have to go outside again until we met him in Brooklyn on his way home.

When I think of it now, I **marvel at** how much courage it must have taken for a grown man to subject himself to such indignity and stress. And at how he did it — without bitterness or complaint.

He never talked about himself as an object of pity, nor did he show any envy of the more fortunate or able. What he looked for in others was a "good heart", and if he found one, the owner was good enough for him.

Now I am older. I believe this is a proper standard by which to judge people, even though I still don't know precisely what a "good heart" is. But I know the times I don't have one myself.

Unable to engage in many activities, my father still tried to participate in some way. When a local baseball team found

设法去上班。这实在是值得骄傲的一件事。

下雪或地上结了冰时，即便有人帮忙，父亲还是举步维艰。每当此时，我或我的姐妹们就用儿童雪橇把他拉过纽约布鲁克林区的街道，一直送他到地铁的入口处。一到那儿，他便手抓扶手一路走到底下的台阶才放开手，因为那儿通道里的空气暖和些，所以地面上没有结冰。到了曼哈顿，地铁站就在他办公楼的地下一层，所以在我们从布鲁克林接他回家之前他无须再走出楼来。

如今，当我想起这些时，我惊叹父亲作为一个成年男子要经受这种侮辱和压力得需要多么大的勇气啊！他竟然做到了，没有痛苦和抱怨。

父亲从来不觉得自己值得同情，他也从不嫉妒别人的幸运和能力。他期待别人所给予的只是“一份善心”，当他得到时，这善意对他来说已经足够了。

现在我已经长大成人，理解了“善心”是评价人的恰当标准，尽管我仍不很清楚它的确切涵义，但我知道自己有时缺乏善心。

父亲虽不能参加许多活动，但他仍设法以某种方式参与进来。当他发现一个地方棒球队缺少一个领

itself without a manager, he kept it going. He was a knowledgable baseball fan and often took me to Ebbets Field to see the Brooklyn Dodgers play. He liked to go to dances and parties, where he could have a good time just sitting and watching.

On a memorable occasion a fight broke out at a beach party, with everyone **punching and shoving**. He wasn't content to sit and watch, but he couldn't stand unaided on the soft sand. In frustration he began to shout, "I'll fight anyone who will sit down with me!" Nobody did. But the next day people kidded him by saying it was the first time any fighter was urged to **take a dive** before the **bout** began.

I now know he participated in some things **vicariously** through me, his only son. When I played ball (poorly), he "played" too. When I joined the Navy, he "joined" too. And when I came home on leave, he saw to it that I visited his office. Introducing me, he was really saying, "This is my son, but it is also me, and I could have done this too, if things had been different." Those words were never said aloud.

He has been gone many years now, but I think of him often. I wonder if he sensed my reluctance to be seen with him during our walks. If he did, I am sorry I never told him how sorry I was, how

队时，便充当了他们的领队。他是个棒球迷，拥有丰富的棒球知识，他过去常带我去埃比茨棒球场观看布鲁克林鬼精灵队的比赛。他喜欢参加舞会和晚会，他坐在那儿看着别人开心自己也觉得很享受。

记得有一次的海滩派对上，有人打架，其他人围在旁边推推攘攘。他不甘于坐在那里当观众，但又无法在松软的沙滩上自己站起来。于是，失望之下，他吼了起来："谁想坐下来和我打？"没有人响应。但是第二天，人们和他开玩笑说，比赛还没开始，拳击手就被劝倒下，这还是头一次。

现在我知道有一些事情他是通过我——他唯一的儿子参与进来的。当我打球时(尽管我打得很差)，他也在"打球"。当我参加海军时，他也"参加"。当我回家休假时，他一定要让我去他的办公室。在介绍我时，他实际上是说，"这是我儿子，但也是我自己，假如我的情况不是这样的话，我自己也会去参军的。"说这些话的时候，他的声音总是很低。

现在父亲已经去世很多年了，但我时常想起他。我不知道他是否意识到我曾经不愿意别人看到我和他走在一起。假如他的确曾意识到这一点，我现在感到很遗憾，因

unworthy I was, how I regretted it. I think of him when I complain about **trifles**, when I am **envious** of another's good fortune, when I don't have a "good heart".

At such times I put my hand on his arm to regain my balance, and say, "You set the pace. I will try to adjust to you."

为我从没告诉过他我是多么愧疚、多么不孝、多么悔恨。每当我抱怨一些琐事，妒忌别人的好运，失去"善心"时，我就会想起父亲。

此时，我会挽起他的胳膊来保持自己的内心平衡，并且说："你走你的，我想法儿跟上你。"

魅力词汇

crippled ['kripld] *adj.* 残疾的
squirm [skwəːm] at 因……而局促不安
let on 表露
adjust to 调整以适应……
nasty ['nɑːsti] *adj.* 恶劣的
sleigh [slei] *n.* 雪橇
handrail ['hændreil] *n.* 扶手
marvel at 对……感到惊讶
punch and shove 推推攘攘
take a dive 假装被击倒
bout [baut] *n.* 比赛，较量
vicariously [vi'keəriəsli] *adv.* 代理地
trifle ['traifl] *n.* 琐事
envious ['enviəs] *adj.* 嫉妒的

温情絮语

That having a child fall asleep in your arms is one of the most peaceful feelings in the world.

有个孩子在你的臂弯中入睡是世界上最安宁的感觉。

5 A Father's Love 深深的父爱

爸爸不爱说话，仿佛脾气很大，照片中也常常找不到他，但他却教会了我骑自行车，教会了我独立。

文苑漫步

Daddy just didn't know how to show love. It was Mom who held the family together. He just went to work every day and came home; she'd have a list of sins we'd committed and he'd scold us about them.

Once when I stole a candy bar, he made me take it back and tell the man I stole it and that I'd pay for it. But it was Mom who understood I was just a kid.

I broke my leg once on the playground swing and it was Mom who held me in her arms all the way to the hospital. Dad pulled the car right up to the door of the emergency room and when they asked him to move it saying that space was reserved for emergency vehicles, he shouted, "What do you think this is? A tour bus?"

At my birthday parties, Dad always seemed sort of out of place. He just busied

译林畅游

爸爸总是不善于表达爱，是妈妈把我们全家紧紧团结在一起。爸爸每天只知道去工作，然后回家；而妈妈对我们生活中的调皮捣蛋都了解得一清二楚，爸爸只会拿这些指责我们。

有一次，我偷了商店里的一块糖，他愣是让我还回去，还要我向店主坦白并付款。倒是妈妈理解我，说我只不过是个孩子。

我曾在荡秋千时摔断了腿，妈妈一路抱着我去医院。爸爸直接把车子开到急救室门口，有人让他把车开走，说那是救护车停靠的地方，爸爸便大声吼道：“你以为这是什么？是旅游车吗？”

在我的生日宴会上，爸爸总是忙得不可开交，他吹气球、摆桌

himself blowing up balloons, setting up tables, and **running errands**. It was Mom who carried the cake with the candles on it for me to blow out.

When I **leaf through** picture albums, people always ask, "What does your Dad look like?" "Who knows? He was always **fiddling around with** the camera taking everyone else's picture. I must have **a zillion** pictures of Mom and me smiling together."

I remember when Mom told him to teach me how to ride a bicycle. I told him not to let it go, but he said it was time. I fell and Mom ran to pick me up, but he waved her off. I was so mad that I showed him, got right back on that bike and rode it myself. He didn't even feel embarrassed and just smiled.

When I went to college, Mom did all the writing. He just sent checks and a little note about how great his lawn looked now that I wasn't playing football on it.

Whenever I called home, he acted like he wanted to talk, but he always said, "I'll get your mother."

When I got married, it was Mom who cried. He just blew his nose loudly and left the room.

All my life he said, "Where are you

子、四处跑腿，是妈妈把生日蛋糕拿来，点燃蜡烛，让我吹灭。

当我翻看相册时，别人总会问："你爸爸长什么模样啊？""谁知道呢？他总是摆弄相机，只知道给大伙儿照相。我和妈妈一起欢笑的合影就有好多好多呢。"

我还记得妈妈让爸爸教我骑自行车的情形。我不让爸爸松手，而他却说我能自己骑了。我摔倒了，妈妈跑过来把我扶起，爸爸却挥手让她走开，这使我非常恼火，我想证明给他看，于是我再次跨上车子，真的可以自己骑了。爸爸竟然一点都不觉得不好意思，只是微微笑了笑。

我上大学时，妈妈经常写信给我，而爸爸只知道寄钱，顶多附上一张便条，告诉我他的草坪因为我不在上面踢球了现在长得好极了。

每次我往家里打电话，爸爸总像是有话要说，可他总是说："我叫你妈妈来接电话。"

我结婚时，妈妈哭得特别伤心，而爸爸只是大声擤着鼻涕，走出房间。

在我的一生中，爸爸只会说：

going? What time are you coming home? No, you cannot go."

Daddy just didn't know how to show love, unless...

Is it possible he showed it and didn't recognize it?

"你要去哪儿？你打算什么时候回来？不，你不能去。"

爸爸就是不知如何表达爱，除非……

是否有可能他已经表达了爱，而他自己并未意识到？

魅力词汇

run errands ['erənd] 跑腿

leaf through 翻阅

fiddle ['fidl] around with 摆弄

a zillion ['ziliən] 许多

温情絮语

That simple walks with my father around the block on summer nights when I was a child did wonders for me as an adult.

我孩提时在夏天夜晚陪着我父亲在街区周围的散步，是我成年后所心驰神往的。

6 Love Is the Best Legacy
最好的遗产是爱

在一次大意失子之后，他的妻子也抛弃了他，于是他变成了一个酒鬼，甚至于最后孤独地死在了旧金山的一个汽车旅馆。然而他唯一留下的孩子竟是一个最善良、最会关心人、最有爱心的人，是什么原因引起如此大的差异呢？

文苑漫步

As a young man, Al was a skilled artist, a potter. He had a wife and two fine sons. One night, his older son developed a severe stomachache. Thinking it was only some common **intestinal** disorder, neither Al nor his wife took the condition very seriously. But the **malady** was actually **acute appendicitis** and the boy died suddenly that night.

Knowing the death could have been prevented if he had only realized the seriousness of the situation, Al's emotional health **deteriorated** under the enormous burden of his guilt. To make matters worse his wife left him a short time later, leaving him alone with his 6-year-old younger son. The hurt and pain of the two situations were more than Al could handle, and he

译林畅游

年轻时，Al 就已经是一个技艺精湛的陶艺家了。他有了妻室和两个健壮的儿子。但是一天夜里，他大儿子肚子疼得厉害，他想这也只不过是普通的肠道疾病，就没太在意，他妻子也是。然而那病却是急性阑尾炎，这个儿子那天夜里就这么死了。

如果他那时意识到情况的严重性，孩子的死本来是可以避免的，一想到这些 Al 内心就无比愧疚，情绪也一天比一天糟糕。更糟的是，不久他的妻子抛弃了他，把他们 6 岁的小儿子留给了他。丧子之痛加上妻离之苦让 Al 无法喘息，他开始酗酒来麻痹自己，最后他成了一个名副其实的酒鬼。

turned to alcohol to help him cope. In time Al became an **alcoholic**.

As the **alcoholism** progressed, Al began to lose everything he possessed — his home, his land, his art objects, everything. Eventually Al died alone in a San Francisco **motel** room.

Al 就这样喝酒度日，慢慢地失去了他所拥有的一切——房子、土地、艺术作品等等，最后孤独地在旧金山的一个汽车旅馆里死去。

When I heard of Al's death, I reacted with the same **disdain** the world shows for one who ends his life with nothing material to show for it. "What a complete failure!" I thought. "What a totally wasted life!"

当我听说 Al 的死讯时，我的反应和世人一样，鄙视他没有留下什么财产。"多失败啊！"我思索着，"完全没有意义的一生。"

As time went by, I began to reevaluate my earlier harsh judgment. You see, I knew Al's now adult son, Ernie. He is one of the kindest, most caring, most loving men I have ever known. I watched Ernie with his children and saw the free flow of love between them. I knew that kindness and caring had to come from somewhere.

随着时间的流逝，我开始重新审视从前我对 Al 刻薄的评价。你们知道，我认识 Al 已成年的儿子，Ernie。他是我认识的最善良、最懂得关心人、最有爱心的男人了。每每看着他和他的孩子们，我都能感觉到他们之间爱的自然流动。我意识到这种善良和关心一定有所渊源。

I hadn't heard Ernie talk much about his father. It is so hard to defend an alcoholic. One day I worked up my courage to ask him. "I'm really puzzled by something," I said. "I know your father was basically the only one to raise you. What on earth did he do that you became such a special person?"

Ernie 很少提及他的父亲，毕竟他就是想为父亲辩驳也很难。一天，我鼓起勇气问了他："有些事情让我很疑惑。"我说道，"我知道事实上可以说是你父亲一个人抚养你成人，但是他是怎样把你培养成这么特别的一个人的呢？"

Ernie sat quietly and reflected for a few moments. Then he said, "From my earliest memories as a child until I left

Ernie 坐在那里沉思了一会儿，说道："从我还是孩子时最早的回忆到 18 岁离开家，Al 每天晚上都

home at 18, Al came into my room every night, gave me a kiss and said, 'I love you, son.'"

Tears came to my eyes as I realized what a fool I had been to judge Al as a failure. He had not left any material possessions behind. But he had been a kind loving father, and he left behind one of the finest, most giving men I have ever known.

会来到我的房间，吻我一下然后对我说'我爱你，儿子。'"

听到这些，我抑制不住自己，眼泪涌出来了，我认识到自己是多么的愚蠢，居然认为 Al 是个失败的人。他确实没留下什么财产，但是他曾经是一个很有爱心的父亲，他的儿子是我认识的最好、最有爱心的人。

魅力词汇

intestinal [in'testinl] *adj.* 肠的，肠内的
malady ['mælədi] *n.* 疾病
acute [ə'kjuːt] *adj.* 急性的，剧烈的
appendicitis [əˌpendi'saitis] *n.* [医] 阑尾炎
deteriorate [di'tiəriəreit] *v.* 恶化，变坏
alcoholic [ˌælkə'hɔlik] *n.* 嗜酒者，酒鬼
alcoholism ['ælkəhɔlizəm] *n.* 酗酒
motel [məu'tel] *n.* 汽车旅馆
disdain [dis'dein] *n.* 鄙视，轻蔑

温情絮语

That there's nothing sweeter than sleeping with your babies and feeling their breath on your cheeks.

和孩子们一起睡，感受他们的呼吸喷在你的脸上，世界上没有比这更甜蜜的事情。

7 Father's Gift 父亲的礼物

他以为那个包装精美的礼品盒里有他期待已久的礼物，然而却是失望。争吵，出走。多年之后，他才发现，那件父亲精心准备的礼物包含着良苦用心。

文苑漫步

A young man was getting ready to graduate from college. For many months he had admired a beautiful **sports car** in a **dealer**'s showroom, and knowing his father could well afford it, he told him that was all he wanted.

As Graduation Day approached, the young man **awaited** signs that his father had **purchased** the car. Finally, on the morning of his graduation, his father called him into his private study. His father told him how proud he was to have such a fine son, and told him how much he loved him. He handed his son a beautifully wrapped gift box. Curious, and somewhat disappointed, the young man opened the box and found a lovely, **leather-bound** *Bible*, with the young man's name **embossed** in gold.

译林畅游

有位年轻人即将大学毕业。数月来，他一直渴望得到某汽车商产品陈列室中的一辆跑车。他知道，他那富有的父亲肯定买得起这辆车，于是，他便跟父亲说他唯一想要的就是那辆跑车。

在毕业典礼即将来临的日子里，年轻人等待着父亲买下跑车的消息。终于，在毕业典礼那天上午，父亲将他叫到自己的书房，并告诉他，有这么出色的儿子他感到非常自豪而且非常爱他。他递给儿子一个包装精美的礼品盒。年轻人带着好奇和些许失望的心情打开礼品盒，却发现里面是一本精美的皮封面精装本《圣经》，上面以金子凸印着年轻人的名字。

Angry, he shouted at his father and said "With all your money, you give me a *Bible*?" and **stormed out** of the house.

Many years passed and the young man had become very successful in business. He had a beautiful home and wonderful family, but realized his father now was getting old, and thought perhaps he should go see him. He had not seen him since that graduation day. Before he could make arrangements, he received a **telegram** telling him his father had **passed away**, and **willed** all of his possessions to his son. He needed to come home immediately and take care of things.

When he arrived at his father's house, sudden sadness and regret filled his heart. He began to search through his father's important papers and saw the still **gift-wrapped** *Bible*, just as he had left it years ago. With tears, he opened the *Bible* and began to turn the pages. As he was reading those words, a car key dropped from the back of the *Bible*. It had a tag with the dealer's name, the same dealer who had the sports car he had wanted. On the tag was the date of his graduation, and the words "PAID IN FULL".

年轻人怒气冲冲地向父亲喊道："你有那么多钱，却只给我一本《圣经》？"说完，便愤怒地冲出房子。

许多年过去了，年轻人已事业有成。他拥有一所漂亮的房子，一个温馨的家庭。但当意识到父亲年事已高，他想，或许应该去看看他。自从毕业那天起他就一直没见过父亲。然而还未等他做好安排，他收到一封电报，告知他父亲已逝世，并已立下遗嘱将其所有财产转给儿子。他要立即回父亲家处理后事。

当他到达父亲的房子里时，内心突然感到一阵悲伤与懊悔。他开始仔细搜寻父亲的重要文件，突然发现了那本包装依旧完好的《圣经》——还跟数年前他丢下它时一样。他眼含泪水打开《圣经》并一页一页地翻着。他在品读那些文字时，从《圣经》的背面掉出一把钥匙。钥匙上挂着一个标签，上面写着一个汽车经销商的名字——正是他曾渴望的那辆跑车的经销商。标签上还有他的毕业日期及"款已付清"的字样。

魅力词汇

sports car 跑车

dealer ['diːlə] *n.* 经销商；商人

await [ə'weit] *v.* 等候，等待

purchase ['pəːtʃəs] *v.* 购买

leather-bound ['leðə,baund] *adj.* 皮边儿的，用皮革包边儿的

emboss [im'bɔs] *v.* 使凸出；在……上作浮雕图案；装饰

storm out 猛冲出去

telegram ['teligræm] *n.* 电报

pass away 去世，逝世

will [wil] *v.* 遗赠

gift-wrapped ['gift,ræpt] *adj.* 用花纸包装的

温情絮语

That I wish I could have told my Dad that I love him one more time before he passed away.

我真希望在父亲去世之前能再说一次我爱他。

Happy are the families where the government of parents is the reign of affection, and of the children the submission to love.

幸福的家庭，父母靠慈爱当家，孩子也是出于对父母的爱而顺从。

8 A Letter to the Daughters By Barack Obama
奥巴马给女儿们的一封信

这些是我想要让你们得到的东西：在一个梦想不受限制、无事不能成就的世界中长大，成为具有慈悲心、坚持理想，能帮忙打造这样一个世界的女性。我要每个孩子都有和你们一样的机会，去学习、梦想、成长、发展。这就是我带领我们一家展开这趟大冒险的原因。

文苑漫步

Dear Malia and Sasha,

I know that you've both had a lot of fun these last two years on the **campaign trail**, going to picnics and parades and state fairs, eating all sorts of junk food your mother and I probably shouldn't let you have. But I also know that it hasn't always been easy for you and Mom, and that as excited as you both are about that new puppy, it doesn't **make up for** all the time we've been apart. I know how much I've missed these past two years, and today I want to tell you a little more about why I decided to take our family on this journey.

When I was a young man, I thought life was all about me — about how I'd make my way in the world, become successful, and get the things I want. But then

译林畅游

亲爱的 Malia 和 Sasha：

我知道这两年你们俩随我一路竞选都有过不少乐子，野餐、游行、逛州博览会，吃了各种或许我和你妈妈不该让你们吃的垃圾食物。然而我也知道，你们俩和你妈妈的日子，有时候并不惬意。新来的小狗虽然令你们兴奋，却无法弥补我们不在一起的所有时光。我明白这两年我错过的太多了，今天我要再向你们说说为何我决定带领我们一家人踏上这趟旅程。

当我还年轻的时候，我认为生活就是围绕着我转：我如何在这世上得心应手，成功立业，得到我想要的。后来，你们俩走进我的世

the two of you came into my world with all your curiosity and **mischief** and those smiles that never fail to fill my heart and **light up** my day. And suddenly, all of my big plans for myself didn't seem so important anymore. I soon found that the greatest joy in my life was the joy I saw in yours. And I realized that my own life wouldn't count for much unless I was able to ensure that you had every opportunity for happiness and fulfillment in yours. In the end, girls, that's why I ran for President: because of what I want for you and for every child in this nation.

界，带来的种种好奇、淘气和微笑，总能填满我的心，照亮我的日子。突然之间，我为自己谱写的伟大计划显得不再那么重要了。我很快便发现，我在你们生命中看到的快乐，就是我自己生命中最大的快乐。而我也同时体会到，如果我不能确保你们此生能够拥有追求幸福和自我实现的一切机会，我自己的生命也没多大价值。总而言之，女儿们，这就是我竞选总统的原因：我要让你们俩和这个国家的每一个孩子，都能拥有我想要给你们的东西。

I want all our children to go to schools worthy of their potential — schools that challenge them, inspire them, and **instill** in them a sense of wonder about the world around them. I want them to have the chance to go to college — even if their parents aren't rich. And I want them to get good jobs: jobs that pay well and give them benefits like health care, jobs that can let them spend time with their own kids and retire with dignity.

我要让我们的所有儿童都在能够发掘他们潜能的学校就读——这些学校要能挑战他们，激励他们，并灌输给他们对身处的这个世界的好奇心。我要他们有机会上大学，哪怕他们的父母并不富有。而且我要他们能找到好的工作：薪酬高还附带医疗保险的工作，让他们有时间陪孩子，并且能带着尊严退休。

I want us to push the boundaries of discovery so that you'll live to see new technologies and inventions that improve our lives and make our planet cleaner and safer. And I want us to push our own human boundaries to reach beyond the

我要大家向探索的极限挑战，让你们在有生之年能够看见可以改善我们生活、使这个地球更干净更安全的新科技和新发明。我也要大家向自己的人际界限挑战，跨越使我们看不到对方长处的种族、地域、

divides of race and region, gender and religion that keep us from seeing the best in each other.

性别和宗教藩篱。

Sometimes we have to send our young men and women into war and other dangerous situations to protect our country — but when we do, I want to make sure that it is only for a very good reason, that we try our best to settle our differences with others peacefully, and that we do everything possible to keep our servicemen and women safe. And I want every child to understand that the blessings these brave Americans fight for are not free — that with the great privilege of being a citizen of this nation comes great responsibility.

有时候为了保卫我们的国家，我们不得不把青年男女派到战场或其他危险的地方——然而当我们这么做的时候，我们确保师出有名，我们竭尽全力以和平方式化解与他人的争执，也想尽了一切办法保障男女官兵的安全。我要每个孩子都明白，这些勇敢的美国人在战场上捍卫的福祉是无法白白得到的。在享有作为这个国家公民的伟大特权之际，重大的责任也随之而来。

That was the lesson your grandmother tried to teach me when I was your age, reading me the opening lines of *The **Declaration** of Independence* and telling me about the men and women who marched for equality because they believed those words put to paper two centuries ago should mean something.

这正是我在你们这个年纪时，你们的祖母想要教给我的功课，她把独立宣言开头几行念给我听，告诉我有一些男女为了争取平等而游行抗议，因为他们认为两个世纪前白纸黑字写下来的这些句子，不应只是空话。

She helped me understand that America is great not because it is perfect but because it can always be made better — and that the unfinished work of perfecting our union falls to each of us. It's a **charge** we pass on to our children, coming closer with each new generation to

她让我了解到，美国之所以伟大，不是因为它完美，而是因为我们可以不断让它变得更好——而让我们的国家变得更加完美的未竟工作，就落在我们每个人的身上。这是我们交给孩子们的责任，每过一代，美国就更接近我们的理想。

what we know America should be.

I hope both of you will **take up** that work, righting the wrongs that you see and working to give others the chances you've had. Not just because you have an **obligation** to give something back to this country that has given our family so much — although you do have that obligation. But because you have an obligation to yourself. Because it is only when you **hitch** your **wagon** to something larger than yourself that you will realize your true potential.

我希望你们俩都愿接下这个工作，看到不对的事要想办法改正，努力帮助别人获得你们有过的机会。这并非因为国家给了我们一家人这么多，你们也当有所回馈——虽然你们的确有这个义务，而是因为你们对自己负有义务。因为，唯有把你们的马车套在更大的东西上，你才会明白自己真正的潜能。

These are the things I want for you — to grow up in a world with no limits on your dreams and no achievements beyond your reach, and to grow up into **compassionate**, committed women who will help build that world. And I want every child to have the same chances to learn and dream and grow and **thrive** that you girls have. That's why I've taken our family on this great adventure.

这些是我想要让你们得到的东西：在一个梦想不受限制、无事不能成就的世界中长大，成长为富有慈悲心、坚持理想，能帮忙打造这样一个世界的女性。我要每个孩子都有和你们一样的机会，去学习、梦想、成长和发展。这就是我带领我们一家人展开这趟冒险的原因。

I am so proud of both of you. I love you more than you can ever know. And I am grateful every day for your patience, **poise**, **grace**, and humor as we prepare to start our new life together in the White House.

我深以你俩为荣，你们永远不会明白我有多爱你们，在我们准备一同在白宫开始新生活之际，我没有一天不为你们的忍耐、沉稳、明理和幽默而心存感激。

Love, Dad

爱你们的父亲

魅力词汇

campaign trail 竞选游说之行
make up for 弥补，补偿
mischief ['mistʃif] *n.* 淘气，顽皮
light up 照亮，点亮
instill [in'stil] *v.* 逐渐灌输
declaration [ˌdeklə'reiʃn] *n.* 宣言，宣布
charge [tʃɑːdʒ] *n.* 责任，职责
take up 接受，承担
obligation [ˌɔbli'geiʃn] *n.* 义务；职责
hitch [hitʃ] *v.* 钩住；套住
wagon ['wægən] *n.* 四轮马车
compassionate [kəm'pæʃənit] *adj.* 慈悲的；富于同情心的
thrive [θraiv] *v.* 茁壮成长
poise [pɔiz] *n.* 沉着，镇静
grace [greis] *n.* 魅力；优雅

温情絮语

That when your newly born grandchild holds your little finger in his little fist, that you're hooked for life.

当刚刚降生的曾孙用他的小拳头握住你的小拇指的时候，你发现你对生命如此地着迷。

9 Who Will Be Your Angel? 你的"守护天使"是谁?

当一个年幼无依的生命从温暖的天堂降至寒冷的人间，是谁为他取暖？当他习惯了歌唱，在他尚未能发声时，是谁为他轻吟？

文苑漫步

Once upon a time there was a child ready to be born. One day the child asked God: "They tell me you are going to send me to earth tomorrow but how am I going to live there being so small and helpless?"

God replied: "Among the many angels, I have chosen one for you. She will be waiting for you and will take care of you."

"But," said the child, "in Heaven I don't need anything else but sing and smile. That's what I need to be happy!"

God said: "Your angel will sing for you and will also smile for you every day. And you will feel your angel's love and be happy."

"And," said the child, "how am I going to be able to understand when people talk to me, if I don't know the language that men talk?"

"That's easy," said God, "Your angel will tell you the most beautiful and sweet

译林畅游

从前，有一个婴儿即将诞生。一天，这个婴儿问上帝："有人告诉我，你明天将把我送到地球上，但是我这么年幼无助，如何生活呢？"

上帝回答道："我为你从众多的天使中挑选了一位。她将等候你的降临并照顾你。"

"但是，"孩子说道，"在天堂里，除了唱歌、微笑，我不需要其他任何事情，唯有它们能使我快乐！"

上帝说："你的天使每天都将为你唱歌并对你微笑。你将感受到天使的爱并因此而快乐。"

"还有，"小孩接着说，"如果我不懂得人类的语言，当他们同我说话时，我将怎样才能听懂呢？"

"那很简单，"上帝说，"你的天使将让你听到最美丽动听的语

words you will ever hear, and with much **patience** and care, your angel will teach you how to speak."

The child looked up at God saying: "And what am I going to do when I want to talk to you?"

God smiled at the child saying: "The angel will place your hands together and will teach you how to **pray**."

The child said: "I've heard on earth there are bad men. Who will protect me?"

God put his arm around the child, saying: "Your angel will **defend** you — even if it means risking life!"

The child looked sad, saying: "But I will always be sad because I will not see you anymore."

God hugged the child: "Your angel will always talk to you about me and will teach you the way to come back to me, even though I will always be next to you." At that moment there was much peace in Heaven, but voices from earth could already be heard.

The child, in a hurry, asked softly: "Oh, God, if I am about to leave now, please tell me my Angel's name!"

God replied: "Your angel's name is of no importance... you will simply call her MOMMY!"

言，她有足够的耐心和爱心去教你如何讲话。"

小孩仰起头对上帝说："当我想和你说话时，我该怎么办？"

上帝微笑着对孩子说："天使会把你的双手合在一起，教你祈祷。"

小孩继续说："我听说地球上有坏人。到时谁将保护我呢？"

上帝用双手抱住小孩，说道："你的天使会保护你——即使那意味着要用她的生命去冒险。"

小孩开始悲伤起来，说道："但我还是会难过，因为我再也见不到你了。"

上帝抱着小孩说："尽管我会一直陪伴在你身边，你的天使还是会经常谈论起我，并教导你如何回到我的身边。"就在那一刻，尽管天堂里十分安静，但是已经能听到地球上的声音了。

小孩急切而温和地说："哦，上帝，如果我现在即将离开，请您告诉我天使的名字吧！"

上帝回答道："天使的名字并不重要……你可以简称其为'妈妈'！"

魅力词汇

once upon a time 从前

patience ['peiʃəns] *n.* 耐心，耐性

pray [prei] *v.* 祈祷，祈求

defend [di'fend] *v.* 保卫，保护

10 Please Dress Me in Red 请为我穿上红衣

我可能就要死了，我不害怕。我死时，请给我穿上红色的衣服。妈妈答应我她也会来天堂的。她来的时候我会在玩，我得保证她能找到我。

文苑漫步

I have worked with **numerous** children infected with the **virus** that causes AIDS. The relationships that I have had with these special kids have been gifts in my life. They have taught me so many things, but I have especially learned that great courage can be found in the smallest of **packages**. Let me tell you about Tyler.

Tyler was born infected with HIV; his mother was also infected. From the very beginning of his life, he was dependent on **medications** to enable him to survive. When he was 5, he had a **tube surgically inserted** in a **vein** in his chest. This tube was connected to a pump, which he carried in a small backpack on his back. Medications were hooked up to this pump and were continuously supplied through this tube to his bloodstream. At times, he also needed **supplemented** oxygen to support

译林畅游

我曾经和许多感染艾滋病病毒的孩子打过交道。我和这些特殊的孩子之间的关系是生活赋予我的恩赐。他们教会我许多东西，我尤其懂得了即使在最弱小的人物身上也能发现其所蕴含的巨大勇气。让我给你讲讲 Tyler 的故事。

Tyler 出生时就感染了艾滋病病毒；他的母亲也是感染者。自他来到人间就一直靠药物维持生命。他 5 岁时做手术，胸部插了一根管子，管子连着他背的小背包里的泵。泵不断地将药物通过管子输入他的血液。有时他还需要补充氧气帮助呼吸。

his breathing.

Tyler wasn't willing to give up one single moment of his childhood to this deadly disease. It was not unusual to find him playing and racing around his backyard, wearing his medicine-laden backpack and dragging his tank of oxygen behind him in his little wagon. All of us who knew Tyler **marvelled at** his pure joy in being alive and the energy it gave him. Tyler's mom often teased him by telling him that he moved so fast she needed to dress him in red. That way, when she peered through the window to check on him playing in the yard, she could quickly spot him.

Tyler 不愿把童年的一分一秒屈服于这种致命的疾病。经常能看见他背着装药的背包，拖着载有氧气罐的小车在他家后院玩耍奔跑。我们所有认识 Tyler 的人都惊叹生命带给他那纯朴的欢乐和赋予他的活力。Tyler 的妈妈经常逗他说，他跑得那么快，得给他穿件红衣服。这样，她透过窗户看他在院子里玩耍时，能一眼发现他。

The **dreaded** disease eventually wore down even **the likes of** a little **dynamo** like Tyler. He grew quite ill and, unfortunately, so did his HIV-infected mother. When it became apparent that he wasn't going to survive, Tyler's mom talked to him about death. She comforted him by telling Tyler that she was dying too, and that she would be with him soon in heaven.

这种可怕的疾病最终还是拖垮了像 Tyler 这样精力充沛的小孩子。他的病情日益严重；不幸的是，身染艾滋病病毒的妈妈也病入膏肓。眼看着 Tyler 即将撒手人寰时，妈妈和他谈起死亡。她安慰 Tyler 说，她也将要离开人世，不久会和他在天堂见面。

A few days before his death, Tyler **beckoned** me over to his hospital bed and whispered, "I might die soon. I'm not scared. When I die, please dress me in red, Mom promised me she's coming to heaven too. I'll be playing when she gets there, and I want to make sure she can find me."

Tyler 病逝前几天，招呼我到他病床前，低声对我说："我可能就要死了，我不害怕。我死时，请给我穿上红色的衣服。妈妈答应我她也会来天堂的。她来的时候我会在玩，我得保证她能找到我。"

魅力词汇

numerous ['njuːmərəs] *adj.* 许多的
virus ['vaiərəs] *n.* 病毒
package ['pækidʒ]
n. [口]整体具有某种特色的人
medication [ˌmedi'keiʃn] *n.* 药物
tube [tjuːb] *n.* 管
surgically ['səːdʒikəli]
adv. 如外科手术般地
insert [in'səːt] *v.* 插入
vein [vein] *n.* 血管
supplement ['sʌplimənt] *v.* 补充（文中为其过去分词形容词化）
marvel at 对……惊奇
dreaded [dredid] *adj.* 令人畏惧的
the likes of
[口]像……这样的人（或事）
dynamo ['dainəməu]
n. [口]精力充沛的人
beckon ['bekən]
v.（以点头、手势等表示）召唤

温情絮语

The greatest thing in family life is to take a hint when a hint is intended—and not to take a hint when a hint is not intended.

家庭生活中最重要的不仅是成员之间的心领神会，还需要心有灵犀一点通。

第二篇

一杯牛奶的温度

1 Choice of Companions 择友

忠实的朋友，是稳固的保障；谁寻得了他就是寻得了宝藏。

文苑漫步

A good companion is better than a fortune, for a fortune cannot purchase those elements of character which make **companionship** a blessing. The best companion is one who is wiser and better than ourselves, for we are inspired by his wisdom and virtue to nobler deeds. Greater wisdom and goodness than we possess lifts us higher mentally and morally.

"A man is known by the companion he keeps." It is always true. Companionship of a high order is powerful to develop character. Character makes character in the associations of life faster than anything else. Purity **begets** purity, like begets like; and this fact makes the choice of companion in early life more important even than that of teachers and **guardians**.

It is true that we cannot always choose all of our companions. Some are

译林畅游

一位好朋友胜过一笔财富，因为财富买不来朋友身上的珍贵品质，这些品质使得友谊成为一种福祉。最好的朋友是那些比我们更睿智、更出色的人，他们的智慧和美德鞭策着我们，让我们的行为变得更加高尚。他们的才智和美德超过我们，从而促使我们不断提高自己的精神境界和道德水平。

"观察一个人的朋友便可了解这个人。"这句话总没错。高层次的交友对于品格的形成有着巨大的作用。在生活交往中，品格对于品格的影响胜过其他一切因素。近朱者赤，近墨者黑，这一事实告诉人们，在年轻时代，择友甚至比选择老师和监护人还重要。

不可否认，总有一些朋友是我们无法选择的。有些朋友是由于生

thrust upon us by business or the social relations of life, we do not choose them, we do not enjoy them; and yet, we have to associate with them more or less. The experience is not altogether without compensation, if there be principle enough in us to **bear the strain**. Still, in the main, choice of companions can be made, and must be made. It is not best or necessary for a young person to associate with "Tom, Dick, and Harry" without **forethought** or purpose. Some fixed rules about the company he or she keeps must be observed. The subject should be uttermost in the thoughts, and **canvassed** often.

Companionship is education, good or not; it develops manhood or womanhood, high or low; it lifts soul upward or drags it downward; it ministers to virtue or vice. There is no half way work about its influence. If it **ennobles**, it does grandly; if it demoralizes, it does **devilishly**. It saves or destroys **lustily**. Nothing in the world is surer than this. Sow virtue, and the harvest will be virtue. Sow vice, and the harvest will be vice. Good companionships help us to sow virtue; evil companionships help us to sow vice.

意往来和社会交际被推到我们面前的。这些朋友不是我们自己选择的，我们也并不享受和他们在一起的时间。然而我们还得或多或少地同他们交往。但如果我们坚守内心的原则，承受一些压力，这样的经历也并非毫无益处。总的来说，我们可以选择自己的朋友，也必须选择朋友。一个年轻人如果没有远见，随便地与张三、李四或王五结交朋友，那是不妥当或完全没有必要的。需要注意的是，结交朋友时必须确立一些原则。这一点务必在思想上引起重视，并时时拿来检点自己。

无论益友还是损友，都会使我们得到教育；友谊或多或少地塑造了我们的男性特质或女性特质；它可以提升我们的灵魂，也可以使我们变得卑微；它可以滋生美德，也可以催生邪恶。它的影响是长远的。友谊，如果使人高尚，就会使人如天使般庄重；如果使人堕落，就会使人如魔鬼般邪恶。它可以及时拯救一个人，也可以快速摧毁一个人。世上没有什么比这更确定的事了。播种美德，收获的就是美德；播种邪恶，收获的就是邪恶。好的朋友帮助我们播种美德，坏的朋友促使我们播种邪恶。

魅力词汇

companionship [kəm'pænjənʃip] *n.* 友谊
beget [bi'get] *v.* 招致
guardian ['gɑːdiən] *n.* 监护人
thrust [θrʌst] *v.* 推
bear the strain 承受压力
forethought ['fɔːθɔːt] *n.* 远见
canvass ['kænvəs] *v.* 检查
ennoble [i'nəubl] *v.* 使高尚
devilishly ['devəliʃli] *adv.* 魔鬼般地
lustily ['lʌstili] *adv.* 有力地

温情絮语

The best kind of friend is the kind you can sit on a porch swing with, never say a word, and then walk away feeling like it was the best conversation you've ever had.

最好的朋友就是那种可以和你一起坐在门廊秋千上，不说一句话，然后离开，却感觉就像你们已经彼此敞开心扉。

2 The Silence of Male's Friendship
男人间无声的友谊

男人间的友谊，并不经常通过言语来表达，他们于无声中蕴含着真情。

文苑漫步

The silence of men in general is over talked about and **overcriticized**. To be sure, men never open up as much as women want them to, but there is a wordless understanding in which we function fairly well, especially in friendships.

I believe, in fact, that most women would prefer a man to be **gloomily uncommunicative** than to **spill his guts at the drop of a hat**.

The push for men to express their feelings presumes that we have feelings, and we do have a few, but they remain **submerged**, and tearing of them often violates their **authenticity**.

I am no biologist, but my guess is that the male human animal was programmed for silence. I would go so far as to argue that men were programmed to be isolated from one another and that aloneness is our natural state. Silence in male friendships is

译林畅游

一般而言，人们总是过多谈论和指责男人的沉默寡言。可以肯定的是，男人从未像女人所希望的那样开诚布公地说出自己的心里话，但默默的理解，在男人当中却很管用，尤其是在维持友谊的时候。

我相信，大多数女人实际上都宁愿男人郁郁寡欢不言不语，而不喜欢男人像竹筒倒豆子似的，什么都说。

人们催促男人把情感表露出来，这说明男人并非没有感情。是的，我们确实有一些情感，但这些情感常常隐而不露，很难真实地表达出来。

我不是生物学家，但我猜想男人这种动物大概天生就被设计得寡言少语。我进一步推测到，男人天生就被设计成相互孤立的动物，孤独是我们的自然状态。男人间无声的友谊使得彼此能独立地存在。

our way of being alone with each other.

Once men have established a friendship that itself is the word. The affection is obvious, at least to us. A main component of our silence is an appreciation of the affection.

一旦男人间建立起友谊，友谊本身就是一种语言。至少对我们来说，这种情感是明显的。我们沉默的很大一部分是用来欣赏这份情感。

魅力词汇

overcriticize [ˌəuvə'kritiˌsaiz] *v.* 过分指责

gloomily ['gluːmili] *adv.* 沮丧地

uncommunicative [ˌʌnkə'mjuːnikətiv] *adj.* 沉默寡言的

spill one's guts at the drop of a hat 像竹筒倒豆子似的，什么都说

submerged [səb'məːdʒd] *adj.* 隐而不露的

authenticity [ˌɔːθen'tisəti] *n.* 真实

温情絮语

Always put yourself in the other's shoes. If you feel that it hurts you, it probably hurts the person too.

始终要换位思考。如果你觉得它会伤害你，它可能也会伤害他人。

3 Saving David 拯救大卫

有时我们以为我们什么都做不了，但一个眼神却可以让另一个人重燃希望；有时，我们以为世界很无情，但一个拥抱，可以让我们感到温暖。

文苑漫步

Years ago, when I was working as a **psychologist** at a children's institution in England, an **adolescent** boy showed up in the waiting room, it was David.

David wore a black raincoat that was buttoned all the way up to his neck. His face was pale, and he stared at his feet while **wringing** his hands nervously. He had lost his father as an infant, and had lived together with his mother and grandfather ever since. But when David turned 13, his grandfather died and his mother was killed in a car accident. He was very depressed, refusing to talk to others.

The first two times we met, David didn't say a word. He sat in the chair and only looked up at the children's drawings on the wall. As he was about to leave after the second visit, I put my hand on his shoulder. He didn't **shrink** back, but he

译林畅游

许多年前，我是英国一所儿童机构的心理医生，有一天，一个十几岁的男孩出现在候诊室，他叫David。

David 穿着一件黑色的雨衣，扣子一直扣到脖颈。他脸色苍白，眼睛紧盯着自己的双脚，同时还紧张地扭搓着双手。David 很小的时候就失去了父亲，一直同母亲和祖父生活在一起。在 13 岁那年，他的祖父去世了，母亲也在一次车祸中丧生。他情绪低落，不跟任何人说话。

在我们头两次见面时，David 一句话也没说。他坐在椅子上，抬起头时也只是看着我身后墙上孩子们画的画。他第二次来后，在他将要离开的时候，我将手放在他的肩上，他没有退缩着躲开，也没有看

didn't look at me either.

"Come back next week," I hesitated a bit. Then I said, "I know it hurts."

He came, and I suggested we play a game of **chess**. He **nodded**. After that we played chess every Wednesday afternoon — in complete silence and without making any eye contact. It's not easy to cheat in chess, but I admit that I made sure David won once or twice.

It seemed as if he enjoyed my company. But why did he never look at me? "Perhaps he senses that I respect his suffering." I kept wondering and playing with him, until some months later, suddenly, he looked up at me, "It's your turn," he said.

After that day, David started talking. He got friends in school and joined a bicycle club. He wrote to me a few times, after that the letters stopped. Now he had really started to live his own life.

Maybe I gave David something. At least I learned a lot from him. I learned how time makes it possible to overcome what seems to be an **insuperable** pain. I learned to be there for people who need me. And David showed me how one—without any words—can reach out to another person. All it takes is a **hug**, a shoulder to cry on, a friendly touch, a **sympathetic** nature, and an ear that listens.

我一眼。

“下周还来吧。”我犹豫了一下说，“我知道你很难过。”

他的确来了，我提议两人下象棋，他点头同意了。之后，我们每周三下午下棋——但都不说话，他也从不和我对视。下棋时作弊并不容易，不过我得承认，我的确有意让David赢过一两次。

看上去他很喜欢和我在一起，但是为什么他从不看我一眼呢？“也许他觉得我尊重他的苦楚。”与他下棋时我一直带着这样的疑问，直到几个月后，突然，David抬头看着我，说道：“该你了。”

自那天起，David开始说话了。他在学校里有了朋友，并加入了一个自行车俱乐部。他给我写过几次信，在那之后，他就不再写信了。现在他已经真正开始了自己的生活。

也许我给予过David某种东西，至少我从他那里学到了很多。我懂得了时间使人克服看上去无法逾越的痛苦，我学会了帮助需要我帮助的人。David还使我明白，一个人怎样才能不通过言语而去帮助他人。这所需的只是一个拥抱，一个痛哭时可依偎的肩头，一次友好的抚慰，一种同情的本性，以及一双聆听的耳朵。

魅力词汇

psychologist [sai'kɔlədʒist]
n. 心理学研究者；心理学家
adolescent [ˌædəu'lesnt]
adj. 青春期的，青少年的
wring [riŋ] *v.* 绞，拧，扭
shrink [ʃriŋk] *v.* 退缩
chess [tʃes] *n.* 棋，国际象棋
nod [nɔd] *v.* 点头
insuperable [in'sjuːpərəbl]
adj. 不能逾越的，不能克服的
hug [hʌg] *n.* 拥抱
sympathetic [ˌsimpə'θetik]
adj. 表示同情的

温情絮语

A careless word may kindle strife. A cruel word may wreck a life. A timely word may level stress. But a loving word may heal and bless.

口无遮拦会引发争执。一句无情的话语会毁掉一生。 适时温语可以消弭压力。但是，只有关爱之声才能疗伤和祈福。

4 Develop Your Own Helping Rituals
伸出你的友爱之手

如果你想让自己的生活安宁祥和，最好做一些友善平和的事情。我最喜欢的一种方式是培养自己乐于助人的习惯。这些小小的善行让你有机会去帮助别人，让你意识到待人友善、乐于助人的感觉有多好。

文苑漫步

If you want your life to stand for peace and kindness, it's helpful to do kind, peaceful things. One of my favorite ways to do this is by developing my own helping **rituals**. These little acts of kindness are opportunities to be of service and **reminders** of how good it feels to be kind and helpful.

We live in a rural area of the San Francisco Bay Area. Most of what we see is beauty and nature. One of the exceptions to the beauty is the **litter** that some people throw out of their windows as they are driving on the rural roads. One of the few drawbacks to living out the **boondocks** is that public services, such as litter collection, are less available than they are closer to the city.

A helping ritual that I practice regu-

译林畅游

如果你想让自己的生活安宁祥和，最好做一些友善平和的事情。我最喜欢的一种方式是培养自己乐于助人的习惯。这些小小的善行让你有机会去帮助别人，让你意识到待人友善、乐于助人的感觉有多好。

我们住在旧金山圣弗朗西斯科湾地区的郊外。我们目所能及的几乎都是美丽的自然风光。与这美景不太和谐的是有人驱车行驶在乡间小路上时随手从车窗往外扔垃圾。而居住在这种偏远的地方的一个缺点就是缺少必要的公共服务，例如，垃圾的收集就不如靠近市区那样方便。

我跟我的两个孩子经常做的一

larly with my two children is picking up litter in our surrounding area. We've become so accustomed to doing this that my daughters will often say to me in animated voices, "There's some litter, Daddy, stop the car!" And if we have time, we will often pull over and pick it up. It may seem strange, but we actually enjoy it. We pick up litter in parks, on sidewalks, practically anywhere. Once I even saw a complete stranger picking up litter close to where we live. He smiled at me and said, "I saw you doing it, and it seemed like a good idea."

Picking up litter is only one of endless supplies of possible helping rituals. You might like holding a door open for people, visiting lonely elderly people in nursing homes, or **shoveling** snow off someone else's driveway. Think of something that seems effortless yet helpful. It's fun, personally **rewarding**, and sets a good example. Everyone wins.

件事就是捡拾我们周围地区的垃圾。对此我们已经习以为常，我的女儿们经常会兴奋地对我说，"爸爸，这儿有垃圾，请停一下车！"只要时间来得及，我们总是将车开到路边并将垃圾捡起来。这似乎有点不可思议，但我们真的喜欢这样做。我们在公园里，人行道上，几乎任何地方捡拾垃圾。曾经有一次，我在我们家附近看到一位陌生人在捡垃圾。他笑着对我说，"我看到你这么做了，看来是个好主意。"

捡垃圾只不过是无数善意行为中的一种而已。你可以为别人开门，或者去敬老院看望那些孤独的老人，或者清除别人行车道上的积雪。想出一些似乎毫不费力但又非常有益的事情。这真的很有趣，自己会感觉很好，也为别人树立了榜样。每个人都会从中受益。

魅力词汇

ritual ['ritʃuəl] *n.*（宗教等的）仪式，例行公事，老规矩

reminder [ri'maində] *n.* 令人回忆起……的东西，提醒……的东西

litter ['litə] *n.* 废弃物，垃圾

boondocks ['buːndɔks] *n.* 偏僻的荒野

shovel ['ʃʌvl] *v.* 铲

rewarding [ri'wɔːdiŋ] *adj.* 值得的

5 The Basis of Love 爱的基础

如果真爱是在金钱的土壤成长，未免难逃世俗的悲哀；如果真爱只是情义或血缘的代名词，未免有些无奈的狭隘。真正的爱，不需要任何诠释，不附着任何条件，是单纯的发自内心“没有任何关系”的关系。

文苑漫步

The following story took place long ago in Israel. One day when government officials were rebuilding a **barn**, they found a mouse hole in a corner and used smoke to force the mice inside the hole to come out. A while later they indeed saw mice running out, one after another.

Then, everyone thought that all the mice had escaped. But just as they were about to start to clean up, they saw two mice **squeezing** out the exit of the hole. After some endeavor, the mice finally got out. The strange thing was that after they came out of the hole, they did not run away immediately. Instead, one chased after the other near the exit of the hole. It seemed that one was trying to bite the **tail** of the other.

译林畅游

很久以前，在以色列发生了下面一段故事：有一天政府人员在翻新谷仓，发现墙角有一个老鼠洞，于是众人用烟熏的方式，希望逼使里面的老鼠出来。待了一会，果然看到老鼠一只只地逃窜出来。

众人正忖度老鼠大概已经逃光了，可以上前打扫之际，却见还有两只老鼠在洞口处推挤，经过一番努力，双双才逃出来。但很奇怪的是，两只老鼠出了洞口以后，却不立即逃走，而是其中的一只老鼠追赶另一只，像是要咬对方的尾巴似的。

Everyone was puzzled, so they stepped closer to take a look. They realized that one of the mice was blind and could not see anything, and the other one was trying to allow the blind mouse to bite on his tail so that he could pull the blind one with him to escape.

众人都很纳闷，便走上前去细看，这才发现原来其中一只老鼠瞎眼看不见，而另一只正设法使对方咬着自己的尾巴，然后带领同伴一起逃走。

After witnessing what happened, everyone was speechless and lost in thought. During meal time, the group of people sat down in a circle and started to chat about what happened to the two mice.

众人见状，都默然不语，陷入沉思中。吃饭的时候，众人又围着坐下，并开始讨论刚才的两只老鼠。

One serious Rome official said: "I think the relationship between those two mice was that of emperor and minister." The others thought for a while and said: "That was why!" Thus the Rome official showed his **arrogance superciliously**.

一个严肃的罗马长官说："我认为刚才的两只老鼠是君臣主仆的关系。"众人思考一会儿后说："原来如此！"于是罗马长官摆出一副高傲的模样。

A smart Israeli said: "I think the relationship between those two mice was husband and wife." Again the others thought for a while, and all felt it made sense; so they expressed assent. Therefore, the Israeli's **countenance** showed self-satisfaction.

聪明的以色列人说："我认为刚才的两只老鼠是夫妇关系。"众人又思考了一会，觉得不错，连声称是。于是以色列人露出一副飘飘然得意的嘴脸。

A Chinese, who was accustomed to the firm tradition of loyalty to parents, said: "I think the relationship between those two mice was that of mother and son." Once again the others thought for a while, and felt this was more reasonable. So they expressed assent yet another time.

强调孝义的中国人说："我认为刚才的两只老鼠是母子关系。"众人又思考了一会，更觉合理，又连声称是。于是中国人的脸上立刻堆满了老道的谦虚。

Therefore, the face of the Chinese **conveyed** professional **humility**.

At that moment, one pure-minded Samaritan who was **squatted** on the ground resting his chin in his palms, bewilderedly looked at other people, and asked: "Why did those two mice have to have a certain relationship?"

此时，单纯的撒玛利亚人蹲在地上托着下巴，呆呆地望着众人，问道："为什么两只老鼠一定要有什么关系呢？"

Suddenly, the atmosphere froze. **Stupefied**, the group looked back at the Samaritan and remained speechless. The Rome official, the Israeli and the Chinese who had spoken earlier all lowered their heads in shame, and did not dare to respond.

空气在刹那之间凝固了，众人呆呆地望着这个撒玛利亚人，不发一语。先前说话的罗马长官、以色列人和中国人都面露惭色地低下头不敢作声。

In fact, the true love is not established on benefit, friendship and loyalty or blood relationship. Instead, it is based on no relationship.

事实上，真正的爱并非建立于利益、情义或血缘的关系上，而是建立于"没有任何关系"上。

魅力词汇

barn [baːn] *n.* 谷仓
squeeze [skwiːz] *v.* 挤
tail [teil] *n.* 尾巴
arrogance ['ærəgəns] *n.* 傲慢自大
superciliously [sjuːpə'siliəsli] *adv.* 目空一切地
countenance ['kauntənəns] *n.* 面容，表情
convey [kən'vei] *v.* 表达，转达
humility [hjuː'miləti] *n.* 谦逊，谦恭
squat [skwɔt] *v.* 蹲坐，蹲
stupefied ['stjuːpifaid] *adj.* 惊愕的

6 The Zen of Cat (1) 猫的禅宗（1）

“那你最常在什么地方见到我呢？”

……

“那么，无论什么时候你想见我，你只要闭上你的眼睛就可以了。”

文苑漫步

The Man was very sad. He knew that the Cat's days were numbered. The doctor had said there wasn't anything more that could be done, that he should take the Cat home and make him as comfortable as possible.

The Man **stroked** the Cat on his lap and sighed. The Cat opened his eyes, **purred** and looked up at the Man. A tear rolled down the Man's cheek and landed on the Cat's forehead. The Cat gave him a slightly annoyed look.

"Why do you cry, Man?" the Cat asked. "Because you can't bear the thought of losing me? Because you think you can never replace me?" The Man nodded "yes."

"And where do you think I'll be when I leave you?" the Cat asked. The

译林畅游

男人非常伤心。他知道猫余下的日子不多了。医生说已经没得治了，他只能把猫带回家，并尽可能地让他在剩下的时间里过得舒服些。

男人把猫放在腿上，叹了口气。猫睁开眼睛，呼噜呼噜地叫着，抬眼看了看男人。一滴眼泪从男人的脸颊边滑落，落在了猫的额头上。猫有点不高兴地看了他一眼。

“你哭个什么啊，伙计？”猫问道，“因为你无法承受将要失去我的念头？因为你认为永远都没有什么能代替我？”男人点了点头，“是啊。”

“那么你认为我离开你以后，到什么地方去了呢？”猫问道。男

Man **shrugged** helplessly. “Close your eyes, Man,” the Cat said. The Man gave him a questioning look, but did as he was told.

“What color are my eyes and fur?” the Cat asked. “Your eyes are gold and your fur is a rich, warm brown,” the Man replied.

“And where is it that you most often see me?” asked the Cat. “I see you… on the kitchen windowsill watching the birds… on my favorite chair… on my desk lying on the papers I need… on the pillow next to my head at night.” “Then, whenever you wish to see me, all you must do is close your eyes,” said the Cat.

人无望地耸了耸肩。“闭上眼睛吧，伙计。”猫说。男人疑惑地看了他一眼，但还是听话地闭上了眼睛。

“我的眼睛和毛皮是什么颜色的？”猫问。“你的眼睛是金色的，你的毛皮是浓郁而温暖的褐色的。”男人回答道。

“那你最常在什么地方见到我呢？”猫问。“我经常见到你……在厨房的窗台上看鸟……在我最喜欢的椅子上……躺在桌子上我需要用的文件上……晚上睡在我脑袋边的枕头上。”“那么，无论什么时候你想见我，你只要闭上你的眼睛就可以了。”猫说。

魅力词汇

stroke [strəuk] *v.* 轻抚；轻揶

pur [pəː] *v.* 发出喉音；咕噜咕噜叫

shrug [ʃrʌg] *v.* 耸肩

温情絮语

Two heads are better than one.

三个臭皮匠，顶个诸葛亮。

7 The Zen of Cat (2) 猫的禅宗（2）

无生无死，无死无生。生命因为有死亡才宝贵，才有意义。死亡因为新生才有希望。

文苑漫步

"Pick up that piece of string from the floor — there, my 'toy.'" The Man opened his eyes, then reached over and picked up the string. It was about two feet long and the Cat had been able to **entertain** himself for hours with it. "Now take each end of the string in one hand," the Cat ordered. The Man did so.

"The end in your left hand is my birth and the end in your right hand is my death. Now bring the two ends together," the Cat said. The Man **complied**.

"You have made a **continuous** circle," said the Cat. "Does any point along the string appear to be different, worse or better than any other part of the string?" The Man inspected the string and then shook his head "no."

"Close your eyes again," the Cat said. "Now lick your hand." The Man widened his eyes in surprise.

译林畅游

"把地上的那段绳子捡起来——那里，我的'玩具'。"男人睁开眼睛，伸手捡起了绳子。绳子大约有两英尺长，猫曾经能够玩着绳子自娱自乐一玩就是几个小时。"现在用两只手捏住绳子的两端。"猫命令道。男人照做了。

"你左手捏着的那端就是我的出生，而右手的那端就是我的死亡。现在把两端连在一起。"猫说道。男人又照做了。

"你做出了一个连贯的圆圈，"猫说，"这个绳子上的任意一点同其他点有什么不同吗？比绳子的其他部分更好或者更差吗？"男人审视着那根绳子，然后摇了摇头。"没有。"

"再次闭上你的眼睛，"猫说，"现在舔舔你的手。"男人惊讶地睁大了眼睛。

"Just do it," the Cat said. "Lick your hand. Think of me in all my familiar places. Think about all the pieces of string."

The Man felt foolish, licking his hand, but he did as he was told. He discovered what a cat must know, that licking a paw is very calming and allows one to think more clearly. He continued licking and the corners of his mouth turned upward into the first smile he had shown in days. He waited for the Cat to tell him to stop, and when he didn't, he opened his eyes. The Cat's eyes were closed. The Man stroked the warm, brown fur, but the Cat was gone.

The Man shut his eyes hard as the tears poured down his face. He saw the Cat on the windowsill, then in his bed, then lying across his important papers. He saw him on the pillow next to his head, saw his bright gold eyes and darkest brown on his nose and ears. He opened his eyes and through his tears looked over at the circle of string he still held **clutched** in his hand.

One day, not long after, there was a new Cat on his lap. She was a lovely calico and white… very different from his earlier beloved Cat and very much the same.

"照我说的做吧，"猫说。"舔舔你的手，想想我在所有我熟悉的地方，想想所有的绳子。"

男人舔着自己的手，觉得自己很蠢，不过他还是照做了。他发现了猫所知道的秘密——舔爪子能让你平静下来，并让你能够思考得更加清楚。他继续舔着，他的嘴角开始上翘，好多天来第一次露出了微笑。他等待着猫叫停，可是没等到，于是他睁开了眼睛。猫的眼睛已经闭上了。他摸了摸猫温暖的褐色皮毛，可是猫已经去了。

男人用力地闭上了眼睛，泪如泉涌。他看到猫蹲在窗台上，然后是他的床上，然后躺在他的重要文件上。他看到猫在他脑袋边的枕头上，看到他明亮的金黄色的眼睛还有鼻子和耳朵上深褐色的毛发。他睁开眼睛，透过泪水看向他依然捏在手里的绳圈。

不久以后的某一天，他的膝上有了一只新的猫咪。她是一只可爱的白色花斑猫——与之前那只他深爱的猫是那么的不同，然而又是那么的相同。

魅力词汇

entertain [ˌentəˈtein] *v.* 娱乐
comply [kəmˈplai] *v.* 顺从，答应
continuous [kənˈtinjuəs] *adj.* 连续的，继续的，连绵不断的
clutch [klʌtʃ] *v.* 紧紧抓住（某人/某物）

8 Compassion 怜悯之心

一样的工作，然而不一样的心带来不一样的效果。怜悯来自于人们内心深处那一份未泯灭的良知，那里是我们的自我价值所在之地。

文苑漫步

My dad works for a food organization that travels to rural areas to offer food, medical assistance as well as entertainment. Recently I went with him to one of their conventions. I was there simply to give people directions, hand them a **flyer** and send them on their way. It was hot and tiring, and I wasn't having much fun. Honestly, I didn't really care, and ended up doing it **halfheartedly**.

Then I saw two girls who had the same task I did, but were smiling and happy. They walked up to people who looked lost and asked them if they needed help, instead of waiting for people to find them. An elderly woman **wobbled** over to one while the other approached a toothless, foul-smelling man with **rags draped** over his sickly body. I saw the first girl talking courteously to the old woman

译林畅游

我爸爸为一个食品组织工作。这个组织经常到偏远地区为那里的人提供食品、医疗援助和娱乐服务。最近，我跟他一起参加了他们的一次日常工作。我在那儿只是简单地给人指示方向、发传单以及引路。那天天气酷热，让人十分疲惫，我一点兴致都没有。坦白地说，我并不是很用心，最后只是敷衍了事。

然后，我看到两个女孩子干着跟我一样的工作，但是却面带笑容，满心欢喜。她们走到看似迷路的人面前，询问他们是否需要帮助，而不是等着别人来找她们。一个老妇人摇摇晃晃地走向其中一个女孩，而另一个女孩则走向一个掉了牙的满身恶臭的男人，那人病恹恹的身子上搭着块破布。我看到第一个女孩彬彬有礼地和那个老妇人交谈，然后笑着给了她一个让她安心的拥抱。与此同时，第

and then smile as she gave her a reassuring hug. Meanwhile the second girl said, "Hello, sir. Is there something I can help you with today?" SIR? SIR!! She spoke to this man as though he were important! It seemed **preposterous**. Was I hearing her correctly? Why would she talk to a **bum** from the street as though he was a **colonel** in the army?

She showed compassion. Because she cared about this man and wanted him to feel loved and important, she showed respect. He raised his chin just a **tad** when she called him "Sir". Rolling his shoulders back, he felt her reaching out to him in that simple phrase, and his tired, wrinkled face **sparkled**. As for the old woman — I stood in **awe**. Never in my life had I seen a moment that displayed such care and love. Yes, this is what compassion is all about.

To love another is not only to recognize the need, but also to express warm sympathy toward that need. It is giving people what they need even when they are too afraid to ask. After seeing the compassion those girls so freely expressed, I knew I could do my job better.

A little girl walked over to me, holding her mother's hand. I smiled, because I cared. I cared about what she needed and wanted, about her sorrows and disappointments. I truly cared! It gave me happiness

二个女孩说道："你好，先生。今天有什么事情我可以帮你的吗？"先生？先生！！她跟这个男人说话的语气就像他是个重要人物似的！那简直太荒谬了。我没听错吧？为什么她跟一个街上的流浪汉说话就像他是个军队的上校似的？

她表现出的是怜悯之心。因为她关心这个男人，希望他感觉到被人爱护并且觉得自己很重要，所以她表现出了尊重。当她叫他"先生"的时候，那男人只是微微抬起下巴。他把肩膀转回去的同时，从那个简单的词中感受到她向他伸出援手，而他疲倦的皱纹满布的面孔溢出光彩。至于老妇人呢——我站在那里肃然起敬。在我的生命中，从没有过一个时刻，让我看到这样的关心和爱护。没错，这就是怜悯之心的含义。

关爱别人并不仅仅是明白他（她）的需要，还要对这种需要表示出温暖的怜悯之心。关爱别人就是向有需要的人提供所需——甚至在他们太害怕而不敢提出的时候。看到那两个女孩如此直率地展现出她们的怜悯之心，我知道我可以做得更好。

一个小女孩牵着她妈妈的手向我走来。我面带微笑，因为我关心。我关心她的需要和希望，她的悲伤和失望。我真的关心！那样做让我

and a glow that can only be felt when you do something right. Happiness grew to **perseverance** — to keep going because I could do something to impact another. And so I not only experienced the glow, but also kept it burning in my heart.

Taking time to show compassion in my life has made a difference in my character and who I am. It is definitely the ultimate principle to live by. Compassion is the key. Holding it, I open every room to let the sunshine flow in.

感到喜悦与暖意——那是只有你做了正确的事才会感受得到的。喜悦让人坚持不懈——继续干下去，因为我可以做出影响其他人的事情来。也因为这样，我不但体验到了这份暖意，而且还使之在我心中继续燃烧。

在生活中花些时间来展现怜悯之心，让我的性格和自我价值发生了改变。那绝对是我一生要遵循的原则。怜悯之心是其核心所在。秉持这份怜悯之情，打开每一间小屋，让阳光都倾泻进来。

魅力词汇

flyer [flaiə] *n.* 传单
halfheartedly ['hɑːfˌhɑːtidli] *adv.* 不认真地；不热心地
wobble ['wɔbl] *v.* 摇晃，摇摆
rag [ræg] *n.* 破布，碎屑
drape [dreip] *v.* 用布帘覆盖
preposterous [pri'pɔstərəs] *adj.* 可笑的；荒谬的
bum [bʌm] *n.* 流浪汉
colonel ['kəːnəl] *n.* 陆军上校
tad [tæd] *n.* 少量
sparkle ['spɑːkl] *v.* 使闪耀；使发光
awe [ɔː] *n.* 敬畏
perseverance [ˌpəːsiː'viərəns] *n.* 坚持不懈

温情絮语

Good company on the road is the shortest cut.

行路有良伴就是捷径。

9 Black Charcoal, White Shirt
黑木炭，白衬衫

送人玫瑰，手有余香；同样，送人黑炭，身留污迹。你愿人怎样待你，你就要怎样待人。

文苑漫步

8-year-old Pico stormed home after school, after the door he wildly **stomping** his feet. His father was working in the yard and saw Pico angry. So he called Pico and wanted to talk with him.

Reluctant to be around his father, Pico said angrily: "Dad, I am very angry."

Pico's father was quietly listening to his son while working. Pico said: "Joaquin made me **disgrace** the former friends. I hope he comes across a few particularly bad luck things."

His father went to a corner, found a bag of **charcoal**, and said to Pico: "Son, you regard that white shirt over there as Joaquin, and the plastic bag of charcoal as some bad luck things. Use charcoal to hit the white shirt. Imagine that every time you hit one on the shirt Joaquin encountered a bad luck thing. When you finish

译林畅游

8岁的Pico放学以后气冲冲地回到家里，进门以后使劲地跺脚。父亲正在院子里干活，看到Pico生气的样子，就把他叫了过来，想和他聊聊。

Pico不情愿地走到父亲身边，气呼呼地说："爸爸，我现在非常生气。"

Pico的父亲一边干活，一边静静地听儿子诉说。Pico说："Joaquin让我在以前的朋友跟前丢脸，我希望他遇上几件特别倒霉的事情。"

他父亲走到一个角落，找到一袋木炭，对Pico说："儿子，你把那边的那件白衬衫当作Joaquin，把这一塑料袋的木炭当作一些倒霉的事情。你用木炭去砸白衬衫，假想每砸中一块，Joaquin就遇到一件倒霉的事情。看看当你把木炭砸完以后会怎样。"

hitting all the charcoal, see what will happen."

Pico thought this game was fun. He picked up charcoal to throw into the shirt. However the shirt was hung in the distant rope. He finished throwing all the charcoal, but not a few on the shirt.

Pico觉得这个游戏很好玩，他拿起木炭就往衬衫上砸去。可是衬衫挂在距离较远的绳子上，他把木炭扔完了，也没有几块扔到衬衫上。

Father asked Pico: "How do you feel now?"

父亲问 Pico："你现在感觉如何？"

He said: "It exhausted me, but I am happy because I threw in quite a few pieces of charcoal, the white shirt with several black trace."

他说："累死我了，但我很开心，因为我扔中了好几块木炭，白衬衫上有好几个黑印子了。"

Father saw his son did not understand his intentions, so he let Pico look in a large mirror. What he could only see from his face was white teeth.

父亲看到儿子没有明白他的用意，于是便让 Pico 去一面很大的镜子里照照。Pico 从他的脸上只能看到白白的牙齿。

Then the father said: "You see, the white shirt did not become particularly dirty, but you have become a 'black people'. You want a lot of bad luck things on others; the result is the most unfortunate thing falls on ourselves. There, our bad thoughts may fulfill a part on others, others suffer bad luck, but the **stains** left to us are difficult to remove."

父亲这时说道："你看，白衬衫并没有变得特别脏，而你自己却成了一个'黑人'。你想让别人遇到很多倒霉事，结果最倒霉的事却落到我们自己身上了。有时候，我们的坏念头虽然在别人身上兑现了一部分，别人倒霉了，但留在我们身上的污点也难以去除。"

魅力词汇

stomp [stɔmp] *v.* 跺脚

disgrace [dis'greis] *v.* 使……丢脸

charcoal ['tʃɑːkəul] *n.* 木炭

stain [stein] *n.* 污点

10 The Old Fisherman 老渔夫的故事

生命并不是一帆风顺的幸福之旅，而是时时摆动在幸与不幸，沉与浮、光明与黑暗之间的模式里。一个可爱的灵魂不会因为一路风风雨雨，而忘记天边的彩虹；一颗感恩的心灵，不会因为一时的痛苦而愤愤不平。上帝的花园中那最美的一株，并不在于那曾经栽培它的花盆如何。

文苑漫步

Our house was directly across the street from the clinic entrance of Johns Hopkins Hospital in Baltimore. We lived downstairs and rented the upstairs rooms to **out-patients** at the clinic.

One summer evening as I was **fixing** supper, there was a knock at the door. I opened it to see a truly awful-looking man. "Why, he's hardly taller than my 8-year-old," I thought as I stared at the **stooped**, **shriveled** body. But the **appalling** thing was his face, **lopsided** from **swelling**, red and raw. Yet his voice was pleasant as he said, "Good evening. I've come to see if you've a room for just one night. I came for a treatment this morning from the eastern shore, but there's no bus until morning."

He told me he'd been hunting for a

译林畅游

我家住在巴尔的摩市，与约翰斯·霍普金森医院门诊部的正门只隔了条马路。我们住楼下，楼上的屋子租给来诊所求诊的病人。

一个夏日的傍晚，我正在准备晚餐时，忽然听见有人敲门。打开门后，我见到一个相貌丑陋的老人。看着他那蜷曲、枯瘦的身体我心想："天啊，他简直还没有我8岁时高呢。"更骇人的是他的脸——因浮肿而显得扭曲，红红的而且很粗糙。不过他说话时的声音倒也和善："晚上好，我想问一下，你这儿有没有屋子借住一晚。我早上从东海岸赶来治病，明天早上才有回家的大巴。"

他告诉我他从中午起就在找房

room since noon but with no success. No one seemed to have a room. "I guess it's my face... I know it looks terrible, but my doctor says with a few more treatments..."

For a moment I hesitated, but his next words convinced me. "I could sleep in this **rocking** chair on the porch. My bus leaves early in the morning."

I told him we would find him a bed, but to rest on the porch. I went inside and finished getting supper. When we were ready, I asked the old man if he would join us. "No, thank you. I have plenty." And he held up a brown paper bag.

When I had finished the dishes, I went out on the porch to talk with him for a few minutes. It didn't take long time to see that this old man had an oversized heart crowded into that tiny body. He told me he fished for a living to support his daughter, her five children, and her husband, who was hopelessly **crippled** from a back injury.

He didn't tell it by way of complaint. In fact, every other sentence was **preface** with a thanks to God for a blessing. He was grateful that no pain accompanied his disease, which was apparently a form of skin cancer. He thanked God for giving him the strength to keep going.

At bedtime, we put a camp **cot** in the children's room for him. When I got

子，但没找到。好像没人有空房。"我猜想是我的脸……我晓得我的脸看上去很可怕，但医生说再多治几次……"

我迟疑了片刻，但他接下来的话语说服了我。"我可以睡在走廊的摇椅上，明天一大早就去赶大巴。"

我告诉他我们会给他找一张床，但只能搁在走廊里。回屋布置好晚餐准备开饭时，我问老人要不要过来一起吃。他举起一只褐色纸包说："不了，谢谢你，我这儿有足够的。"

饭后，我到走廊上同他聊了几分钟。不久，便发现这位老人瘦小的身躯里却有着伟岸的心灵。他告诉我，以钓鱼为生是为了扶持他女儿，女儿的五个孩子，还有女婿——一个因脊椎受伤彻底致残的人。

他不是以抱怨的口吻讲述这些事，实际上，每句话的开始都对上帝的保佑充满谢意。他感激他所患的病——显然是某种皮肤癌——没有疼痛，他感谢上帝赐予他继续活下去的力量。

就寝时，我在孩子们的房间给他放了张野营用的小床。第二天早

up in the morning, the **bed linens** were neatly folded and the little man was out on the porch. He refused breakfast. But just before he left for his bus, **haltingly**, as if asking a great favor, he said, "Could I please come back and stay the next time I have a treatment? I won't put you out a bit. I can sleep fine in a chair."

He paused for a moment and then added, "Your children made me feel at home. Grownups are bothered by my face, but children don't seem to mind."

I told him he was welcome to come again.

On his next trip he arrived a little after 7:00 in the morning. As a gift, he brought a big fish and a quart of the largest oysters I had ever seen. He said he had **shucked** them that morning before he left so that they'd be nice and fresh. I knew his bus left at 4:00 a.m. and I wondered what time he had to get up in order to do this for us.

During the years he came to stay overnight with us, there was never a time that he did not bring us fish or oysters or vegetables from his garden. Other times we received packages in the mail, always by special delivery... fish and oysters packed in a box with fresh young **spinach** or **kale**... every leaf carefully washed. Knowing that he must walk three miles to mail these, and knowing how little money

晨我起来时，小床上的被褥已齐整地叠好，老人站在外面的走廊上。他谢绝了早餐。就在即将离开去乘巴士时，他犹豫再三，像是要请求一个天大的恩惠，问道："下次来看病时，我还能回到这儿住吗？我不会给你们添乱的，我只要在椅子上就能睡好。"

他顿了一会，补充道："你们的小孩让我感觉像是在家里一样自在。大人们因我的脸而烦恼，可孩子们好像不那么介意。"

我告诉他欢迎下次再来。

第二次，老人早上 7 点多就到了。他带了一条大鱼和一夸脱牡蛎作为礼物，那是我所见过的最大的牡蛎。他说早上出发前剥了壳，这样能保证新鲜又美味。我知道他乘的巴士凌晨 4 点发车，我在想，为给我们准备这些东西，他得多早就起来啊。

那些年他在我们家借宿，每次都带鱼、牡蛎，或是他家园子里的蔬菜。还有几次我们收到他特意寄来的东西——盒子里新鲜嫩菠菜或甘蓝叶包裹的鱼和牡蛎……每片叶子都仔细清洗过。得知他得步行三英里邮寄，得知他自己的收入那么低，这些礼物在我们心里变得倍加珍贵。

he had made the gifts doubly precious.

When I received these little **remembrances**, I often thought of a comment our next-door neighbor made after he left that first morning. "Did you keep that awful-looking man last night? I turned him away! You can lose roomers by **putting up** such people!"

每当我收到这些小小的礼物时，常想起老人首次借宿的次日清晨，我们隔壁的邻居对我说："昨晚你收留那丑八怪老头了吗？我把他支出去了！你要留他过夜非吓跑房客不可！"

Maybe we did lose roomers once or twice. But oh! If only they could have known him, perhaps their illness would have been easier to bear. I know our family will always be grateful to have known him. From him, we learned what it was to accept the bad without **complaint** and the good with **gratitude** to God.

可能我家的确曾经一两次失去房客，但是啊，如果他们能认识这位老人，或许他们的病痛将不再那么难以承受。我知道，我的家人总是为认识这位老人而心存感激。从他那里，我们学到了坦然面对不幸而毫无怨言，并怀着感恩的心接受上帝赐予的美好。

Recently I was visiting a friend who has a greenhouse. As she showed me her flowers, we came to the most beautiful one of all... a golden **chrysanthemum**, bursting with blooms. But to my great surprise, it was growing in an old **dented**, **rusty** bucket.

最近，我拜访了一位朋友，她有一个花房。她带我观看她的花时，我们来到花房中最美丽的一处——一株绽放的金菊。但令我特别惊奇的是，它竟然生长在一个凹陷的、生了锈的铁桶里。

I thought to myself, "If this were my plant, I'd put it in the loveliest container I had!" My friend changed my mind.

我心里想，"如果这是我的花，我会把它放到我最可爱的花盆里去！"朋友改变了我的想法。

"I ran short of pots," she explained, "and knowing how beautiful this one would be, I thought it wouldn't mind starting out in this old **pail**. It's just for a little while, until I can put it out in the garden."

"当时我缺花盆"，她解释道，"既然知道它会那么好看，我想它也不介意在这旧桶里开花。用不了多久，我就会把它移栽到花园里去。"

She must have wondered why I

她一定很奇怪我为何笑得如此

laughed so **delightedly**, but I was imagining such a scene in heaven. "Here's an especially beautiful one," God might have said when he came to the soul of the sweet old fisherman. "He won't mind starting in this small body."

All this happened long ago. And now, in God's garden, how tall this lovely soul must stand.

开心，我那时正想象着天堂中这样一幅情景。当上帝来到老渔夫可爱的灵魂前时可能会说："这样一个特别可爱的灵魂，并不介意栖息于瘦小的身躯。"

这些都发生在很久以前。而现在，那美好的灵魂该是多么高大地伫立于上帝的花园里啊！

魅力词汇

out-patient ['ɑutpeiʃnt] *n.* 门诊病人
fix [fiks] *v.* 准备，安排
stoop [stuːp] *v.* 屈身，弯腰
shrivel ['ʃrivəl] *v.* 使枯萎；使皱缩
appalling [ə'pɔːliŋ]
adj. 可怕的；令人震惊的
lopsided [ˌlɔp'sɑidid]
adj. 不平衡的，倾向一方的
swelling ['sweliŋ] *n.* 肿胀
rocking ['rɔkiŋ] *adj.* 摇摆的
cripple ['kripl] *v.* 使跛；使残废
preface ['prefəs] *n.* 前言；引语
cot [kɔt] *n.* 简易床；轻便小床
bed linen 床用织物，床单和枕套
haltingly ['hɔːltiŋli]
adv. 迟疑不决地；犹豫地
shuck [ʃʌk] *v.* 剥去
spinach ['spinitʃ] *n.* 菠菜
kale [keil] *n.* 甘蓝；洋白菜
remembrance [ri'membrəns] *n.* 纪念品
put up 供给住宿
complaint [kəm'pleint] *n.* 抱怨
gratitude ['grætitjuːd]
n. 感激之情，感恩的心
chrysanthemum [kri'sænθəməm]
n. [植] 菊花
dented ['dentid] *adj.* 有凹痕的
rusty ['rʌsti] *adj.* 生锈的，腐蚀的
pail [peil] *n.* 桶，提桶
delightedly [di'lɑitidli]
adv. 高兴地，欣喜地

11 A Perfect Heart 完美的心

不去尝试，固然没有心痛与失败，但也失去了成功的喜悦。不去付出，自然不会有所损失，但永远也无法收获回报的快乐。人生需要收获，也许更需要付出。

文苑漫步

One day a young man was standing in the middle of the town **proclaiming** that he had the most beautiful heart in the whole valley. A large crowd gathered, and they all admired his heart for it was perfect. There was not a flaw in it.

Suddenly, an old man appeared and said, "Why, your heart is not nearly as beautiful as mine!"

The crowd and the young man looked at the old man's heart. It was full of scars. It had places where pieces had been removed and other pieces put in, but they didn't fit quite right, and there were several **jagged** edges. In fact, in some places there were deep **gouges** where whole pieces were missing.

The young man laughed. "Comparing your heart with mine, mine is perfect and

译林畅游

一天，一个年轻人站在镇子的中央，宣称他拥有整个山谷最美丽的心。一大群人围了过来，纷纷称赞年轻人的心，因为这颗心完美无瑕。

突然一位老者出现了，说道：“嗨，你的心可不如我的心美丽啊！”

这群人和年轻人都看了看老者的心，只见上面布满伤痕。心上的一些部分被取走了，另外补上了其他人的，但并不十分吻合，还有几处边缘参差不齐。事实上，他的心上有些地方留下了深深的凹痕，整瓣整瓣的心都不见了。

年轻人笑道：“跟你的心相比，我的心完美无比，而你的心却满是

yours is a mess of scars."

"Yes," said the old man, "Yours looks perfect but I would never trade with you. You see, every scar represents a person to whom I have given my love. I tear out a piece of my heart and give it to them, and often they give me a piece of their heart that fits into the empty place in my heart. "

"But because the pieces aren't exact, I have some rough edges, which I cherish, because they remind me of the love we shared."

"Sometimes I have given pieces of my heart away, and the other person hasn't returned a piece of his or her heart to me. These are the empty gouges — giving love is taking a chance."

"Although these gouges are painful, they stay open, reminding me of the love I have for those people too, and I hope someday they may return and fill the space I've been waiting. So now do you see what true beauty is?"

The young man walked up to the old man, reached into his perfect heart, and **ripped** a piece out. He offered it to the old man.

The old man placed it in his heart, then took a piece from his old scarred heart and placed it in the wound in the young man's heart. It fit, but not perfectly, as there were some jagged edges.

疤痕。"

"没错，"老者说，"你的心看上去很完美，但是我永远不会和你交换。你瞧，每处伤痕都代表一个我曾爱过的人。我撕下自己的一片心给他们，他们往往也会给我一片他们的心，填补我心中缺失的那部分。"

"但是由于每片心大小并不完全相同，我的心有些粗糙的边缘，不过我很珍惜，因为它们让我想起我们之间分享过的爱。"

"有时我把自己的几片心送出去，另一个人却没有向我回馈他/她的心。这些便成了空着的深痕——付出爱本来就是一种冒险。"

"尽管这些凹痕让我感到痛苦，但它们敞开着，让我想起我对他们付出的爱，并希望有朝一日能得到回馈，填满这等待已久的空间。所以，现在你明白什么才是真正的美了吗？"

年轻人走到老者面前，把手伸进自己完美的心中，撕下了一片，赠给了老者。

老者把这片心放进自己的心里，然后从自己那颗苍老而又伤痕累累的心上撕下一片，放入年轻人心上的伤口里。虽然能够放进去，但不十分吻合，因为有的边缘凹凸不平。

The young man looked at his heart, not perfect anymore but more beautiful than ever, since love from the old man's heart flowed into his.

They embraced and walked away side by side.

How sad it must be to go through life with a whole untouched heart!

年轻人看了看自己的心，它虽然不再完美，却比以往更加美丽，因为老者心中的爱流入了他的心田。

他们互相拥抱，然后并肩前行。

如果人这一生一直保持着一颗完整未动的心是多么可悲啊！

魅力词汇

proclaim [prə'kleim] *v.* 宣告，公布

jagged ['dʒægid] *adj.* 锯齿状的；参差不齐的

gouge [gaudʒ] *n.* 沟，半圆凿

rip [rip] *v.* 撕

温情絮语

Once we dreamt that we were strangers,
we woke up to find that we were dear to each other.

有一次，我们梦见彼此不相识，
我们醒了，却知道我们原是相亲相爱的。

12 The Warmth of a Glass of Milk
一杯牛奶的温度

帮助别人就是帮助自己，一杯在小男孩饥饿之时所赠予的牛奶，换来的是自己生命垂危之时的及时救助。上帝的爱通过人类的心灵和双手传播。

文苑漫步

One day, a poor boy who was trying to pay his way through school by selling goods from door to door found that he had only one **dime** left. He was hungry so he decided to beg for a meal at the next house.

However, he **lost his nerve** when a lovely young woman opened the door. Instead of a meal he asked for a drink of water. She thought he looked hungry so she brought him a large glass of milk. He drank it slowly, and then asked, "How much do I owe you?"

"You don't **owe** me anything," she replied. "Mother has taught me never to accept pay for a kindness." He said, "Then I thank you from the bottom of my heart." As Howard Kelly left that house, he not only felt stronger physically, but it also

译林畅游

一天，一个贫穷的小男孩为了攒够学费正挨家挨户地推销商品。他非常饥饿，却发现自己只剩下一角钱。于是他决定向下一户人家讨口饭吃。

然而，当一位美丽的年轻女子打开房门的时候，这个小男孩却有点胆怯了。他没有要饭，只乞求给他一口水喝。这位女子看到他饥饿的样子，就倒了一大杯牛奶给他。男孩慢慢地喝完牛奶，问道："我应该付多少钱？"

她答道："一分钱也不用付。我妈妈教导我，施以爱心，不图回报。"男孩说："那么，就请接受我由衷的感谢吧！"Howard Kelly 离开这户人家时，感觉自己浑身是劲儿，而且更加相信上帝和整个人类。

increased his faith in God and the human race. He was about to give up and quit before this point.

而在这之前，他都打算要放弃了。

Years later the young woman became **critically** ill. The local doctors were **baffled**. They finally sent her to the big city, where specialists can be called in to study her rare disease. Dr. Howard Kelly, now famous was called in for the **consultation**. When he heard the name of the town she came from, a strange light filled his eyes. Immediately, he rose and went down through the hospital hall into her room.

数年之后，那位年轻女子得了重病，当地医生对此束手无策。最后，他们把她送到大城市医治，在那里召集专家对她这种罕见的病进行会诊治疗。大名鼎鼎的 Howard Kelly 医生也被召集参加了这次会诊。当他听到病人来自的那个城镇的名字时，眼神变得非常奇怪。他马上起身穿过医院走廊直奔她的病房。

Dressed in his doctor's **gown** he went in to see her. He recognized her at once. He went back to the consultation room and determined to do his best to save her life. From that day on, he gave special attention to her case.

身穿医袍的 Kelly 进了病房去看她，他一眼就认出了她。回到会诊室后，他下定决心要竭尽所能来挽救她的生命。从那天起，他就特别关照她的病情。

After a long struggle, the battle was won. Dr. Kelly requested the business office to pass the final bill to him for appro-val. He looked at it and then wrote something on the side. The bill was sent to her room. She was afraid to open it because she was positive that it would take the rest of her life to pay it off. Finally she looked, and the note on the side of the bill caught her attention. She read these

经过艰苦的努力，手术成功了。Kelly 医生要求财务室把最终的费用通知单送到他那里审批，他看了一下，便在通知单的旁边写了一些字。当费用通知单送到她的病房时，她不敢打开看。因为她确信，治病的费用将会用尽她的余生来偿还。最后，她还是看了医药费通知单，旁边的那行小字引起了她的注意，她不禁读了出来：

words...

"Paid in full with a glass of milk."

(Signed) Dr. Howard Kelly

Tears of joy flooded her eyes as she prayed silently: "Thank You, God. Your love has spread through human hearts and hands."

"医药费已付：一杯牛奶的价钱。"

（签名）Howard Kelly 医生

喜悦的泪水溢出了她的眼睛，她默默地祈祷着："谢谢你，上帝，你的爱已通过人类的心灵和双手传播了。"

魅力词汇

dime [daim] *n.* 一角硬币

lose one's nerve 失去勇气

owe [əu] *v.* 欠

critically ['kritikəli] *adv.* 严重地

baffle ['bæfl] *v.* 使……困惑；难住

consultation [ˌkɔnsəl'teiʃn] *n.* [医] 会诊；咨询；磋商

gown [gaun] *n.* 长袍

温情絮语

That just one person saying to me, "You've made my day!" makes my day.

有人告诉我"你让我很快乐"，这使我很快乐。

13 A Pair of Precious Hands
宝贵的双手

聪明的女孩终于为自己挑得了一个可以托付终身的小伙子。相比于那些满载着稀世珍宝的求婚者，他有何长处竟赢得了姑娘的芳心呢？

文苑漫步

There was once a **shepherd** who had a daughter whose great beauty attracted a lot of young men from all over the country.

One day, the shepherd asked his daughter, "My dear daughter, tell me, what kind of man do you want to be your husband?" His daughter said, "My dear father, my future husband can be poor but also a wealthy man." "How could that be? Poor and rich are two opposite things!" said her father. "Dear father, a poor person also has his wealth," said his daughter. The shepherd then announced that his daughter was ready for marriage.

One day, there were many **eligible** men gathered outside the shepherd's home. He came out and said, "All right, gentlemen, those who think they are eligible, please come forward and tell me your **qualifications**!" A few well-dressed

译林畅游

从前，有个牧羊人，他有一个非常美丽的女儿，她的美吸引了方圆几百里的许多年轻小伙子。

一天，牧羊人问女儿："亲爱的孩子，告诉我，你想要什么样的人做你的丈夫呢？"女儿回答说："亲爱的父亲，我将来的丈夫是个既贫穷又富有的人。""这怎么可能呢？贫穷和富有是相对的啊！"牧羊人说。女儿说，"亲爱的父亲，贫穷的人也有他自己的财富。"然后，牧羊人就发出了招婿的通告。

一天，许多符合条件的求婚男子云集在牧羊人的房子外面。牧羊人走出帐篷，对大家说："好，各位认为自己有资格来求婚的人士，请上前来说说自己的条件吧！"几个衣着华丽的小伙子走上前来，他们

gentlemen came forward followed by their servants and camel loads of gifts carried by camels. "We are rich men; we have gold and silver mines, silk, fur and red carpets. Please choose one of us." The shepherd's daughter just smiled. Then came five young men with some jewelry boxes. "These golden boxes contain rare jewelry. You will be the most wealthy person if you choose one of us to be your husband." "All of you are not my idea of an ideal husband," said the disappointed lady.

One by one young men came forward but they were **rejected** by her. The shepherd began to worry. Suddenly, a plainly dressed young man appeared. The shepherd asked, "Young man, you look so poor. What can you offer my daughter?" "My wealth is always with me and it is my hands," the young man said, "I am a good **tailor**. I am also a good **carpenter**. I can make tables and chairs within an hour. Moreover, I can also put up a tent for you all!" The lady smiled. The young man continued, "I can cook too. I can cook delicious meals. However, I do not have any **property**, servants or jewelry. But, with my pair of hands, I do have a whole life of wealth!" "That's great!" shouted the shepherd's daughter excitedly. "You are more wealthy than any of them because you have a pair of precious hands. You are my

的仆人牵着满载礼品的骆驼跟在后面。“我们都是有钱人。我们拥有金山银山、丝绸、皮毛和红毡。请从我们当中选一个吧。”牧羊人的女儿只是报以微笑。接着，五位手捧珠宝盒子的小伙子走上前来。“这些金盒子里装满了稀世珍品。如果你选择我们其中之一作为你的丈夫，你将成为最富有的人。”“你们都不是我心目中的理想丈夫。”牧羊人的女儿失望地说。

小伙子们一个个走上前来求婚，但都被她拒绝了。牧羊人开始着急起来。突然，有个衣着朴素的青年走了过来。牧羊人问:“年轻人，你看上去很穷。那么，你有什么宝物要献给我女儿吗？”“我的财富一向随身携带，它就是我的双手，”青年说，“我是一个技艺精湛的裁缝师；我还是一个熟练的木匠，我能在一个小时内，给你们订制一套桌椅；而且，我还能给你们搭一个帐篷。”牧羊人的女儿笑了。青年继续说，“我还会烹饪，我能做出最美味的饭菜。然而，我既没有财产，也没有仆人，更没有金银珠宝。但我有一双手，有了这双手，我就拥有了一生用之不尽的财富！”“太好了！”牧羊人的女儿激动地高声喊道，“你比他们中任何人都富有！因为你有一双宝贵的手，你正是我

idea of an ideal husband!"

A pair of hardworking hands can create much wealth.

心目中的理想丈夫！"

一双勤劳的手，可以创造无限的财富。

魅力词汇

shepherd ['ʃepəd] *n.* 牧羊人
eligible ['elidʒəbl] *adj.* 符合条件的
qualification [ˌkwɔlifi'keiʃn] *n.* 资格
reject [ri'dʒekt] *v.* 拒绝
tailor ['teilə] *n.* 裁缝
carpenter ['kɑːpəntə] *n.* 木匠，木工
property ['prɔpəti] *n.* 资产，财产

温情絮语

That I can always pray for someone when I don't have the strength to help him in some other way.

如果从各种方面我都没有能力帮助某个人的时候，我就为他祈祷。

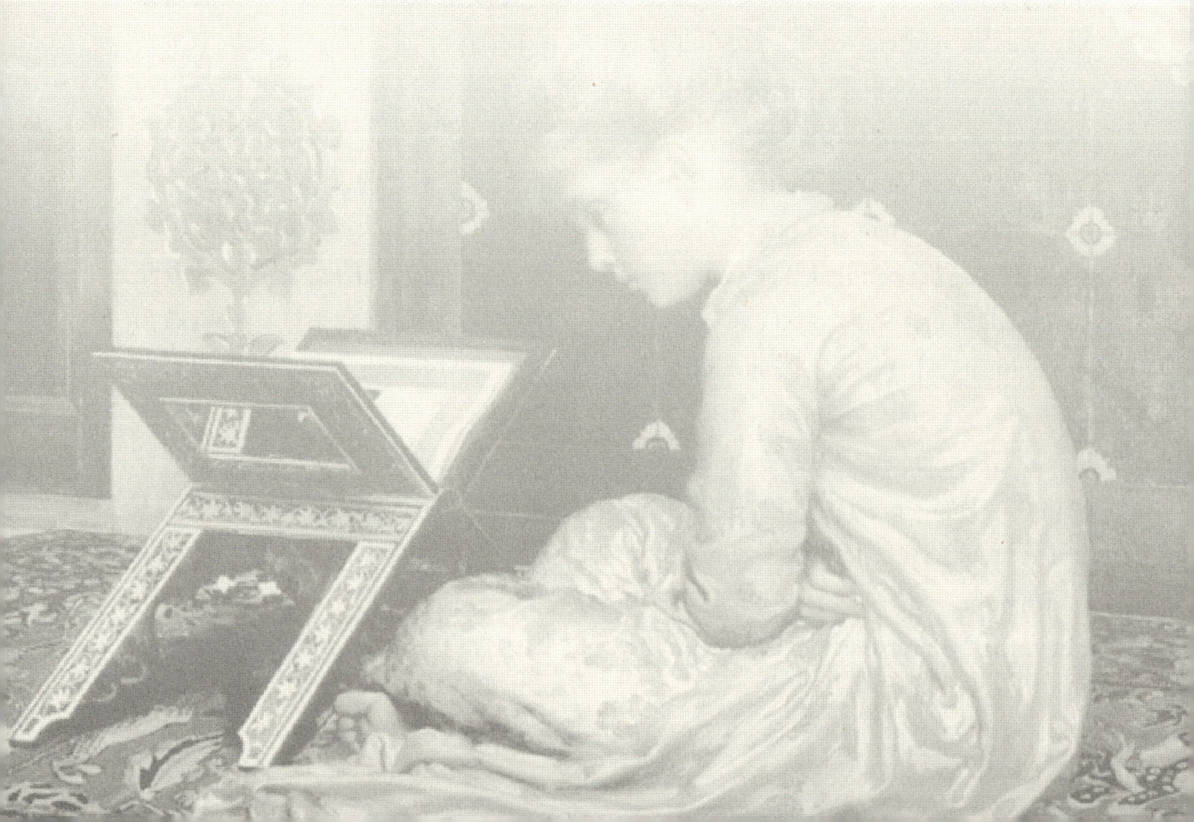

14 The Splashes of Life 生命的波纹

你的一个微笑，也许就会影响一个人一天的心情；你的一个小小的善举，也许就会挽救一条珍贵的生命；你的一个厌恶的眼神，也许就会扼杀一个热切求知的心灵；你的一句轻狂之言，也许就会改变一个人的一生。你的一个举动影响了一个人，那个人也许又会因此而影响到身边更多的人……

文苑漫步

My grandfather took me to the fish pond on the farm when I was about 7, and he told me to throw a stone into the water. He told me to watch the circles created by the stone. Then he asked me to think of myself as that stone person.

"You may create lots of **splashes** in your life, but the waves that come from those splashes will disturb the peace of all your fellow creatures," he said, "Remember that you are responsible for what you put in your circle and that circle will also touch many other circles."

"You will need to live in a way that allows the good that comes from your circle to send the peace of that goodness

译林畅游

在我7岁那年，祖父带我到农场的鱼塘。他让我捡一颗石头扔到水中，并嘱咐我仔细观察石头所激起的波纹。然后，他叫我把自己也看成是那颗石头。

"在生命的水面上，你可能会激起许多波纹，而这些波纹也会打扰到你周围众生的宁静。"祖父对我说，"记住，你需要对你所激起的波纹负责，因为它们会碰到别人的波纹。"

"你应当努力通过自己的波纹将平和静谧传递给他人。而那些带着愤怒或嫉妒的水花，也会将坏

to others. The splash that comes from anger or **jealousy** will send those feelings to other circles. You are responsible for both."

的情绪传递。两种情况，你都要负责任！"

That was the first time I realized that each person creates the inner peace or **discord** that flows out into the world. We cannot create world peace if we are **riddled** with inner conflict, hatred, doubt, or anger.

那是我第一次明白，每个人心中的平静或不安，都会传播给整个世界。如果我们的内心充斥着矛盾、仇恨、怀疑或愤怒，就不能创造一个和平的世界。

We **radiate** the feelings and thoughts that we hold inside, whether we speak them or not. Whatever is splashing around inside of us is spilling out into the world, creating beauty or discord with all other circles of life.

无论是否说出来，我们都在向外传递自己的感情和思想。无论我们内心激起的波纹是哪一种，都会溅向这个世界，并与他人的波纹一起，创造美好或不和谐的生活。

魅力词汇

splash [splæʃ] *n.* 飞溅的水，波纹
jealousy ['dʒeləsi] *n.* 妒忌
discord ['diskɔːd] *n.* 不调和，分歧
riddled ['ridld] *adj.* 充满的，充斥的
radiate ['reidieit] *v.* 放射，散发

温情絮语

That sometimes all a person needs is a hand to hold and a heart to understand.

有时候一个人所需要的只是一只可以握住的手和一颗可以理解他的心。

第三篇

伴你一生

1 Yesterday Once More
追忆似水年华

爱是一生的承诺。从相识、相知到相爱，两个人一路走来，经历人生的风雨，感受岁月的变迁。年华似水，当年的恋人已不再年轻甚至即将辞世，回首走过的一生，感恩伴侣的相伴厮守，不禁让人泪流满面。

文苑漫步

Can it really be sixty-two years ago that I first saw you?

It is truly a lifetime, I know. But as I **gaze into** your eyes now, it seems like only yesterday that I first saw you, in that small cafe in Hanover Square.

From the moment I saw you smile, as you opened the door for that young mother and her newborn baby. I knew. I knew that I wanted to share the rest of my life with you.

All through my life I have relived that very first day. Many, many times I have sat and thought about that first day, and how for a few fleeting moments I am there, feeling again what it is like to know true love for the very first time. It pleases me that I can still have those feelings now after all those years, and I know I will always have them to comfort me.

译林畅游

我第一次见到你，真的是六十二年前吗?

岁月如梭，我知道我们已携手走过一生。但是如今，当我凝望着你的眼睛，当年在汉诺威广场的那间小咖啡馆里的邂逅仍历历在目，恍如就发生在昨天。

见到你的那一刻，你正微笑着为一位年轻的母亲和她的小宝宝开门。那一刻我就想到要与你共度余生。

我一生当中无数次忆起那天的情景。多少次我坐在那里，不断回味那天的点滴，捕捉那些闪动的瞬间，重新体会一见钟情的美丽。欣喜的是，那么多年以后，我仍然拥有那些爱恋的感觉，这些体验将会一直伴随我，安抚我。

Not even as I shook and **trembled** uncontrollably in the **trenches**, did I forget your face. I would sit **huddled** into the wet mud, terrified, as the **hails of bullets and mortars** crashed down around me. I would clutch my rifle tightly to my heart, and think again of that very first day we met. I would cry out in fear, as the noise of war beat down around me. But, as I thought of you and saw you smiling back at me, everything around me would become silent, and I would be with you again for a few precious moments, far from the death and destruction. It would not be until I opened my eyes once again, that I would see and hear the **carnage** of the war around me.

即便当我在战壕中控制不住地颤抖，我也不曾忘记你的容颜。我蜷缩在稀泥中，身边是枪林弹雨，硝烟弥漫，一颗心惊恐不安。我把步枪紧紧地攥在胸前，又回想起了我们初识的那一天。身旁战火呼啸，我恐惧得想要大声呼喊。但是，当我想起你，看到你微笑地回头望着我时，周围的一切忽然沉寂下来，在这珍贵的瞬间，我觉得自己暂时远离了死亡和毁灭，重新回到了你的身旁。我拼命想留住这美好，直到睁开眼，周围却依然是血与火的生死战场。

I cannot tell you how strong my love for you was back then, when I returned to you on leave in the September, feeling battered, **bruised** and fragile. We held each other so tight I thought we would burst. I asked you to marry me the very same day and I **whooped** with joy when you looked deep into my eyes and said “yes” to being my bride.

九月休假回到你身边，我伤痕累累，疲惫不堪，我无法诉说战火纷飞时我对你的爱有多深。我们只能紧紧地抱在一起，仿佛要把对方挤碎。也就在那天，我向你求婚，当你深深凝望着我说“愿意”做我的新娘时，我兴奋地大喊大叫。

I remember being so over-enjoyed, when a year later, you gently held my hand to your waist and whispered in my ear that we were going to be a family.

一年后，你轻轻地把我的手放到你的腹前，对我轻声耳语道我们快要有宝宝了时，我欣喜若狂。

I know both our children love you dearly; they are outside the door now, waiting.

我知道我们的孩子都深深地爱着你，他们现在就等在门外。

Do you remember how I **panicked**

你还记得 Jonathon 出生的时候

like a mad man when Jonathon was born? I can still picture you laughing and smiling at me now, as I **clumsily** held him for the very first time in my arms. I watched as your laughter faded into tears, as I stared at him and cried my own tears of joy.

我那手足无措的慌张样吗？当我笨拙地第一次把他抱在怀里，我还记得你笑话我的样子，我看着他，看着你由笑而落泪，我自己也流下了高兴的眼泪。

I know you are tired, my dear, and I must let you go. But I love you so much and it hurts to do so.

亲爱的，我明白，你累了，我必须放手让你走。可是我对你的爱是如此之深，你的离去让我倍觉伤感！

I must go now, my darling. Our children are waiting outside. They want to say goodbye to you.

亲爱的，我必须走了。孩子们都等在外面，他们想和你道别。

I wipe the tears away from my eyes and bend my **frail** old legs down to the floor, so that I can kneel beside you. I lean close to you and take hold of your hand and kiss your **tender** lips for the very last time.

我擦去眼角的泪水，弯下衰弱的老腿以便能跪在你的身旁。我轻轻靠近你，握住你的双手，最后一次吻你的芳唇。

Sleep peacefully my dear.

亲爱的，安静地睡吧。

I am sad that you had to leave me, but please don't worry. I am content, knowing I will be with you soon. I am too old and too empty now to live much longer without you.

你的离去让我伤心欲绝，不过别担心。想到自己不久就能去陪伴你，我感到些许安慰。如今我垂垂老矣，身体空乏，没有你的陪伴，我在人世也待不了多久了。

I know it won't be long before we meet again in that small cafe in Hanover Square.

我知道很快我们就能在汉诺威广场的那间小咖啡馆里再相逢。

Goodbye, my darling wife.

再会了，我的爱妻。

魅力词汇

gaze into 凝望
tremble ['trembl] *v.* 战栗
trench [trentʃ] *n.* 战壕
huddled ['hʌdld] *adj.* 蜷缩的
hails of bullets and mortars 枪林弹雨
carnage ['kaːnidʒ] *n.* 残杀
bruised [bruːzd] *adj.* 擦伤的
whoop [huːp] *v.* 大叫
panic ['pænik] *v.* 恐慌
clumsily ['klʌmzili] *adv.* 笨拙地
frail [freil] *adj.* 虚弱的
tender ['tendə] *adj.* 温柔的

2 Life Together 伴你一生

相爱容易，相守难。这对老夫妻仿佛最熟悉的陌生人，生活在一起，但却不知对方最想要的是什么，以致最终错过……

文苑漫步

One fine day, an old couple around the age of 70, walked into a lawyer's office. **Apparently**, they were there to file a divorce. Lawyer was very puzzled, after having a chat with them, he got their story.

This couple had been quarreling all their forty over years of marriage and nothing ever seemed to go right.

They hang on because of their children, afraid that it might affect their upbringing. Now, all their children have already grown up, have their own family and there's nothing else the old couple have to worry about. All they wanted was to lead their own life free from all these years of unhappiness from their marriage, so both agreed on a divorce.

Lawyer was having a hard time trying to get the papers done, because he felt that after forty years of marriage at the age

译林畅游

一个阳光明媚的日子，一对70岁左右的老夫妇走进了一家律师事务所。显然，他们是来办理离婚手续的。律师很纳闷，在和他们聊完之后，才知道了其中的原由。

这对夫妇结婚四十年来一直在争吵，生活似乎从来没有平静过。

他们之所以坚持到今天，是担心离婚会影响孩子的成长。如今，孩子们都已长大并成家立业，老夫妇觉得没有什么可顾虑的了。他们现在只想摆脱这么多年来婚姻所带来的不快，过自己想要的生活，于是协商离婚。

律师极其艰难地为他们草拟了一份离婚协议书，因为他觉得，经过婚后四十年的相濡以沫，现在两

of 70, he couldn't understand why the old couple would still want a divorce. While they were signing the papers, the wife told the husband, "I really love you, but I really can't carry on anymore, I'm sorry."

"It's OK, I understand," said the husband. Looking at this, the lawyer suggested a dinner together, just three of them. The wife thought, why not, since they were still going to be friends.

At the dining table, there was a silence of **awkwardness**. The first dish was roasted chicken. Immediately, the old man took the **drumstick** for the old lady, "Take this, it's your favorite."

Looking at this, the lawyer thought maybe there was still a chance, but the wife was **frowning** when she answered, "This is always the problem that you always think so highly of yourself, never thought about how I feel. Don't you know that I hate drumsticks?"

Little did she know that, over the years, the husband had been trying all ways to please her. Little did she know that drumsticks was the husband's favorite. Little did he know that she never thought he understood her at all. Little did he know that she hated drumsticks even though all he wanted was the best for her.

That night, both of them couldn't sleep, **toss and turn** , toss and turn... After

个老人都70多岁了，他就是弄不明白为什么这对老夫妇仍然坚持要离婚。当他们签署文件时，妻子遗憾地告诉丈夫："我真的很爱你，但我再也不能忍受下去了，我非常抱歉。"

"没关系，我理解，"丈夫说道。看到这一幕，律师建议三人一起吃个饭。老夫人想了想，为什么不呢，因为以后他们仍然是朋友。

餐桌上，这对夫妇沉默不语，尴尬的气氛顿时弥漫开来。第一道菜是烤鸡。老夫人的丈夫立马夹了一个鸡腿给她："尝尝这个，这是你最喜欢吃的鸡腿。"

见到这种情景，律师心想，也许他们还有弥合的机会，然而，当妻子接过丈夫所夹的菜时，眉毛却很不自然地皱了一下，答道："这就是问题所在，你总是自以为是，从来没有顾及过我的感受，难道你就不知道我很讨厌吃鸡腿吗？"

她一点也不清楚，这些年来，她的丈夫一直想尽办法讨她开心；她一点也不知道，鸡腿是她丈夫最喜爱吃的食物。他一点也不清楚，他的妻子认为他完全不了解她；他一点也不知道，他妻子讨厌吃鸡腿，尽管他把自己最爱吃的都给了她。

那晚，夫妇二人辗转反侧都没有睡着……过了几个小时，老先生

hours, the old man couldn't take it anymore. He knew that he still loved her, and he couldn't carry on life without her. He wanted her back, he wanted to tell her, he was sorry. He wanted to tell her, "I love you."

再也忍受不了了。他知道自己还爱着她，他的生活不能没有她。他想要她回来，他想对她说抱歉，他想告诉她："我爱你。"

He picked up the phone, started dialing her number. Ringing never stopped. He never stopped dialing.

于是，他拿起电话，开始拨妻子的电话号码，铃声响个不停，他一直不停地在按着重拨键。

On the other side, she was sad. She couldn't understand how come after all these years, he still didn't understand her at all. She loved him a lot, but she just couldn't take it anymore. Phone was ringing, she refused to answer knowing that it was him. "What was the point of talking now that it was over? I had asked for it and now I wanted to keep it this way. If not I would lose face." She thought. Phone was still ringing. She has decided to **pull out the cord**.

在另一边，老夫人也很伤心，她搞不清楚为什么经过这么多年的相处她丈夫仍然一点都不了解她。事实上，她也非常爱她的丈夫，但她再也不愿意跟他一起生活了。电话铃声一直在响，她知道是她丈夫打来的，但她不愿接他的电话。"现在谈论还有什么意思呢？一切都已经结束了。首先提出离婚的是我，现在我想保持这种现状。要不然我岂不是很丢脸。"她心想道。电话铃声仍然在响，她索性把电话线拔了。

Little did she remember, he had heart problems.

她一点也不曾记起，她的丈夫有心脏病。

The next day, she received news that he had passed away. She rushed down to his apartment, saw his body, lying on the couch still holding on the phone. He had a heart attack when he was still trying to get through her phone line. As sad as she could be, she would have to clear his belongings. When she was looking through the drawers, she saw this insurance policy,

第二天，她被告知老先生已去世。她冲到老先生的公寓，看见他躺在沙发上手里仍握着电话。就在他试图打通她的电话时，他的心脏病发作了。尽管她很悲伤，老夫人仍不得不亲自动手清理他的遗物。当她认真细致地翻着一个抽屉时，她发现了一张保险单。保险日期从他们结婚之日算起，保险的受益人

dated from the day they got married, **beneficiary** is her. Together in that file there was this note.

"To my dearest wife, by the time you are reading this, I'm sure I'm no longer around. I bought this policy for you, though the amount is only $100. I hope it will be able to help me continue my promise that I have made when we got married. I might not be around anymore, but I want this amount of money to continue taking care of you, just like the way I will if I could have lived longer. I want you to know I will always be around, by your side. I love you."

Tears flowed like river. When you love someone, let them know. You never know what will happen the next minute. Learn to build a life together. Learn to love each other for who they are, not what they are.

是她。在这个文件夹里，还有一张她丈夫亲手写的便条。

"献给我最亲爱的妻子：当你读着这张便条的时候，我确信我已不在人世。我为你买了这份保险。虽然金额总数才区区 100 美元，但我希望它能帮助我继续履行我们结婚时我所许下的诺言。我不能再陪你一起度过你的余生，但我希望保险金额里的钱能帮助我实现照顾你后半生生活的愿望，就像我还活着时那样照顾你。我同时也想让你知道，我会一直在你的周围，在你的身边。我爱你。"

老夫人的眼泪像江河一样喷涌而出。当你爱着一个人的时候，一定要让他们知道。你无法预料下一刻会发生什么。学会一起经营生活。学会相互爱护，不是因为他们拥有什么，而是因为他们本身。

魅力词汇

apparently [ə'pærəntli] *adv.* 明显地
awkwardness ['ɔːkwədnis] *n.* 尴尬
drumstick ['drʌmstik] *n.* 鸡腿
frown [fraun] *v.* 皱眉
toss and turn 辗转反侧
pull out the cord 拔断电话线
beneficiary [ˌbeni'fiʃəri] *n.* 受益人

3 If You Love Her Enough (1)
如果你足够爱她（1）

“他爱我，照顾我、关心我”“我病弱时，他帮助我”……一个妻子对丈夫最高的评价莫过于她真实地知道“他爱她”，那么他又是如何做到这一点的呢？

文苑漫步

My friend John always has something to tell me. He knows so much that young men have to have older and more worldly wise men to tell them, for instance, who to trust, how to care for others, and how to live life to the fullest.

Recently, John lost his wife Janet. For eight years she fought against cancer, but in the end her sickness **had the last word**.

One day John took out a folded piece of paper from his wallet. He had found it, so he told me, when he tidied up some drawers at home. It was a small love letter Janet had written. The note could look like a school girl's **scrawls** about her dream guy. All that was missing was a drawing of a heart with the names John and Janet written in it. But the small letter was written by a woman who had had seven

译林畅游

我的朋友 John 总会有些事儿给我讲，他深知年轻人必须让比自己年长、阅历更丰富的男人多多启发。比如说，什么样的人值得信任、如何关心别人以及怎样才能活得最充实。

最近，John 的妻子 Janet 离开了他。她与癌症抗争了八年，但最终还是输给了病魔。

一天，John 从钱包里拿出一张叠起来的纸。他告诉我，这是他在家收拾抽屉时找到的。那是 Janet 写的一封短小的情书。纸上的内容就像是一个女生想念她的梦中情人时胡写出来的，旁边就差再画上一颗写着 John 和 Janet 的名字、被箭穿过的心了。但是这封短信的作者是一位养育了七个孩子的母亲——一个为活下来而抗争，生命可能只

children; a woman who fought for her life and who probably only had a few months to live.

It was also a beautiful **recipe** for how to keep a marriage together. Janet's description of her husband begins thus: "Loved me. Took care of me. Worried about me."

Even though John always had a ready answer, he never joked about cancer apparently.

Sometimes he came home in the evening to find Janet in the middle of one of those **depressions** cancer patients so often get. In no time he got her into the car and drove her to her favorite restaurant.

He showed consideration for her, and she knew it. You cannot hide something for someone who knows better.

"Helped me when I was ill," the next line reads. Perhaps Janet wrote this while the cancer was in one of the horrible and wonderful lulls. Where everything is — almost — as it used to be, before the sickness broke out, and where it doesn't hurt to hope that everything is over, maybe forever.

剩下几个月的女人。

这封信同时也是一个绝妙的秘方，它告诉我们如何保持婚姻和谐。Janet 是如此描述她的丈夫的：“他爱我，照顾我，关心我。”

虽然 John 对一切都心中有数，但他从不拿癌症开玩笑。

有时他晚上回到家，发现 Janet 陷入了癌症患者经常会遇到的种种忧郁中，他二话不说，立刻就开车带着 Janet 到她最喜欢的餐馆去。

John 对 Janet 十分体贴，Janet 知道这一点。如果一个人比你更加了解一件事，你是无法将这件事对其隐瞒的。

信的下一行写道：“我病弱时，他帮助我。”Janet 写下这句时，她的病情可能正处在某个恐怖却又美好的暂缓期。在病情急剧恶化之前的这个阶段，一切都和以前一样——几乎一样吧。这时候，你可以不痛不痒地企盼一切都结束了，也许永远地结束了。

魅力词汇

have the last word 有决定权
scrawl [skrɔːl] *v.* 乱涂
recipe ['resipi] *n.* 处方，秘诀
depression [di'preʃn] *n.* 沮丧

4 If You Love Her Enough (2)
如果你足够爱她（2）

人终究都会老去，但是爱情不会，亲情不会。在一个人生命之中有一两个值得永远去爱的人是一件很幸福的事情。

文苑漫步

"Forgave me a lot."

"Stood by my side."

And a piece of good advice for everyone who looks on giving constructive criticism as a kind of sacred duty: "Always praising."

"Made sure I had everything I needed," she goes on to write.

After that she has turned over the paper and added: "Warmth. Humor. Kindness. Thoughtfulness." And then she writes about the husband she has lived with and loved most of her life: "Always there for me when I needed you."

The last words she wrote sum up all the others. I can see her for me when she adds **thoughtfully**: "Good friend."

I stand beside John now, and cannot even **pretend** to know how it feels to lose someone who is as close to me as Janet

译林畅游

"容忍我很多的不对。"

"守在我身边。"

对于那些喜欢将发表建设性批评意见作为神圣职责的人，信中还有一条很好的建议："不停地赞扬。"

"确保我能得到我所需要的任何东西，"她接着写道。

她将纸翻到背面又添上："温柔。幽默。善良。贴心。"然后，她又这样描述了那个与她一同生活的丈夫——她大半生最爱的人："在我需要时你一直守候在那里。"

她写的最后一句话总结了其他所有内容，我可以看到她是如何若有所思地在纸上加上了这句话——"好朋友。"

我现在站在John身边，却无法假装了解自己失去一个像Janet对John那样重要的人的感觉。John需要找人说话，有些话他必须说出来，

was to him. I need to hear what he has to say much more than he needs to talk.

"John," I ask, "How do you stick together with someone through thirty-eight years — not to mention the sickness? How do I know if I can bear to stand by my wife's side if she becomes sick one day?"

"You can," he says quietly, "If you love her enough, you can."

而我却更急切地要听他的那些话。

"John，"我问道，"先不提对方生病的状况，就光说这三十八年，你是怎么跟一个人和谐地生活过来的？如果某天我妻子生病了，我怎么知道我能不能挺住一直守在她身边呢？"

"你能，"John 静静地回答，"只要你爱她够深，你就能做到。"

魅力词汇

thoughtfully ['θɔːtfəli] *adv.* 认真思考地

pretend [pri'tend] *v.* 假装

温情絮语

Coffee is lonely without cups. I am lonely without you.

没有杯子，咖啡是寂寞的；没有你，我是孤独的。

5 Grandpa's Bee 祖父的蜜蜂

等到爷爷89岁的那个夏天，他只能坐在草地的椅子上，看蔬菜长大，玫瑰开花。夏日渐渐消逝，爷爷在丰收前去世了。奶奶生命的秋天，是枫叶一般的色彩，不是春光胜似春光，时值霜天季节，却格外显得神采奕奕。从那时开始，奶奶便相信是因为爷爷那年夏天没能亲自帮她，才派了蜜蜂到这里，让奶奶的小花园欣欣向荣。

文苑漫步

A long time before I was born, my Grandma and Grandpa moved into the house on Beechwood Avenue. They had a young family of four little girls. The little girls slept in the **attic** in a big feather bed. It was cold there on winter night. Grandma put hot bricks under the covers at the foot of the bed to keep the little girls warm.

During the Great Depression, work was hard to find, so Grandpa did whatever jobs he could. He dug **ditches** during the week and on weekend he and Grandma dug a garden to grow some of their own food.

The house on Beechwood Avenue had a big front yard with shade trees and fruit trees. In the middle of the yard was a water **pump** where the four little girls

译林畅游

早在我出生以前，奶奶和爷爷搬到比奇乌大道住。他们膝下养有四个可爱女儿。女孩们睡在阁楼的一张大羽毛床上。那里冬夜寒冷。奶奶得在床脚下垫热砖给女儿们取暖。

大萧条时期，工作很难找，爷爷什么苦工都做。在平时他挖沟渠，周末便和奶奶在花园里挖挖锄锄，种点自己的粮食。

比奇乌大道的房子前面有个大院子，院子里种着浓荫遮蔽的大树和果树。院子中央是一个水泵，小女孩们就在这里抽水来做饭、打扫

pumped water for cooking, cleaning and watering the garden. On one side of the yard, Grandma and Grandpa planted tomatoes, beans, **squash**, **cucumbers**, peppers and strawberries to feed their growing family. They planted roses, **lilacs** and **irises** on the other side of the yard, around the statue of the Blessed Mother.

卫生、灌溉花园。奶奶和爷爷在院子的一边种上番茄、豆子、南瓜、黄瓜、辣椒和草莓，供应这个大家庭的吃用。在另一边，他们围着圣母的雕像种了玫瑰、丁香和蝴蝶花。

Everybody worked to keep the garden growing. All summer long, the family ate food from the garden and enjoyed the beautiful flowers. Grandma put up strawberry jam, tomatoes, beans, peppers, pears and peaches in canning jam. They were good to eat through the long winter.

人人都辛勤地耕种花园，使它更加丰盛。整个夏天，一家人吃着花园种出的食物，欣赏着花园里的美丽花朵。奶奶还把做好的草莓酱、番茄、豆子、辣椒、梨子和桃子装进罐子里，使它们的美味能保持一整个漫长的冬天。

The family grew up, and before too many years had passed, the grandchildren came to visit. Grandma and Grandpa still planted their garden every spring. Everyone still enjoyed the good food from the garden and always took some home.

多年过去，孩子们长大，孙子孙女们也来到了世上。奶奶和爷爷仍然每年春天都耕种花园。人人都能分享花园种出的好东西，也总能带上一些回家。

Grandchilden grow up, and grandparents grow older. It became harder for Grandma and Grandpa to keep up the garden. So they made it a little smaller. There was still plenty to eat from the garden and lovely flowers to enjoy.

孙子孙女们长大了，爷爷、奶奶年迈古稀。维护花园花去他们更多的精力，所以他们缩小了些花园的面积。但里面种出来的食物还足够吃，花朵也还招人喜爱。

Then one summer when Grandpa was 89 years old, all he could do was watch from his lawn chair as the vegetables grew and the roses bloomed. Summer slowly faded, and Grandpa died before it was time to bring in the harvest.

等到爷爷 89 岁的那个夏天，他只能坐在草地的椅子上，看蔬菜长大，玫瑰开花。夏日渐渐消逝，爷爷在丰收前去世了。

It was a lonely winter for Grandma. She sat near the window, looking out at the yard and wondering if she could plant the garden in the spring. It would be hard to care for it by herself. When spring came, she planted only a little garden.

对奶奶来说，这是个寂寞的冬天。她坐在窗边，望着外边的院子，考虑着来年春天还能不能耕种花园。只靠她自己来打理太难了些。当春天来到时，她只稍微种了一点。

One sunny day in the early summer, Grandma heard a **commotion** in the front yard and looked out the window to see a frightening sight—a gigantic **swarm** of bees filled the air between two tall trees. There was thousands of bees in the air, so many that the swarm reached the treetops! The buzzing sound was tremendous. Grandma watched as the bees made their way into a hole up in one of the trees. Before long, every one of those bees had disappeared into its new home.

初夏的一天，阳光灿烂，奶奶听到前院传来一阵骚动声，她望向窗外，看到可怕的一幕。两棵大树上满满缀着大团的蜜蜂。空中还飞舞着成千上万只，多不胜数的蜂群一直排到树梢上！嗡嗡声不绝于耳。奶奶看见这些蜜蜂先后钻进一棵树上高高的树洞中。很快，所有的蜜蜂都搬进新家，消失了。

Grandma wondered what in the world she could do. Should she hire someone to get rid of bees? That would cost more than she could afford. She decided to wait and think it over.

奶奶不禁发愁起来。她是否该请人清走这些蜜蜂呢？但是她根本支付不起费用。于是她决定等一等，再想想办法。

During the next few days, the bees were busy making their own business. Grandma could always see a few bees buzzing in and out around the opening high in the tree. Before long, she decided the bees won't bother anyone, so she went about her business and didn't give them any other thought.

随后几天，蜜蜂忙碌个不停。奶奶总能看到有一些蜂儿从高高的树洞里嗡嗡地飞进飞出。不久，她看出蜜蜂并无妨碍，于是自顾自地干活，不再理会它们。

That summer, Grandma's little garden grew and grew. The neighbors would stop to admire the huge crop of vegetables

那年夏天，奶奶的小花园硕果累累。邻居们都驻足羡慕里面生长出丰盛的蔬菜，纳闷怎么自己花园

and puzzle over their own gardens weren't doing well. No matter, because Grandma had enough give some away. Of course, everyone who came to visit was treated to a meal of good things from the garden.

的长势就没有这么喜人。没关系，因为奶奶有好多可以送人。登门来访的人当然都用花园里的美味来招待。

One day, Grandma's brother Frank visited from Arizona. As Grandma made Frank a delicious lunch of squash pan cakes and homemade apple sauce, she told him the story about the swarm of bees.

一天，奶奶的弟弟 Frank 从亚利桑那州前来拜访。奶奶给他做了一顿香喷喷的午饭，有南瓜饼，有自制的苹果酱，她还把蜜蜂的故事告诉了 Frank。

Frank said, "in Arizona, the farmers often hired beekeepers to set up beehives near their fields. The bees pollinated the crops and helped them to grow."

Frank 说："在亚利桑那，农夫们常常雇请养蜂人在农田附近搭蜂箱。蜜蜂授粉有助于庄稼成长。"

That was when Grandma realized that her bees had helped with her garden all summer.

奶奶才意识到，原来是这些蜜蜂在夏季助成了花园的丰收。

"So that's why my little garden had such a big crop!" she exclaimed.

"这才是我的小花园大丰收的原因！"她大声地说道。

From that time on, Grandma always believed that since Grandpa couldn't be there to help her that summer, he had sent the bees to take his place and make Grandma's little garden grow and grow.

从那时开始，奶奶便相信是因为爷爷那年夏天没能亲自帮她，才派了蜜蜂到这里，让奶奶的小花园欣欣向荣。

魅力词汇

attic ['ætik] *n.* 阁楼
ditch [ditʃ] *n.* 沟，渠
pump [pʌmp] *n.* 泵
squash [skwɔʃ] *n.* 南瓜
cucumber ['kju:kʌmbə] *n.* 黄瓜，胡瓜
lilac ['lailək] *n.* 丁香花
iris ['airis] *n.* 鸢尾（花）
commotion [kə'məuʃn] *n.* 混乱，喧闹，骚动
swarm [swɔ:m] *n.* 蜂群

6 In Life We Are Happiest When...
生活中，我们最幸福时

生命中我们有很多的失望、沮丧和烦恼，我们根本不需要再去寻找。我们美妙的世界充满了美丽、光明和希望。但是，当我们放眼四周时，为什么浪费时间寻找不快、失望和烦恼，而看不到面前美好的事物呢？从今天起，学会做一个快乐的人。

文苑漫步

A man and his girlfriend were married. It was a large celebration.

All of their friends and family came to see the lovely ceremony and to partake of the festivities and celebrations. All had a wonderful time.

The bride was **gorgeous** in her white wedding **gown** and the groom was very **dashing** in his black **tuxedo**. Everyone could tell that the love they had for each other was true.

A few months later, the wife came to the husband with a **proposal**, "I read in a magazine, a while ago, about how we can strengthen our marriage," she offered. "Each of us will write a list of the things that we find a bit annoying with the other person. Then, we can talk about how we

译林畅游

一个男人和他的女朋友结婚，举行了一场盛大的结婚庆典。

所有的朋友和家人都来到结婚典礼上参加欢宴和庆祝活动。大家都很开心。

穿着白色婚纱的新娘漂亮迷人，穿着黑色礼服的新郎英俊潇洒。每个人都能看出他们彼此的爱是真诚的。

几个月后，妻子跟丈夫提议说："我刚才在杂志上看到一篇文章，说的是怎样巩固婚姻。"她说："我们两个人各自把对方的小毛病列在一张纸上，然后我们商量一下怎样解决，让我们的生活更幸福。"

can fix them together and make our lives happier together."

The husband agreed. So each of them went to a separate room in the house and thought of the things that annoyed them about the other. They thought about this question for the rest of the day and wrote down what they came up with.

丈夫同意了。于是他们各自去了不同的房间去想对方的缺点。那一天余下的时间里，他们都在思考这个问题，并且把他们想到的都写下来。

The next morning, at the breakfast table, they decided they would go over their lists.

第二天早上，吃早饭的时候，他们决定谈谈彼此的缺点。

"I'll start," offered the wife. She took out her list. It had many items on it, enough to fill 3 pages. In fact, as she started reading the list of the little **annoyances**, she noticed that tears were starting to appear in her husband's eyes.

"我先开始吧。"妻子说。她拿出她的单子，上面列举了很多条，事实上，足足写满了三页。当她开始念的时候，她注意到丈夫眼里含着泪花。

"What's wrong?" she asked. "Nothing," the husband replied, "keep reading your list."

"怎么啦？"她问。"没什么，"丈夫答道，"继续念吧。"

The wife continued to read until she had read all three pages to her husband. She neatly placed her list on the table and **folded** her hands over the top of it.

妻子又接着念。整整三页都念完之后她把单子整齐地放在桌上，两手交叉放在上面。

"Now, you read your list and then we'll talk about the things on both of our lists," she said happily.

"现在该你念了，然后我们谈谈列出来的缺点。"她高兴地说。

Quietly the husband stated, "I don't have anything on my list. I think that you are perfect the way that you are. I don't want you to change anything for me. You are lovely and wonderful and I wouldn't

丈夫平静地说："我什么也没写，我觉得像你这样就很完美了，我不想让你为我改变什么。你很可爱迷人，我不想让你改变。"

want to try and change anything about you."

The wife, touched by his honesty and the depth of his love for her and his acceptance of her, turned her head and wept.

In life, there are enough times when we are disappointed, depressed and annoyed. We don't really have to go looking for them. We have a wonderful world that is full of beauty, light and promise. Why waste time in this world looking for the bad, disappointing or annoying when we can look around us, and see the wondrous things before us?

妻子被丈夫的诚实和对她深深的爱和接纳感动了，她转过头哭了起来。

生命中我们有很多的失望、沮丧和烦恼，我们根本不需要再去寻找。我们美妙的世界充满了美丽、光明、希望。但是，当我们放眼四周时，为什么浪费时间寻找不快、失望和烦恼，而看不到我们面前的美好事物呢？

魅力词汇

gorgeous ['gɔːdʒəs]
adj. 极好的，非常漂亮的
gown [gaun] *n.* 女长服，礼服
dashing [dæʃiŋ] *adj.* 英俊潇洒的
tuxedo [tʌk'siːdəu] *n.* 燕尾服
proposal [prə'pəuzəl] *n.* 提议
annoyance [ə'nɔiəns] *n.* 烦恼，烦扰
fold [fəuld] *v.* 折叠

温情絮语

You and I remain the same in different time, at different places, among different people; time is changing, space is changing and everything is changing except my miss to you!

不同的时间，不同的地点，不同的人群，相同的只有你和我；时间在变，空间在变，不变的只有对你无限的思念！

7 Love of Two Mutes 无声之爱

为了一段传奇般的爱情，她突然住进了医院，从此再没人听到他们讲过一句话。他们用手、用笔、用眼神交流，分享喜悦和悲伤。然而终有一天，他走了，谎言也揭穿了……

文苑漫步

He was a **mute**. Although he could understand others' speech, he could not express his own actual feeling. She was his neighbor, a girl who was bound by a common **destiny** with her grandmother, calling him brother.

He really looked like an elder brother: led her to go to school; accompanied her to play; listened to her **chirp** with a smile.

He only used the hand signal to communicate with her. Possibly she was able to read each of his look. From elder brother's gaze, she knew how much he loved her.

Afterwards, She finally past the tests and went to college. She was extremely happy. He then started to go out to make money, and then sent continuously to her. She had never rejected.

Finally, she graduated and began to work. Then, she said firmly to him, "Elder brother, I must marry you!" He looked like

译林畅游

他是个哑巴，虽然能听懂别人的话，却无法表达自己的感受。她是他的邻居，一个和外婆相依为命的女孩，她一直喊他哥哥。

他的确有哥哥的样子，带她上学，陪她一起玩耍，含笑听她唧唧喳喳讲话。

他只用手势和她交谈，可能她能读懂他的每一个眼神。从哥哥注视她的目光里，她知道他有多么喜欢自己。

后来，她终于考上了大学，非常开心。他便开始出去拼命挣钱，然后源源不断地寄给她。她从来没有拒绝。

终于，她毕业了，参加了工作。然后，她坚定地对他说："哥哥，我要嫁给你！"他像一只受惊的兔子

only the frightened rabbit and escaped. He refused to see her again, regardless of how she **entreated**.

一样逃掉了，无论她怎样哀求，他再也不肯见她。

"Do you think I pity you? Do you think I appreciate you? No, I've fallen in love with you since I was 12," she said, but no reply.

她说："你以为我同情你吗？你以为我想报答你吗？不，我12岁时就爱上你了。"但她依然没得到答复。

One day, she was sent to hospital suddenly. He was scared and went to see her. Doctor said that, in her throat steadily a **lump**, although **excised**, destroyed the vocal cord actually. She possibly could not deliver the speech again. On the hospital bed, she gazed at him tearfully. Eventually, they were married.

有一天，她突然住进了医院。他吓坏了，跑去看他。医生说，她喉咙里长了一个瘤，虽然切除了，却破坏了声带，她可能再也讲不了话了。病床上，她泪眼婆娑地注视着他。最终，他们结婚了。

Very many years, nobody listened to them to deliver a speech. They used the hand and the pen, conversed with the look, and shared what was joyful and what was sad. They had become the couple which the loved men and women envied. People said, how happy that pair of mute husband and wife!

多年来，没有人听他们讲过一句话。他们用手、用笔、用眼神交谈，分享喜悦和悲伤。他们成了相恋男女羡慕的一对。人们说，那对哑巴夫妻多么幸福呀！

Love could not prevent god of death arrival. He abandoned her and past away first.

爱情抵挡不住死亡的降临，他撇下她一个人先走了。

The people feared she could not undergo the attack of losing the lover and came to comfort her. By then, she took back her dull gazes at his portrait, and said suddenly that, "He went away."

人们怕她经受不住失去爱侣的打击来安慰她，这时，她收回注视他遗像的呆痴目光，突然开口说："他还是走了。"

The rumor revealed...

谎言揭穿了……

魅力词汇

mute [mjuːt] *n.* 哑巴
destiny ['destini] *n.* 命运
chirp [tʃɜːp] *v.* 吱喳讲话
entreat [in'triːt] *v.* 恳求
lump [lʌmp] *n.* 肿块
excise [ek'saiz] *v.* 切除

8 Flower at the Mountain Cliff
悬崖上的花朵

外国的月亮比中国的圆；别人碗里的饭比自己碗里的香。我们总是看轻自己已有的东西，而去看重那些没有得到的，盲目地憧憬一些根本不需要或根本不存在的东西。当一个人成天被爱包围时，她就很容易忽视爱的存在，转而羡慕别的东西，直到失去爱的那一天，她才会重新意识到原来自己是那么幸福。

文苑漫步

My husband is a scientist by profession. I love him for his steady nature, and I love the warm feeling when I lean against his broad shoulders.

Three years in the **courtship** and now, two years into marriage, I have to admit, I am getting tired of it. The reasons for loving him has now transformed into the cause of all the **restlessness**. I am a sentimental woman and is extremely sensitive and **exquisite** when it comes to relationships and feelings. I yearn for romantic moments, like a little boy yearning for candy.

My husband is a stark contrast to me. His lack of sensitivity and of all, inability of bringing romantic moments into our marriage has disheartened me about love.

译林畅游

我的丈夫是一位科学家。我喜欢他稳重的性格，也享受靠在他宽阔肩膀上那份温暖的感觉。

在经历三年的热恋和两年的婚姻后，如今，我必须承认，自己开始感到厌倦了。当初爱上他的理由如今却变成了不安的因素。我是个多愁善感的女人，在情感上，心思细密、极度敏感。我渴望浪漫，就像小男孩渴望糖果一样。

而我的丈夫却恰恰相反。他不够敏感，更不懂得给婚姻带来浪漫，这使我对爱情感到沮丧。

One day, I finally decided to tell him my decision, that I want a divorce.

"Why?" he asked, shocked.

"I am tired, there aren't reasons for everything in the world," I answered.

He kept silent for a long time, seeming to be in deep thoughts with a cigarette lighted the entire night. My feelings of disappointment is getting intense, a man who can't even express his **detainment**, what else can I hope from him? And finally he asked, "What can I do to change your mind?"

Somebody said it right, it's hard to change a person's personality, and I guess I have started losing faith in him. I looked deep into his eyes and I slowly answered: "Here is a question, if you can find the answer in my heart, I will change my mind. Let's say, I love a flower at a mountain cliff, and we are both sure that picking the flower will cause death. Will you still do it for me?"

He said, "I will give you your answer tomorrow." My heart just sank low after hearing his reply.

The next morning, he was not around, and I saw a piece of paper with his **scratchy** writing, underneath a glass of warm milk.

It goes: "Dear, I would not pick that flower for you, but please allow me to further explain the reason."

This first line has already broken my

一天，我终于下定决心向他提出离婚。

“为什么？”丈夫感到很震惊。

“我厌倦了，世界上不是所有事情都需要理由的。”我回答道。

他沉默了良久，点了支烟似乎陷入了沉思，整整一夜烟都没有灭。我越发感到失望了，一个男人甚至不知道如何表达他的挽留之意，我还能对他有什么指望呢？最后，他终于问了句：“我要怎么做才能改变你的心意呢？”

老话说得没错：本性难移。我想我已经对他失去了信心。我凝视着他的眼睛，慢慢地说道：“我这儿有一个问题，如果你能说出我心中的答案，我就改变想法。这么说吧，如果我喜欢悬崖上的一朵花，我们也都清楚去采它会有生命危险。你还会为我这样做吗？”

他说：“我明天给你答案吧。”听到这个回答，我的心猛地一沉。

第二天早晨没见着他，只看见一杯热牛奶下边压着一张字迹潦草的纸条。

上面写道：“亲爱的，我不会为你去采那朵花，但请听我解释其中的原因。”

第一行字已经叫人心碎，但我

heart. I continued reading.

"You can only type with the computer and yet you always mess up the programs in the PC and cry in front of screen. I have to save my fingers so that I can help to restore the programs.

You always leave the house keys behind. I have to save my legs to rush home to open the door for you.

You love traveling yet you always lose your way in a new city. I have to save my eyes to lead you around.

You always have **cramps** whenever your 'good friend' approaches every month. I have to save my palm so that I can calm the cramp at your **tummy**.

You like to stay indoor, and I worry that you will be infected by **infantile autism**. I have to save my mouth, tell you jokes and stories to cure your boredom.

You always stare at the computer for long hours, and that's no good for your eyes. I have to save my eyes so that when we grow older, I can help to clip your nails, and help to remove those annoying white hair.

I will hold your hand, **stroll** down the beach, enjoy the sunshine and the beautiful sand, tell you the color of flowers, which is just like the **glow** on your young face...

Thus, my dear, before I am sure there is someone who loves you more than I do, I would not pick the flower, and die."

My tears fell on the letter, and blurred

还是继续读了下去。

"你用电脑的时候只会打打字，却总是把程序弄得一团糟，只好坐在屏幕前哭。我得留着我的手指帮你恢复程序。

你总是忘带房门钥匙，我得留着双腿冲回家为你开门。

你热爱旅游，但每到一个新城市总是迷路，我得留着眼睛为你指路。

每个月'老朋友'来的时候，你总是肚子痛，我得留着手掌揉你的小肚子，为你止痛。

你喜欢待在屋里，我担心你会患上自闭症，因此还得留着嘴巴给你讲笑话，讲故事，为你解闷。

你总是连着好几个小时看电脑，这对眼睛不好，因此我得留着眼睛。这样等咱们老了，我还可以帮你剪指甲，拔掉那些讨厌的白头发。

我会拉着你的手，在海滩上散步，享受阳光和美丽的沙滩，告诉你那些花儿的颜色就像你年轻时的脸庞一样光彩照人……

因此，亲爱的，在我确定有人能够比我更爱你之前，我不会冒着生命危险去采那朵花。"

我的眼泪流了下来，掉在了纸

the ink of his handwriting while I resumed my reading...

"And now, dear...you have finished reading my answer. If you are satisfied with this answer, please open the door of our house. I am standing there, with your favorite bread and fresh milk..."

I rushed to pull open the door, and saw his anxious face, with his hand held tight on the milk and bread... Oh I am sure no one ever loved me as much, and now I have decided to leave the flower alone...

That's life, or some said, love. When one is surrounded by love, the feeling of excitement fades away, and one tends to forget that true love lies in between the peace and dullness.

Love shows in any form, even a very little and **corny** form, it has never been a model; it could be the most incurious form. Flowers, romantic moments are only the **buckish** form on the surface of the relationship. Under all these, the pillar of true love stands and that's our life.

Love, but not words win the arguments.

条上，模糊了他的字迹。我继续读下去……

"现在，亲爱的……你已经看完了我的答案，如果你对这答案满意的话，请打开房门，我就站在门口，正端着你最喜欢的面包和鲜奶……"

我冲过去拉开门，看见丈夫满脸的焦急，手里紧紧端着牛奶和面包……哦，这一刻我确信从来没有人如此爱我，我打定主意再也不要那朵花了……

这就是生活，或者像某些人说的那样，这就是爱。一个人被爱包围时，激动的感觉就会慢慢消失。他很容易忘记，平淡和无趣中蕴含着真爱。

爱可以通过很多种方式表现出来，有些毫不起眼，有些很老套，没有固定的模式；有的表达方式甚至非常无趣。鲜花、浪漫时光，这些都只是爱情浮华的表面，而真爱的基石存在于这些的下面，这才是我们真实的生活。

爱，不是一句空话。

魅力词汇

courtship ['kɔːtʃip] *n.* 求爱期
restlessness ['restlisnis] *n.* 坐立不安
exquisite ['ekskwizit] *adj.* 细腻的
detainment [di'teinmənt] *n.* 挽留
scratchy ['skrætʃi] *adj.* 潦草的
cramp [kræmp] *n.* 绞痛
tummy ['tʌmi] *n.* 肚子
infantile autism 自闭症
stroll [strəul] *v.* 散步
glow [gləu] *n.* 亮丽的眼色
corny ['kɔːni] *adj.* 老套的
buckish ['bʌkiʃ] *adj.* 浮华的

9 The Silent Guardian 默默的守护者

有的爱是无法用言语来表达的。比起动人的言语，默默的付出更能打动人心。富兰克林说过这样一句话："语言的巨人，行动的矮子。"说比做容易，但我们最看重的恰恰是做。爱人之间最需要的不是华丽的词句，而是默默的呵护和关怀。

文苑漫步

When it comes to flowery speech or emotional expression, my husband, Dave, is a man of few words. That was one of the first things I learned about him when we married thirty-one years ago.

One of the next things I discovered is that Dave has little use for rosebushes. He had no second thoughts about **yanking** out mature plants to widen the driveway when we purchased our home. To him, roses represent hours of **pruning** and **spraying**, **mulching** and fertilizing. As far as he's concerned, a **lawn mower** and a **hedge trimmer** are all you need for the perfect garden.

On the other hand, I treasure my roses. I consider every minute of their care well worth the beautiful, **fragrant** results.

译林畅游

我的丈夫Dave不擅长说漂亮的俏皮话，也不懂得如何充满深情地表达爱意。三十一年前我们结婚时，我就了解这一点。

我随后还了解到，Dave觉得玫瑰丛是没用的东西。在我们刚买房子时，他毫不犹豫地把那些成熟的植物拔掉以扩宽我们的行车道。对他而言，玫瑰意味着数小时的修剪、喷雾、护根和施肥。在他看来，割草机和树枝修剪机就足以能建造一个完美的花园。

相反，我视我的玫瑰为珍宝。我认为对它们每一分钟的细心呵护都是值得的，因为我收获的将是玫瑰的美丽和芳香。

One winter, I spent several evenings **drooling over** rose catalogs and planning a small garden. In the spring, I ordered several English varieties of self-rooted plants. I removed an area of **sod**, worked and reworked the ground, and planted the foot-long starts. During the heat of summer, I watered them daily. In my mind, I saw the fruits of my labor: masses of color and fragrance perfuming the air just outside my kitchen window.

But as it sometimes does, life **spun** us around and redirected our attention. In the fall, I began to have pain in my lower abdomen. At first I passed it off as nothing serious. But instead of getting better, the pain intensified. I went to see my doctor. He ordered tests; when the results came back, he asked to see me in his office right away. He also requested that Dave come with me.

Our worst fears became reality: **colon cancer**. I'd need surgery immediately. After a short recovery period, I'd undergo a six-month course of **chemotherapy**.

We cried and prayed and cried some more. We had one week to inform our family and friends. Then, trusting God and my doctors, I entered the hospital.

One month later, as I lay on the sofa still **recuperating** from surgery, Dave and I watched the TV weather forecast. It

一个冬天，我连续几个晚上都痴迷于玫瑰的分类，计划把它们种成一个小花园。在春天，我整理好几个英国品种的自根植物。我腾出一块草皮，松了两遍土，然后栽了一些一英尺高的花苗。炎热的夏天，我每天都给它们浇水。我心里已看到了自己劳动的成果：厨房窗外弥漫着沁人的芳香，鲜艳的花朵四处绽放。

但就像往常那样，生活在我们的周围旋转，重新转移我们的注意力。那年秋天，我开始感觉到小腹疼痛。刚开始，我觉得不严重所以没把它当回事。但接下来疼痛并没有好转，反而加剧。我去看了医生。医生给我安排了检查，结果出来时，医生让我马上去他办公室。他同时要求Dave一起陪我去。

我们最坏的担忧变成了现实：结肠癌。我需要立即手术。经过短暂的恢复期后，我将需要六个月的化疗。

我们哭泣、祈祷，然后哭得更伤心了。我们有一星期的时间通知亲友。接下来，怀着对上帝和医生的信任，我住进了医院。

一个月后，仍然在术后恢复期的我躺在沙发上，和 Dave 一起看天气预报。天气预报里说会有极端

promised bitter cold temperatures and possible Snow.

"Oh," I moaned to myself, "I never did get the roses mulched."

Dave just sat and watched the end of the forecast. Then, always the practical, on-top-of-things handyman, he said, "I'd better go to **winterize** the outside faucets." He **bundled up** and headed toward the garage.

Fifteen minutes later, I hobbled to the kitchen for a glass of water. What I saw from the window brought tears to my eyes. There was Dave, bending over the roses, carefully helping mulch around every plant.

I smiled and watched as my quiet husband said "I love you". You know, sometimes words aren't needed at all.

的低温天气，还可能伴有大雪。

"哦"，我自语道，"我还没给玫瑰护根呢。"

Dave只是坐着，看着天气预报的片尾。一向讲求实效、总把事情安排得妥妥当当的他说道："我最好去为外面的水龙头做御寒准备。"他捆好工具朝仓库走去。

十五分钟后，我一瘸一拐地走向厨房想要拿一杯水。厨房窗外的那一幕让我热泪盈眶。那是Dave，他正俯身，细心地为每一株玫瑰护根。

我微笑地看着眼前这一幕，因为Dave默默地说出了那句"我爱你"。要知道，爱有时并不需要太多的语言。

魅力词汇

yank [jæŋk] *v.* 猛拉
prune [pruːn] *v.* 修剪
spray [sprei] *v.* 喷雾
mulch [mʌltʃ] *v.* 做护根
lawn mower 割草机
hedge trimmer 树枝修剪机
fragrant ['freigrənt] *adj.* 芳香的
drool over 痴迷于
sod [sɒd] *n.* 草皮
spun [spʌn] *v.* 旋转
colon cancer 结肠癌
chemotherapy [ˌkiːməʊ'θerəpɪ] *n.* 化疗
recuperate [ri'kuːpəreit] *v.* 恢复
winterize ['wintəraiz] *v.* 为过冬作准备
bundle up 捆扎

10 One True Love 唯一真爱

世上到底有没有真爱，有人说有，有人说没有。佛曰：“信则有，不信则无。”相信真爱，用心去感受周围人的爱，你就会遇到真正的爱。真正的爱是生命中最伟大的礼物，它将超越生命而永存。

文苑漫步

He never believed that true love existed. His parents divorced when he was young and he didn't think that true love was able to survive in today's world.

He was proven wrong.

His grandparents were always **supportive** to the kids and tried to help them when their parents divorced. He knew they loved each other. He just wasn't sure whether it was true love. He had never heard them say, "I love you" or show any affection other than hugging. They had been married for over fifty years and he thought that their true love was gone.

But again he was wrong. His grandfather, Ralph, was struck ill in his junior year of college and he didn't know how serious it was until he fell and hurt his hip. While in the hospital, the doctors found out a **tumor** in his lung. They told him that he had lung cancer and due to

译林畅游

他从不相信世上存在真爱。年少的时候他的父母就离婚了，他认为当今世界上不可能存在真正的爱。

后来的事实证明，他错了。

父母离婚后，他的祖父母一直支持孩子们，并尽力帮助他们。他知道祖父母相互爱恋着。他只是不能确定那是否是真爱。他从未听他们说过“我爱你”，除了拥抱外，他们也没有其他爱的表示。他们结婚已经五十多年了，他认为他们的真爱早已烟消云散。

但是他又错了。大三时，他的祖父病了。他不知道祖父的病情有多严重，直到祖父跌倒，伤了臀部。在医院里，医生发现祖父的肺部有一个肿瘤。医生告诉祖父，他得了肺癌。考虑到原有的疾病，医生不能给他做手术；他太虚弱了，

previous illnesses, they could not operate and he was too weak for chemotherapy.

也不能接受化疗。

It was around Thanksgiving Day and by Christmas his condition **worsened**. The cancer spread and in late January his sister away at college too, called him crying and said she was on her way home because the doctors told the family that their grandfather had only a week to live, that by the weekend he would no longer be with them. The family came in from around the country and stayed next to his side.

事情发生在感恩节前后，到圣诞节时，祖父的病情恶化了。癌症病毒迅速扩散，一月末，同样在外地上大学的妹妹哭着给他打了个电话，说她在回家的路上，因为医生告诉这家人他们的祖父只能活一周了，到周末他会离他们而去。全家人从全国各地赶回来，守候在祖父身旁。

It was there he realized that true love does exist today and will survive beyond death. Every night as his grandfather grew more **fragile**, he would whisper sweet words to his grandmother, Madge. The night before he died, grandmother was walking out of his room and he said to her "I love you, Madgie baby".

就在那时，他才意识到当今世上确有真爱，并且这种爱可以超越死亡。每晚，当身体变得越来越虚弱时，祖父会用甜蜜的话语同祖母Madge低声交谈。就在祖父去世前一天晚上，当祖母走出房间时，祖父还对祖母说“我爱你，亲爱的Madge。”

The next morning he received a phone call at work that grandfather had passed during the night. Throughout his short battle with cancer, he realized how much two people can love each other and he realized how much it means to be loved and give love. It is the greatest gift on earth and it lasts beyond life because you never forget your one true love.

第二天早晨上班时，他接到一个电话：他的祖父昨晚去世了。在他的祖父与癌症病魔的短暂抗争中，他认识到两位老人爱得是多么深，他还认识到被爱和爱意味着什么。这是世界上最伟大的礼物，它将超越生命而永存，因为你永远也不会忘记你的唯一真爱。

魅力词汇

supportive [sə'pɔːtiv] *adj.* 支持的

tumor ['tjuːmə] *n.* 肿瘤

worsen ['wɜːsən] *v.* 恶化，变得更坏

fragile ['frædʒail] *adj.* 虚弱的

11 The Measure of Love
爱无止境

爱是可以衡量的吗？如果可以，究竟什么才能衡量爱呢？既然找不到衡量爱的标准，那就无限制地去爱吧，因为爱无止境。家庭因为夫妇的相爱而温馨和睦，世界因为人人相爱而和平安宁。

文苑漫步

Freda Bright says, "Only in **opera** do people die of love." It's true. You really can't love somebody to death. I've known people to die from no love, but I've never known anyone to be loved to death. We just can't love one another enough.

A heart-warming story tells of a woman who finally decided to ask her boss for a raise in salary. All day she felt nervous and **apprehensive**. Late in the afternoon she **summoned the courage** to approach her employer. To her delight, the boss agreed to a raise. The woman arrived home that evening to a beautiful table set with their best dishes. Candles were softly glowing. Her husband had come home early and prepared a festive meal. She wondered if someone from the offi ce had **tipped him off**, or he just somehow knew that she would not get turned down? She found him

译林畅游

弗里达・布赖特说过：“只有在歌剧中，人们才会因爱而死。”是的。你不可能把一个人爱死。我听说过人们因缺少爱而死，但我从未听过有人会因为被爱得太多而死。我们永远都爱得不够。

有这样一个温馨的故事：有个女人终于鼓足勇气向老板请求加薪。那一整天她都忐忑不安，忧虑重重。下午晚些时候，她鼓起勇气走向老板。令她十分高兴的是，老板同意给她加薪。那晚女人回到家里，发现一个漂亮的桌子上摆满了各种佳肴。烛光轻轻地摇曳着。她的丈夫已经早早回家，准备了一顿丰盛的晚餐。她很纳闷，难道办公室有人已把这个消息透露给了丈夫？又或者丈夫料定她的加薪要求不会被拒绝？她发现丈夫在厨房，

in the kitchen and told him the good news. They embraced and kissed, then sat down to the wonderful meal. Next to her plate the woman found a beautifully lettered note. It read: "Congratulations, darling! I knew you'd get the raise! These things will tell you how much I love you."

Following the supper, her husband went into the kitchen to clean up. She noticed that a second card had fallen from his pocket. Picking it off the floor, she read: "Don't worry about not getting the raise! You deserve it anyway! These things will tell you how much I love you."

Someone has said that the measure of love is when you love without measure. What this man feels for his spouse is total acceptance and love, whether she succeeds or fails. His love celebrates her victories and **soothes** her wounds. He stands with her, no matter what life throws in their direction. Upon receiving the Nobel Peace Prize, Mother Teresa said: "What can you do to promote world peace? Go home and love your family. And love your friends. Love them without measure."

就把这个好消息告诉了他。他们相拥而吻，接着坐下来享用可口的饭菜。这时，女人在自己的盘子旁边发现了一张书写漂亮的字条。上面写着："亲爱的，祝贺你！我知道你一定会得到加薪。准备了这些饭菜是想告诉你，我是多么爱你。"

晚饭结束后，丈夫去厨房收拾东西。她注意到又一张卡片从他的口袋里掉了出来。女人把卡片捡起来，读道："不用因为没有得到加薪而难过！不管怎样，你的工作都是很出色的！准备了这些饭菜是想告诉你，我是多么爱你。"

有人曾说，爱的限度就是无限度的爱。这个男人给予了妻子全部的包容和爱，不计较她成功与否。他的爱包含了成功时的祝福和失败时的安慰。无论生活把他们引向什么方向，他都始终与妻子在一起。特雷莎修女在获得诺贝尔和平奖时说道："你能为促进世界和平做什么？回家去爱你的家人吧。也去爱你的朋友。毫无保留地去爱他们。"

魅力词汇

opera ['ɒprə] *n.* 歌剧
apprehensive [æpri'hensiv] *adj.* 忧虑的
summon the courage 鼓起勇气
tip sb. off 透露给某人
soothe [suːð] *v.* 安慰

12 Going Home 回家

我的刑期已满，正要赶回家；我必须知道有哪些东西还属于我。
若你收到了我的信，告诉你我将重获自由；
那么，你知道该怎么做；
如果你还要我的话，
在老橡树上系条黄丝带……
我无法相信我所看到的——老橡树上挂满了上百条黄丝带。
——《老橡树上的黄丝带》

文苑漫步

I first heard this story a few years ago from a girl I had met in New York's Greenwich Village. Probably the story is one of those mysterious bits of **folklore** that reappear every few years, to be told a new in one form or another. However, I still like to think that it really did happen, somewhere, sometime.

They were going to Fort Lauderdale, three boys and three girls and when they boarded the bus, they were carrying sandwiches and wine in paper bags, dreaming of golden beaches as the gray cold of New York vanished behind them.

As the bus passed through New Jersey, they began to notice Vingo. He sat

译林畅游

几年前我在纽约的格林尼治村从一位遇到的姑娘那儿第一次听到这个故事。它也许是那种隔几年就会改头换面地被重新传播一次的神奇的民间传说。然而我仍然愿意相信它是在某地某时真正发生过的事情。

三个男孩和三个女孩带着纸袋装的三明治与葡萄酒，坐车前往佛罗里达的劳德达拉要塞。他们向往着金色的海滩，将灰蒙蒙的寒冷的纽约甩在了身后。

当他们穿过新泽西州时，坐在前排的一个叫Vingo的男人引起了

in front of them, dressed in a plain, **ill-fitting** suit, never moving, his dusty face masking his age. He kept chewing the inside of his lip a lot, frozen into some personal **cocoon** of silence.

他们的注意。他穿着一套不起眼亦很不合身的衣服，一动不动，满是灰尘的脸掩盖了他的年龄，他不停地咬着下嘴唇，陷入沉思中。

Deep into the night, outside Washington, the bus pulled into Howard Johnson's, and everybody got off except Vingo. He sat rooted in his seat, and the young people began to wonder about him, trying to imagine his life: perhaps he was a sea captain, a runaway from his wife, an old soldier going home. When they went back to the bus, one of the girls sat beside him and introduced herself.

夜深了，公共汽车停在华盛顿郊外的霍华德·约翰逊连锁餐馆，除了Vingo，其他人都下了车，他仍纹丝不动地坐在那里。这班年轻人开始猜想：也许他是个船长，也许是从家出走的，或者是一个归家的老兵。当他们又回到车上时，他们中的一个女孩坐到Vingo的身边，并向他作了自我介绍。

"We're going to Florida," she said brightly. "I hear it's really beautiful."

"我们都是去佛罗里达的，"那个女孩轻快地说，"我听说那里很美。"

"It is," he said quietly, as if remembering something he had tried to forget.

"是的。"他静静地回答道，他似乎记起了过去曾试图忘却的往事。

"Want some wine?" she said. He smiled and took a **swig**. He thanked her and retreated again into his silence. After a while, she went back to the others, and Vingo nodded in sleep.

"来点葡萄酒吧？"那个女孩说。他微笑着喝了一大口，说了声谢谢后又陷入了沉默中。后来女孩回到那班人中，Vingo 则低着头睡着了。

In the morning, they awoke outside another Howard Johnson's, and this time Vingo went in. The girl insisted that he join them. He seemed very shy, and ordered black coffee and smoked nervously as the young people chattered about sleeping on beaches. When they returned to the bus, the girl sat with Vingo again, and after a while, slowly and painfully, he told his story. He had been

早上，他们醒来时公共汽车停在了另一个霍华德·约翰逊连锁餐馆前，这回Vingo也进去了。那个女孩极力邀请他加入他们。但他看起来很腼腆，当那班年轻人谈论着在海滨该怎么过夜时，他则独自一人待在一边喝黑咖啡，还不停地抽烟，显得有些局促不安。当他们回到车上时，那个女孩又坐到他身边，过了一会儿，Vingo才缓慢而痛

in jail in New York for the past four years, and now he was going home.

"Are you married?"

"I don't know."

"You don't know?" she said.

"Well, when I was in jail I wrote to my wife," he said. "I told her that I was going to be away a long time, and that if she couldn't stand it, if the kids kept asking questions, if it hurt too much, well, she could just forget me, I'd understand. Get a new guy, I said she's a wonderful woman, really something and forget about me. I told her she didn't have to write me for nothing. And she didn't. Not for three and a half years."

"And you're going home now, not knowing?"

"Yeah," he said shyly, "Well, last week, when I was sure the parole was coming through, I wrote her again. We used to live in Brunswick, just before Jacksonville, and there's a big oak tree just as you come into town. I told her that if she'd take me back, she should put a yellow handkerchief on the tree, and I'd get off and come home. If she didn't want me, forget it, no handkerchief, and I'd go on through."

"Wow," the girl exclaimed, "Wow."

She told the others, and soon all of them were in it, caught up in the approach of Brunswick, looking at the pictures Vingo showed them of his wife and three

苦地诉说起他的经历。他在纽约的监狱里待了四年，现在要回家了。

"你结婚了吗？"

"我不知道。"

"你不知道？"那女孩很奇怪。

"是这样，我在狱中时曾给我妻子写过一封信，"他说，"我告诉她我要离开很长一段时间，如果她忍受不了，如果孩子不断追问，如果这使她非常痛苦，那么她可以忘了我，我会理解的。我叫她重新嫁人，我知道她是个很不错的女人，真的不一般。我让她忘了我，我让她别给我写回信，因为这没有用，她也真没回信，我已有三年半没有她的音信了。"

"那么你就这样盲目地回家去？"

"也不是，"他略带腼腆地说，"上周当我确知假释得到批准时，我又给她写过一封信。过去我们住在布伦斯威克，就在杰克逊维尔前面，在进城去的路上有一棵高大的橡树。我告诉她，如果她愿意我回来就在树上挂一方黄手帕，我就下车回家。如果她不愿我回去，就忘掉这件事，看不见手帕，我也就不下车了。"

"噢，是吗？"那个女孩惊讶极了。

她把这事告诉了同伴们，于是他们都盼着快点到布伦斯威克。Vingo 又给他们看了一张他妻子与

children. The woman was handsome in a plain way, the children still unformed in the much-handled **snapshots**.

Now they were twenty miles from Brunswick, and the young people took over window seats on the right side, waiting for the approach of the great oak tree. The bus acquired a dark, **hushed** mood, full of the silence of absence and lost years. Vingo stopped looking, tightening his face into the ex-con's mask, as if fortifying himself against still another disappointment.

Then Brunswick was ten miles, and then five. Then, suddenly, all of the young people were up out of their seats, screaming and shouting and crying, doing small dances of joy. All except Vingo.

Vingo sat there stunned, looking at the oak tree. It was covered with yellow handkerchiefs, 20 of them, 30 of them, maybe hundreds, a tree that stood like a banner of welcome **billowing in** the wind. As the young people shouted, the old con rose and made his way to the front of the bus to go home.

三个孩子的照片。这是一张被摸旧了的照片：一个面容端庄的妇女与三个年岁还小的孩子。

现在他们离布伦斯威克只有二十英里了，那班年轻人占据了车右边靠窗的座位，等待着那棵橡树的出现。车里一片阴暗和肃静。充满着逝去岁月的沉重的气氛。Vingo 则低下头，一副囚犯们所特有的绷紧的面容，不敢往外看，好像是防备着又一次失望的打击。

离布伦斯威克只有十英里了，五英里了。突然，那班年轻人全都叫着从座位上跳了起来，高兴得手舞足蹈，只有 Vingo 例外。

Vingo 目瞪口呆地坐在那儿，望着窗外的橡树，那上面挂满了黄手帕。20 块，30 块，也许有好几百块，这棵树站在那儿，就像一面欢迎的大旗，在风中飘扬。在年轻人的呼喊声中，那个往日的囚徒站起来，走到车门前，然后向家走去。

魅力词汇

folklore ['fəʊklɔː]
n. 民俗学，民间风俗，民间传说
ill-fitting ['il'fitiŋ] *adj.* 不合身的
cocoon [kə'kuːn] *n.* 茧
swig [swig] *n.* 大口喝，吞咽
snapshot ['snæpʃɒt] *n.* 快照
hushed [hʌʃt] *adj.* 安静的
billow in 在……中飘动

第四篇

— 浪漫路 —
曲曲折折

1 Ole and Trufa 两片树叶的爱情

有句诗这样写道："生命诚可贵，爱情价更高；若为自由故，二者皆可抛。"热恋中的人经常爱得死去活来，为了对方甚至甘愿放弃自己的生命。因为他们想要一直抓住对方，不管生前还是死后。如此的执着带来的是烦恼和恐惧，因为他们不知道只有解放自己、进入永恒才能拥有无上的快乐。生而何欢，死亦何惧！对待爱情也应如此，这样才会爱得潇洒，爱得欢喜。

文苑漫步

The forest was large and thickly overgrown with all kinds of leaf-bearing trees. Usually, it is cold this time of year and it even happens that it snows, but this November was relatively warm. You might have thought it was summer except that the whole forest was **strewn** with fallen leaves — some yellow as **saffron**, some red as wine, some the color of gold and some of mixed color. The leaves had been torn down by the rain, by the wind, some by day, some at night, and they now formed a deep carpet over the forest floor. Although their juices had run dry, the leaves still **exuded a pleasant aroma**. The sun shone down on them through the living branches, and worms and flies which

译林畅游

在一座很大很茂密的森林里，生长着许多树，树的叶子多种多样。通常，一年中的这个时候天气会变得寒冷，甚至会下雪，但是这个十一月份却还有些暖和。如果不是整座森林都洒满了落叶——桔黄的、酒红的、金黄的，还有多种颜色混合在一起的，你甚至会以为这是夏天。日夜的风吹雨淋把这些叶子从树上撕扯下来，它们在森林的地面上形成了一层厚厚的毯子。尽管汁液已经干枯，这些叶子依然散发着宜人的香味。阳光穿过树枝照在叶子上，那些想尽办法在秋日的风暴中存活下来的虫子、苍蝇在树叶上爬动着。树叶下面的空间为蟋蟀、田鼠以及许多在地面上寻求庇

had somehow survived the autumn storms crawled over them. The space beneath the leaves provided hiding places for **crickets**, field mice and many other creatures who sought protection in the earth.

On the tip of a tree which had lost all its other leaves, two still remained hanging from one **twig**: Ole and Trufa. For some reason unknown to them, Ole and Trufa had survived all the rains, all the cold nights and winds. Who knows the reason one leaf falls and another remains? But Ole and Trufa believed the answer lay in the great love they bore one another. Ole was slightly bigger than Trufa and a few days older, but Trufa was prettier and more delicate. One leaf can do little for another when the wind blows, the rain pours, or the **hail** begins to fall. Still, Ole encouraged Trufa at every opportunity. During the worst storms, when the thunder clapped, the lightning flashed and the wind tore off not only leaves but even whole branches, Ole pleaded with Trufa: "Hang on, Trufa! Hand on with all your might!"

At times during cold and stormy nights, Trufa would complain: "My time had come, Ole, but you hand on!"

"What for?" Ole asked. "Without you, my life is senseless. If you fall, I'll fall with you."

"No, Ole, don't do it! So long as a

护的不知名生物提供了藏身之所。

有一棵树的叶子几乎全掉光了，除了树梢一根细枝上还挂着的两片树叶，它们的名字叫 Ole 和 Trufa。Ole 和 Trufa 也不清楚为什么它们能在所有的暴雨、寒夜和狂风中存活下来。有的叶子被吹落而有的却没有，这其中的原因谁又知道呢？可是 Ole 和 Trufa 认为答案在于它们深深地爱着对方。Ole 比 Trufa 早出生几天，外形略大于 Trufa，可是 Trufa 更漂亮更精致。每当刮风、下雨或冰雹天气时，它们彼此爱莫能助。然而，Ole 总是抓住一切机会鼓励 Trufa。当最恶劣的暴风雨来临时，雷鸣电闪，狂风不仅刮落树叶，甚至刮断整根树枝，Ole 恳求着 Trufa："坚持，Trufa！尽全力坚持住！"

有时在寒冷的暴风雨之夜，Trufa 会抱怨："我的时间到了，Ole，可是你要坚持住！"

"为什么？" Ole 问。"没有你，我的生命将毫无意义，如果你掉下去，我将跟你一起掉下去！"

"不，Ole，别这样！一片树叶只

leaf can stay up it mustn't let go."

"It all depends if you stay with me," Ole replied. "By day I look at you and admire your beauty. At night I sense your fragrance. Be the only leaf on a tree? No never!"

"Ole, your words are so sweet but they're not true," Trufa said. "You know very well that I'm no longer pretty. Look how **wrinkled** I am, how **shriveled** I've become! Only one thing is still left me — my love for you."

"Isn't that enough? Of all our powers love is the highest, the finest," Ole said. "So long as we love each other we remain here, and no wind, rain or storm can destroy us. I'll tell you something, Trufa — I never loved you as much as I love you now."

"Why, Ole? Why? I'm all yellow."

"Who says green is pretty and yellow is not? All colors are equally handsome."

And just as Ole spoke these words, that which Trufa had feared all these months happened — a wind came up and tore Ole loose from the twig. Trufa began to **tremble and flutter** until it seemed that she, too, would soon be torn away, but she held fast. She saw Ole fall and sway in the air, and she called to him in leafy language: "Ole! Come back! Ole! Ole!"

But before she could even finish, Ole

要能留在树上就不应该松手往下掉。"

"这完全取决于你是否留下来陪我。" Ole 回答，"白天我看着你，爱慕你的美丽，夜里感觉着你的芬芳。只有我一片树叶留在树上？决不！"

Trufa 说："Ole，你的话真让我高兴，可是你说得不对。你很清楚我不漂亮了，看我多皱，变得多么枯萎了啊！我唯一剩下的就是——我对你的爱。"

Ole 说："那不就够了吗？爱是所有力量中最高尚、最美好的。只要我们在这里彼此相爱，就没有风、雨或暴风雪能摧毁我们。Trufa，我要告诉你，我从未像现在这么爱你。"

"为什么，Ole？为什么？我已经完全枯黄了。"

"谁说绿色漂亮黄色就不漂亮了？所有的色彩都同样漂亮。"

Ole 刚说完这些话，Trufa 几个月来一直害怕的事发生了——一阵风刮来，扯松了细枝上的 Ole。Trufa 开始颤抖、晃动，似乎她很快也要被刮落了，可是她迅速抓稳了。她看到 Ole 掉了下去，在空中摇晃着，她用叶子的语言大喊道："Ole！回来啊，Ole！ Ole！"

可是她甚至都没把话说完，

vanished from sight. He blended in with the other leaves on the ground, and Trufa was left all alone on the tree.

Trufa didn't think a night could be so long as this one — so dark, so frosty. She spoke to Ole and hoped for an answer, but Ole was silent and gave no sign of his presence.

Trufa said to the tree: "Since you've taken Ole from me, take me too."

But even this prayer the tree didn't acknowledge.

After a while, Trufa **dozed off**. This wasn't sleep but a strange **languor**. Trufa awoke and to her amazement found that she was no longer handing on the tree. The wind had blown her down while she was asleep. This was different from the way she had used to feel when she awoke on the tree with the sunrise. All her fears and anxieties had now vanished. The awakening also brought with it an awareness she had never felt before. She knew now that she wasn't just a leaf that depended on every **whim** of the wind, but that she was part of the universe. Through some mysterious force, Trufa understood the miracle of her **molecules**, atoms, **protons** and **electrons** — the enormous energy she represented and the divine plan of which she was a part.

Next to her lay Ole, and they greeted

Ole 就从她的视野里消失了。他跟地上的其他落叶混在一起，而 Trufa 被孤伶伶地留在了树上。

Trufa 从没想过一个夜晚能像今晚——这么漫长，这么黑暗，这么严寒。她呼唤着 Ole，希望能听到一声回答，可是 Ole 沉默着，没有给出一点他存在的迹象。

Trufa 对树说道："既然你从我身边带走了 Ole，就把我也一起带走吧。"

可是甚至连树也没有注意到这个祈求。

片刻后，Trufa 打瞌睡了。这不是睡，而是一种奇怪的无精打采。醒来后，她吃惊地发现她不在树上了。在她睡着的时候，风已把她刮了下来。这不同于她平日长在树上享受着阳光沐浴时醒来的感觉。此刻，她所有的恐惧和担心全都消失了。这次的苏醒带给她一种从未有过的感觉。如今，她知道自己已不再是依附于风的一时兴致的树叶了，而成了宇宙的一部分。借助某种神秘的力量，Trufa 了解了自身分子、原子、质子和电子的奇迹——她所代表的巨大能量以及作为其中一份子的神圣计划。

Ole 就躺在她身旁，它们怀着

each other with a love they hadn't been aware of before. This wasn't a love that depended on chance or **caprice**, but a love as mighty and eternal as the universe itself. That which they had feared all the days and nights between April and November turned out to be not death but **redemption**. A breeze came and lifted Ole and Trufa in the air and they soared with the **bliss** known only by those who have freed themselves and have joined with eternity.

前所未有的爱问候对方。这不是建立在偶然或任性基础上的爱，而是像宇宙本身一样巨大和永恒的爱。从四月份到十一月份期间所有的日日夜夜里他们所担心的结果，不是死亡而是救赎。一阵微风过来，把它们吹到了空中，它们带着无比的喜悦向上飞去，这种快乐只有解放自己进入永恒才能体会到。

魅力词汇

strew [struː] *v.* 洒满
saffron ['sæfrən] *n.* 橘黄色
exude a pleasant aroma 散发出宜人的香味
cricket ['krikit] *n.* 蟋蟀
twig [twig] *n.* 细枝
hail [heil] *n.* 冰雹
wrinkled ['riŋkld] *adj.* 有皱纹的
shriveled ['ʃrivəld] *adj.* 枯萎的
tremble and flutter 颤抖摇摆
doze off 打瞌睡
languor ['læŋgə] *n.* 无精打采
whim [wim] *n.* 一时兴致
molecule ['mɒlikjuːl] *n.* 分子
proton ['prəʊtɒn] *n.* 质子
electron [i'lektrɒn] *n.* 电子
caprice [kə'priːs] *n.* 任性
redemption [ri'dempʃn] *n.* 救赎
bliss [blis] *n.* 极乐

温情絮语

It hurts to love someone and not be loved in return.But what is more painful is to love someone and never find the courage to let that person know how you feel.

没有回报的爱是一种伤害。但更痛苦的是爱一个人却没有勇气让那个人知道你的感受。

2 Detour to Romance
浪漫路曲曲折折

所谓“好事多磨”，一对恋人经历了千辛万苦才最终走到一起，这段曲曲折折的浪漫路让他们更懂得了彼此的真情，更珍惜来之不易的幸福。

文苑漫步

Located in the **checkroom** in Union Station as I am, I can see everybody that comes up the stairs.

Harry came in a little over three years ago and waited at the head of the stairs for the passengers from the 9:05 train.

I remember seeing Harry that first evening. He wasn't much more than a thin, anxious kid then. He was all dressed up and I knew he was meeting his girl and that they would be married twenty minutes after she arrived.

Well, the passengers came up and I had to get busy. I didn't look toward the stairs again until nearly time for the 9:18 and I was very surprised to see that the young fellow was still there.

She didn't come on the 9:18 either, nor on the 9:40, and when the passengers from the 10:02 had all arrived and left,

译林畅游

因为我在联合车站的行李寄存处工作，所以我看得见每一个上这个楼梯的人。

三年多前 Harry 来到这儿，站在楼梯口等待 9 点零 5 分到达的火车上的旅客。

我还记得那一晚第一次见到 Harry 时的情景。那时，他瘦瘦的，神情焦虑，就像个孩子似的。他穿戴整齐，我知道他是在等女朋友，而且在她到达二十分钟之后他们就要结婚了。

旅客们过来了，我忙碌起来。等到 9 点 18 分的那趟车快到的时候我再往楼梯方向看去，我吃惊地发现那个年轻人还在那里。

她没乘 9 点 18 分的那趟车来，9 点 40 分的车上也没她。等 10 点零 2 分那趟车的旅客全都到达并离

Harry was looking pretty desperate. Pretty soon he came close to my window so I called out and asked him what she looked like.

"She's small and dark," he said, "and 19 years old and very neat in the way she walks. She has a face," he said, thinking a minute, "that has lots of **spirit**. I mean she can get mad but she never stays mad for long, and her eyebrows come to a little point in the middle. She's got a brown fur, but maybe she isn't wearing it."

I couldn't remember seeing anybody like that.

He showed me the telegram he'd received: ARRIVE THURSDAY. MEET ME STATION. LOVE LOVE LOVE LOVE. MAY. It was from Omaha, Nebraska.

"Well," I finally said, "why don't you phone to your home? She's probably called there if she got in ahead of you."

He gave me a sick look. "I've only been in town two days. We were going to meet and then drive down South where I've got a job. She hasn't any address for me." He touched the telegram.

When I came on duty the next day he was still there and came over as soon as he saw me.

"Did she work anywhere?" I asked.

He nodded. "She was a typist. I telegraphed her former boss. All they know is

开后，Harry显得很失望。很快他走近我的窗口，我招呼他，问他等的人长什么模样。

"她个子不高，皮肤有点黑，"Harry说，"年龄是19岁，走起路来很精干。她的脸，"他想了一会儿说道，"很有朝气。我的意思是她会生气，但从来不会持续很久。她的眉心有一个小点。她有一件褐色毛皮大衣，不过今天不一定穿着。"

我想不起来看见过有谁长得像那样。

他给我看他收到的电报：周四到。车站接我。爱你爱你爱你爱你。——May。电报来自内布拉斯加州的奥马哈市。

"呃，"我最后说，"你干吗不往家里打个电话？如果她比你先到，她可能已给你家打过电话。"

他难过地看了我一眼。"我到城里才两天。我们打算见面之后开车去南方，我在那儿找到了一份工作。她也没给我任何地址。"他摸了摸电报。

第二天我去值班时Harry还在那儿。一看见我，他就走了过来。

"她在哪儿工作过吗？"我问。

他点了点头。"她本来是个打字员。我给她以前的老板拍了电报。

that she left her job to get married."

Harry met every train for the next three or four days. Of course, the railroad lines made a **routine checkup** and the police looked into the case. But nobody was any real help. I could see that they all figured that May had simply played a trick on him. But I never believed that, somehow.

One day, after about two weeks, Harry and I were talking and I told him about my theory. "If you'll just wait long enough," I said, "you'll see her coming up those stairs some day." He turned and looked at the stairs as though he had never seen them before.

The next day when I came to work, Harry was behind the counter of Tony's magazine stand. He looked at me rather **sheepishly** and said, "Well, I had to get a job somewhere, didn't I?"

So he began to work as a clerk for Tony. We never spoke of May anymore and neither of us ever mentioned my theory. But I noticed that Harry always saw every person who came up the stairs.

Toward the end of the year Tony was killed in some argument over gambling, and Tony's widow left Harry in complete charge of the magazine stand. And when she got married again some time later, Harry bought the stand from her. He bor-

他们只知道她辞职，结婚去了。"

Harry 在后来的三四天接了每趟车。当然，铁路方面做了例行检查，警察也参与了这件事。但实际上谁也没帮上忙。我看得出来，他们都觉得 May 只不过是跟他开了个玩笑，但不知怎么我却压根不这么认为。

有一天，大约是过了两周之后，Harry 和我聊天，我跟他谈了我的想法。"假如你等的时间够长的话，"我说，"总有一天，你会看见她走上楼梯的。"他转过身看着楼梯，仿佛过去从来没见过似的。

第二天我去上班时，Harry 已经站在 Tony 杂志摊的柜台后面了。他不大好意思地看着我说，"呃，我总得在哪儿找个工作，是不是？"

于是，他开始给 Tony 当店员。我们再也没谈起 May 的事，也没人再提我的见解。但我注意到 Harry 总要看看每一个上那个楼梯的人。

到年底时，Tony 由于赌博时发生争执被人杀了。Tony 的妻子将杂志摊完全交给 Harry 打理。过了些时候她再次结婚，Harry 就从她那儿把杂志摊买了过来。他借了钱，装了个冷饮柜，不久小生意就做得不错了。

rowed money and installed a **soda fountain** and pretty soon he had a very nice little business.

Then came yesterday. I heard a cry and a lot of things falling. The cry was from Harry and the things falling were a lot of dolls and other things which he had upset while he was jumping over the counter. He ran across and grabbed a girl not ten feet from my window. She was small and dark and her **eyebrows** came to a little point in the middle.

昨天，我听到一声叫喊和许多东西掉到地上的声音。叫喊声是Harry发出的，掉在地上的那些玩具是他在翻越柜台时碰倒的。他越过去抓住一个女孩，那个女孩就在离我窗户不到十英尺的地方。她个子小小的，皮肤黑黑的，眉心处有一个小点。

For a while they just hung there to each other laughing and crying and saying things without meaning. She'd say a few words like, "It was the bus station I meant" and he'd kiss her speechless and tell her the many things he had done to find her. What apparently had happened three years before was that May had come by bus, not by train, and in her telegram she meant "bus station", not "railroad station". She had waited at the bus station for days and had spent all her money trying to find Harry. Finally she got a job typing.

好一会儿他们就那么待着，相对着笑呀，哭呀，讲些没什么意义的话。她好像说"我指的是汽车站。"而他则把她吻得说不出话来，告诉她自己为找她所做的许多事情。显然，三年前May是乘汽车而不是火车来的，她电报里指的是"汽车站"而不是"火车站"。她在汽车站等了好几天，为找Harry花掉了所有的钱。最后，她找了一份打字的工作。

"What?" said Harry. "Have you been working in town? All the time?"

"什么？" Harry说，"你在城里工作？一直都在？"

She nodded.

她点点头。

"Well, Heavens. Didn't you ever come down here to the station?" He pointed across to his magazine stand. "I've been there all the time. I own it. I've watched

"哦，上帝。你从来就没来过这个车站？"他用手指向他的杂志摊。"我一直都在这儿。那个摊是我的。我一直注意着走上这个楼梯

everybody that came up the stairs."

She began to look a little pale. Pretty soon she looked over at the stairs and said in a weak voice, "I never came up the stairs before. You see, I went out of town yesterday on a short business trip. Oh, Harry!" Then she threw her arms around his neck and really began to cry.

After a minute she backed away and pointed very **stiffly** toward the north end of the station. "Harry, for three years, for three solid years, I've been right over there working right in this very station, typing, in the office of the station master."

的每一个人。"

她的脸色开始变得苍白。过了一会儿，她站在楼梯上看过去，用微弱的声音说道，"我以前从来没有上过这个楼梯。你瞧，我昨天出城办了点公事。噢，Harry！"然后，她用胳膊搂住 Harry 的脖子，真的哭了起来。

过了一会儿，她往后一站，胳膊僵硬地指着车站的最北端。"Harry，三年来，整整三年来，我一直就在车站工作，就在那儿，在站长办公室里打字。"

魅力词汇

checkroom ['tʃekruːm] *n.* 行李寄存处
spirit ['spirit] *n.* 精神，活力
routine checkup 例行检查
sheepishly ['ʃipiʃli] *adv.* 羞怯地，腼腆地，不好意思地
soda fountain 冷饮柜台
eyebrow ['aibraʊ] *n.* 眉心
stiffly ['stifli] *adv.* 僵硬地

温情絮语

A sad thing in life is when you meet someone who means a lot to you, only to find out in the end that it was never meant to be and you just have to let go.

生命中令人悲伤的是，当你遇到了某个对你来说极为重要的人，却发现根本没有所谓的命中注定，最后你只得放手。

3 Rose-Tree 玫瑰树

爱慕月亮的人并不将它据为己有，能远远望着，就已足够。玫瑰树的根须中燃烧着爱情中没有实现的渴望，枝繁叶茂的玫瑰树开出深红的花儿，谱写着爱人的忠贞和热烈。

文苑漫步

The old lady had always been proud of the great rose-tree in her garden, and was fond of telling how it had grown from a cutting she had brought years before from Italy, when she was first married. She and her husband had been travelling back in their carriage from Rome (it was before the time of railways) and on a bad piece of road south of Siena they had broken down, and had been forced to pass the night in a little house by the road-side. The accommodation was **wretched** of course; she had spent a sleepless night, and rising early had stood, wrapped up, at her window, with the cool air blowing on her face, to watch the dawn. She could still, after all these years, remember the blue mountains with the bright moon above them, and how a far-off town on one of the peaks had gradually grown whiter and

译林畅游

这位老太太总以她花园中那棵巨大的玫瑰树为荣。她会津津有味地告诉你多年前她刚结婚时从意大利带回来的一根枝条是怎样长成参天大树的。当年她和丈夫乘马车从罗马归来（那时还未通铁路），途经锡耶纳南部时，有一段路很难走，结果马车坏了，他们只好就宿于路边的一间小店。当然，住宿条件很恶劣，她彻夜难眠，很早就起身穿好衣服，站在窗前等待黎明。凉风不时从窗外袭来。时隔多年，她依然记得一轮明月挂在那蓝色的群山上，远山上的小城一点一点地变白，直到月亮渐渐落下，初升的太阳为群山抹上一层淡淡的粉色。突然之间，一束光辉照亮小城，小城扇扇窗户亮了起来，反射出耀眼的光芒，最后，整座小城如满天繁星般在蓝天下熠熠生辉。

whiter; till the moon faded, the mountains were touched with the pink of the rising sun, and suddenly the town was lit as by an **illumination**, one window after another catching and reflecting the sun's beam, till at last the whole little city twinkled and sparkled up in the sky like a nest of stars.

That morning, finding they would have to wait while their carriage was being repaired, they had driven in a local **con-veyance** up to the city on the mountain, where they had been told they would find better **quarters**; and there they had stayed two or three days. It was one of the **min-iature** Italian cities with a high church, a **pretentious piazza**, a few narrow streets and little palaces, **perched**, all **compact** and complete, on the top of a mountain, within and **enclosure** of walls hardly larg-er than an English kitchen garden. But it was full of life and noise, echoing all day and all night with the sounds of feet and voices.

那天上午，得知必须等一段时间马车才能修好，他们便乘当地的交通车去了那个山顶小城，听说在那儿可以找到好一些的住处。之后，他们在那儿逗留了两三天。那是个意大利小城，有一座高大的教堂，一个虚华的市场，一些窄窄的街道，几座小小的宫殿，周密而完美地立于山顶。被城墙围着的城区并不比英国人的菜园子大多少，但这里生机勃勃，喧闹嘈杂，昼夜回荡着脚步声和话语声。

The Cafe of the simple inn where they stayed was the meeting place of the notabilities of the little city; the mayor, the lawyer, the doctor, and a few others; and among them they noticed a beautiful, slim, talkative old man, with bright black eyes and snow-white hair — tall and straight and still with the figure of a youth, although the waiter told them with pride that the earl was very old — would in fact be 80 in the following year. He was the last of his

他们居住在当地一个名流云集的简易酒店里，有市长、律师、医生，还有其他几个人。在他们当中，一位英俊、瘦高个儿而又健谈的老人引起他们的注意。他有乌黑明亮的眼睛，雪白的头发，个子高高的，腰板很直，像年轻人一样。但是酒店的侍者却自豪地告诉他们实际上这位伯爵已届高龄，明年是他的80岁寿辰。侍者还说到伯爵是他们家族的最后一人，曾是豪门大户，但

family, the waiter added — they had once been great and rich people — but he had no **descendants**; in fact the waiter mentioned with **complacency**, as if it were a story on which the locality prided itself, that the earl had been unfortunate in love, and had never married.

一生无子嗣。但事实上，这个侍者还甚是得意地说，伯爵情场失意，终生未娶。这似乎是一件在当地值得炫耀的事情。

The old gentleman, however, seemed cheerful enough; and it was plain that he took an interest in the strangers, and wished to make their acquaintance. This was soon effected by the friendly waiter; and after a little talk the old man invited them to visit his **villa** and garden which were just outside the walls of the town. So the next afternoon, when the sun began to descend, and they saw in glimpses through door-ways and windows, blue shadows beginning to spread over the brown mountains, they went to pay their visit. It was not much of a place, a small, modernized, **stucco** villa, with a hot **pebbly** garden, and in it a stone basin with **torpid** gold-fish, and a statue of Diana and her **hounds** against the wall. But what gave a glory to it was a **gigantic** rose-tree which **clambered** over the house, almost **smothering** the windows, and filling the air with the perfume of its sweetness. “Yes, it was a fine rose”, the earl said proudly when they praised it, and he would tell the lady about it. And as they sat there, drinking the wine he offered them, he **alluded** with the cheerful indifference of old age to his

然而，这位老先生似乎过得挺开心；他显然对陌生人很感兴趣，愿意与之结交。很快这位和善的侍者促成了他们之间的相识。聊了一会儿，老人就邀请他们参观他在城外的别墅和花园。因此，第二天下午，日落之时，当他们从门口和窗口瞥见蓝色的阴影覆盖了褐色的山峦时，就动身去造访这位老伯爵了。其实别墅比较一般，只是一座灰泥粉饰的现代小别墅，铺有石头的花园里有些热，石盆中的金鱼无精打采，戴安娜和她的猎犬的雕像倚墙而立。然而，一颗巨大的玫瑰树为这座别墅增色不少，它高过屋顶，几乎遮住了窗户，散发出诱人的花香。“嗯！确实是一棵美丽的玫瑰树。”在他们的赞美声中老先生自豪地说，而且他很乐意为这位女士讲述玫瑰树的故事。当他们坐在那儿，喝着老人提供的葡萄酒时，老伯爵忘却了自己已届高龄，向大家娓娓道起自己当年的爱情故事，就好像他理所当然地认为他们早已经听说过似的。

love-affair, as though he took for granted that they had heard of it already.

"The girl lived across the valley there beyond that hill. I was a young man then, for it was many years ago. I used to ride over to see her; it was a long way, but I rode fast, for young men, as no doubt the lady knows, are impatient. But the girl was not kind, she would keep me waiting, oh, for hours; and one day when I had waited very long I grew very angry, and as I walked up and down in the garden where she had told me she would see me, I broke one of her roses, broke a branch from it; and when I saw what I had done, I hid it inside my coat... so; and when I came home I planted it, and the lady sees how it has grown. If the lady admires it, I must give her a cutting to plant also in her garden; I am told the English have beautiful gardens that are green, and not burnt with the sun like ours."

The next day, when their mended carriage had come up to fetch them, and they were just starting to drive away from the inn, the earl's old servant appeared with the rose-cutting neatly wrapped up, and the **compliments** and wishes for a nice trip from her master. The town collected to see them depart, and the children heard a rush of feet behind them for a few moments, but soon they were far down towards the valley; the little town with all its noise and life was high above them on its mountain peak.

"多年以前，那个女孩就住在那座山背后的山谷对面。当时我还是个年轻人。我常骑马去见她；虽然路很长，但年轻人性子急——女士无疑是知道的，所以我骑得很快。但那位小姐很不友善，总是让我等啊等，一等就是几个小时。一天，久候不来之后，我勃然大怒。我在她说好会见我的那个花园里不停地踱步，借着怒火砍了她的一棵玫瑰树，把上面的一根树枝折走了。当我意识到自己的所作所为之后，我将它藏进外套。事情就是这样。回家之后我把它种到花园里，它现在的成长情形这位女士已经看到了。当然这位女士要是喜欢的话，我愿意送根插条给她种在她家的花园里。听说英国人的花园很漂亮，到处绿油油的，不像我们的园子都被太阳烤焦了。"

翌日，马车已经修好，上山来接他们。正要乘车离开小酒店时，伯爵的老仆人来了。送了他们一根包扎得整整齐齐的玫瑰插条，并转达了老伯爵的问候与祝辞，祝他们旅途愉快。全城人都聚在一起目送他们离去，孩童们追着马车跑了一会儿。开始还能听到身后阵阵的脚步声，但不久马车就驶入山谷，喧闹的小城依然在他们上面高高立于山巅。

She had planted the rose at home, where it had grown and flourished in a wonderful manner; and every June the great mass of leaves and **shoots** still broke out into a passionate **splendour** of **scent** and crimson colour, as if in its root and fibres there still burnt the anger and **thwarted** desire of that Italian lover. Of course the old earl must have died many years ago; she had forgotten his name, and had even forgotten the name of the mountain city that she had stayed in, after first seeing it twinkling at dawn in the sky, like a nest of stars.

她将玫瑰插条种在家里，长势十分良好，枝繁叶茂。每年的六月，枝繁叶茂的玫瑰树都会开出深红的花儿，花香四溢，就好像它的根须中依然燃烧着那个意大利爱人的愤怒和爱情中没有实现的渴望。当然，老伯爵已经辞世多年；她也忘记了老伯爵的名字，连曾经住过的小山城的名字也遗忘了。只记得初见时，它犹如满天的繁星在黎明的薄暮中熠熠生辉。

魅力词汇

wretched ['retʃid] *adj.* 劣等的，破旧的
illumination [i,ljuːmi'neiʃn] *n.* 照明
conveyance [kən'veɪəns] *n.* 运输工具
quarter ['kwɔːtə] *n.* 住处（用复数形式）
miniature ['minitʃə]
adj. 微型的，小规模的
pretentious [pri'tenʃəs]
adj. 虚饰的，炫耀的
piazza [pi'ætsə] *n.* 露天市场
perch [pɜːtʃ] *v.* 位于，使坐落于
compact [kəm'pækt]
adj. 紧密的，紧凑的
enclosure [in'kləʊʒə] *n.* 围墙
descendant [di'sendənt] *n.* 后裔，子孙
complacency [kəm'pleisənsi] *n.* 自满
villa ['vilə] *n.* 别墅
stucco ['stʌkəʊ] *n.*（建筑业）粉饰灰泥
pebbly ['pebli] *adj.* 多卵石的
torpid ['tɔːpid] *adj.* 不活泼的
hound [haʊnd] *n.* 猎犬
gigantic [dʒai'gæntik] *adj.* 巨大的
clamber ['klæmbə] *v.* 攀登，爬上
smother ['smʌðə] *v.* 笼罩，覆盖，使窒息
allude [ə'ljuːd] *v.* 提及，说起
compliment ['kɒmplimənt] *n.* 问候
shoot [ʃuːt] *n.* 嫩枝
splendour ['splendə] *n.* 光彩壮丽
scent [sent] *n.* 气味
thwarted [θwɔːtid] *adj.* 挫败的

4 On Love 论爱

爱是恒久忍耐，又有恩慈； 爱是不嫉妒，爱是不自夸，不张狂，不做害羞的事，不求自己的益处，不轻易发怒，不计算人的恶，不喜欢不义，只喜欢真理；凡事包容，凡事相信，凡事盼望，凡事忍耐。爱是永不止息。

文苑漫步

When love **beckons to** you, follow him,

Though his ways are hard and **steep**.

And when his wings enfold you, **yield to** him,

Though the sword hidden among his **pinions** may wound you.

And when he speaks to you, believe in him,

Though his voice may shatter your dreams as the north wind lays waste the garden.

For even as love crowns you, so shall he **crucify** you.

Even as he is for your growth, so is he for your **pruning**.

Even as he ascends to your height and **caresses** your tenderest branches that **quiver** in the sun,

译林畅游

当爱召唤你的时候，跟随他，

虽然他的路程艰险而陡峻。

当他的翅翼围卷你的时候，降服于他，

虽然那藏在羽翮中间的剑刃也许会伤害你。

当他对你说话的时候，信从他，

虽然他的声音会把你们的梦想击碎，如同北风吹荒了林园。

爱虽给你加冠，他也把你钉在十字架上。

他虽栽培你，但也修剪你。

他虽升到你的最高处，抚惜你在阳光中颤动的枝叶，

So shall he descend to your roots and shake them in their clinging to the earth.

他也会降到你的根下，摇动你根柢的一切关节，使之归土。

Like **sheaves** of corn he gathers you unto himself. He **threshes** you to make you naked.

如同一捆稻粟，他把你束聚起来。他舂打你使你赤裸。

He sifts you to free you from your **husks**.

他筛分你使你脱壳。

He **grinds** you to whiteness.

他磨碾你直至洁白。

He **kneads** you until you are **pliant**;

他揉搓你直至柔韧；

And then he assigns you to his sacred fire, that you may become sacred bread for God's sacred feast.

然后他送你到他的圣火上去，使你成为上帝盛宴上的圣饼。

All these things shall love do unto you that you may know the secrets of your heart, and in that knowledge become a fragment of Life's heart.

这些都是爱要给你们做的事情，使你知道自己心中的秘密，在这知识中，你便成了"生命"心中的一部分。

But if in your fear you would seek only love's peace and love's pleasure.

假如在你的疑惧中，只寻求爱的和平与逸乐。

Then it is better for you that you cover your nakedness and pass out of love's **threshing-floor**.

那不如掩盖真实的自我而躲过爱的考验。

Into the seasonless world where you shall laugh, but not all of your laughter, and weep, but not all of your tears.

而走入那没有季候的世界，在那里你将欢笑，却不是开怀大笑，你将哭泣，却并非尽情地哭。

Love gives **naught** but itself and takes naught but from itself.

爱只将自己付出，也只得到自己。

Love possesses not nor would it be possessed;

爱不占有也不被占有；

For love is sufficient unto love.

因为爱在爱中满足了。

When you love you should not say, "God is in my heart," but rather, "I am in the heart of God."

当你爱的时候，你不要说"上帝在我心中"，却要说"我在上帝的心里。"

And think not you can direct the course of love, if it finds you worthy, directs your course. Love has no other desire but to fulfill itself.

不要想你能引导爱的路程，因为若是他觉得你值得，他就引导你。爱没有别的愿望，只要成全自己。

But if you love and must have desires, let these be your desires:

但若是你爱，而且需求渴望，就让以下的作你的渴望吧：

To melt and be like a running brook that sings its **melody** to the night.

融化你自己，像溪流般对清夜吟唱歌曲。

To know the pain of too much tenderness.

明了过度温存所带来的痛苦。

To be wounded by your own understanding of love;

让你对于爱的了解伤了你自己。

And to bleed willingly and joyfully.

而且心甘情愿喜乐地受伤。

To wake at dawn with a winged heart and give thanks for another day of loving;

清晨醒来，以轻快的心来致谢这爱的又一天；

To rest at the noon hour and meditate love's **ecstasy**;

日中静息，默念爱的浓欢；

To return home at **eventide** with gratitude;

晚潮退时，怀着感恩之心回家；

And then to sleep with a prayer for the beloved in your heart and a song of praise upon your lips.

然后带着为内心所爱之人的祈祷和赞美之歌入眠。

魅力词汇

beckon to 向……示意，打招呼
steep [stiːp] *adj.* 险峻的，陡峭的
yield to 让步
pinion ['pinjən] *n.* 鸟翼
crucify ['kruːsifai] *v.* 把……钉在十字架上处死
prune [pruːn] *v.* 修剪，砍掉
caress [kə'res] *v.* 抚摩
quiver ['kwivə] *v.* 颤动
sheaf [ʃiːf] *n.* 束，捆（复 sheaves）
thresh [θreʃ] *v.* 打谷
husk [hʌsk] *n.* 外壳，皮
grind [graind] *v.* 磨擦，磨碎
knead [niːd] *v.* 揉
pliant ['plaiənt] *adj.* 柔韧的，顺从的
threshing-floor *n.* 打谷场
naught [nɔːt] *n.* 无价值（零）
melody ['melədi] *n.* 旋律，曲调
ecstasy ['ekstəsi] *n.* 狂喜
eventide ['iːvəntaid] *n.* 黄昏

5 Love and Time 爱和时间

爱的价值，有谁知道？是富有吗？是虚荣吗？是悲伤吗？抑或是幸福？只有时间，只有它知道爱到底有多么宝贵。

文苑漫步

Once upon a time, there was an island where all the feelings lived: Happiness, Sadness, Knowledge, and all of the others, including Love. One day it was announced to the feelings that the island would sink, so all **constructed** boats and left. Except for Love.

Love was the only one who stayed. Love wanted to **hold out** until the last possible moment.

When the island had almost sunk, Love decided to ask for help.

Richness was passing by Love in a grand boat. Love said,

"Richness, can you take me with you?"

Richness answered, "No, I can't. There is a lot of gold and silver in my boat. There is no place here for you."

Love decided to ask **Vanity** who was also passing by in a beautiful **vessel**.

译林畅游

从前有一个岛，所有的情感都住在那里： 幸福、悲伤、知识和所有其他的情感，爱也不例外。一天，所有的情感听说小岛即将沉没，因此都纷纷建造小船，准备离开，除了爱。

爱是唯一留下来的，因为它渴望能坚持到最后一刻。

小岛即将沉没了，爱决定恳求帮助。

富有驾着一艘豪华的船从爱身边经过，爱说：

"富有，你能带上我吗？"

富有答道："不行，我的船上载满金银财宝，没有你的地方。"

虚荣坐在美丽的小船中也从爱身边驶过，爱决定向虚荣寻求帮助：

"Vanity, please help me!"

"I can't help you, Love. You are all wet and might damage my boat," Vanity answered.

Sadness was close by, so Love asked, "Sadness, let me go with you."

"Oh…Love, I am so sad that I need to be by myself!"

Happiness passed by Love, too, but she was so happy that she did not even hear when Love called her.

Suddenly, there was a voice, "Come, Love, I will take you." It was an elder. So **blessed** and **overjoyed**, Love even forgot to ask the elder where they were going. When they arrived at dry land, the elder went her own way. Realizing how much was owed the elder, Love asked Knowledge, another elder, "Who helped me?"

"It was Time," Knowledge answered.

"Time?" asked Love. "But why did Time help me?"

Knowledge smiled with deep wisdom and answered, "Because only Time **is capable of** understanding how valuable Love is."

"虚荣，请你帮帮我。"

虚荣回答："我帮不了你，爱，你全身湿透，会损坏我的船。"

悲伤的船靠近了，于是爱请求："悲伤，带上我和你一起走吧。"

"哦……爱，我太难过了，想一个人待着。"

幸福也经过爱的身边，但她太开心了，甚至没听见爱在呼唤她。

突然，一个声音喊道："来吧，爱，我带你走。"声音来自一位老者。爱太高兴了，甚至忘了问他们即将去何方。当他们来到岸上，老者自己离开了。爱突然意识到老者给了它多大的帮助。于是，爱问另一位老者——知识："谁帮助了我？"

知识答道："是时间。"

"时间？"爱问，"但是时间为什么帮助我？"

知识睿智地笑了笑，答道："因为只有时间懂得爱的价值。"

魅力词汇

construct [kən'strʌkt] *v.* 构造，建造

hold out 坚持

vanity ['vænətɪ] *n.* 虚荣

vessel ['vesəl] *n.* 船

blessed ['blesid] *adj.* 幸福的

overjoyed [əʊvə'dʒɒid] *adj.* 狂喜的，极度高兴的

be capable of 能够

6 How to Find True Love (1) 如何发现真爱（1）

在人生旅途中，徘徊于千万个十字路口，只为寻找今生的幸福。虽然世界上有很多有缘无份，也有很多遗憾和无奈，但请相信爱情不是幻想，只要你耐心等待，终有一日，当你抬起头，会发现那个人正深情地凝望着你，仿佛你是一支蜡烛，是照亮黑暗世界的唯一光明。

文苑漫步

I began to learn about love in dancing school, at age 11. I remember thinking on the first day I was going to fall madly in love with one of the boys and spend the next years of my life kissing and waltzing.

During class, however, I sat among the girls, waiting for a boy to ask me to dance. To my complete shock, I was consistently one of the last to be asked. At first I thought the boys had made a terrible mistake. I was so funny and pretty, and I could beat everyone I knew at tennis and climb trees faster than a cat. Why didn't they **dash** toward me?

Yet class after class, I watched boys dressed in blue blazers and gray pants head toward girls in flowered **shifts** whose perfect **ponytails** swung **back and forth**

译林畅游

我11岁在一所舞蹈学校上学时开始对爱有所了解。记得去学校的第一天我就在想，自己将疯狂地爱上某个男孩子，并与他在亲吻和跳华尔兹中度过接下来的时光。

在课堂上，我坐在一群女孩子中，等着男孩来邀我跳舞。然而令我完全震惊的是，我总是最后一个被邀请的。起初我认为是男孩子的严重失误：我如此风趣如此可爱，打网球胜过所有我认识的人，爬起树来比猫还要快，他们为什么不争先恐后地冲过来邀请我呢？

一堂又一堂课，我看着那些穿着蓝色运动上衣和灰色裤子的男孩们一头扎向那些穿着花边衬衫的女孩子，她们漂亮的马尾辫有节奏地

like **metronomes**. They fell easily into step with one another in a way that was completely mysterious to me. I came to believe that love belonged only to those who **glided**, who never **shimmied** up trees or even really touched the ground.

晃来晃去。他们的舞步总是很合拍，这完全让我感到不可思议。我开始相信，爱只属于那些优雅文静的女孩子，而不会属于像我这样晃悠着爬树甚至重重摔在地上的女孩。

By the time I was 13, I knew how to subtly **tilt** my head and make my tears fall back into my eyes, instead of down my cheeks, when no one asked me to dance. I also discovered the "**powder room**", which became my softly lit, reliable **retreat**. Whenever I started to cry, I'd excuse myself and run in there.

13岁时，我已经学会了在没人请我跳舞时，如何巧妙地仰起头，将眼泪忍住，不让它们流下脸颊。我还发现了"化妆室"，那里灯光柔和，成了我可靠的躲避之处。每次我要哭的时候，就借故跑到那里去。

I finally stopped crying when I met Matt, who was quiet and hung out on the edges of the room. When we danced for the first time, he wouldn't even look at me in the eyes. But he was cute, and he told great stories. We became good buddies, dancing every dance together until the end of school.

后来我遇见了Matt，终于不再哭泣。他静静地出现在房间的一边。我们第一次跳舞时，他甚至不敢正视我。但是他很可爱，而且会讲很好听的故事。我们成了好朋友，每次都一起跳舞，这样一直到毕业。

I learned from him my most important early lesson about romance: that the **potential** for love exists in corners, in the most unlikely as well as the most obvious places.

从他那儿我学到了有关恋爱的最重要的早期课程：爱的可能性无处不在，既在最显眼之处，也在最不起眼的地方。

For years my love life continued to be one long tragic-comic novel. In college I fell in love with a tall English major who rode a motorcycle. He **stood me up** on our sixth date — an afternoon of sky diving. I

多年来，我的爱情生活一直就像一部悲喜相交的长篇小说。上大学时，我爱上了英语系一个骑摩托车的高个子男孩。我们约好一天下午去跳伞，那是我们的第六次约会，

jumped out of the plane alone and landed in a parking lot.

In my mid-20s I moved to New York City where love is as hard to find as a legal parking spot. My first Valentine's Day there, I went on a date to a crowed bar on the Upper West Side. Halfway through dinner, my date excused himself and never returned.

At the time I lived with a beautiful roommate. Flowers piled up at our door like **snowdrifts**, and the light on the answering machine always **blinked** in a **panicky** way, overloaded with messages from her admirers. **Limousines** purred outside, with dates waiting for her behind **tinted** windows.

In my mind, love was something behind a tinted window, part **apparition**, part shadow, definitely unreachable. Whenever I spotted happy-looking couples, I'd wonder where they found love, and want to follow them home for the answer.

After a few years in the city I got my dream job — writing about weddings for a magazine called *7 Days*. I had to find interesting engaged couples and **write up** their love stories. I got to ask total strangers the things I'd always wanted to know.

I found out at least one sure answer to the question "How do you know it's love?" You know when the everyday things surrounding you — the leaves, the

他失约了。我只好独自从飞机上跳下，降落在一个停车场上。

二十四五岁时，我搬到了纽约。在那里，找寻真爱如同寻找一个合法的停车位一样困难。在纽约的第一个情人节，我前往西区一间拥挤的酒吧赴约，晚餐吃了一半，我的约会对象借故离席后，再也没有回来。

当时与我同住的是个漂亮女孩，门口的鲜花多得像雪堆，录音电话上的指示灯疯狂地闪个不停，里面录满了爱慕她的人的留言。豪华轿车停在外面，邀她赴约的人在有色玻璃车窗后等待着她。

在我的脑海里，爱情就像是有色玻璃后的某种东西，半隐半现，难以企及。每当我看到一对对脸上洋溢着幸福的情侣，我就想问问他们是如何找到真爱的，并想跟随他们一起回家，探个究竟。

在纽约待了几年之后，我终于得到了自己梦寐以求的工作——为一个名为《七日谈》的杂志写婚礼报道。我的任务就是寻找一些有趣的订了婚的情侣，并将他们的爱情故事写出来。这使我终于有机会向那些陌生人打听我一直想知道的事情。

我发现至少有一个确切的答案可以回答“你怎么知道这是爱”这个问题。当你周围一些原来平常的

shade of light in the sky, a bowl of strawberries — suddenly **shimmer** with a kind of unreality.

东西，像树叶、天空中的光影、一碗草莓，忽然间蒙上了一层梦幻的色彩，你会知道这就是爱。

You know when the tiny details about another person, ones that are insignificant to most people, seem fascinating and incredible to you. One groom told me he loved everything about his future wife, from her handwriting to the way she scratched on their apartment door like a cat when she came home. One bride said she fell in love with her **fiancé** because "one night, a **moth** was flying around a light bulb, and he caught it and let it out the window. I said, 'That's it. He's the guy.' "

一个人的某些方面在大多数人看来可能是微不足道的，但对恋爱中的人来说却是迷人而奇妙的。一位新郎曾告诉我，他爱未婚妻的一切，从她的字体到她回家时像猫一样挠门的习惯。有一位新娘爱上她的未婚夫则是因为"有一晚，一只飞蛾在灯泡周围飞来飞去，他捉住了它，然后将它从窗户放了出去。当时我想：'没错，他就是我要找的人。'"

You also know it's love when you can't stop talking to each other. Almost every couple I've ever interviewed said that on their first or second date, they talked for hours and hours. For some, falling in love is like walking into a **soundproof confessional booth**, a place where you can tell all.

当你们滔滔不绝地相互倾诉时，你也会知道那就是爱。我采访过的每一对情侣几乎都说，他们在第一次或第二次约会时，一谈就是几个小时。对一些人来说，坠入爱河就像是走进一间隔音的忏悔室，在那里你可以倾诉一切。

Finding love can be like discovering a **gilded** ballroom on the other side of your **dingy** apartment, and at the same time like finding a pair of great old blue jeans that are exactly your size and seem as if you've worn them forever. I can't tell you how many women have told me they knew they were in love because they forgot to wear makeup around their boyfriend. Or because they felt at ease hanging around him

找到爱情就像是在你昏暗公寓的另一边，发现了一个豪华舞厅；同时又像是找到了一条非常合身而且仿佛你已经穿了很久的质地很好的蓝色旧牛仔裤。我无法说清究竟有多少女人告诉过我，她们确信自己在恋爱，因为她们在男友面前忘记了化妆；或者因为穿着法兰绒的睡衣在他身边晃来晃去也觉得很自在。灰姑娘的故事即使在现代，也

in **flannel pajamas**. There's some modern truth to **Cinderella**'s tale — it's love when you're incredibly comfortable, when the shoe fits perfectly.

有其真实性：当你感到无比惬意时，当那双舞鞋恰恰合你的脚时，那肯定就是爱。

Finally, I think you're in love if you can make each other laugh at the very worst times — when the **IRS** is **auditing** you or when you are driving a **convertible** in a rainstorm or when your hair is turning gray. As someone once told me, 90 percent of being in love is making each other's life funnier and easier, all the way to the **deathbed**.

最后一点，如果你们在最糟的时候——比方说，在国内收入署审查你的账目的时候，在暴风雪中开着敞篷车的时候，或者当你的头发变灰白的时候，还能使彼此开心地发笑，那你们就是在相爱。正如有人曾告诉我的那样，真爱中的 90% 都会让对方的生活变得更轻松有趣，直到生命的终结。

魅力词汇

dash [dæʃ] *v.* 猛冲
shift [ʃift] *n.*［方言］衬衫
ponytail ['pəuniteil] *n.* 马尾辫
back and forth（前后）来回地，反复地
metronome ['metrənəum] *n.* 节拍器
glide [glaid] *v.* 滑行，滑翔
shimmy ['ʃimi] *v.* 摇摆，颤动
tilt [tilt] *v.* 翘起；倾斜
powder room 化妆室
retreat [ri'triːt] *n.* 避难所
potential [pə'tenʃəl] *n.* 可能性
stand sb. up 让某人空等一场
snowdrift ['snəudrift] *n.* 雪堆
blink [bliŋk] *v.* 闪烁
panicky ['pæniki] *adj.* 惊慌失措的
limousine ['liməziːn] *n.* 豪华轿车
tinted [tintid] *adj.* 带色彩的
apparition [æpə'riʃn] *n.* 显形，幻影
write up 详细记述，报道
shimmer ['ʃimə] *v.* 闪烁，闪光
fiancé [fi'aːnsei] *n.* 未婚夫
moth [mɔθ] *n.* 蛾
soundproof ['saundpruːf] *adj.* 隔音的
confessional [kən'feʃənl] *adj.* 忏悔的
booth [buːð] *n.* 小隔间，小房间
gilded ['gildid] *adj.* 富有的，奢侈的
dingy [dindʒi] *adj.* 昏暗的
flannel ['flænl] *n.* 法兰绒
pajamas [pə'dʒaːməz] *n.* 睡衣
Cinderella [ˌsində'relə] *n.* 灰姑娘
IRS *abbr.*（美国）国内收入署（Internal Revenue Service）
audit ['ɔːdit] *v.* 查（账等）
convertible [kən'vəːtɪbl] *n.* 敞篷汽车
deathbed ['deθbed] *n.* 弥留之际

7 How to Find True Love (2) 如何发现真爱（2）

看了许多人的爱情故事，询问了许多人，虽被看为是爱情专家，但爱情对我来说依然是一个谜。终于，在那一家文具店，爱情找到了我，我还记得他那褪色的牛仔裤，而他也忘不了我那双满是沙子的运动鞋。我终于明白：爱情不是幻想，而是像地铁一样执着而真实，只要坚持等待，就一定不会错过。

文苑漫步

Seven years ago I started writing about love and weddings for *The New York Times* in a column called "**Vows**". And now that I have been on this **beat** for so long, a strange thing has happened: I'm considered an expert on love. The truth is, love is still mostly a mystery to me. The only thing I can confidently say is this: Love is as plentiful as oxygen. You don't have to be thin, naturally **blond**, super-successful, socially connected, knowledgeable about politics or even particularly charming to find it.

I've interviewed many people who were down on their luck **in every way** — a **ballerina** with chronic back problems, a physicist who had been on 112 (he counted) disastrous blind dates, a **clarinet**

译林畅游

七年前，我开始为《纽约时报》的"誓言"专栏写关于恋爱和婚姻的报道。由于我从事这一行业很长时间，竟发生了一件怪事：我被人看成是爱情专家。事实上，爱情对我来说仍旧是一个谜。我唯一能自信地说的就是：爱情就像氧气一样丰富。为了找到它，你不需要有苗条的身材、天生的金发、巨大的成就、良好的社会关系、渊博的政治知识甚至富有魅力。

我采访过许多遭受各种厄运的人：患上慢性背疾的芭蕾舞女演员，与112个（他自己数的）从未谋面的人有过失败约会的物理学家，一位几乎付不起房租又是单身

player who was a single dad and could barely pay the rent. But love, when they found it, brought humor, candlelight, home-cooked meals, fun, adventure, poetry and long conversations into their lives.

父亲的单簧管吹奏者。但是当他们找到真爱时，爱情就会把幽默、烛光、家常便饭、乐趣、冒险精神、诗歌和畅谈带进他们的生活。

When people ask me where to find love, I tell a story about one of my first job interviews. It was with an editor at a famous literary magazine. I had no experience or skills, and he didn't for one second consider hiring me. But he gave me some advice I will never forget. He said, "Go out into the world. Work hard and concentrate on what you love to do, writing. If you become good, we will find you."

当人们问我在哪里能找到真爱时，我就会给他们讲我第一次工作面试时的故事。当时面试我的是一家著名文学杂志社的一名编辑。那时，我没有任何经验和技巧，他也根本没有想要雇用我，但他给我提了一些让我终身难忘的建议。他说："到社会中去，集中精力努力做好你想做的事——写作。如果你做得好，我们会找到你的。"

That's why I always tell people looking for love to wait for that "I won the lottery" feeling — wait, wait, wait! Don't read articles about how to trap, **seduce** or **hypnotize** a mate. Don't worry about your lipstick or your height, because it's not going to matter. Just live your life well, take care of yourself, and don't **mope** too much. Love will find you.

这就是为什么我一直告诉那些追求爱情的人，让他们去等待那种"我中奖了"的感觉，等待，等待，再等待！你不必去读那些教你如何俘获、引诱或使男人着迷的文章，也不必去担心那些诸如口红或身高之类的小事，因为这并不重要。只要好好生活，照顾好自己，别太忧郁，爱情终会找到你。

Eventually it even found me. At 28, I met my husband in a **stationery store**. I was buying a typewriter ribbon, and he was looking at **Filofaxes**. I remember that his eyes perfectly matched his faded jeans. He remembers that my **sneakers** were full of sand. He still talks about those sneakers and how they **evoked** his childhood —

最终，爱情也找到了我。28 岁那年，在一家文具店，我遇到了现在的丈夫。当时，我正在买打字机用的色带，他则在看备忘记事本。我还记得，他的眼睛与他那条褪色的牛仔裤很相配。而他则忘不了我那双满是沙子的运动鞋。至今他还说起我那双运动鞋，并且说它们是

bonfires by the ocean, driving on the sand in an old jeep — all those things that he cherished.

How did I know that it was true love? Our first real date lasted for nine hours; we just couldn't stop talking. I had never been able to dance in my life, but I could dance with him, perfectly in step. I have learned that it's love when you finally stop **tripping over** your toes.

A year after we met, we married.

I have come to cherish writing the "Vows" column. With each story I hear, I have proof that love, optimism, **guts**, grace, perfect partners and good luck do, in fact, exist. Love, in my opinion, is not a fantasy, not the stuff of romance novels or fairy tales. It's as **gritty** and real as the subway, it comes around just as regularly, and as long as you can **stick it out** on the platform, you won't miss it.

如何唤起了他对童年的回忆——海边的篝火，驾着老式吉普车在沙滩上兜风——所有这些都是他最珍贵的回忆。

我怎么知道这是真爱呢？我们第一次真正的约会持续了整整九个小时，我们竟有说不完的话！遇到他之前，我从来跳不好舞，但我却能和他一起跳，舞步还非常合拍。我终于明白，是爱情使我不再绊脚。

认识一年后，我们结婚了。

我开始珍视我所主笔的"誓言"专栏。我所听到的每一个故事都向我证实了，爱情、乐观、勇气、风度、完美的伴侣以及好运的确存在。在我看来，爱情不是幻想，不是浪漫小说和童话故事的素材。爱就像地铁一样坚定而真实，就像地铁一样会按时来到，只要你坚持在月台上等待，你就不会错过它。

魅力词汇

vow [vaʊ] *n.* 誓言
beat [biːt] *n.* 新闻记者负责采访的区域
blond [blɒnd] *adj.* 金发的
in every way 在各方面
ballerina [ˌbæləˈriːnə] *n.* 芭蕾舞女演员
clarinet [ˌklæriˈnet] *n.* ［乐］单簧管
seduce [siˈdjuːs] *v.* 引诱
hypnotize [ˈhipnətaiz] *v.* 使着迷
mope [məʊp] *v.* 忧郁
stationery store 文具店
Filofax [ˈfiːləufæks] *n.* 备忘记事本
sneaker [ˈsniːkə] *n.* 运动鞋
evoke [iˈvəʊk] *v.* 引起，唤起
bonfire [ˈbɒnˌfaiə] *n.* 篝火
trip over 绊倒
gut [gʌt] *n.* 胆量
gritty [ˈgriti] *adj.* 坚韧不拔的，坚定的
stick it out ［俚语］坚持到底

8 Shelley to Elizabeth Hitchhiker
雪莱致伊丽莎白·西琴勒

雪莱是英国文学史上最有才华的抒情诗人之一。英国著名诗人威廉·华兹华斯曾称其为“最优秀的艺术家”，同时期的拜伦称其为“我所认识的最优秀最无私的人”，他更被誉为“诗人中的诗人”。雪莱一生见识广泛，不仅是柏拉图主义者，更是个伟大的理想主义者。他创作的诗歌节奏明快，积极向上。“道德中最大的秘密是爱。”“冬天来了，春天还会远吗？”他的这些名言令人叫绝，千古称颂。《雪莱致伊丽莎白·西琴勒》更是字里行间尽显优美，也更让我们领略爱的真谛。

文苑漫步

Your letter of the 1st **hath** this moment reached me. I answer it according to our agreement, which shall be **inviolable**. Truly did you say that, at our arising in the morning, Nature assumes a different aspect.

Who could have **conjectured** the circumstances of my last letter? Friend of my soul, this is terrible, dismaying: it makes one's heart sink, it **withers** vital energy...

Dear being, I am **thine** again; the happiness shall again predominate over this **fleeting tribute** to self-interest. Yet who would not feel now? Oh, it were as **reckless** a task to endeavor to **annihilate**

译林畅游

我刚才收到你1号的来信，按我们之间的约定给你回信，这一约定是不可违背的。你确实说过，在我们早晨起来的时候，大自然总是有不同的面貌。

谁能猜想到我上次写信的境况呢？我心灵的知己，这太可怕，太令人沮丧了：我的心为之一沉，浑身的锐气消磨殆尽……

亲爱的人儿，我又是你的了，这幸福又将压倒我这短暂的孤芳自赏。然而在这种时候，谁又不会有相同的感受呢？啊，如果一息尚存而欲对其不闻不问岂非与使第六感

perception while sense existed, as to **blunt** the sixth sense to such impressions as these!

对这样一些印象变得迟钝且同样地不顾后果了吗？

Forgive me, dearest friend? I pour out my whole soul to you. I write by fleeting intervals: my pen runs away with my senses. The impassionateness of my **sensations** grows upon me. Your letter, too, has much affected me.

最亲爱的朋友，宽恕我好吗？我把整个心都掏给你了。几度举笔，笔不从心。但我理智的情感终于又涌上我的心头，你的信也深深地影响着我。

Never, with my **consent**, shall that **intercourse** cease which has been the day-dawn of my existence, the sun which has shed warmth on the cold **drear** length of the anticipated prospect of life. Prejudice might demand the sacrifice, but she is an **idol** to whom we bow not.

我从不认为我们之间的交往会永远终止，你与我的交往给我带来了生命的曙光，是洒在我冰凉而漫长的人生旅途上所期待的温暖阳光。偏见可能要求人们以牺牲为代价，那只不过是幽灵，你我都不会向这个幽灵屈服。

The world might demand it; its opinion might require; but the cloud which flees over **yon** mountain were as important to our happiness, to our usefulness. This must never be, never **whilst** this existence continues; and when time has enrolled us in the list of the departed, surely this friendship will survive to bear our identity to heaven.

世俗可能要我们做出牺牲，舆论也会提出要求；但遥望飘过远方山岭的云彩，不是也乐在其中，有益于我们的身心吗？这绝不可能，只要一息尚存，决不屈服，决不低头；即使时光把我们列入告别的名单中，毫无疑问，我们这段友情在天国中也一同相聚。

What is love, or friendship? Is it something material? A ball, an apple, a plaything which must be taken from one to be given to another? Is it capable of no extension, no communication? Lord Kaimes defines love to be a **particularization** of the general passion.

何谓爱情？何谓友情？是一些物质的东西吗？是球、苹果、玩偶这些可以信手拈来、随意给人的实物吗？是不能深化、不能交流的吗？ Kaimes 勋爵给爱情下的定义是，爱情是一般激情的特殊体现。

But this is the love of sensation,

但这是肉欲之爱，情欲之爱，

of **sentiment**, the absurdest of absurd vanities: it is the love of pleasure, not the love of happiness. The one is a love which is self-centered, self-interested: It desires its own interest; it is the parent of jealousy. Its object is the plaything which it desires to **monopolize**. Selfishness, monopoly, is its very soul, and to communicate to others part of this love were to destroy its essence, to annihilate this chain of **straw**.

是荒谬绝伦的逢场作戏：是寻欢作乐的爱，不是幸福的爱。这是一种自私自利的爱：它只求利己，是嫉妒之源。其目的在于独占它所想要的玩物，其本质是私心、垄断，即便是和他人分享这种爱的一部分就是在摧毁它的本质，使脆如纤草的爱泯灭殆尽。

But love, the love which we worship, virtue, heaven, **disinterestedness**, in a word, friendship, which has as much to do with the senses as with **yonder** mountains; that which seeks the good of all, the good of its object first, not because that object is a minister to its pleasures, not merely because it even contributes to its happiness, but because it is really worthy, because it has powers, sensibilities, is capable of **abstracting** itself, and loving virtue's own loveliness...

但我们崇拜的爱，象征美德、天意和无私，简言之，真情，它既能感知，又与远方的山脉息息相通；它寻求大家的益处，首先是对方的益处，不是因为对方给予欢乐，有愧于心，而是因为它值得，它有力量，有情感，并能无私奉献，因为美德的可爱而爱美德……

Desiring the happiness of others, not from the obligation of fearing hell or desiring heaven, but for pure, simple, **unsophisticated** virtue. You will soon hear again. **Adieu**, my dearest friend. Continue to believe that when I am insensible to your existence, I shall cease to exist.

不是因为怕下地狱或想升天堂而为他人求得幸福，而是出于纯朴无华的美德。你不久又会收到我的信。再见了，我最亲爱的朋友。请你继续相信这一点：我什么时候对阁下无动于衷，我便将不复存在。

魅力词汇

hath [hæθ]
v. 有（have 的第三人称单数现在式）
inviolable [in'vaiələbl] *adj.* 不可违背的
conjecture [kən'dʒektʃə] *v.* 推测
wither ['wiðə] *v.* 使衰弱
thine [θain] *pron.*（古）你的
fleeting ['fliːtiŋ] *adj.* 飞逝的，转瞬间的
tribute ['tribjuːt] *n.* 称赞
reckless ['reklis]
adj. 鲁莽的，不顾后果的
annihilate [ə'naiəleit] *v.* 歼灭
blunt [blʌnt] *v.* 使迟钝
sensation [sen'seiʃn] *n.* 感觉
consent [kən'sent] *n.* 同意，赞成
intercourse ['intəkɔːs] *n.* 交往
drear [driə] *adj.* 阴郁的，悲伤的
idol ['aidəl] *n.* 幽灵
yon [jɒn] *adj.*（古）那边的
whilst [hwailst]
conj. 当……的时候（=while）
particularization [pəˌtikjulərai'zeiʃn]
n. 特殊化
sentiment ['sentimənt] *n.* 感情，情绪
monopolize [mə'nɔpəlaiz] *v.* 垄断，独占
straw [strɔː] *n.* 稻草
disinterestedness [dis'intrəstidnis]
n. 公正无私
yonder [jɒndə] *adj.* 那边的，远处的
abstract ['æbstrækt] *v.* 提取
unsophisticated [ˌʌnsə'fistikeitid]
adj. 简单而自然的
adieu [ə'djuː] *interj.*（感叹词）再见

温情絮语

It's true that we don't know what we've got until we lose it, but it's also true that we don't know what we've been missing until it arrives.

只有失去才明白曾经拥有过，这话一点没错；同样的事实；直到我们所期待之物到来之时，我们才明白一直错过了什么。

9 Soul Mates Really Exist
心心相印的伴侣

俗话说："找到王子之前，需要亲吻很多只青蛙。"上帝会让你遇到几个不合适的人，然后才让你遇到合适的人。心心相印并不是遥不可及的梦想，只要相信，总能找到那个他/她。

文苑漫步

Dear Rymen,

That night that our paths crossed was as if a **magnetic** force joined us. It seemed as if I forgot to wake up that morning and face true reality. As our eyes connected it seemed too fresh and real to be a dream. The fire, the strength, the longing to be loved, words were not needed as we stared and watched as the world closed in and stopped at these two souls connected like the center point of an eye.

I remember when we first spoke, as if we have known one another for years. Our conversations went on as if the seasons were changing with no disconnection of the line. Never could I have asked the Lord for anything more **assuring** or **hypnotizing** than the **soothing** tone of your voice and the words **lingering off** them.

译林畅游

亲爱的 Rymen：

我们相遇的那个晚上好像有一股磁力把我们两个连接在一起。就好像那天早上，我忘记醒来去面对现实。我们四目相对，感觉那么清新真实，以至于我们都确定这不是梦境。我们彼此对望、深情注视，似乎整个世界缩小，停止运转，而这两个紧密相连的灵魂就是所有的中心，此刻，激情的火焰，巨大的力量，对爱的渴望，所有这些都无需语言来表达。

我还记得我们第一次谈话时，感觉就像已认识多年的朋友。我们不停地聊着，就好像四季的交替一样自然。你讲话的言辞语调是那么抚慰人心，我向上帝所求的没有什么比这更鼓舞我，令我着迷。即便整夜阴雨连绵，你也能让我的白天

You made my days sunny even though the nights rained on endlessly.

We completed one another; you thought that no good woman existed and then you met me. How I long for you to know that the feeling is mutual, that I have never met a man that can read through me and explore my inner core. Please keep in mind that I will not **take** your heart, that I hold, **for granted**. I will replace it with mine, so you know I wouldn't be able to breathe without it.

You are a splendid jewel she released and I grasped. Never would I let a soul take you away or bring harm near you. The day I looked into the **recesses** of your soul — correction: my soul, I knew no force could ruin the joining of two souls.

Soul mates do exist and now I have learned that there is beauty beyond all imperfections. It took us both years of hurt and pain and it has paid off. It's true when they say, "God makes you meet a few wrong people, before you meet the right one, so you will be able to appreciate and understand their worth."

Thank you for all that you have given me and that you continue too.

Love always.

Angel

阳光普照。

我们补全了彼此；你原以为世上不存在好女人，然后你遇到了我。我多么希望你知道，我也有这种感觉，以前我从未遇到一个能读懂我、探究我内心的男人。请相信，我不会把自己目前拥有你的心看作是理所当然的。我会用我的心去交换，要知道，没有了你，我将无法呼吸。

你是一颗灿烂的宝石，她放手了，我却抓住了。我再也不会让任何人把你带走或伤害到你。我进入你灵魂深处的那天——纠正一下，我看到的是我自己的灵魂，我明白没有任何力量能破坏两个灵魂的结合。

灵魂伴侣的确存在，如今我懂得一切不完美的背后都蕴含着美。我们两个在经历了数年的伤害和痛苦后，都得到了补偿。有句话说得没错："上帝先让你遇到几个不合适的人，然后才让你遇到合适的人，这样你才会珍惜并了解他们的价值。"

感谢你为我所做的一切，以及今后对我的付出。

永远爱你！

Angel

魅力词汇

magnetic [mæg'netik] *adj.* 磁的；有磁力的

assuring [ə'ʃuəriŋ] *adj.* 使人有信心的

hypnotizing ['hipnətaiziŋ] *adj.* 让人着迷的

soothing ['suːðiŋ] *adj.* 抚慰的

linger off 围绕，徘徊

take... for granted 认为……理所当然

recess [ri'ses] *n.* 深处，凹处

温情絮语

It takes only a minute to get a crush on someone, an hour to like someone, and a day to love someone—but it takes a lifetime to forget someone.

迷上一个人只需一分钟，喜欢一个人只需一小时，爱上一个人只需一天，但忘记一个人却需要一辈子。

Don't go for looks, they can deceive. Don't go for wealth, even that fades away. Go for someone who makes you smile because it takes only a smile to make a dark day seem bright.

不要迷恋于容貌，容貌会欺骗你。不要追逐财富，财富也会消失。找一个能让你微笑的人，因为仅仅一个微笑就能让一个阴暗的日子变得明亮起来。

第五篇

莫待花谢时

1 Happiness Is a Journey 幸福是段旅程

寻找幸福的过程本身就是幸福。所以我们要珍惜所拥有的点点滴滴。我们总是在追寻幸福，但生活却总是留有遗憾。其实我们匆匆找寻，却忽略了沿途的风景。幸福其实就是很简单的事情啊，保持良好的心态，有个好脾气，不要为生活的琐事烦恼。其实生活中总有点滴的幸福。我们不妨放慢脚步，欣赏生命的过程。

文苑漫步

We always convince ourselves that life will be better after we get married, have a baby, then another. Then we are frustrated that the kids aren't old enough and we'll be more content when they are. After that we're frustrated that we have teenagers to deal with, and we will certainly be happy when they are out of that stage.

We always tell ourselves that our life will be complete when our **spouse gets his or her act together**, when we get a nice car, and are able to go on a nice vocation when we retire. The truth is, there's no better time than right now. Our life is always filled with challenges. It's best to admit this to ourselves and decide to be happy anyway.

One of my favorite quotes comes from

译林畅游

我们总是说服自己，等到结婚、生子后日子会更好。然后我们又因为孩子不够懂事感到挫败，想着他们长大了生活会好一点。当孩子们到了青春期的时候，我们会很无奈。我们深信当他们过了那个年龄段后，我们可以快乐一点。

我们总是对自己说，当我们的另一半有条理地生活时，当我们买了一辆好车，可以在年老退休后开去度假时，我们的人生就会很圆满。可事实上，再也没有比当下更好的时候了。我们的人生总是充满了挑战。我们最好承认活在当下的意义，然后快快乐乐。

我最喜欢艾尔弗雷德·苏泽说

Alfred Souza. He said: "For a long time it had seemed to me that life was about to begin real life. But there were always some **obstacles** in the way, something to be gotten through first, some unfinished business, time still to be served, a debt to be paid. Then life would begin. At last it dawned on me that these obstacles were my life." This perspective has helped me to see that there is no way to happiness. Happiness is the way. So treasure every moment that you have.

过的一段话。他说："一直以来，我感觉真正的生活就要来了。但是在这之前总有些障碍，一些问题必须先搞定，比如未完成的工作，要履行的义务，待付的账单。当这些事解决后你才能开始自己的一天。后来我才觉悟到解决这些生活琐事就是我的人生。"这样的想法使我认识到幸福是没有办法去追寻的。因为寻找幸福的过程本身就是幸福。所以珍惜你所拥有的点点滴滴。

And remember that time waits for no one. So stop waiting until you finish school, until you go back to school; until you get married, until you get divorced; until you have kids; until you retire; until you get a new car or home; until spring; until you are born again to decide that there is no better time than right now to be happy...

而且还要牢记时光不等人。所以别等到你毕业之后、重返校园之时再去享受（幸福）；不要步入婚姻之中，甚至离婚后才去享受（幸福）；别等到你已有孩子；别等到你退休；别等到你有了新车或新居；别等到春天；别等到你重获新生后才认识到人生本是：莫待来日，及时行乐……

Happiness is a journey, not a **destination**. So, work like you don't need money, love like you've never been hurt, and dance like no one's watching.

幸福是一次旅行，而不是终点站。所以，不要想着为钱而工作，敞开心扉不怕伤害地去爱，旁若无人地去跳舞。

魅力词汇

spouse [spaʊz] *n.* 配偶，夫或妻

get one's act together （使某人的生活处事）有头绪

obstacle ['ɒbstəkl] *n.* 障碍（物），妨碍

destination [ˌdesti'neiʃn] *n.* 目的地，终点

2 If I Had My Life to Live Over
如再活一次，一切将会不同

人生短暂，不可虚度。每个人只能活一回，然后生命就消失了。与其在失去的时候懊悔，倒不如从现在便开始改变自己的生活态度。如果将每天都看作世界末日的前一天，那么我们会更加珍惜现在所拥有的一切。生活如此美妙，请你不要暴躁。即使生活不尽如人意，也要微笑着走下去。

文苑漫步

I would have gone to bed when I was sick instead of pretending the earth would go into a holding pattern if I weren't there for the day.

I would have burned the pink candle **sculpted** like a rose before it melted in storage.

I would have talked less and listened more.

I would have invited friends over to dinner even if the carpet was stained, or the sofa faded.

I would have eaten the **popcorn** in the "good" living room and worried much less about the dirt when someone wanted to light a fire in the **fireplace**.

I would have taken the time to listen to my grandfather **ramble** about his youth.

译林畅游

生病的时候我就卧床休息，而不是假装自己一天不工作，地球就会停止转动。

我会将雕成玫瑰花状的粉红蜡烛点上，而不让它在闲置中融化。

我会少说多听。

即使地毯弄脏了，沙发褪色了，我也会请朋友过来吃饭。

我会在“讲究”的客厅里吃爆米花。有人想在壁炉里生火，我也不会那么操心炉灰的问题。

我会花时间听爷爷唠叨他年轻时候的事情。

I would never have insisted the car windows be rolled up on a summer day because my hair had just been **teased** and **sprayed**.

我决不会因为夏天头发刚刚梳理过、喷过发胶，就一定要把车窗玻璃摇起来。

I would have sat on the lawn with my children and not worried about grass stains.

我会和孩子们一起坐在草坪上，不会担心衣服上染上草渍。

I would have cried and laughed less while watching television — and more while watching life.

看电视时，我要少哭一点，少笑一点；观察生活时，我要多哭一点，多笑一点。

I would never have bought anything just because it was practical, wouldn't show soil, or was **guaranteed** to last a lifetime. Instead of wishing away nine months of **pregnancy**, I'd have cherished every moment and realized that the **wonderment** growing inside me was the only chance in life to assist God in a miracle.

我买东西不会只看它很实用，不显脏，或能保证用一辈子。我不会在盼望中度过 9 个月的妊娠期，我要珍惜每一刻，要意识到体内生长的神奇是我今生帮助上帝创造奇迹的唯一机会。

When my kids kissed me **impetuously**, I would never have said, "Later. Now go get washed up for dinner." There would have been more "I love you", more "I'm sorry". But mostly, given another shot at life, I would seize every minute, look at it and really see it, live it and never give it back.

孩子们毛手毛脚地亲我，我决不会说："一会儿。先去洗手洗脸，准备吃饭。"我要更多地说"我爱你""对不起"。但总的来说，如果再让我活一回，我会把握每一分钟，留心生活，真正关注生活，品味生活，决不使岁月蹉跎。

Stop **sweating** the small stuff. Don't worry about who doesn't like you, who has more, or who's doing what. Instead, let's cherish the relationships we have with those who do love us. Let's think about what God has blessed us with and what we are doing

不为小事烦心。不要担心谁不喜欢你，谁更富有，或者谁在干什么。让我们珍惜同真心关爱我们的人之间的那份感情。让我们多想想上帝赐予我们的福分，多想想我们每天做了哪些有益于自己思想、身

each day to promote ourselves mentally, physically, emotionally, as well as spiritually.

Life is too short to let it pass you by. We only have one shot at this and then it's gone. I hope you all have a blessed day.

体、感情和精神方面的事。

人生短暂，不可虚度。每个人只能活一回，然后生命就消失了。祝愿大家生活幸福。

魅力词汇

sculpt [skʌlpt] *v.* 雕刻
popcorn ['pɒpkɔːn] *n.* 爆米花
fireplace ['faiəpleis] *n.* 壁炉
ramble ['ræmbəl] *n.* 漫谈
tease [tiːz] *v.* 梳理
spray [sprei] *v.*（液体）喷洒
guarantee [gærən'tiː] *v.* 保证
pregnancy ['pregnənsi] *n.* 怀孕
wonderment ['wʌndəmənt] *n.* 惊奇，惊叹
impetuously [im'petjuəsli] *adv.* 性急地
sweat [swet] *v.* 担心，焦虑，不安

温情絮语

Dream what you want to dream, go where you want to go, be what you want to be. Because you have only one life and one chance to do all the things you want to do.

做你想做的梦，去你想去的地方，做你想做的人。因为你只有一次生命，只有一个机会去做所有你想要做的事。

3 You Have a Choice 你可以选择

“今天囊中羞涩，我可以难过；但我懂得了理性地消费、远离浪费，所以，我也可以高兴。今天为自己的健康状况，我可以满腹牢骚；但自己仍然活着，所以，我也可以欢呼雀跃……”人经常在困难的时候想起痛苦，在开心的时候想起幸福，如果每个人都能变换一下思维，反方向思考的话，那么我们的生活将会更加美好。

文苑漫步

I woke up early today, excited over all I get to do before the clock strikes midnight. I have responsibilities to fulfill today. I am important.

My job is to choose what kind of day I am going to have.

Today I can complain because the weather is rainy or I can be thankful that the grass is getting watered for free.

Today I can feel sad that I don't have more money or I can be glad that my finances encourage me to plan my purchases wisely and guide me away from waste.

Today I can **grumble** about my health or I can rejoice that I am alive.

Today I can **lament** over all that my parents didn't give me when I was grow-

译林畅游

今晨，我早早起来，为自己在午夜之前将要做的一切事情而兴奋不已。我有责任让今天过得充实，我很重要。

选择怎样去过每一天，这是我的工作。

今天下雨了，我可以抱怨；但草坪可以免费浇水了，所以，我也可以感激。

今天囊中羞涩，我可以难过；但我懂得了理性地消费、远离浪费，所以，我也可以高兴。

今天为自己的健康状况，我可以满腹牢骚；但自己仍然活着，所以，我也可以欢呼雀跃。

今天因父母给予的太少，我可以悲伤；但他们给予了我生命，所

ing up or I can feel grateful that they allowed me to be born.

Today I can cry because roses have thorns or I can celebrate that thorns have roses.

Today I can mourn my lack of friends or I can excitedly **embark** upon a quest to discover new relationships.

Today I can murmur **dejectedly** because I have to do housework or I can feel honored because the Lord has provided shelter for my mind, body and soul.

Today stretches ahead of me, waiting to be shaped. And here I am, the sculptor who gets to do the shaping.

What today will be like is up to me. I get to choose what kind of day I will have!

以，我也可以万分感激。

今天因为玫瑰上有刺，我可以哭泣； 但带刺的茎上有玫瑰花，所以，我也可以欢欣庆祝。

今天因为缺少朋友，我可以难过； 但能寻求并发掘新的友谊，所以，我也可以感到兴奋。

今天因为必须做家务，我可以抱怨沮丧； 但是主赐予了我思想、身体和灵魂的避难所，所以，我也可以深感荣耀。

今天就展现在我的面前，等着我去雕琢。而我这个雕刻家，就在这儿等着去雕刻它。

今天会怎么样，完全取决于我自己。我将选择我的生活。

魅力词汇

grumble ['grʌmbl] *v.* 发牢骚
lament [lə'ment] *v.* 哀悼，悔恨
embark [im'bɑːk] *v.* 着手，从事
dejectedly [di'dʒektidli] *adv.* 沮丧地

温情絮语

Let's write that letter we thought of writing "one of these days".
曾"打算有那么一天"去写的信，就在今天写吧。

4 Wake Up Your Life
唤醒自己的生活

“路漫漫其修远兮，吾将上下而求索。”探索人生之路，漫长又艰难，错误是免不了的，迷失方向也是会有的。但只要做个有心人，永远保持自己的那份追求，及时唤醒心中的那轮明月，那么胜利之门便会悄悄地为你打开。唤醒自己对生活的热爱，打开心门，迎接灿烂的阳光，让我们时时看到生活最美的一面。

文苑漫步

Years ago, when I started looking for my first job, wise advisers urged, “Barbara, be **enthusiastic**! Enthusiasm will take you further than any amount of experience.” How right they were. Enthusiastic people can turn a boring drive into an adventure, extra work into opportunity and strangers into friends.

“Nothing great was ever achieved without enthusiasm,” wrote Ralph Waldo Emerson. It is the paste that helps you hang in there when the going gets tough. It is the inner voice that whispers, “I can do it!” when others shout, “No, you can't.”

It took years and years for the early work of Barbara Mc Clintock , a **geneticist** who won the 1983 Nobel Prize

译林畅游

很多年以前，当我找第一份工作时，一些明智之士向我强烈建议：“Barbara，要充满热情！热情比任何经验都更有益。”这话多么正确，满腔热情的人可以把乏味无聊的车程变成充满激情的探险，把加班变成机会，把陌生人变成朋友。

“没有热情就不会有任何伟大的成就。”拉尔夫·沃尔多·爱默生写道。当事情很棘手的时候，热情是帮助你坚持下去的黏合剂。当别人对你叫喊“你不行”时，热情是你心底发出的声音：“我能行。”

巴巴拉·麦克林托克，这个在1983年获得诺贝尔医学奖的遗传学家，她早年的工作直到很多年后才被公众所认可。但她并没有放弃实

in medicine, to be generally accepted. Yet she didn't **let up** on her experiments. Work was such a deep pleasure for her that she never thought of stopping.

验。对于她来说，工作是一种如此巨大的快乐，以至于她从未想过要停止它。

We are all born with wide-eyed, enthusiastic wonder as anyone knows who has ever seen an infant's delight at the **jingle** of keys or the **scurrying** of a beetle. It is this childlike wonder that gives enthusiastic people such a youthful air, whatever their age.

我们生来就充满好奇，满腔热情——凡是看到过婴儿听到钥匙声或看见乱爬的甲虫就兴奋不已的人都会明白这一点。不论他们年龄的大小，就是这种孩童般天真烂漫的好奇心给了热情的人们一种青春的气息。

At 90, cellist Pablo Casals would start his day by playing Bach. As the music flowed through his fingers, his stooped shoulders would straighten and joy would reappear in his eyes. Music, for Casals, was an **elixir** that made life a never ending adventure. As author and poet Samuel Ullman once wrote, "Years wrinkle the skin, but to give up enthusiasm wrinkles the soul."

大提琴演奏家帕布罗·卡萨尔斯在90岁高龄时，还坚持以演奏巴赫的曲子开始自己每天的生活。随着音乐从他的指尖流出，他弯着的肩膀挺直起来，快乐再度溢满他的眼眸。对卡萨尔斯来说，音乐是一副灵丹妙药，它使人生变成了无止境的探索之旅。正如作家兼诗人的塞缪尔·厄尔曼曾写过："岁月使皮肤起了皱纹，但如果失去热情，便会使灵魂起皱纹。"

How do you rediscover the enthusiasm of your childhood? The answer, I believe, lies in the word itself. "Enthusiasm" comes from the Greek and means "God within." And what is God within is but an **abiding** sense of love — proper love of self (self-acceptance) and, from that, love of others.

你怎样才能找回孩提时代的热情呢？我相信，答案就在"热情"这个词本身。"热情"一词源于希腊语，原意是"内在的上帝"。这里所说的"内在的上帝"不是别的，而是一种持久不变的爱——适当的自爱（自我接受），并推及于他人。

Enthusiastic people also love what they do, **regardless of** money or title or power. If we cannot do what we love as a full-time career, we can as a part-time

不考虑金钱、地位和权力，热情的人们同样热爱他们所做的事情。如果我们不能把热爱的事作为正式职业，我们也可把它当作业余

avocation, like the head of state who paints, the nun who runs marathons, the executive who handcrafts furniture.

Elizabeth Layton of Wellsville, Kansas, was 68 before she began to draw. This activity ended bouts of depression that had **plagued** her for at least thirty years, and the quality of her work led one critic to say, "I am **tempted** to call Layton a genius." Elizabeth has rediscovered her enthusiasm.

We can't afford to waste tears on "might-have-beens". We need to turn the tears into sweat as we go after "what-can-be".

We need to live each moment wholeheartedly, with all our senses — finding pleasure in the **fragrance** of a back-yard garden, the **crayoned** picture of a 6-year-old, the **enchanting** beauty of a rainbow. It is such enthusiastic love of life that puts a sparkle in our eyes, a lilt in our steps and smoothes the wrinkles from our souls.

消遣：比如有国家元首喜欢画画的，有修女参加马拉松长跑的，有行政官员手工制作家具的。

堪萨斯州韦尔斯维尔市的伊丽莎白·莱顿68岁的时候才开始画画。这一爱好结束了曾纠缠她至少达三十年之久的忧郁症，而她的作品水准之高使得一个评论家说：“我不禁要称莱顿为天才。”伊丽莎白又找回了她的热情。

我们不应该把眼泪浪费在“早该”之类的后悔上。我们需要把眼泪化为汗水，去追求“可能”之物。

我们需要全心全意去度过生命中的每一分钟——在后花园的芬芳中，在6岁小孩的蜡笔画中，在美得醉人的彩虹中，寻找快乐。正是这种对生活的热爱，让我们双目有神，让我们步履矫健，让我们灵魂的皱纹展平。

魅力词汇

enthusiastic [inˌθjuːziˈæstik] *adj.* 满腔热情的，热心的

geneticist [dʒiˈnetisist] *n.* 遗传学家

let up 减少，减缓，停止

jingle [ˈdʒiŋgl] *n.* 叮当声

scurry [ˈskʌri] *v.* 疾走

elixir [iˈliksə] *n.* 长生不老药，仙丹妙药

abiding [əˈbaidiŋ] *adj.* 永久的，持久的，不变的

regardless of 不管，不顾

avocation [ˌævəˈkeiʃn] *n.* 副业，嗜好，消遣

plague [pleig] *v.* 使苦恼

tempt [tempt] *v.* 引诱，诱惑，勾引

fragrance [ˈfreigrəns] *n.* 芳香，香味，香水

crayon [ˈkreiən] *v.* 以蜡笔作画

enchanting [inˈtʃɑːntiŋ] *adj.* 迷人的

5 Life's a Cafeteria 生活就像自助餐

生活确实很像自助餐，你需要自己去选择你想要的东西，并且为你自己的选择付账。

文苑漫步

A friend's grandfather came to America from Eastern Europe. After **settling down** at Ellis Island, he went into a **cafeteria** in lower Manhattan to get something to eat. He sat down at an empty table and waited for someone to **take** his **order**. Of course nobody did. Finally, a woman with a tray full of food sat down opposite him and **informed** him how a cafeteria worked.

"Start out at that end," she said. "Just go along the line and **pick out** what you want. At the other end they'll tell you how much you have to pay."

"I soon learned that's how everything works in America," the grandfather told a friend."Life's a cafeteria here. You can get anything you want as long as you are willing to pay the price. You can even get

译林畅游

一个朋友的祖父从东欧到美国来。在埃利斯岛安顿下来后，他去曼哈顿下城的一家自助餐厅吃饭。他在一张空桌子边坐下，等待侍者来点餐，当然没有人来招呼他。最后，一位女士拿着满满一托盘食物走过来坐在他对面，并告诉他自助餐厅怎样选餐。

她说："从餐厅的那端开始，沿着队伍向前走，挑选你想要的东西，在餐厅的另外一端会有人告诉你该付多少钱。"

"接着我很快了解到这就是美国人的生活方式，"朋友的祖父对一个朋友说，"在这里，生活就像自助餐。你可以得到你想要的任何东西，只要你愿意负担它们的价格。

success. But you'll never get it if you wait for someone to bring it to you. You have to get up and get it yourself."

你也可以取得成功。但是如果你什么都不做，只等着别人把它送到你身边的话，那是永远都不可能的。你必须行动起来，必须自己去追求它。"

魅力词汇

settle down 安定下来
cafeteria [kæfɪ'tiəriə] *n.* 自助餐厅
take order 点餐
inform [in'fɔːm] *v.* 通知，告诉
pick out 挑选出

温情絮语

It's never too late to mend.

过而能改，善莫大焉；亡羊补牢，犹未晚也。

Time stays not the fool's leisure.

时间不等闲逛的傻瓜。

6 Hour in the Sun 阳光下的时光

有人认为今天最重要，因为今天是我们能够把握与珍惜的；有人认为明天最重要，因为我们可以期待明天有美好的事物发生；可是昨天应该更值得我们珍惜，因为昨天有我们最宝贵的回忆和最难得的心境。你还能回忆起往日时光里，我们在艳阳下的追逐嬉闹吗？

文苑漫步

I was rich, if not in money, in sunny hours and summer days.

—Henry David Thoreau

When Thoreau wrote that line, he was thinking of the Walden Pond he knew as a boy.

Woodchoppers and the Iron Horse had not yet greatly damaged the beauty of its setting. A boy could go to the pond and lie on his back against the seat of a boat, lazily drifting from shore to shore while the **loons** dived and the swallows dipped around him. Thoreau loved to recall such sunny hours and summer days "when **idleness** was the most attractive and productive business".

I too was a boy in love with a pond, rich in sunny hours and summer days. Sun

译林畅游

我虽不富甲天下，却拥有无数个艳阳天和夏日。

——亨利・大卫・梭罗

写这句话时，梭罗想起孩提时代的瓦尔登湖。

当时，伐木工人和火车尚未严重破坏湖畔的美丽景致。小男孩可以仰卧小舟，泛舟湖中。自一岸缓缓漂向另一岸，周遭有鸟儿戏水，燕子翻飞。梭罗喜欢回忆这样的艳阳天和夏日，"在这样的日子里，慵懒是最迷人、最有收获的事情！"

我也曾经是热爱湖塘的小男孩，拥有无数个艳阳天与夏日。如

and summer are still what they always were, but the boy and the pond changed. The boy, who is now a man, no longer finds much time for idle drifting. The pond has been **annexed** by a great city. The **swamps** where **herons** once hunted are now drained and filled with houses. The bay where water lilies quietly floated is now a harbor for motor boats. In short, everything that the boy loved no longer exists — except in the man's memory of it.

今阳光、夏日依旧，男孩和湖塘却已不再。那男孩如今已长大成人，不再有那么多时间泛舟湖上。而湖塘也为大城市所并。曾有苍鹭觅食的沼泽，如今已枯竭殆尽，上面盖满了房舍。睡莲静静漂浮的湖湾，现在成了汽艇的避风港。总之，男孩所爱的一切已不复存在——它们只留在他的回忆中。

Some people insist that only today and tomorrow matter. But how much poorer we would be if we really lived by that rule! So much of what we do today is **frivolous** and futile and soon forgotten. So much of what we hope to do tomorrow never happens.

有些人坚持认为只有今日和明日才是重要的，可是如果真的照此生活，我们将是何其可怜！我们今日做的许多事情是徒劳且不足道的，很快就会被遗忘。许多我们期待明天将要做的事也从来没有发生过。

The past is the bank in which we store our most valuable **possession**: the memories that give meaning and depth to our lives.

过去是一所银行。我们将最宝贵的财产——记忆珍藏其中。记忆赐予我们生命的意义和深度。

Those who truly treasure the past will not **bemoan** the passing of the good old days, because days **enshrined** in memory are never lost. Death itself is powerless to **still** a remembered voice or erases a remembered smile. And for one boy who is now a man, there is a pond which neither time nor tide can change, where he can still spend a quite hour in the sun.

真正珍惜过去的人，不会悲叹旧日美好时光的逝去。因为藏于记忆中的时光永不流逝。死亡本身无法止住一个记忆中的声音，或擦除一个记忆中的微笑。对现已长大成人的那个男孩来说，那儿将有一个湖塘，既不因时间而改变，也不会被潮汐所淹没，他仍可以继续在阳光下享受片刻的安静时光。

魅力词汇

loon [luːn] *n.* 潜鸟
idleness ['aidlnəs] *n.* 懒惰，闲散
annex [ə'neks] *v.* 并吞，强占，合并
swamp [swɒmp] *n.* 沼泽，湿地
heron ['herən] *n.* 苍鹭
frivolous ['frivələs] *adj.* 无足轻重的
possession [pə'zeʃn] *n.* 财产，所有物
bemoan [bi'məʊn] *vt.* 悲叹，认为遗憾
enshrine [in'ʃrain] *v.* 铭记
still [stil] *v.* 使静止，止住

温情絮语

One today is worth two tomorrows.

一个今天胜似两个明天。

Time and I against any two.

我和时间携起手来，一人抵两人。

7 Relish the Moment
品味现在

我们行色匆匆，向着目的地不知疲倦地奔波着，可是却忽略了沿途的美景。结果固然吸引人，可是过程也是难能可贵的。在人生的旅途中，我们向着各自的目标前进，是否感到疲累了，那么就慢下来，欣赏沿途的美景吧。

文苑漫步

Tucked away in our **subconscious** is an **idyllic** vision. We see ourselves on a long trip that spans the continent. We are traveling by train. Out the windows, we drink in the passing scene of cars on nearby highways, of children waving at a crossing, of cattle grazing on a distant hillside, of smoke pouring from a power plant, of row upon row of corn and wheat, of flatlands and valleys, of mountains and rolling hillsides, of city skylines and village halls.

But **uppermost** in our minds is the final destination. On a certain day at a certain hour, we will pull into the station. Bands will be playing and flags waving. Once we get there, so many wonderful

译林畅游

我们的潜意识里藏着一派田园诗般的风光。我们仿佛身处一次横贯大陆的漫漫旅程之中。乘着火车，我们醉心于窗外一掠而过的景色：附近高速公路上奔驰的汽车、十字路口挥着手的孩童、远山上吃草的牛群、从电厂排放出的袅袅尘烟、一片片的玉米和小麦、平原与山谷、群山与绵延的丘陵、天空映衬下城市的轮廓，以及乡间的庄园宅第。

然而我们心里想得最多的却是最终的目的地。在某一天的某一时刻，我们将会抵达进站。迎接我们的将是乐队演奏和彩旗飘舞。一旦到了那儿，多少美梦将成为现实，

dreams will come true and the pieces of our lives will fit together like a completed **jigsaw puzzle**. How restlessly we pace the aisles, damning the minutes for **loitering** — waiting, waiting, waiting for the station.

"When we reach the station, that will be it!" we cry. "When I'm 18." "When I buy a new 450SL Mercedes Benz!" "When I put the last kid through college." "When I have paid off the **mortgage**!" "When I get a **promotion**." "When I reach the age of **retirement**, I shall live happily ever after!"

Sooner or later, we must realize there is no station, no one place to arrive at once and for all. The true joy of life is the trip. The station is only a dream. It constantly **outdistances** us.

It isn't the burdens of today that drive men mad. It is the regrets over yesterday and the fears of tomorrow. Regret and fear are twin thieves who rob us of today.

So stop pacing the aisles and counting the miles. Instead, climb more mountains, eat more ice cream, go barefoot more often, swim more rivers, watch more sunsets, laugh more, cry less. Life must be lived as we go along. The station will come soon enough.

我们破碎的生活也将变得完整，如同一块整理好了的拼图。可是我们现在在车厢里不耐烦地踱来踱去，咒骂火车的拖拖拉拉。我们期待着，期待着，期待着火车进站的那一刻。

"当我们到站的时候，一切就都好了！"我们呼喊着。"当我18岁的时候。""当我有了一辆新奔驰450SL的时候！""当我供最小的孩子念完大学的时候！""当我偿清贷款的时候。""当我升职的时候。""当我到了退休年龄的时候，就可以从此过上幸福的生活啦！"

可是我们终究会认识到人生的旅途中并没有终点站，也没有能够"一到永逸"的地方。人生的真正乐趣在于旅行的过程，而车站不过是个梦，它始终遥遥领先于我们。

真正令人发疯的不是今日的负担，而是对昨日的悔恨及对明日的恐惧。悔恨与恐惧是一对孪生窃贼，将今天从你我身边偷走。

那么就不要在过道里徘徊吧，别老惦记着你离车站还有多远。何不换一种活法，爬更多高山，多吃点儿冰淇淋，经常光着脚板儿溜达，在更多的河流里畅游，多看看夕阳西下，多点欢笑，少让泪水滴答。生活得一边过一边瞧，车站就会很快到达。

魅力词汇

tuck away 隐藏
subconscious [sʌb'kɒnʃəs] *n.* 潜意识
idyllic [i'dilik] *adj.* 田园诗的
uppermost ['ʌpəməʊst]
adj. 最主要的，最重要的
jigsaw puzzle 拼图玩具
loiter ['lɒitə] *v.* 闲荡，徘徊
mortgage ['mɔːgidʒ] *n.* 按揭，抵押贷款
promotion [prə'məʊʃn] *n.* 晋升
retirement [ri'taiəmənt] *n.* 退休
outdistance [aʊt'distəns]
v. 远远超过，把……远远抛在后头

温情絮语

That opportunities are never lost; someone will take the ones you miss.

机会从不落空，你错过的总有人得到。

Time is a file that wears and makes no noise.

光阴如锉，细磨无声。

8 Allow Your Own Inner Light to Guide You
让内心之光指引你

理想的生活来源于对自己心灵的关爱。倾听你的内心，找回属于每个人的那份真性情，让内心的灯指引你。

文苑漫步

There comes a time when you must stand alone. You must feel confident enough within yourself to follow your own dreams. You must be willing to **make sacrifices**.

You must be capable of changing and rearranging your **priorities**, so that your final goal can be achieved.

Sometimes, familarity and comfort need to be challenged. There are times when you must take a few extra chances and create your own realities.

Be strong enough to at least try to make your life better. Be confident enough that you won't settle for a **compromise** just to get by.

Appreciate yourself by allowing yourself the opportunities to grow, develop, and find your true sense of purpose in this life.

译林畅游

生活有时需要你独自去面对。此时，你内心要足够自信去追随自己的梦想，并要做好为之牺牲的准备。

为实现你的最终目标，你必须能做出改变并具备判断事情轻重缓急的能力。

有时，你需要挑战熟悉和安逸；有时，你需要抓住更多的机会，创造自己的未来。

你要足够坚强，起码要让自己的生活更美好。要给自己足够的自信，不能轻易妥协。

要欣赏自己，给自己成长、发展的机会，并找到自己人生的真正意义。

Don't stand in someone else's shadow when it's your sunlight that should lead the way.

不要活在别人的阴影里，属于你的阳光会指引你前进。

Work hard at what you like to do and try to overcome all **obstacles**.

努力去做自己喜欢的事，尽力克服所有的障碍。

Laugh at your mistakes and praise yourself for learning from them.

笑对自己的过失，从中吸取教训，并引以为荣。

Pick some flowers and appreciate the beauty of nature.

摘些花朵，欣赏大自然的美丽。

Say hello to strangers and enjoy the people you know.

向陌生人问好，享受熟人的陪伴。

Don't be afraid to show your emotions; laughing and crying will make you feel better.

别害怕流露真情，纵情大笑、放声哭泣，会让你感觉更好。

Love your friends and family with your entire being and they are the most important part of your life.

全身心地去爱你的家人、朋友，他们是你生命中最重要的部分。

Feel the **calmness** on a quite sunny day.

在阳光灿烂的日子里，感受安宁。

Find a rainbow and live your world of dreams. Always remember life is better than it seems.

寻找彩虹，活在梦想的世界。永远记住，生活比看上去的更美好。

魅力词汇

make sacrifices 做出牺牲
priority [prai'ɔrəti] *n.* 优先
compromise ['kɒmprəmaiz] *n.* 妥协
obstacle ['ɒbstəkl] *n.* 障碍，绊脚石
calmness ['kaːmnis] *n.* 安宁

9 The 50 Percent Theory of Life
我的座右铭：生活半对半

生活中既有阳光灿烂的日子，也有阴雨连绵的时候，正因为如此，人生才显得五彩斑斓，多姿多彩。祸兮福之所倚，福兮祸之所伏。风雨过后是彩虹，张开双臂勇敢地拥抱生活吧！

文苑漫步

Half the time things are better than normal; the other half, they are worse. I believe life is a **pendulum** swing. It takes time and experience to understand what normal is, and that gives me the perspective to deal with the surprises of the future.

Let's benchmark the **parameters**: Yes, I will die. I've dealt with the deaths of both parents, a best friend, a beloved boss and cherished pets. Some of these deaths have been violent, before my eyes, or slow and **agonizing**. Bad stuff, and it belongs at the bottom of the scale.

Then there are those high points: romance and marriage to the right person; having a child and doing those Dad things like coaching my son's baseball team, **paddling** around the creek in the boat while he's swimming with the dogs,

译林畅游

生活有时一帆风顺，有时艰难曲折，好坏参半。我把生活看作来回晃动的钟摆。读懂生活的常态需要时间和阅历，也正是这样才给了我一个视角去面对未来生活中出其不意的各种事情。

让我们考量一下生活的参数：是的，我注定会死去。我已经历了双亲的仙逝，一位友人的亡故，一位敬爱的老板的过世，还有心爱宠物的离去。其中一些变故突如其来，直击眼前；有些却长期折磨，痛苦不堪。糟糕的事儿，它们驻留谷底。

当然生活也不乏熠熠光彩：拥有浪漫爱情，与适合的对象结婚；养育孩子，承担一个父亲应尽的责任，如训练儿子的棒球队，当他和狗在水中嬉戏时，摇桨划船前瞻后顾，感受他如此强烈的同情心——

discovering his compassion so deep it manifests even in his kindness to snails, his imagination so vivid he builds a spaceship from a scattered pile of Legos.

But there is a vast **meadow** of life in the middle, where the bad and the good flip-flop **acrobatically**. This is what convinces me to believe in the 50 percent theory.

One spring I planted corn too early in a bottomland so flood-prone that neighbors laughed. I felt **chagrined** at the wasted effort. Summer turned brutal — the worst heat wave and drought in my lifetime. The air-conditioner died, the well went dry, the marriage ended, the job lost, the money gone. I was living lyrics from a country tune — music I **loathed**. Only a surging Kansas City Royals team, bound for their first World Series, **buoyed** my spirits.

Looking back on that horrible summer, I soon understood that all succeeding good things merely **offset** the bad. Worse than normal wouldn't last long. I am owed and savor the halcyon times. They reinvigorate me for the next **nasty** surprise and offer assurance that I can thrive. The 50 percent theory even helps me see hope beyond my Royals' recent slump, a field of struggling **rookies** sown so that some year soon we can reap an October harvest.

Oh, yeah, the corn crop? For that one

即使对蜗牛也充满善意，发现他如此活跃的想象力——用零散的积木堆出太空飞船。

但生活中有一片巨大的草坪，在那儿各种好事坏事像耍杂技一样地轮流上演。这就是让我信奉生活半对半理论的原因。

有一年春天，我在一片容易被淹的低洼地过早地种下了玉米，以至于邻居们都嘲笑我。我懊恼自己的辛苦努力将要白白浪费。结果那个夏天更是难耐无比——最糟糕的热浪来袭，酿成我有生以来遭遇过的最严重的旱灾。空调坏了，水井枯了，婚姻破裂了，工作没了，积蓄也耗尽了。我正经历某个乡村调频里描绘的情节，我讨厌这种音乐。只有一支人气攀升的堪萨斯皇家棒球队的小组因他们第一次出征世界大赛而团结起来使我精神振奋。

回想那个可怕的夏天，我很快就明白了所有的好坏事不过是正负抵消。不顺心的境遇不会持续很久。我要尽情享受我应得的太平时光。它们给我新的活力以应对接下来突如其来的险境，并确保我再度辉煌。对半理论甚至让我在我喜爱的皇家棒球队最近的低潮中看到希望——新手们努力地在这块土地上耕种，假以时日我们就可以收获十月的金秋。

哦，对了，玉米收成？那个炎

blistering summer, the ground moisture was just right, planting early allowed **pollination** before heat withered the tops, and the lack of rain spared the standing corn from floods. That winter my crib **overflowed with** corn — fat, healthy three-to-a-stalk ears filled with **kernels** from heel to tip while my neighbors' fields yielded only brown, empty husks.

Although plantings past may have fallen below the 50 percent expectation, and they probably will again in the future, I am still sustained by the crop that flourishes during the drought.

热的夏天，庄稼地的湿度恰到好处，过早地种植反而使授粉避开酷热在顶梢干枯前完成，干旱少雨使得长在洼地里的玉米免遭水灾。那年冬天，我的谷仓堆满了玉米——饱满结实的玉米每株秆上结三个，每个玉米从头到尾长满了玉米粒，而我的邻居们地里长出来的只是暗沉干瘪的壳。

尽管过去播种的收获可能没有达到50%的期望，而且将来也可能是这样，我仍然要为经历旱季依然丰收的玉米而坚守阵地。

魅力词汇

pendulum ['pendjʊləm] *n.* 钟摆
parameter [pə'ræmitə] *n.* 参数
agonizing ['ægənaiziŋ] *adj.* 使人痛苦的
paddle ['pædl] *v.* 用桨划船
meadow ['medəʊ] *n.* 草地
acrobatically [ˌækrəu'bætikli] *adv.* 杂技般地
chagrined ['ʃægrind] *adj.* 懊恼的
loathe [ləʊð] *v.* 讨厌
buoy [bɒi] *v.* 鼓励
offset [ɒf'set] *v.* 抵消
nasty ['nɑːsti] *adj.* 危险的
rookie ['rʊki] *n.* 新手
blistering ['blistəriŋ] *adj.* 酷热的
pollination [ˌpɒnə'neiʃn] *n.* 授粉
overflow with 充满着
kernel ['kɜːnəl] *n.* 核，仁

10 Today and Tomorrow 今天和明天

时间，如天上的云彩，翩然而来，又飘然而去，这便有了昨天、今天和明天，也便有了人生的多姿多彩、生活的纷繁杂乱。今天是昨天的果，明天的花，无论昨天是激越、宁静，还是哀叹、凄婉，都已成为过眼云烟；明天虽有无限的向往与憧憬，但毕竟都是虚无缥缈的梦幻。只有今天，才是真正存在的时段，才是我们要有所作为的时段。珍惜今天！

文苑漫步

A white-bearded ancient man was walking over the hills and **valleys** of the world. On his back he carried a bag which moved uneasily as if something was trying to escape from it, but he settled it between his shoulders and walked on.

He was Father Time, traveling forever, and the bag he bore was filled with Tomorrows, all struggling to get out.

Each night at 12:00, he opened the bag and flew out a Tomorrow, just one, with its wings of blue, and its shining **feathers** rising with hope. All the rest were kept back by Time's strong hands and pushed deep in the bag.

Down flew the Tomorrow beating its lovely feathers, but as it touched the earth,

译林畅游

一位胡子花白的老人在世界各地的山脉及峡谷间穿行。他背着一个袋子，袋子里的东西在不安分地躁动着，好像要往外跑似的。他把袋子在肩膀上放好，继续前行。

他就是时间老人，他永远在前行。而装在袋子里的是明天，它们都争着想往外跑。

每天午夜 12 点，时间老人就会打开袋子，放飞一个明天，只放飞一个！它挥动着蓝色的翅膀，展示着它闪闪发光的羽毛，带着希望飞走了。时间老人用其有力的双手把剩下的明天塞进袋子底部。

明天挥动着可爱的翅膀飞向大地。可当它到达地面时，它的蓝色

off fell its blue wings and it changed to an ordinary white bird which could not fly. It had become a Today. Everyone knows that Today isn't as wonderful as Tomorrow, for Today can be held in one's hands, accepted, unloved, but Tomorrow is full of **mystery** and beauty. It is desired by all the world. Even those who with little hope sigh, "Tomorrow may bring a change. Tomorrow's life will be different."

翅膀脱落了，变成一只不会飞的白色的普通的鸟。它变成了今天。每个人都知道今天没有明天好，因为每个人可以把今天抓在手中，接受它，却不去爱它，但是明天充满神奇和美丽。所有人都想拥有明天，即使那些心中没有希望的人也会叹息说："明天也许会带来一些变化，明天的生活会很不一样。"

Everybody tried to catch the Tomorrow before it fell to the ground. They thought if they knew beforehand what the Tomorrow carries, they could prepare for it. So they put great nets on the trees, seeking to catch one before it changed his feather. Yet although they tried every means, the birds **escaped** and flew to the ground as Todays.

每个人都想在明天到达地面前抓住它。他们认为，如果能事先知道明天带来的是什么，他们便会有所准备。所以他们在树上挂好大网，试图在明天收起翅膀之前抓住它。然而，尽管他们用尽了一切方法，也没能抓住明天，它还是来到了地面，变成了今天。

魅力词汇

valley ['væli] *n.* 山谷，溪谷
feather ['feðə] *n.* 羽毛
mystery ['mistri] *n.* 神秘的事物
escape [i'skeip] *v.* 逃脱，溜走

11 Ten Years 十年

当青春、梦想还有爱情都凋零的时候，当我们大腹便便，甚至开始头发稀疏的时候，我们究竟丢失了什么？

文苑漫步

10 years ago, we were children of our parents;

10 years later, we become parents of our children.

10 years ago, I had a home full of joys and affection;

10 years later, I feel warmth of family then and not till then.

10 years ago, I yearned for leaving far away from home;

10 years later, I am longing to return my drifting heart home.

10 years ago, I shouted and thunder at my parents;

10 years later, I wish my parents scold me again even in my dream.

10 years ago, you were my deskmate;

10 years later, you become the wife of the other guy.

10 years ago, I sang *My Deskmate*

译林畅游

十年前我们是父母的孩子；

十年后我们是孩子的父母。

十年前我有充满欢乐和温情的家；

十年后我才体会家的温暖。

十年前我渴望离家去远方；

十年后我渴望从远方回家。

十年前我对父母大吵大嚷；

十年后我希望父母再骂我一次，即使在梦中。

十年前你是我的同桌；

十年后你成了别人的妻子。

十年前我唱着《同桌的你》；

for you;

10 years later, I am thinking of you, my dear deskmate.

10 years ago, the only problem we faced was exam;

10 years later, we have to face all except for exam.

10 years ago, I remembered your sweet smile at me at your downstairs;

10 years later, I **unwittingly** saw you **nagging** at your child with a stony face at your downstairs.

10 years ago, I yearned for marriage at every moment;

10 years later, I am longing to fall in love one more time.

10 years ago, we felt shy when talking about love;

10 years later, awkwardness only can be seen on our face when talking about love.

10 years ago, I yearned for love but didn't know what true love was;

10 years later, I have known what love is but love is long gone.

10 years ago, I fell in love first time;

10 years later, I had my first divorce.

10 years ago, I rode home whistling brightly;

10 years later, I drive on road bounding for social intercourse, answering phones in succession.

十年后我想着你，亲爱的同桌。

十年前我们面临的唯一问题是考试；

十年后我们除了考试所有的问题都要面对。

十年前我在你家楼下记住了你嫣然的回眸一笑；

十年后我无意中在你家楼下看到你训斥孩子的严厉面孔。

十年前我渴望马上结婚；

十年后我渴望再谈一次恋爱。

十年前我们谈及爱情，总是羞涩；

十年后我们谈及爱情，却是生涩。

十年前我渴望爱情，但不知道什么是爱情；

十年后我知道了什么是爱情，却不再拥有爱情。

十年前我有了初恋；

十年后我初次离婚。

十年前我骑着自行车，吹着欢快的口哨，走在回家的路上；

十年后我开着私家车，接着不断的电话，走在应酬的路上。

10 years ago, I dreamed of staying in a five star hotel;

十年前我渴望住进五星级饭店；

10 years later, I am longing to return home even if living in a five star hotel.

十年后我住进五星级饭店，却想回家。

10 years ago, I yearned for traveling by air once;

十年前我渴望坐一次飞机；

10 years later, I am afraid of taking plane most.

十年后我最害怕的就是坐飞机。

10 years ago, I hoped that I was the boy sitting opposite the girl when I passed by the window of coffee shop after playing football;

十年前我踢完球，走过咖啡屋的窗前，希望女生对面的男生是我；

10 years later, I hope I am that boy who passes by the window of the coffee shop just now after playing football.

十年后我望着咖啡屋外走过的刚刚踢过球的孩子们，希望我是其中一个。

10 years ago, native dishes are tasteless to me;

十年前吃家乡菜感觉没有滋味；

10 years later, I have no taste for all food except for native dishes.

十年后除了家乡菜什么都吃不出味。

10 years ago, I was forced to sit at the desk and attend a lecture carefully by parents and teacher;

十年前我们被父母和老师逼到课桌前，认真听讲；

10 years later, I want to attend a lecture again but can not find a desk.

十年后我想再次听讲，却找不到课桌。

10 years ago, I despised of **drunkard** in front of restaurant gate and sworn not drinking alcoholic all my life;

十年前我鄙视饭店门前的酒鬼，发誓一辈子也不喝酒；

10 years later, I become that drunkard.

十年后我就是饭店门前的那个酒鬼。

10 years ago, I felt blushed when touching a girl;

十年前我碰女生一下，都会脸红；

10 years later, I am accused of sexual

十年后我成了性骚扰的控诉

harassment.

对象。

10 years ago, I thought that I were a sky-reaching tree;

十年前我以为自己是一棵大树；

10 years later, I realize that I am nothing more than a tiny grass.

十年后我才明白自己只不过是一棵小草。

10 years ago, youth was unrepentant to us;

十年前我们可以说青春无悔；

10 years later, youth is far away from us.

十年后我们只能说青春不在。

魅力词汇

unwittingly [ˌʌnˈwitiŋli] *adv.* 不知情地，无意地

nag [næg] *v.* 不断挑剔或批评

drunkard [ˈdrʌŋkəd] *n.* 酒鬼

harassment [ˈhærəsmənt] *n.* 困扰，烦扰，烦恼

温情絮语

What may be done at any time will be done at no time.

常将今日推明日，推到后来无踪迹。

12 Rush 匆匆

时间最不偏私，给任何人一天都是二十四小时；时间也最偏私，给任何人一天都不是二十四小时。一天有多长，只看你如何利用。赢得了时间，就赢得了一切。时间匆匆而过，我们有追逐着它的，有与其并列前行的，更有领跑于时间之前的。你想做哪一种？莫让余生都在嗟叹那匆匆而过的时间吧。

文苑漫步

Swallows may have gone, but there is a time of return; willow trees may have died back, but there is a time of regreening; peach **blossoms** may have fallen, but they will **bloom** again. Now, you the wise, tell me, why should our days leave us, never to return? If they had been stolen by someone, who could it be? Where could he hide them? If they had made the escape themselves, then where could they stay at the moment?

I don't know how many days I have been given to spend, but I do feel my hands are getting empty. Taking stock silently, I find that more than eight thousand days have already slid away from me. Like a drop of water from the point of

译林畅游

燕子去了，有再来的时候；杨柳枯了，有再青的时候；桃花谢了，有再开的时候。但是，聪明的，你告诉我，我们的日子为什么一去不复返呢？——是有人偷了他们吧：那是谁？又藏在何处呢？如果是他们自己逃走了吧：现在又到了哪里呢？

我不知道他们给了我多少日子；但我的手确乎是渐渐空虚了。在默默里算着，八千多日子已经从我手中溜去；像针尖上一滴水滴在大海里，我的日子滴在时间的流里，没有声音，也没有影子。我不禁头

a needle disappearing into the ocean, my days are dripping into the stream of time, soundless, traceless. Already sweat is starting on my forehead, and tears **welling** up in my eyes.

涔涔而泪潸潸了。

Those that have gone have gone for good, those to come keep coming; yet in between, how **swift** is the **shift**, in such a rush? When I get up in the morning, the **slanting** sun marks its presence in my small room in two or three **oblongs**. The sun has feet, look, he is treading on, lightly and **furtively**; and I am caught, **blankly**, in his **revolution**. Thus — the day flows away through the sink when I wash my hands, wears off in the bowl when I eat my meal, and passes away before my day-dreaming gaze as reflect in silence. I can feel his haste now, so I reach out my hands to hold him back, but he keeps flowing past my **withholding** hands. In the evening, as I lie in bed, he strides over my body, glides past my feet, in his **agile** way. The moment I open my eyes and meet the sun again, one whole day has gone. I bury my face in my hands and **heave** a sigh. But the new day begins to flash past in the sigh.

去的尽管去了，来的尽管来着，去来的中间，又怎样地匆匆呢？早上我起来的时候，小屋里射进两三方斜斜的太阳。太阳他有脚啊，轻轻悄悄地挪移了；我也茫茫然跟着旋转。于是——洗手的时候，日子从水盆里过去；吃饭的时候，日子从饭碗里过去；默默时，便从凝然的双眼前过去。我觉察他去的匆匆了，伸出手遮挽时，他又从遮挽着的手边过去，天黑时，我躺在床上，他便伶伶俐俐地从我身边跨过，从我脚边飞去了。等我睁开眼和太阳再见，这算又溜走了一日。我掩着面叹息。但是新来的日子的影儿又开始在叹息里闪过了。

What can I do, in this **bustling** world, with my days flying in their escape? Nothing but to hesitate, to rush. What have I been doing in that eight-thousand-day

在逃去如飞的日子里，在千门万户的世界里的我能做些什么呢？只有徘徊罢了，只有匆匆罢了；在八千多日的匆匆里，除徘徊外，又

rush, apart from hesitating? Those **bygone** days have been **dispersed** as smoke by a light wind, or **evaporated** as mist by the morning sun. What traces have I left behind me? Have I ever left behind any **gossamer** traces at all? I have come to the world, **stark** naked; am I to go back, in a blink, in the same stark nakedness? It is not fair though: why should I have made such a trip for nothing!

剩些什么呢？过去的日子如轻烟，被微风吹散了，如薄雾，被初阳蒸融了；我留着些什么痕迹呢？我何曾留着像游丝样的痕迹呢？我赤裸裸来到这世界，转眼间也将赤裸裸地回去吧？但不能平的，为什么偏要白白走这一遭啊？

You the wise, tell me, why should our days leave us, never to return?

你聪明的，告诉我，我们的日子为什么一去不复返呢？

魅力词汇

blossom ['blɒsəm] *n.* 花
bloom [bluːm] *v.* 开花，繁盛
well [wel] *v.* 涌出
swift [swift] *adj.* 快的，迅速的
shift [ʃift] *n.* 转换，更替
slanting ['slaːntiŋ] *adj.* 倾斜的，歪斜的
oblong ['ɒblɒŋ] *n.* 长方形
furtively ['fəːtivli] *adv.* 偷偷地，暗中地
blankly ['blæŋkli] *adv.* 茫然地
revolution [ˌrevə'luːʃn] *n.* 旋转
withhold [wið'həuld] *v.* 保留，抑制
agile ['ædʒail] *adj.* 敏捷的，灵活的
heave [hiːv]
v. (费力地)发出(叹息等)，喘息
bustling ['bʌsliŋ]
adj. 熙熙攘攘的，忙乱的
bygone ['baigɒn] *adj.* 过去的
disperse [dɪ'spɜːs] *v.* 分散，传播，散开
evaporate [i'væpəreit] *v.* 蒸发
gossamer ['gɒsəmə] *n.* 薄纱
stark [staːk]
adj. 完全的 *adv.* 一丝不挂地

温情絮语

There is no time like the present.

现在正是时候。

13 Don't Wait for Withering 莫待花谢时

花开堪折直须折，莫待无花空折枝。美好的事物都是转瞬即逝的，如果不懂得珍惜眼前的美好，日后将是无尽的徒劳的悔恨。

文苑漫步

Each spring brings a new blossom of wildflowers in the **ditches** along the highway I travel daily to work.

There is one particular blue flower that has always caught my eye. I've noticed that it blooms only in the morning hours, the afternoon sun is too warm for it. Every day for approximately two weeks, I see those beautiful flowers.

This spring, I started a wildflower garden in our yard. I can look out of the kitchen window while doing the dishes and see the flowers. I've often thought that those lovely blue flowers from the ditch would look great in that bed alongside other wildflowers.

Everyday I drove past the flowers thinking, "I'll stop on my way home and dig them." "Gee, I don't want to get my good clothes dirty..."Whatever the reason, I

译林畅游

每年春天，在我每天上班途经的高速公路旁边的沟渠里，都会盛开着一片鲜艳的花朵。

有一簇独特的蔚蓝的花朵总会吸引我的目光。我早已觉察到它只有在早晨的时光里才会盛开，这也许是因为下午的温度太高了。大约两周的时间，我每一天都要看看那些美丽的花。

今年春天，我在自己的院子里面开辟了一片花园。我能在洗碗的时候透过厨房的窗户看到外面的花。我常想，要是沟渠里那可爱的蔚蓝色花簇也移栽在花床中并和其他野花放置到一起，那样该多好看。

每天我开车路过那簇蔚蓝色花朵的时候都在想着，“回家的时候我就去把它们挖走吧。”“哎，我不想把自己漂亮的衣服弄脏了……”

never stopped to dig them. My husband even gave me a folding shovel one year for my trunk to be used for that expressed purpose.

One day on my way home from work, I was saddened to see that the highway department had mowed the ditches and the pretty blue flowers were gone. I thought to myself, "Way to go, you waited too long. You should have done it when you first saw them blooming this spring."

A week ago we were shocked and saddened to learn that my oldest sister-in-law has a terminal brain **tumor**. She is 20 years older than my husband and unfortunately, because of age and distance, we haven't been as close as we all would have liked.

I couldn't help but see the connection between the pretty blue flowers and the relationship between my husband's sister and us. I do believe that God has given us some time left to plant some wonderful memories that will bloom every year for us. And yes, if I see the blue flowers again, you can bet I'll stop and **transplant** them to my wildflower garden.

不管是什么理由吧，我始终没有停下车来去把它们挖走。为了那个想法，有一年我丈夫甚至在我的汽车后备箱里放了一把折叠铲。

有一天，在下班回家的路上，我沮丧的发现路政处已经把那沟渠修整一番，而那些漂亮的蔚蓝花簇也已经不见了。我心里想，"早该动手了，你等了太长时间。你应该在春天里第一次看到它们开放的时候就把它们带回家去了。"

一个礼拜前，得知我丈夫的姐姐患了晚期脑瘤，我们很震惊也为她感到很难过。她比我丈夫大 20 岁，很遗憾的是由于年龄和距离的一些原因，我们的关系并不像我们想得那样亲密。

我不禁想到，那些漂亮蓝花和我们同姐姐的关系之间的关联。我相信上帝年年都留给我们一段时间去播种那些美好的回忆。而且我深信，如果重来一次，我要是能再看到那些蓝色的小花，不用说，我肯定会停下车来，然后把它们移栽到我的花园里。

魅力词汇

ditch [ditʃ] *n.* 沟渠

tumor ['tjuːmə] *n.* 肿瘤，肿块

transplant [træns'plɑːnt] *v.* 移栽，移植

14 Every Day Is a Gift 每一天都是特殊的日子

每一天、每一分钟、每一瞬间都是上帝赐予的礼物。生命随时可能结束，就让我们享受生活吧，享受现在的每一天，享受现在的一切，无需再珍藏那些能给我们生活带来欢笑和光彩的东西，别给自己留下没必要的遗憾和留恋。

文苑漫步

My brother-in-law opened the bottom drawer of my sister's **bureau** and lifted out a tissue-wrapped package. "This," he said, "is not a slip. This is **lingerie**." He **discarded** the tissue and handed me the **slip**.

It was exquisite, silk, handmade and **trimmed** with a **cobweb** of **lace**. The price tag with an **astronomical** figure on it was still attached.

"Jan bought this the first time we went to New York, at least Eight or Nine years ago. She never wore it. She was saving it for a special occasion."

Well, I guess this is the occasion.

He took the slip from me and put it on the bed, with the other clothes we were

译林畅游

妹夫打开了妹妹衣柜的底层抽屉，拿出一个用纸包装的包裹。“这个，”他说，“不是件普通衬裙，而是一件做工非常精细的衬裙。”他把薄纸撕开，递给我那件衬裙。

它的确精致无比，丝绸材质、全手工缝制，周围还有一圈网状花边。价签都尚未拆去，上面的数字高得惊人。

“这是Jan在我们第一次去纽约时买的，至少已经是八九年前的事了。她从没有穿过它。她留着它，想等一个特殊的日子再穿。”

唉，我想现在便是那特殊的日子了。

妹夫从我手中拿过衬裙放在床上，和其他要带给殡仪服务人员的

taking to the **mortician**. His hands **lingered** on the soft material for a moment, then he **slammed** the drawer shut and turned to me, "Don't ever save anything for a special occasion. Every day you're alive is a special occasion."

衣服放在一起。他的手在那柔软衣服上停留了一会儿，随即砰然关上抽屉，转身对我说："永远不要把任何东西留给什么特殊的日子。你活着的每一天就是一个特殊的日子。"

I remembered those words through the funeral and the days that followed when I helped him and my niece attend to all the sad chores that follow an unexpected death. I thought about them on the plane returning to California from the mid-western town where my sister's family lives. I thought about all the things that she hadn't seen or heard or done. I thought about the things that she had done without realizing that they were special.

在葬礼上，帮妹夫、侄女处理妹妹意外死亡的所有后事的那几天，我一直记着这些话。我乘飞机从位于中西部的妹妹家的小镇上返回加州时，还在想这些话。我想着妹妹没有去看、去听或去做的事。我想着她虽然做过却没有意识到其特殊性的事。

I'm still thinking about his words, and they've changed the weeds in the garden. I'm spending more time with my family and friends and less time in committee meetings. Whenever possible, life should be a pattern of experience to savour, not endure. I'm trying to **recognize** these moments now and cherish them.

我至今还在想着妹夫说的话，正是它们改变了我心里的杂念。我花更多的时间与家人朋友在一起，而少花时间在那些委员会议上。无论何时，只要有可能，生活应当是一种"品味"而非一种"忍受"。我在试着欣赏每一刻，并珍惜每一刻。

I'm not "saving" anything; we use our good china and crystal for every special event such as losing a pound, getting the sink unstopped, the first **camellia** blossom... I wear my good **blazer** to the market if I feel like it. My

我不再去"珍藏"任何东西；只要有一件特别的事情，比如说当体重减了一磅时，厨房水槽被疏通了时，当第一朵山茶花绽放时……我们就会使用精美的瓷器和水晶制品。如果我想穿，我就穿上我的品

theory is if I look prosperous, I can **shell out** $28.49 for one small bag of groceries without **wincing**. I'm not saving my good perfume for special parties; clerks in hardware stores and tellers in banks have noses that function as well as my party-going friends.

"Someday" and "one of these days" are losing their grip on my vocabulary. If it's worth seeing or hearing or doing, I want to see and hear and do it now. I'm not sure what my sister would've done had she known that she wouldn't be here for the tomorrow we all take for granted.

I think she would have called family members and a few close friends. She might have called a few former friends to apologize, and mend fences for past **squabbles**. I like to think she would have gone out for a Chinese dinner, her favorite food. I'm guessing. I'll never know.

It's those little things left undone that would make me angry if I knew that my hours were limited. Angry because I put off seeing good friends whom I was going to get in touch with someday. Angry because I hadn't written certain letters that I intended to write one of these days. Angry and sorry that I didn't tell my husband and daughter often enough how much I truly love them.

质优良颜色鲜亮的运动衣去市场购物。我的理论是：如果我看上去还富足的话，我可以毫不畏缩地为一小袋杂货付 28.49 美元。我不再为特殊的派对而珍藏我上好的香水；五金店售货员和银行出纳员们的嗅觉，不会比派对上朋友们来得差。

"有朝一日"和"终有一天"这样的词正从我的字典中淡出。如果值得去看、去听或去做，我当即就要去看、去听、去做。我们总是理所当然地以为自己必然有明天，不知假如妹妹知道她将没有明日，她会做些什么。

我想她会给家人和几位密友打电话。她可能还会给几位昔日朋友打电话主动道歉，摒弃前嫌，重归于好。我想她可能会外出吃顿中餐，那是她最喜欢的。我只是猜想而已。我永远也不会知道。

假如我知道我的时间不多了，那些没来得及做的小事会让我恼火。恼火是因为我一拖再拖没能去看看"有朝一日"会去看的好友们。恼火是因为我还没有写出我"终有一天"要写的信。恼火与遗憾是因为我没能常常告诉我的丈夫和女儿：我是多么真切地爱他们。

I'm trying very hard not to put off, **hold back**, or save anything that would add laughter and **luster** to our lives. And every morning when I open my eyes, I tell myself that every day, every minute, every **breath** truly, is... a gift from God.

我正努力不再拖延、保留或珍藏那些能给我们生活带来欢笑和光彩的东西。每天清晨当我睁开双眼，我便告诉自己每一天、每一分钟、每一瞬间都是……上帝赐予的礼物。

魅力词汇

bureau ['bjʊərəʊ] *n.* 衣柜
lingerie ['lɒnʒəri] *adj.* 做工精细的
discard [di'skaːd] *v.* 丢弃
slip [slip] *n.* 肩带式女长内衣
trim [trim] *v.* 装点
cobweb ['kɒbweb] *n.* 蛛网状的薄织物
lace [leis] *n.* 花边
astronomical [æstrə'nɒmikəl]
adj. 天文的，极大的
mortician [mɔː 'tiʃən] *n.* 丧事承办人
linger ['liŋgə] *v.* 徘徊
slam [slæm] *v.* 砰地关上
recognize ['rekəgnaiz] *v.* 意识到
camellia [kə'miːliə] *n.* [植] 山茶花
blazer ['bleizə]
n. 颜色鲜明的运动上衣，轻便短上衣
shell out [口] 付款
wince [wins] *v.* 畏缩，退避
squabble ['skwɒbl] *n.* 争吵
hold back 保留
luster ['lʌstə] *n.* 光彩
breath [breθ] *n.* 呼吸

温情絮语

When opportunity knocks, open the door even if you're in your bathrobe.

当机遇敲门时，打开门，即便你是穿着浴袍。

Never put off till tomorrow what may be done today.

今日事，今日毕。

第六篇

— 热爱生活 —

1 Love Your Life 热爱生活

亨利·梭罗是美国作家、哲学家，是著名散文集《瓦尔登湖》和论文《论公民的不服从权利》的作者。本文节选自他的名篇《热爱生活》。作为超验主义的代表性人物之一，他的文章文笔隽秀，而且充满哲理的思考。

文苑漫步

However mean your life is, meet it and live it; do not **shun** it and **call it hard names**. It is not so bad as you are. It looks poorest when you are richest. The fault-finder will find faults in paradise. Love your life, poor as it is. You may perhaps have some pleasant, **thrilling**, glorious hours, even in a poor-house. The **setting sun** is reflected from the windows of the **alms-house** as brightly as from the rich man's **abode**; the snow melts before its door as early in the spring. I do not see but a quiet mind may live as contentedly there and have as cheering thoughts, as in a palace. The town's poor seem to me often to live the most independent lives of any. May be they are simply great enough to receive without **misgiving**. Most think

译林畅游

不论你的生活如何卑贱，你要面对它，不要躲避它，更别用恶言咒骂它。它不像你那样坏。你最富有的时候，倒是看似最穷。爱找缺点的人就是到天堂里也能找到毛病。尽管生活贫困，你也要热爱生活。甚至在一个济贫院里，你也还有愉快、高兴、光荣的时候。夕阳反射在济贫院的窗上，像在富户人家窗上一样光亮；门前的积雪一同在早春融化。我只看到，一个从容的人，在哪里也像在皇宫中一样，生活得心满意足而富有愉快的思想。城镇中的穷人，我看，倒往往是过着最独立不羁的生活。也许因为他们很伟大，所以受之无愧。大多数人以为他们是超然的，不靠城镇来养活他们；可是用不正当的手

that they are above being supported by the town; but it often happens that they are not above supporting themselves by dishonest means, which should be more disreputable. Cultivate poverty like a garden herb, like sage. Do not trouble yourself much to get new things, whether clothes or friends. Turn the old, return to them. Things do not change; we change. Sell your clothes and keep your thoughts.

段来养活自己更不光彩，而事实上他们往往不这么做。像圣人一样视贫穷如花园里的芳草吧！别费事找新东西了，无论是新的朋友或新的衣服，找旧的，回到那里去。万物不变，是我们在变。你的衣服可以卖掉，但要保留你的思想。

魅力词汇

shun [ʃʌn] *v.* 避开，规避，避免

call... hard names 咒骂

thrilling ['θriliŋ] *adj.* 令人兴奋的

setting sun 夕阳

alms-house 救济院

abode [ə'bəud] *n.* 住处，住所

misgiving [mis'giviŋ] *n.* 疑虑

sage [seidʒ] *n.* 圣人，哲人

温情絮语

The happiest of people don't necessarily have the best of everything, they just make the most of everything that comes along their way.

最快乐的人不一定拥有所有一切最好的东西，他们只是充分珍惜了生命中所遇到的一切。

2 A Psalm of Life 人生礼颂

“我们命定的归宿不是快乐，也不是悲伤； 而是埋头实干，每天进步一点点。”有人白日做梦，幻想一夜暴富，终日沉浸在自己的“乌托邦”里，也有人怨天尤人，抱怨社会不公，总是挑剔自己的工作或是生活。空想不会变成现实，抱怨也不会改变现状。我们最应该做的其实就是脚踏实地做好自己应该做的事情，保持良好的心态，努力实现自己的人生价值。

文苑漫步

Tell me not in **mournful** numbers,
Life is but an empty dream!
For the soul is dead that **slumbers**
And things are not what they seem.
Life is real! Life is **earnest** !
And the grave is not its goal;
Dust thou art, to dust returnest,
Was not spoken of the soul.
Not enjoyment, and not sorrow,
Is our **destined** and our way;
But to act,
That much tomorrow.
Find us farther than today.
Art is long, and time is **fleeting**.
And our hearts, though **stout** and brave.
Still, like **muffled** drums, are beating
Funeral marches to the grave.
In the world's broad field of battle,
In the **bivouac** of Life,

译林畅游

请别用哀伤的诗句对我讲，
人生只不过是虚梦一场！
因为沉睡的灵魂如死一般，
事物并不像看起来那样。
人生是真实的！人生是热烈的！
人生的目标决不是走向坟墓；
你是尘土，也应归于尘土，
这并不是指我们的灵魂。
我们命定的归宿，
不是快乐，也不是悲伤；
而是在未来的日子里，
埋头实干，
每天进步一点点。
光阴流逝，而艺海无涯，
我们跳动的心哪，虽然勇敢坚强，
却像被蒙住的鼓，
把殡葬的哀乐擂响。
在这辽阔的世界战场，
在这人生的宿营地，

Be not like dumb, driven cattle!	别做无言的牲畜，任人驱赶，
Be a hero in the **strife** !	要做一名英雄浴血奋战！
Trust no future, howe'er pleasant!	别相信未来，哪怕未来多么欢乐!
Let the dead past bury its dead!	过去的事情就将它埋葬！
Act, act in the living Present!	上帝在上，我们胸怀勇气，
Heart within, and God O'erhead!	行动吧，趁现在活着的好时光!
Lives of great men all remind us	伟人的生平都使我们想起，
We can make our lives **sublime**,	我们能使生命变得高尚！
And departing, leave behind us	当我们离开人世，
Footprints on the sands of time;	能在时间的流沙上留下足迹；
Footprints that perhaps another;	也许有个遭了船灾的苦难弟兄，
Sailing o'er life solemn main,	在庄严的人生大海中飘航，
A **forlorn** and **shipwrecked** brother,	见到我们的脚印，
Seeing, shall take heart again,	又会满怀信心。
Let us, then, be up and doing,	让我们起来干吧，
With a heart for any fate;	下定决心，不管命运如何；
Still achieving,	不断成功，
still pursuing,	不断追求，
Learn to labour and to wait.	要学会苦干和耐心等待。

魅力词汇

mournful ['mɔːnfəl] *adj.* 令人伤心的
slumber ['slʌmbə] *v.* 睡眠，安眠
earnest ['əːnist] *adj.* 热切的
destined ['destind] *adj.* 命中注定的
fleeting ['fliːtiŋ] *adj.* 疾驰的，飞逝的
stout [staut] *adj.* 不屈不挠的，坚强的
muffled ['mʌfld] *adj.* 裹严的，蒙住的
bivouac ['bivuæk] *n.* 野营，露营地
strife [straif] *n.* 争吵，斗争，冲突
sublime [sə'blaim] *adj.* 崇高的
forlorn [fə'lɔːn] *adj.* 孤立无助的
shipwrecked ['ʃiprekt] *v.* 遇海难

3 Write Your Own Life 谱写你的生活乐章

作者通过用笔写字这一简单的意象向大家透露出生活的真谛，人应当如何选择自己的生活。生命的诞生是一种过程，生命的延续也是一种过程。每个人都在用自己的人生书写一个轨迹，每个人都在用自己的人生绘出一幅篇章。而这轨迹是否优美，篇章是否精彩就取决于个人的汗水和辛劳，努力和奋斗了。

文苑漫步

Suppose someone gave you a pen — a **sealed**, **solid-colored** pen.

You couldn't see how much ink it had. It might run dry after the first few **tentative** words or last just long enough to create a masterpiece (or several) that would last forever and make a difference in the scheme of things.

You don't know before you begin.

Under the rules of the game, you really never know.

You have to **take a chance**!

Actually, no rule of the game states you must do anything. Instead of **picking up** and using the pen, you could leave it **on a shelf** or in a drawer where it will dry up, unused.

译林畅游

假设有人给了你一支笔，一支密封的、纯色的水笔。

里面有多少墨水你看不到。很可能刚刚试写几字便用干耗尽；也可能足以完成一部或几部杰作，永存于世，使世事为之大变。

而这一切你在动笔之前却是一无所知。

根据游戏的规则，你确实永远也不会知道，

只能冒一下险。

而事实上，也没有规则说你就一定要做些什么。你大可以把笔搁在架子上、放在抽屉里，弃置不用，任墨水蒸发干净。

But if you decide to use it, what would you do with it? How would you play the game?

然而，如果你真的决定使用，你会做什么？怎么来玩这个游戏？

Would you plan and plan before you ever wrote a word?

你会左计划、右计划，然后才下笔吗？

Would your plans be so extensive that you never even got to the writing?

计划会不会太泛太多，根本就达不到写作这一步？

Or would you take the pen in hand, plunge right in and just do it, struggling to keep up with the **twists and turns** of the **torrents** of words that take you where they take you?

或者会不会提笔在手，迫不及待地投入其中，任由笔下的字带着你在词海中上下翻腾、左突右冲？

Would you write cautiously and carefully, as if the pen might run dry the next moment, or would you pretend or believe (or pretend to believe) that the pen will write forever and proceed accordingly?

会不会下笔谨小慎微，似乎墨水随时都将干涸？会不会假装或相信（或假装相信）笔中墨水永不会枯竭，任你挥洒？

And of what would you write: Of love? Hate? Fun? Misery? Life? Death? Nothing? Everything?

你会写些什么？爱情？仇恨？乐趣？痛苦？生命？死亡？虚无？或世事万种？

Would you write to please just yourself? Or others? Or yourself by writing for others?

是会用来自娱？还是取悦他人？还是为人写作而愉悦自身？

Would your **strokes** be **tremblingly** timid or brilliantly bold? Fancy with a flourish or plain?

你的一笔一画会颤抖怯懦还是亮丽大胆？花里胡哨还是朴实无华？

Would you even write? Once you have the pen, no rule says you have to write. Would you **sketch**? **Scribble**? **Doodle** or draw?

你确实会去写吗？你有了这支笔，却也没有规则说你一定就要去写。你会粗粗勾勒，潦潦草草，信手涂鸦，还是认真描画？

Would you stay in or on the lines, or see no lines at all, even if they were there?

你会写在线里还是写在线上，或者对纸上的线格根本就视而不

Or are they? There's a lot to think about here, isn't there?

Now, suppose someone gave you a life...

见？真的有什么线格吗？此时此刻，有很多东西值得思考，不是吗？

那么，假设有人给了你一次生命……

魅力词汇

sealed [siːld] *adj.* 密封的
solid-colored 全身一色的
tentative ['tentətiv] *adj.* 试探性的
under the rules of the game 根据游戏的规则，在游戏的规则下
take a chance 冒险
pick up 捡起，收拾
on a shelf 在架子上
twists and turns 迂回曲折
torrent ['tɔrənt] *n.* 奔流
stroke [strəuk] *n.* 一画，一笔
tremblingly ['tremblinli] *adv.* 颤抖地
sketch [sketʃ] *vt.* 草草地做，敷衍
scribble ['skribl] *vt.* 潦草地书写，乱画
doodle ['duːdl] *v.* 心不在焉地乱写乱画

温情絮语

Love begins with a smile, grows with a kiss, ends with a tear. When you were born, you were crying and everyone around you was smiling. Live your life so that when you die, you're the one smiling and everyone around you is crying.

爱以微笑开始，在亲吻中成长，以泪水结束。当你出生时，你在哭，而周围的人在笑。过好自己的生活，那么当你死去时，你就是那个微笑的人，而你周围的人在哭泣。

4 The Sense of Humor 幽默的意义

幽默，不仅仅是使人们发笑而已，幽默比笑更有深度，其产生的效果远胜于咧嘴一笑。来看看本文所展示的幽默的奇妙效果吧！

文苑漫步

The story goes that a certain court **jester** went too far one day and **insulted** his king. The king became so **infuriated** he sentenced the jester to be executed. His court prayed upon the king to have **mercy** for the man who had served him well for so many years. After a time, the king **relented** only enough to give the jester his choice as to how he would like to die. The jester replied, "If it's all the same to you, my Lord, I'd like to die of old age." Certainly in this case, a good sense of humor saved the man's life.

It's true for us as well. We may not be faced with a situation where our wit will save us from an **execution**, but our sense of humor and the ability to laugh at things has proven health benefits that extend and improve our quality of life.

Norman Cousins, in his book ***Anato-***

译林畅游

这是关于一个宫廷小丑的故事。这天，他故事讲得有点儿过头，得罪了国王。国王非常恼怒，下令将其处死。他的同伴求情，希望国王能够饶过这个服侍他多年的人。后来，国王有些心软了，但只是让他选择如何死而已。小丑回答说："陛下，如果您不反对的话，我愿意老死。"毋庸置疑，出色的幽默感救了这个人的性命。

对我们来说，幽默感同样重要。我们可能不会遇到用智慧来使我们免于被处死的情况，但是幽默感和笑对世事的能力却可以促进身体健康，提高生活质量。

诺曼·库辛在他的名为《解剖

my of an Illness, wrote about how he cured himself of cancer by laughing a good part of each day. He rented films of comedies and watched them for hours on end in his hospital room. He had nothing to lose since he'd been **diagnosed** as **terminal**.

His "experiment" turned out to be a classic example of the healing powers of laughter. If it worked for Cousins with a life-threatening illness, it can work for us to enhance and protect our health. We should laugh often and **heartily**. It's good for our body.

疾病》的书中记录了他如何通过每天大笑一段时间来治愈自己的癌症的故事。他租了一些喜剧电影然后在病房里连续看上几个小时。自从被诊断出癌症晚期之后，他对死亡淡然处之。

他的这个“试验”成为证明大笑的治疗作用的经典例子。如果幽默对这位面临着死亡危险的库辛起作用的话，那么幽默也会促进和保护我们的健康。我们应该经常大笑，而且是发自内心地大笑，这对我们的健康有好处。

魅力词汇

jester ['dʒestə] *n.* （中世纪宫廷或贵族家中的）小丑，爱开玩笑的人

insult [in'sʌlt] *v.* 侮辱；辱骂

infuriate [in'fjuərieit] *v.* 激怒

mercy ['məːsi] *n.* 仁慈，宽容

relent [ri'lent] *v.* 变温和，变宽厚

execution [ˌeksi'kjuːʃn] *n.* 死刑

anatomy [ə'nætəmi] *n.* 解剖学

diagnose ['daiəg'nəuz] *v.* 诊断

terminal ['təːminəl] *adj.* 末端的；晚期的

heartily ['haːtili] *adv.* 衷心地

温情絮语

To see a world in a grain of sand, and a heaven in a wild flower.

Hold infinity in the palm of your hand, and eternity in an hour.

从一粒沙看世界，一朵花看天堂。

把握在你手心里的就是无限，永恒也就消融于一个小时。

5 The Joys of Writing (Excerpts)
写作的乐趣（节选）

丘吉尔是英国政治家，演说家，军事家和作家，曾于1940年至1945年出任英国首相，任期内领导英国在第二次世界大战中联合美国、对抗德国，取得胜利，并自1951年至1955年再度出任英国首相。本文选自他的散文《写作的乐趣》，讲述了丘吉尔本人对于写作的看法。

文苑漫步

The fortunate people in the world — the only really fortunate people in the world, in my mind, are those whose work is also their pleasure. The class is not a large one, not nearly so large as it is often represented to be; and authors are perhaps one of the most important **elements** in its **composition**. They enjoy in this respect at least a real harmony of life. To my mind, to be able to make your work your pleasure is the one class distinction in the world worth **striving** for; and I do not wonder that others are inclined to envy those happy human beings who find their **livelihood** in the gay **effusions** of their fancy, to whom every hour of labour is an hour of enjoyment, to whom repose — however necessary

译林畅游

在我看来，世上幸运的人——世上唯一真正幸运的人，是那些以工作为乐的人。这个阶层的人并不多，还没有人们常说的那样多。也许，作家是其中最重要的组成部分之一。就幸运而言，他们至少享受着生活中真正的和谐美。依我看，能使工作成为乐趣的能力是区分阶级的一个标准，是世人值得为之奋斗的一种崇高的荣誉；而且，我毫不意外别人会羡慕那些幸福的人，因为他们在快乐的喷涌的幻想中找到了生计，对他们来说，每劳动一小时，就是享受一小时，而休息——无论多么有必要——也是令人讨厌的插曲，甚至度假也几乎成了一种损失。无论写得好坏，写成

— is a **tiresome interlude**. And even a holiday is almost deprivation. Whether a man writes well or ill, has much to say or little, if he cares about writing at all, he will appreciate the pleasures of composition. To sit at one's table on a sunny morning, with four clear hours of uninterruptible security, plenty of nice white paper, and a Squeezer pen — that is true happiness. The complete **absorption** of the mind upon an agreeable occupation — what more is there than that to desire? What does it matter what happens outside? The House of Commons may do what it likes, and so may the House of Lords. The heathen may rage furiously in every part of the globe. The bottom may be knocked clean out of the American market. Consols may fall and suffragettes may rise. Never mind, for four hours, at any rate, we will withdraw ourselves from a common, ill-governed, and disorderly world, and with the key of fancy unlock that cupboard where all the good things of the infinite are put away.

多少，只要在意，就可尝到谋章布局的乐趣。在一个阳光明媚的早晨，临桌而坐，整整四个小时不受打扰，有足够数量的雪白稿纸，还有一支“挤压式”妙笔——那才叫真正的幸福。全心全意地投入一项令人愉快的职业——此愿足矣！外面发生什么事又有何妨？下议院想干什么就干什么吧，上议院也一样。异教徒可以在全球各地大发作。美国市场可以彻底崩溃。证券可以下跌；女权运动可以兴起：没有关系，不管怎么说，我们有四个小时可以躲开这俗气的、治理不善的、杂乱无章的世界，并且用想象这把钥匙，去开启藏有大千世界一切宝物的小橱。

魅力词汇

element ['elimənt] *n.* 成分，要素，元素

composition [kɔmpə'ziʃn]
n. 成分，组成成分

strive [straiv] *vi.* 努力，奋斗，力争

livelihood ['laivlihud] *n.* 生计，营生

effusion [i'fjuːʒn] *n.* 流出，溢出

tiresome ['taiəsəm] *adj.* 令人厌倦的

interlude ['intəluːd]
n. 中间，插曲，介在中间的事件

absorption [əb'sɔːpʃn] *n.* 吸收

6 Companionship of Books (Excerpts)
以书为伴（节选）

好书就像是你最好的朋友。它矢志不渝，过去如此，现在如此，将来也一定如此。它总是最有耐心的，最令人愉悦的伴侣。在我们穷困潦倒、临危遇难时，它也不会抛弃我们，对我们总是一如既往地亲切。在我们年轻时，好书陶冶我们的性情，增长我们的知识；当我们年老时，它又会给我们以慰藉和勉励。

文苑漫步

A man may usually be known by the books he reads as well as by the company he keeps; for there is a companionship of books as well as men; and one should always live in the best company, whether it be of books or of men.

A good book may be among the best friends. It is the same today that it always was, and it will never change. It is the most patient and cheerful of companions. It does not turn its back upon us in times of **adversity** or **distress**. It always receives us with the same kindness; amusing and instructing us in youth, and comforting and **consoling** us in age.

Men often discover their **affinity** to each other by the mutual love they have

译林畅游

通常看一个人读些什么书就可以知道他的为人，就像看他同什么人交往就可知道他的为人一样，因为有人以人为伴，也有人以书为伴。无论是书友还是朋友，我们都应该以最好的为伴。

好书就像是你最好的朋友。它矢志不渝，过去如此，现在如此，将来也永远不变。它是最有耐心，最令人愉悦的伴侣。在我们穷困潦倒，临危遭难时，它也不会抛弃我们，对我们总是一如既往地亲切。在我们年轻时，好书陶冶我们的性情，增长我们的知识； 到我们年老时，它又给我们以慰藉和勉励。

人们常常因为喜欢同一本书而结为知已，就像有时两个人因为敬

for a book just as two persons sometimes discover a friend by the admiration which both entertain for a third. There is an old proverb, "Love me, love my dog." But there is more wisdom in this: "Love me, love my book." The book is truer and higher bond of union. Men can think, feel and sympathize with each other through their favorite author. They live in him together, and he in them.

慕同一个人而成为朋友一样。有句谚语说道："爱屋及乌"。其实"爱我及书"这句话蕴涵更多的哲理。书是更为真诚而高尚的情谊纽带。人们可以通过共同喜爱的作家沟通思想，交流感情，彼此息息相通，并与自己喜欢的作家思想相通，情感相融。

A good book is often the best **urn** of a life **enshrining** the best that life could think out; for the world of a man's life is, for the most part, but the world of his thoughts. Thus the best books are treasures of good words, the golden thoughts, which, remembered and cherished, become our constant companions and comforts.

好书如同最精美的宝器，珍藏着人生思想的精华，因为人生的境界主要就在于其思想的境界。因此，最好的书是金玉良言和崇高思想的宝库，这些良言和思想若铭记于心并多加珍视，就会成为我们忠实的伴侣和慰藉。

Books possess the essence of immortality. They are by far the most lasting products of human effort. Temples and statues decay, but books survive. Time is of no account with great thoughts, which are as fresh today as when they first passed through the author's minds ages ago. The only effect of time has been to **sift** out the bad products; for nothing in literature can long survive but what is really good.

书籍具有不朽的本质，是人类努力创造的最为持久的成果。寺庙会倒塌，神像会朽烂，而书却经久长存。对于伟大的思想来说，时间是无关紧要的。多年前初次闪现于作者脑海的伟大思想今日依然清新如故。时间唯一的作用是淘汰不好的作品，因为只有真正的佳作才能经世长存。

Books introduce us into the best society; they bring us into the presence of the greatest minds that have ever lived. We hear what they said and did; we see them

书籍介绍我们与最优秀的人为伍，使我们置身于历代伟人巨匠之间，如闻其声，如观其行，如见其人，同他们情感交融，悲喜与共，

as if they were really alive; we sympathize with them, enjoy with them, **grieve** with them; their experience becomes ours, and we feel as if we were in a measure actors with them in the scenes which they describe.

感同身受。我们觉得自己仿佛在作者所描绘的舞台上和他们一起作为演员登场。

The great and good do not die, even in this world. **Embalmed** in books, their spirits walk abroad. The book is a living voice. It is an intellect to which one still listens.

即使在人世间，伟大杰出的人物也永生不朽。他们的精神被载入书册，传于四海。书是人们至今仍在聆听的智慧之声，永远充满着活力。

魅力词汇

adversity [əd'vəːsiti] *n.* 逆境，不幸
distress [di'stres] *n.* 危难
console [kən'səul] *v.* 安慰，慰问
affinity [ə'finiti] *n.* 喜爱
urn [əːn] *n.* 瓮
enshrine [in'ʃrain] *v.* 保存某物于……
sift [sift] *v.* 筛，筛滤
grieve [griːv] *v.* 感到悲痛，伤心
embalm [im'baːm] *v.* 使不被遗忘

温情絮语

Pain past is pleasure.

过去的痛苦就是快乐。

That when you harbor bitterness, happiness will dock elsewhere.

当你遭遇苦难，幸福总会在某处停靠。

7 Thorough Understanding of Oneself
彻悟自我

面对挫折能够虚怀若谷，大智若愚，保持一种恬淡平和的心境，是彻悟人生的大度。

文苑漫步

In all one's lifetime it is oneself that one spends the most time being with or dealing with. But it is precisely oneself that one has the least understanding of. When you are going upwards in life you tend to overestimate yourself. When you are going downhill you tend to underestimate yourself. It's likely that you think it wise for yourself to know your place and stay **aloof** from worldly wearing a mask of **cowardice**, behind which the flow of **sap** in your life will be **retarded**.

To get a **thorough** understanding of oneself is to gain a correct view of oneself and be a **sober** realist — aware of both one's strength and shortage. You may look forward hopefully to the future but be sure not to expect too much, for ideals can never be fully realized. You may be courageous to meet challenges but it should be clear to you where to direct your efforts.

To get a thorough understanding of oneself needs self-appreciation. Whether

译林畅游

人生在世，和自己相处最多，打交道最多，但是又最不了解的人恰恰是自己。当你一帆风顺时，往往高估自己；不得志时，又往往低估自己。你可能认为安分守己、与世无争是明智之举，而这实际上往往是被怯懦的面具窒息了自己鲜活的生命。

彻底了解自己，就是正确认识自己，做一个冷静的现实主义者，既知道自己的优势，也知道自己的不足。我们可以憧憬人生，但不要期望过高。因为在现实中，理想的实现总是会打折扣的。你可以勇敢地迎接挑战，但是必须清楚自己努力的方向。

要彻底了解自己就要欣赏自己。无论你是一棵参天大树，还是

you liken yourself to a towering tree or a blade of grass, whether you think you are a high mountain or a small stone, you represent a state of nature that has its own reason of existence. If you earnestly admire yourself you'll have a real sense of self-appreciation, which will give you confidence. As soon as you gain full confidence in yourself, you'll be enabled to fight and overcome any **adversity**.

一棵无名小草，无论你想要成为一座高山，还是一块小石头，你都是一种自然状态，都有自己存在的理由。只要你认真地欣赏自己，你就会拥有一个真正的自我，这样你才会拥有信心。一旦拥有了信心你就能战胜任何困难。

To get a thorough understanding of oneself also requires doing oneself a favor when it's needed. In time of anger, do yourself a favor by giving **vent** to it in a quiet place so that you won't be hurt by its flames; in time of sadness, do yourself a favor by sharing it with your friends so as to change a **gloomy** mood into a cheerful one; in time of tiredness, do yourself a favor by getting a good sleep or taking some **tonic**. Show yourself loving concern about your health and daily life. Unless you know perfectly well when and how to do yourself a favor, you won't be confident and ready enough to resist the attack of illness.

要彻底了解自己，就要在需要的时候善待自己。在气愤时善待自己，找个僻静之处宣泄一下，不要被那些无名之火伤害；忧伤时，要善待自己，找个朋友倾诉一番，让低迷的情绪高涨起来；劳累时，要善待自己，睡个好觉或者吃点滋补品，对自己的健康和生活关心备至。唯有知道如何善待自己，你才会信心百倍，从容不迫地准备应对疾病的侵袭。

To get a thorough understanding of oneself is to get a full control of one's life. Then one will find one's life full of color and flavor.

彻底了解了自己，你才能把握自己的生命，你的生活才会丰富多彩、有滋有味！

魅力词汇

aloof [ə'luːf] *adv.* 远离
cowardice ['kauədis] *n.* 怯懦
sap [sæp] *n.* 活力
retard ['ritɑːd] *v.* 妨碍
thorough ['θʌrə] *adj.* 彻底的
sober ['səubə] *adj.* 冷静的，清醒的
adversity [əd'vəːsəti] *n.* 逆境
vent [vent] *n.*（感情的）发泄
gloomy ['gluːmi] *adj.* 沮丧的
tonic ['tɔnik] *n.* 补药

8 Fear of Six Inches 六英尺的恐惧

仅仅六英尺，却是一晚上的胆战心惊。我们的生活是否也是这样呢？我们看不到前路，不知道脚下到底是石头还是万丈深渊，那么我们如何选择呢？

文苑漫步

A man walking in the night **slipped** from a rock. Afraid that he would fall down thousands of feet, because he knew that place was a very deep **valley**, he took hold of a branch that was hanging over the rock. In the night all he could see was a bottomless **abyss**. He shouted, his own shout reflected back — there was nobody to hear.

You can imagine that man and his whole night of scare. Every moment there was death, his hands were becoming cold, he was losing his **grip**... and as the sun came out, he looked down and he laughed. There was no abyss. Just six **inches** down there was a rock. He could have rested the whole night, slept well — the rock was big enough — but the whole night was a **nightmare**.

译林畅游

一个人在赶夜路时，突然从岩石上跌了下去，吓得他赶紧抓住了岩石下的树枝，因为他知道这一带有个深谷，一不小心就会跌入上千英尺的深渊。一晚上，他唯一能看到的就是深不见底的峡谷。他大呼救命，但只听到了自己的回音——没有人能听到他呼救。

你可以想象一下他的处境和整晚的恐惧。死神随时都可能降临。他的手开始发凉，渐渐地抓不住了……当太阳升起的时候，他朝下看了看，笑了。下面压根就没有什么深渊。在他下方六英尺的地方有一块大石头。岩石那么大，他本可以在那儿休息一个晚上，美美地睡上一觉，但昨晚他却在梦魇中度过。

Fear is only six inches deep. Now it is up to you whether you want to go on cling to the branch and turn your life into a nightmare, or whether you would love to leave the branch and stand on your feet.

恐惧只是六英尺的距离而已。接下来，到了你做决定的时候了：你是想要继续抓着树枝过梦魇一般的生活，还是更喜欢把手从树枝上松开，双脚着地？

魅力词汇

slip [slip] *v.* 滑倒
valley ['væli] *n.* 山谷
abyss [ə'bis] *n.* 深渊
grip [grip] *n.* 紧握
inch [intʃ] *n.* 英寸
nightmare ['naitmeə] *n.* 恶梦

温情絮语

Misfortunes tell us what fortune is.

不经灾祸不知福。

If you shed tears when you miss the sun, you also miss the stars.

如果你因失去了太阳而流泪，那么你也将失去群星了。

9 A Story on an Island 孤岛上的故事

上帝在关上一扇门的时候会为你敞开一扇窗户，生活中的困境有时候只是美好事物的表象。苦难和困境总是不时地挡在美好事物的面前，阻止你迈向美好的事物，像阻止王子和白雪公主的王后一样，令人讨厌、畏惧。殊不知美好事物是磨难身后的影子，隐藏在磨难背后，向你微笑、招手。所以无论遭遇什么样的磨难，都不要失去信心，美好的事物就在前面。

文苑漫步

The only survivor of a shipwreck was washed up on a small, uninhabited island. He prayed **feverishly** for God to rescue him, and every day he scanned the horizon for help, but none seemed forthcoming.

Exhausted, he eventually managed to build a little **hut** out of driftwood to protect him from **the elements**, and to store his few possessions.

But then one day, after **scavenging** for food, he arrived home to find his little hut in flames, the smoke rolling up to the sky.

The worst had happened; everything was lost.

He **was stunned with** grief and anger. "God, how could you do this to me!"

译林畅游

在一场船难中，唯一的幸存者漂流到一座荒无人烟的小岛上。他焦躁不安地祈祷上帝能够救他。每天他都注视着海面，看是否有可搭救他的人，但似乎没有人前来。

感觉筋疲力尽时，他最终决定用浮木造一个简陋的小木屋，以保护自己在这险恶的环境中生存，并且保存他所剩无几的东西。

但有一天，在他搜寻完食物回到小屋时，却发现他的小屋陷入熊熊烈火之中，滚滚浓烟不断向天上窜。

最糟糕的事情发生了。他所有的一切通通化为乌有。

他既悲痛又愤怒，茫然不知所措，怒喊道："神啊！你怎么可以这

he cried.

Early the next day, however, he was awakened by the sound of a ship that was approaching the island. It had come to rescue him.

"How did you know I was here?" he asked the **weary** man of the rescuers.

"We saw your smoke signal," they replied.

It is easy to get discouraged when things are going bad. But we shouldn't lose heart, because God is at work in our lives, even in the midst of pain and suffering.

Remember, next time your little hut is burning to the ground, it just may be a smoke signal that **summons** the grace of God. For all the negative things we have to say to ourselves, God has a positive answer for it.

样对我！"

第二天一早，他被一艘正向小岛驶近的船只的鸣笛声吵醒。那是来救他的。

"你们怎么知道我在这里？"他问那些船员中一个充满倦意的人。

"我们看到了你发出的烟雾信号。"他们回答说。

人处于困境时，很容易变得沮丧。但我们不应失去信心，因为上帝一直在我们的生活中，甚至在我们遭遇疼痛和苦难时也是这样。

记住：当下一次你的小木屋烧毁时，那可能只是召唤上帝美妙恩典的烟雾信号而已。所有我们认为负面的事情，上帝都有正面的回答。

魅力词汇

feverishly ['fiːvəriʃli] *adv.* 焦躁不安地
hut [hʌt] *n.* 小屋
the elements ['eliməntş] 自然力（如风、雨和寒冷），恶劣天气
scavenge ['skævindʒ] *v.* 搜寻（事物等）
be stunned with 因……而震惊
weary ['wiəri] *adj.* 疲倦的
summon ['sʌmən] *v.* 传唤，召唤

10 Making Sandcastles 堆沙堡

面对巨浪的时候，小男孩没有悲哀、恐惧，也没有遗憾，相反，他却欢呼雀跃。那是因为他知道这一切总是会发生的，所以，他并不感到惊讶。而成功的男人在面对这岁月的巨浪时，充满了愤怒、恐惧，以及深深的无奈，是什么造成了这两者如此大的差异呢？

文苑漫步

A little boy is on his knees **scooping** and packing the sand with plastic shovels into a bright blue bucket. Then he **upends** the bucket on the surface and lifts it. And, to the delight of the little architect, a castle tower is created.

All afternoon he works, scooping out the moat and packing the walls. Bottle tops are **sentries**. Sticks are bridges. A sandcastle has been built.

Big city. Busy streets. Rumbling traffic.

A man is in his office. At his desk he puts papers into stacks and **assigns** tasks. The phone is on his shoulder and he is knocking the keyboard with his fingers. Contracts are signed and much to the delight of the man, a profit is made.

译林畅游

一个小男孩跪在那儿，正在用塑料铲挖沙子，他把沙子装在一个浅蓝色的桶里，然后把蓝桶倒扣在地上，再把它提起。令这个小建筑师高兴的是：一座城堡的塔楼就这样诞生了。

整个下午，他都在做这件事情：挖掘壕沟，建筑城墙。用瓶盖做岗哨，用木棍做桥梁，就这样，一座城堡建成了。

繁华的城市，熙攘的街道，川流不息的交通。

一个男人在他的办公室里。他坐在办公桌前，把文件堆叠在一起，布置任务。他将电话夹在肩头，手指敲击键盘。合同签字生效，令这个男人高兴的是，一笔盈利就这样到手了。

All his life he works, **formulating** the plans, **forecasting** the future. Profits are sentries. Capital gains are bridges. An empire has been built.

Two builders of two castles. They have much in common. They shape little pebbles into grand buildings. They are **diligent** and determined. And for both the tide will rise and the end will come.

As the waves near, the wise child jumps to his feet and begins to clap. There is no sorrow. No fear. No regret. He knew this would happen. He is not surprised.

And when the great breaker crashes into his castle and his **masterpiece** is sucked into the sea, he smiles. He smiles, picks up his tools, takes his father's hand, and goes home.

The grownup, however, is not so wise. As the wave of years **collapses** on his castle he is terrified. He tries to protect the sandy **monument**. He blocks the waves from the walls he has made. Salt-water soaked and shivering he **snarls** at the incoming tide.

"It's my castle," he protests.

The ocean need not respond. Both know to whom the sand belongs...

I don't know much about sandcastles. But children do. Watch them and learn. Go ahead and build, but build with a child's heart.

整个一生，他都在工作： 制定规划，预测未来。利润就是岗哨，资本增加就是桥梁，一个帝国就这样建成了。

这两座城堡的建筑者有许多共同之处。他们会把细小的沙石变成宏伟的建筑。他们勤奋用功、意志坚决，而对于他们两个而言，涨潮都会发生，一切都会结束。

当巨浪来临时，聪明的小男孩欢呼雀跃，拍手鼓掌，没有悲哀，没有恐惧，没有遗憾。因为他知道这一切都会发生，所以，他并不感到惊讶。

当这巨大的破坏者击碎他的城堡，将他的杰作卷入大海，男孩笑了，收拾好他的工具，拉着父亲的手回家了。

但是，这位成年人就没有这么聪明了。当岁月的巨浪击毁他的城堡时，他害怕了，他试图保护这沙质纪念碑。他试图阻止巨浪袭击他建的城墙。然而，咸咸的海水将他的城堡湮没了，他颤抖着，朝那来临的潮水咆哮着。

“这是我的城堡。”他抗议道。

海洋不需要回应。两者都明白沙子的归宿……

我对沙堡所知甚少，但孩子们知道，看看他们，向他们学习。走上前去建造吧，但是要用一颗孩童的心去建造。

When the sun sets and the tides take—**applaud**.

Salute the process of life and go home.

当太阳升起，潮水将沙堡带走，鼓掌吧。

向生命的过程敬礼，回家。

魅力词汇

scoop [skuːp] *v.* 汲取，舀取，挖空

upend [ʌp'end] *v.* 竖直，颠倒

sentry ['sentri] *n.* 卫兵，哨兵，步哨

assign [ə'sain] *v.* 分配，指派

formulate ['fɔːmjuleit] *v.* 构想出，规划

forecast ['fɔːkaːst] *v.* 预测

diligent ['dilidʒənt] *adj.* 勤奋的

masterpiece ['maːstəpiːs] *n.* 杰作

collapse [kə'læps] *v.* 倒坍，崩溃

monument ['mɔnjumənt] *n.* 纪念碑

snarl [snaːl] *v.* 吼叫，怒骂

applaud [ə'plɔːd] *v.* 拍手喝采

salute [sə'luːt] *v.* 行礼，致意，问候

温情絮语

Life is a chain of moments of enjoyment, not only about survival.

生活是一串串的快乐时光，我们不仅仅是为了生存而生存。

That it's those small daily happenings that make life so spectacular.

正是一些生活的琐碎让生命壮丽。

11 On the Fear of Death
对死亡的恐惧

死亡，是每个人都无法逃避的生命终点。到底我们该如何看待那终将会到来的终点线呢？本文或许可以给我们一些启发……

文苑漫步

Perhaps the best cure for the fear of death is to **reflect** that life has a beginning as well as an end. There was a time when we were not: this gives me no concern. Why then should it trouble us that a time will come when we shall **cease to be**? I have no wish to have been alive a hundred years ago, or in the reign of Queen Anne. Why should I regret and lay it so much to heart that I shall not be alive a hundred years hence, **in the reign of** I cannot tell whom?

To die is only to be as we were born; yet no one feels any **remorse**, or regret, or **repugnance**, in contemplating this last idea. It is rather a relief and disburdening of the mind; it seems to have been a holiday time with us then; we were not called to appear upon the stage of life, to wear robes or **tatters**, to laugh or cry, be **hooted**

译林畅游

也许克服对于死亡的恐惧的最好的办法是思考生命既有开始，就有终结。过去曾有过一段时间，我们并不存在，这也没有让我们多担心。所以当我们有一天不复存在的时候，我们又为什么要担心呢？既然我并不想活在一百年前或者是安妮女王的时代，那么我为什么还要遗憾或在意自己不能生活在一百年以后说不出谁是统治者的时代呢？

死亡只不过是回到出生以前的样子而已。当我们这样想的时候，没有感到懊悔，遗憾或者厌烦，反而感受到心灵的解脱和慰藉。生前我们仿佛在度假一样，我们没有被召唤至人生舞台上，穿上华服或者破衣，在舞台上欢笑或者痛哭，被人唾弃或者被人称赞。相反地，我

or applauded; we had lain **perdu** all this while, sung out of harm's way; and had slept out our thousands of centuries without wanting to be waked up; at peace and free from care, in a long nonage, in a sleep deeper and calmer than that of infancy, wrapped in the softest and finest dust. And the worst that we dread is, after a short **fretful**, **feverish** being, after vain hopes, and idle fears, to sink to final **repose** again, and forget the trouble dream of life!

们潜藏了很久，安详而自在地远离伤害，熟睡了千百个世纪也不愿意被唤醒，舒适惬意而且无忧无虑，长期处于幼年期，远比婴儿的沉睡更加深沉平和，被最轻柔、最细致的尘埃所拥抱。我们最担心的只不过是在短暂的烦躁和狂热的生存，空虚的期盼以及无谓的恐惧之后，再度沉入最终的长眠，忘记生命中的那些噩梦。

魅力词汇

reflect [ri'flekt] *v.* 反映，归咎
cease to be 死去，停止存在
in the reign of 在……的统治下
remorse [ri'mɔːs] *n.* 懊悔，悔恨
repugnance [ri'pʌgnəns] *n.* 厌恶
tatter ['tætə] *n.* 破布，碎纸
hoot [huːt; hut] *v.* 大声叫嚣，鸣响
perdu ['pəːdjuː,ˌpəː'djuː] *adj.* 看不见的
fretful ['fretful] *adj.* 烦燥的，焦燥的
feverish ['fiːvəriʃ] *adj.* 兴奋的
repose [ri'pəuz] *n.* 休息，睡眠，静止

温情絮语

Don't cry cause it is over, smile, cause it happened.

不要因为结束而哭泣，微笑吧，为你的曾经拥有。

12 A Fable 看画

这是由马克·吐温写的一则小寓言故事。每个动物都从那面镜子中看到了自己，然而它们却没有从这些表象中找到镜子的特点。镜子在我们的生命中意味着什么呢？

文苑漫步

Once upon a time an artist who had painted a small and very beautiful picture placed it so that he could see it in the mirror. He said, "This doubles the distance and softens it, and it is twice as lovely as it was before."

The animals out in the woods heard of this through the housecat, who was greatly admired by them because he was so **learned**, and so refined and civilized, and so polite and **well-bred**, and could tell them so much which they didn't know before, and were not certain about afterward. They were much excited about this new piece of **gossip**, and they asked questions, so as to get at a full understanding of it. They asked what a picture was, and the cat explained.

"It is a flat thing," he said; "wonderfully flat, marvelously flat, **enchantingly**

译林畅游

从前，有位画家画了一幅得意之作，并把它挂在一个他能从镜子里看到的地方，他说："这下看上去距离倍增，色调柔和，感觉比先前更好了。"

画家的猫把这件事告诉了森林中的众兽。众兽对这只家猫向来推崇备至，因为它博学多才、温文尔雅、讲文明彬彬有礼、极有修养，能告诉它们很多它们以前不知道，甚至高深莫测的事。听了这条新闻，它们都很激动，于是连连发问，以便充分了解情况。它们问画是什么样的，猫就讲解了起来。

"那是一种平的东西，"它说，"出奇地平，绝妙地平，迷人地平，

flat and elegant. And, oh, so beautiful!"

十分精致，而且，太漂亮了！"

That excited them almost to a **frenzy**, and they said they would give the world to see it. Then the bear asked:

动物们听了之后更加疯狂了，说无论如何要看看这张画。熊问：

"What is it that makes it so beautiful?"

"是什么使得它那么漂亮呢？"

"It is the looks of it," said the cat.

"是它的美貌。"猫说。

This filled them with admiration and uncertainty, and they were more excited than ever. Then the cow asked: "What is a mirror?"

这个答复令众兽更赞叹不已，更觉得高深莫测，它们越发激动。接着牛问："镜子究竟是个什么东西？"

"It is a hole in the wall," said the cat. "You look in it, and there you see the picture, it is so **dainty** and charming and **ethereal** and inspiring in its unimaginable beauty that your head turns round and round, and you almost **swoon** with ecstasy."

"镜子就是挂在墙上的一个洞，"猫说，"朝洞里看进去，你就能见到那张画，在那难以想象的美妙中，它显得那样地迷人，那样地惟妙惟肖，那样地令人鼓舞，你看了以后会有些头晕，有些飘飘然的感觉。"

The ass had not said anything as yet; he now began to throw doubts. He said there had never been anything as beautiful as this before, and probably wasn't now. He said that when it took a whole basketful of **sesquipedalian** adjectives to **whoop up** a thing of beauty, it was time for suspicion.

一直在旁边沉默的驴此时开口提出质疑了。它说以前从没有那样漂亮的东西，也许现在也没有。又说用一整篓形容词来宣扬一样东西的美丽时，就是需要怀疑之时。

It was easy to see that these doubts were having an effect upon the animals, so the cat went off offended. The subject was dropped for a couple of days, but in the meantime curiosity was taking a fresh start, and there was a **revival** of interest **perceptible**. Then the animals **assailed** the ass for spoiling what could possibly have been a pleasure to them, on a mere suspicion that the picture was not beauti-

驴的怀疑论使众兽也产生了怀疑，猫觉得受到了侮辱当下就离开了。这个话题被搁了几天，但与此同时，众兽的好奇心极度膨胀，那种想一睹为快的兴趣又复活了。于是众兽纷纷责备驴把那也许能给它们带来乐趣的事弄糟了，而这种仅仅对那画的漂亮产生的怀疑，却没有任何根据。驴不加理睬，安之若素，说只有一个办法可以证明它和

ful, without any evidence that such was the case. The ass was not troubled; he was calm, and said there was one way to find out who was in the right, himself or the cat: he would go and look in that hole, and come back and tell what he found there. The animals felt relieved and grateful, and asked him to go at once — which he did.

猫谁是正确的。它要去看那洞，然后回来报告它的真实所见。众兽感到既宽慰又感激，请它马上去，于是驴便动身去看那个洞。

But he did not know where he ought to stand; and so, through error, he stood between the picture and the mirror. The result was that the picture had no chance, and didn't show up. He returned home and said:

但是驴不知道该站在什么地方，最后错误地站到画和镜子之间，结果那画没法在镜子中出现，它回去说：

"The cat lied. There was nothing in that hole but an ass. There wasn't a sign of a flat thing visible. It was a handsome ass, and friendly, but just an ass, and nothing more."

"猫撒谎，那洞里什么都没有，没有看见平的东西，只有一只漂亮的、友善的驴，仅仅一头驴，什么都没有。"

The elephant asked: "Did you see it good and clear? Were you close to it?"

象问："你看仔细、看清楚了吗？你挨得近吗？"

"I saw it good and clear, O Hathi, King of Beasts. I was so close that I touched noses with it."

"当然了，我发誓，没有谁比我看得更清楚、更仔细了。噢！万兽之王，我挨得那么近，我的鼻子和它的鼻子都碰上了。"

"This is very strange," said the elephant; "the cat was always truthful before, as far as we could make out. Let another witness try. Go, Baloo, look in the hole, and come and report."

"这就怪了，"象说，"据我们所知，猫以前是可信的，再让一位去试试看。去，巴罗，你再去看看那个洞，然后报告你所看到的。"

So the bear went. When he came back, he said: "Both the cat and the ass have lied; there was nothing in the hole but a bear."

熊接到命令立即前往，回来后它说："猫和驴都说谎，洞里除了有头熊外，啥也没有。"

Great was the surprise and puzzle-

众兽大为惊奇，迷惑不解，现在谁都渴望亲自去尝试一下，搞个

ment of the animals. Each was now anxious to make the test himself and get at the straight truth. The elephant sent them one at a time.

水落石出。于是，象便让他们一个一个地去看那个洞。

First, the cow. She found nothing in the hole but a cow.

母牛先去看了，发现那个洞里除了一头母牛之外什么都没有。

The tiger found nothing in it but a tiger.

虎发现洞里除了一只虎，啥也没有。

The lion found nothing in it but a lion.

狮发现洞里除了一只狮，啥也没有。

The leopard found nothing in it but a leopard.

豹发现洞里除了一只豹，啥也没有。

The camel found a camel and nothing more.

骆驼发现洞里除了一只骆驼，啥也没有。

Then Hathi was wroth, and said he would have the truth, if he had to go and fetch it himself. When he returned, he abused his whole subjectry for liars, and was in an **unappeasable fury** with the moral and mental blindness of the cat. He said that anybody but a near-sighted fool could see that there was nothing in the hole but an elephant.

象听了它们的报告，怒不可遏，决定亲自前往，弄个水落石出。象回来后，不客气地训斥了它的全体庶民，因为它们全都撒谎，对猫的无视道德及盲人摸象的做法更是怒不可遏，它说："除非是个近视的傻瓜，否则，不论谁都能看得出来，那个洞里明明只有一头象。"

魅力词汇

learned ['ləːnid] *adj.* 有学问的，博学的
well-bred ['welːbred] *adj.* 有教养的
gossip ['gɔsip] *n.* 闲聊，随笔
enchantingly [in'tʃaːntiŋli] *adv.* 夺人心魂地
frenzy ['frenzi] *n.* 狂暴，狂怒
dainty ['deinti] *adj.* 优美的，讲究的
ethereal [i'θiəriəl] *adj.* 轻飘的
swoon [swuːn] *v.* 昏晕，晕倒
sesquipedalian [ˌseskwipi'deiliən] *n.* 冗长的单字
whoop up 狂欢，哄抬
revival [ri'vaivəl] *n.* 恢复
perceptible [pə'septəbl] *adj.* 可察觉的
assail [ə'seil] *v.* 攻击
unappeasable ['ʌnə'piːzəbl] *adj.* 无法平息的
fury ['fjuəri] *n.* 狂怒

13 Put the Glass Down 放下玻璃杯

一杯水要让你举一分钟，这没有什么问题。但是若要你举上一个小时甚至举上一整天，那么你就会受不了。生活中的我们也是一样，不能始终背负着重担压力，适时地将其卸下，给自己的心放个假期，这样才能真正地享受生活。

文苑漫步

A lecturer was giving a lecture to his student on stress management.

He raised a glass of water and asked the audience, "How heavy do you think this glass of water is?"

The students' answers **ranged from** 20g to 500g.

"It does not matter on the **absolute** weight. It depends on how long you hold it. If I hold it for a minute, it is OK. If I hold it for an hour, I will have an ache in my right arm. If I hold it for a day, you will have to call an **ambulance**. It is the exact same weight, but the longer I hold it, the heavier it becomes.

"If we carry our burdens all the time, sooner or later, we will not be able to carry on, the burden becoming increasingly

译林畅游

一位讲师正在给他的学生讲如何处理压力。

他端着一杯水，然后问学生："你们认为这杯水有多重？"

学生们的回答从20克到500克不等。

"它的实际重量并不重要，这取决于你端它有多久。倘若我端它一分钟，没问题。如果我端它一个钟头，我的右臂会觉得疼。假如我一整天都端着它，你们就要叫辆救护车了。重量都是一样的，但我端着它越久，它就越重。"

"如果我们总是背负着担子，迟早，我们将无法承担，这个担子会变得愈加沉重。你要做的就是放

heavier. What you have to do is to put the glass down, rest for a while before holding it up again."

下这杯水，休息一下再端起来。"

We have to put down the burden **periodically**, so that we can be **refreshed** and are able to carry on.

我们必须要定期地放下杯子，这样我们才能恢复力气继续端起它。

So before you return home from work tonight, put the burden of work down. Don't carry it back home. You can pick it up tomorrow.

因此，今晚下班回家后，放下工作的担子。不要将它带回家。你可以明天再担起它。

Whatever burdens you are having now on your shoulders, let it down for a moment if you can.

不管你肩上有什么担子，如果可以的话，先放下一会儿。

Life is short, enjoy it!

人生短暂，要学会享受！

魅力词汇

range from 从……到……
absolute ['æbsəluːt] *adj.* 绝对的
ambulance ['æmbjuləns] *n.* 救护车
periodically [ˌpiəri'ɔdikəli] *adv.* 周期性地，定期地
refreshed ['ri'freʃt] *adj.* 恢复精神的

温情絮语

Be yourself and stay unique. Your imperfections make you beautiful, lovable, and valuable.

坚持做唯一的自己，正是你的缺点体现了你的美丽，你的可爱，更体现了你的价值。

14 Clear Your Mental Space
清理心灵的空间

通过给自己空间，真正体会消极情绪，你是在处理这种情绪，而不是将其压制下去然后尽量不加理会。通过给予消极情绪所需的空间和关注，你实际上是在消解其力量。当你沉浸在那种情绪之中，并且明白它只是一种情绪时，你就摆脱了它的控制。你就可以清理头脑继续做事了。

文苑漫步

Think about the last time you felt a negative emotion — like stress, anger, or frustration. What was going through your mind as you were going through that negativity? Was your mind cluttered with thoughts? Or was it **paralyzed**, unable to think?

The next time you find yourself in the middle of a very stressful time, or you feel angry or frustrated, stop. Yes, that's right, stop. Whatever you're doing, stop and sit for one minute. While you're sitting there, completely **immerse** yourself in the negative emotion.

Allow that emotion to consume you. Allow yourself one minute to truly feel that emotion. Don't cheat yourself here. Take the entire minute—but only one minute—to do nothing else but feel that emotion.

When the minute is over, ask yourself,

译林畅游

想一下你最近一次感受到的消极情绪——比如压力、愤怒或挫败感。当你处于那种消极情绪时你在想些什么？你的脑海中是充满了混乱的思绪？还是陷于麻木，无法思考？

下次当你发现自己神经紧张时，或是你感到气愤或沮丧时，停下来。是的，对，停下来。不管你在做什么，停下来坐上一分钟。坐着的时候，让自己完全沉浸在那种消极情绪之中。

让那种消极情绪吞噬你，给自己一分钟的时间去真正地感受那种情绪，不要欺骗自己。花整整一分钟的时间——但只有一分钟——别的什么也不要做，只体会那种情绪。

当一分钟结束时，问自己：“在

"Am I willing to keep holding on to this negative emotion as I go through the rest of the day?"

今天余下的时间里，我是否想继续保持这种消极情绪？"

Once you've allowed yourself to be totally immersed in the emotion and really feel it, you will be surprised to find that the emotion clears rather quickly.

一旦你允许自己完全沉浸在那种情绪当中并真正体会它，你就会惊奇地发现那种情绪很快就消失了。

If you feel you need to hold on to the emotion for a little longer, that is OK. Allow yourself another minute to feel the emotion.

如果你觉得还需要点时间来保持那种情绪，没关系，再给自己一分钟的时间去体会它。

When you feel you've had enough of the emotion, ask yourself if you're willing to carry that negativity with you for the rest of the day. If not, take a deep breath. As you **exhale**, release all that negativity with your breath.

如果你觉得自己已经充分体会了那种情绪，那就问自己是否愿意在今天余下的时间里继续保持那种消极的情绪。如果不愿意，那就深呼吸。呼气的时候，把所有的消极情绪都释放出去。

This exercise seems simple — almost too simple. But, it is very effective. By allowing that negative emotion the space to be truly felt, you are dealing with the emotion rather than stuffing it down and trying not to feel it. You are actually taking away the power of the emotion by giving it the space and attention it needs. When you immerse yourself in the emotion, and realize that it is only emotion, it loses its control. You can clear your head and proceed with your task.

这个方法似乎很简单——几乎是太过简单了，但却非常有效。通过给自己空间真正体会消极情绪，你是在处理这种情绪，而不是将其压制下去然后尽量不加理会。通过给予消极情绪所需的空间和关注，你实际上是在消解其力量。当你沉浸在那种情绪之中，并且明白它只是一种情绪时，你就摆脱了它的控制。你就可以清理思绪继续做事了。

魅力词汇

paralyze ['pærəlaiz] *v.* 使……麻木，使……瘫痪

immerse [i'məːs] *v.* 浸，陷入

exhale [eks'heil] *v.* 呼气

15 "There" Is No Better than "Here"
彼岸无尽头，知足才常乐

与饥饿哭泣的人相比，能够吃饱自然就是幸福；
与寒冷号啼的人相比，得到温暖自然就是幸福；
与辛劳服役的人相比，悠闲度日自然就是幸福；
与身患疾病的人相比，健康强壮自然就是幸福；
与遭受灾祸的人相比，平安无事自然就是幸福；
与夭寿死去的人相比，健康活着自然就是幸福。

文苑漫步

Many people believe that they will be happy once they arrive at some specific goal they set for themselves. However, **more often than not**, once you arrive "there" you will still feel dissatisfied, and move your "there" vision to yet another point in the future. By always **chasing** after another "there" you are never really appreciating what you already have right "here". It is important for human beings to keep "**sober-minded**" about the age-old drive to look beyond the place where you now stand. On one hand, your life is enhanced by your dreams and aspirations. On the other hand, these drives can pull you farther and farther from your enjoy-

译林畅游

许多人都相信，只有实现了自己所设定的某个特定目标，我们才会幸福快乐。然而事实往往并非如此，当你到达彼岸时，你还是会感到不知足，而且又会给未来设定另一个目标。由于你总是劳心费神地去追逐一个又一个的彼岸，你从未真正感恩你已经拥有的一切。不安于现状的欲望人皆有之，由来已久，但重要的是要对它保持清醒的头脑。一方面，因为梦想和渴望，你的生活才变得更加精彩。另一方面，这些欲望又使你离享受现有生活越来越远。假如你能懂得感恩，学会知足，你就会离解决现实生活的挑战越来越近。

ment of your life right now. By learning the lessons of gratitude and abundance, you can bring yourself closer to fulfilling the challenge of living in the present.

Gratitude

To be grateful means you are thankful for and appreciative of what you have and where you are on your path right now. Gratitude fills your heart with the joyful feeling and allows you to fully appreciate everything that arises on your path. As you strive to keep your focus on the present moment, you can experience the full wonder of "here".

There are many ways to **cultivate** gratitude. Here are just a few suggestions you may wish to try:

1. Imagine what your life would be like if you lost all that you had. This will most surely remind you of how much you do appreciate it.

2. Make a list each day of all that you are grateful for, so that you can stay conscious daily of your blessings. Do this especially when you are feeling as though you have nothing to feel grateful for. Or spend a few minutes before you go to sleep giving thanks for all that you have.

3. Spend time offering assistance to those who are less fortunate than you, so that you may gain perspective.

感恩之心

感恩是指对当前所拥有的一切以及所处的人生境遇怀有感激之情，并懂得珍惜。心存感恩，你的心灵就会满溢愉悦，你就能真正领会人生道路上的种种体验。如果你极力地将目光定格在此时此刻，你就能体会它的美妙之处。

有很多方法可以培养感恩之心。你不妨试试以下几种：

1. 试想一下，如果你失去了现在所拥有的一切，你的生活将会怎么样？它肯定会使你回想起原来你是多么喜欢和珍视这一切。

2. 每天，将你感激的那些事物都罗列出来，那样你就能时刻意识到自己的幸运。每天都要这么做，尤其是当你觉得好像没有什么可感恩的时候。或者，你也可以在睡前花几分钟对自己所拥有的一切表示感恩。

3. 花些时间帮助那些不如你幸运的人，这样你也许会对生活有更深刻的认识。

However you choose to learn gratitude is **irrelevant**. What really matters is that you create a space in your consciousness for appreciation for all that you have right now, so that you may live more joyously in your present moment.

Abundance

One of the most common human fears is scarcity. Many people are afraid of not having enough of what they need or want, and so they are always striving to get to a point when they would finally have enough.

Alan and Linda always dreamed of living "the good life". Both from poor working-class families, they married young and set out to fulfill their mutual goal of becoming wealthy. They both worked very hard for years, **amassing** a small fortune, so they could move from their two-bedroom home to a **palatial** seven-bedroom home in the most **upscale** neighborhood. They focused their energies on **accumulating** all the things they believed signified abundance: membership in the local **exclusive** country club, luxury cars, designer clothing, and high-class society friends. No matter how much they accumulated, however, it never seemed to be enough. They were unable to erase the deep fear of scarcity both had acquired in

其实，你选择何种方法去学会感恩，这无关紧要。在你的心灵深处留有一处净土，有意识地去感恩你现在所拥有的一切，这才是最为重要的。这样你也可以更快乐地享受目前的生活。

知足常乐

贫穷是人类最普遍的恐惧之一。许多人担心自己的所需所求不够，所以他们总是不懈努力以求有朝一日能心满意足。

Alan 和 Linda，都来自于贫苦的工薪家庭，他们一直都梦想着能过上“好日子”。他们早早就成了家，然后就开始为他们共同的致富目标奋斗。他们一起拼搏了好多年，积攒了一小笔钱财，从两居室搬到了一套坐落在最高档街区的富丽堂皇的七居室大房子。他们费尽心思去积聚那些他们认为是代表富足的东西：当地唯一的一家乡村俱乐部的会员资格、豪华汽车、名牌服装，以及上流社会的朋友。然而，无论他们积聚了多少，似乎永远不够。他俩谁都无法消除小时候对贫穷的刻骨铭心的恐惧。实际上，他们需要学会的就是知足常乐。之后，在1987年，股票市场遭受重创，Alan 和 Linda 损失惨重。祸不单行，一

childhood. They needed to learn the lesson of abundance. Then the stock market crashed in 1987, and Alan and Linda lost a considerable amount of money. A **bizarre** but costly lawsuit **depleted** another huge portion of their savings. One thing led to another, and they found themselves in a financial disaster. Assets needed to be sold, and eventually they lost the country club membership, the cars, and the house. It took several years and much hard work for Alan and Linda to land on their feet, and though they now live a life far from **extravagant**, they have taken stock of their lives and feel quite blessed. Only now, as they assess what they have left—a solid, loving marriage, their health, a **dependable** income, and good friends — do they realize that true abundance comes not from amassing, but rather from appreciating.

Scarcity consciousness arises as a result of the "hole-in-the-soul **syndrome**". This is when we attempt to fill the gaps in our inner lives with things from the outside world. But like puzzle pieces, you can't fit something in where it does not naturally belong. No amount of external objects, **affection**, love, or attention can ever fill an inner void. We already have enough, so we should revel in our own interior abundance.

场莫名其妙的昂贵的官司又耗尽了他们的一大笔积蓄，这一切使他们陷入了经济困境。他们不得不变卖家产，最后他们丢掉了乡村俱乐部的会员资格，失去了汽车和房子。Alan 和 Linda 努力奋斗了好几年才从困境中走出来。尽管他们现在的生活一点也不奢华，但是他们是自己生活的主宰，幸福而又知足。只有在这时，他们才掂量着那些尚未失去的东西——稳固相爱的婚姻、健康的身体、稳定的收入、真正的朋友，他们终于认识到，真正的富足不是来自财富的积聚，而是来自对所拥有的一切的珍惜。

贫穷感可以归因于“精神空虚综合症”，即我们试图用身外之物来填补内心的空缺。但就如同是拼图游戏一样，你不能把本来不属于那个地方的东西硬塞进去。任何身外之物、情感、关爱和关注都无法填补内心的空虚。我们拥有的已经足够，因此我们应该满足于内心世界的充实。

魅力词汇

more often than not 往往不是
chase [tʃeis] *v.* 追求，争取
sober-minded *adj.* 头脑清醒的
cultivate ['kʌltiveit] *v.* 培养
irrelevant [i'reləvənt] *adj.* 无关的
amass [ə'mæs] *v.* 积聚，收集
palatial [pə'leiʃəl] *adj.* 宫殿般的
upscale ['ʌpskeil] *adj.* 高端的
accumulate [ə'kjuːmjuleit] *v.* 积聚
exclusive [ik'skluːsiv] *adj.* 唯一的
bizarre [bi'zɑː] *adj.* 奇异的，怪诞的
deplete [di'pliːt] *v.* 耗尽，使……空竭
extravagant [ik'strævəgənt] *adj.* 奢侈的
dependable [di'pendəbl] *adj.* 可靠的
syndrome ['sindrəum] *n.* 综合症
affection [ə'fekʃn] *n.* 喜爱，感情

温情絮语

Wisdom in the mind is better than money in the hand.

脑中有知识，胜过手中有金钱。

Good advice is beyond all price.

忠告是无价宝。

16 Please Remember, You Are Special
请记住，你是与众不同的

在生活中，很多事情不是我们主观意愿所能控制的。很多时候我们的行为都被周围的环境所左右。有时，我们甚至会感到自己一无是处。但是不管发生了什么，我们都要坚信，自己是与众不同的，永远不要失去自己的价值。

文苑漫步

A well-known speaker started off his **seminar** by holding up a $20 bill. In the room of 200, he asked, "Who would like this $20 bill?"

Hands started going up. He said, "I am going to give this $20 to one of you, but first, let me do this."

He proceeded to **crumple** the 20 dollar note up. He then asked, "Who still wants it?" Still the hands were up in the air.

"Well," he replied, "what if I do this?" He dropped it on the ground and started to **grind** it into the floor with his shoe. He picked it up, now crumpled and dirty.

"Now, who still wants it?"

Still the hands went into the air.

译林畅游

一位著名演讲家手里拿着一张20美元的纸币，开始了讨论会。在200人的屋子里，他问道："谁想要这20美元纸币？"

开始有人举手。他说："我会把这20美元纸币给你们中间的一位，但是，我会先这么做。"

他开始把这张纸币揉皱，然后他问道："还有人想要它吗？"仍然有很多手举在空中。

"好，"他说道，"如果我这样做会怎么样呢？"他把纸币扔到地上，开始用皮鞋使劲踩踏。然后他拣起又脏又皱的纸币。

"现在，还有人要它吗？"

仍然有很多人举手。

"My friends, you have all learned a very valuable lesson. No matter what I did to the money, you still wanted it because it did not decrease in value. It was still worth $20."

"Many times in our lives, we are dropped, crumpled, and ground into the dirt by the decisions we make and the **circumstances** that come our way. We feel as though we are **worthless**; but no matter what happened or what will happen, you will never lose your value."

"Dirty or clean, crumpled or finely **creased**, you are still priceless to those who love you. The worth of our lives comes, not in what we do or who we know, but by Who We Are."

"You are special — don't ever forget it."

"朋友们，刚刚你们已经得出一个非常宝贵的经验。不管我怎么糟蹋这张纸币，你们仍然想要它，因为它的价值没有降低。它仍然是20美元。"

"在生活中，很多次我们被自己的决定和身边的环境所抛弃、蹂躏，甚至碾入尘土。我们感到自己好像一无是处。但是不管发生了什么，或者将来发生什么，你们都永远不会失去自己的价值。"

"无论你肮脏或者干净，皱巴巴的或者被折磨，对周围爱你的人来说你仍然是无价的。我们生活的价值不在于我们做了什么，或者我们认识谁，而是在于我们是谁。"

"你是与众不同的，永远不要忘记这一点！"

魅力词汇

seminar ['seminɑː] *n.* 讨论会，研讨班
crumple ['krʌmpl] *v.* 弄皱
grind [graind] *v.* 磨碎
circumstance ['səːkəmstəns] *n.* 环境
worthless ['wəːθlis] *adj.* 无价值的
crease [kriːs] *v.* 弄皱

温情絮语

In all one's lifetime it is oneself that one spends the most time being with or dealing with. But it is precisely oneself that one has the least understanding of.

一个人的一生中，与自己相处和打交道最多，却也最不了解自己。

17 The Real Meaning of Peace 宁静的真谛

什么是真正的宁静？一个没有噪音，没有动乱，没有烦扰的地方？这些都不是真正的宁静，真正的宁静是所有这些因素都存在于你的周围，而你的心中依然能保持安宁。心静如水，这才是宁静的真谛。

文苑漫步

There once was a king who offered a prize to the artist who would paint the best picture of peace. Many artists tried. The king looked at all the pictures. But there were only two he really liked, and he had to choose between them. One picture was of a calm lake. The lake was a perfect mirror for peaceful **towering** mountains all around it. **Overhead** was a blue sky with **fluffy** white clouds. All who saw this picture thought that it was a perfect picture of peace.

The other picture had mountains, too. But these were **rugged** and bare. Above was an angry sky, from which rain fell and in which lightning played. Down the side of the mountain **tumbled** a **foaming** waterfall. This did not look peaceful at all.

But when the king looked closely,

译林畅游

从前有个国王，悬赏能画出关于宁静最好的画的画家。很多画家都试过了。国王看了所有的作品，但他真正喜欢的只有两幅。他要从这两幅中选出一幅。一幅画中是一片宁静的湖泊，四周群山环绕，而湖泊就是一面完美的镜子。蓝色的天空中白云飘飘，每个看到这幅画的人都认为这真是一幅表现宁静的完美作品。

另一幅画也有山脉，但却崎岖不平，而且光秃秃的。上面是乌云密布的天空，而且狂风骤雨、闪电雷鸣，一条白色的瀑布从山的一侧倾泻下来。这看起来一点都不宁静。

然而当国王仔细地看了看，他

he saw behind the waterfall a tiny bush growing in a crack in the rock. In the bush a mother bird had built her nest. There, in the midst of the rush of angry water, sat the mother bird on her nest — in perfect peace.

看到在瀑布后面岩石的裂缝中长着一颗小小的灌木。一只鸟妈妈在灌木中搭了一个窝，它就这样安坐在自己的巢穴中，坐在汹涌的瀑布之后——如此宁静。

Which picture do you think won the prize? The king chose the second picture. Do you know why?

"Because," explained the king, "peace does not mean to be in a place where there is no noise, trouble, or hard work. Peace means to be in the midst of all those things and still be calm in your heart. That is the real meaning of peace."

你认为哪幅画得到了国王的悬赏呢？国王选择了第二幅。你知道为什么吗？

国王说："这是因为，宁静并不是指在一个没有噪音、没有烦扰、没有艰苦劳动的地方。宁静意味着所有这些因素都存在于你的周围，而你的心中依然能保持安宁。这才是宁静的真谛。"

魅力词汇

towering ['tauəriŋ] *adj.* 高耸的
overhead [əuvə'hed] *adv.* 在头顶上
fluffy ['flʌfi] *adj.* 蓬松的，松软的
rugged ['rʌgid] *adj.* 不平的
tumble ['tʌmbl] *v.* 倒下
foam [fəum] *v.* 起泡沫

温情絮语

Actions speak louder than words.

行动比语言更响亮。

18 Solitude 寂寞

本文节选自亨利·梭罗的传世名著《瓦尔登湖》。梭罗曾独自一人远离社会在瓦尔登湖畔生活了一段时间。而《瓦尔登湖》大部分内容都是梭罗在那个时期的一些思考。

文苑漫步

I find it **wholesome** to be alone the greater part of the time. To be in company, even with the best, is soon wearisome and **dissipating**. I love to be alone. I never found the companion that was so companionable as solitude. We are for the most part more lonely when we go abroad among men than when we stay in our chambers. A man thinking or working is always alone, let him be where he will. Solitude is not measured by the miles of space that **intervene** between a man and his fellows. The really diligent student in one of the crowded hives of Cambridge College is as solitary as a **dervish** in the desert. The farmer can work alone in the field or the woods all day, **hoeing** or chopping, and not feel lonesome, because he is employed; but when he comes home at night he cannot sit down in a room

译林畅游

我发现花大部分时间独处是有益的。与人为伴，即使最有默契，也很快会觉得乏味和浪费时间。我喜欢独处。没有比独处更宜人的陪伴了。我们走进人堆当中通常会比待在房中更感寂寞。人在思考和工作时总是孤独的，就让他随心而为。独处与否并非是用人与人之间的距离来衡量的。真正勤奋的学生，在剑桥拥挤的教室里感觉犹如苦行僧在沙漠中一样孤独。农夫可以在田里耕锄或在林里伐木一整天都不感到寂寞，因为他一直在工作着；但当他晚上归家，无论如何克制，他就一个人在房间里待不住了。他必须到人群里消遣。就他看来，这是对白天的孤独作出弥补。因此，他就不理解为何学生能花大半天和整夜独自待在屋里而不觉无聊和郁闷；然而他却不明白，学生

alone, at the mercy of his thoughts, but must be where he can see the folks, and **recreate**, and, as he thinks, remunerate himself for his day's solitude; and hence he wonders how the student can sit alone in the house all night and most of the day without **ennui** and the blues; but he does not realize that the student, though in the house, is still at work in his field, and chopping in his woods, as the farmer in his, and in turn seeks the same recreation and society that the latter does, though it may be a more condensed form of it.

在屋里，就等于他在田里和在林里工作，亦同样和他一样在消遣、社交，只不过是一种更浓缩的形式而已。

Society is commonly too cheap. We meet at very short intervals, not having had time to acquire any new value for each other. We meet at meals three times a day, and give each other a new taste of that old musty cheese that we are. We have had to agree on a certain set of rules, called **etiquette** and politeness, to make this frequent meeting tolerable and that we need not come to open war. We meet at the post-office, and at the sociable, and about the fireside every night; we live thick and are in each other's way, and **stumble over** one another, and I think that we thus lose some respect for one another. Certainly less frequency would **suffice** for all important and hearty communications. Consider the girls in a factory — never alone, hardly in their dreams. It would be better if there were but one inhabitant to a square mile, as where I live. The value of a man is not

社交往往廉价。相聚的时间之短促，来不及使彼此获得任何新的有价值的东西。我们在每日三餐的时间里相见，大家重新尝尝我们这种发霉乳酪的味道。我们都必须同意若干条规则，那就是所谓的礼节和礼貌，使得这种经常的聚首能相安无事，避免公开争吵，以至面红耳赤。我们相会于邮局，于社交场所，每晚在炉火边； 我们生活得太拥挤，互相干扰，彼此牵绊，因此我想，彼此已缺乏敬意了。当然，所有重要而热忱的聚会，次数少一点也够了。试想工厂中的女工——永远不能独自生活，甚至梦里也不会。如果像我住的地方一样，一英里只住一个人，那要好得多。人的价值并不在他的皮肤上，所以我们不必要去接触。

in his skin, that we should touch him.

I have a great deal of company in my house; especially in the morning, when nobody calls. Let me suggest a few comparisons, that some one may convey an idea of my situation. I am no more lonely than the **loon** in the pond that laughs so loud, or than Walden Pond itself. What company has that lonely lake, I pray?

我的房屋中有许多伴侣；特别在早上还没有人来拜访我的时候。让我来做几个对比，或许能传达出我的某些状况。我并不比湖中高声大笑的潜水鸟更孤独，也并不比瓦尔登湖更寂寞。我倒要问问这孤独的湖有谁做伴？

And yet it has not the blue devils, but the blue angels in it, in the **azure** tint of its waters. The sun is alone, except in thick weather, when there sometimes appear to be two, but one is a mock sun. God is alone — but the devil, he is far from being alone; he sees a great deal of company; he is legion. I am no more lonely than a single **mullein** or **dandelion** in a pasture, or a bean leaf, or sorrel, or a horse-fly, or a bumblebee. I am no more lonely than the Millbrook, or a weathercock, or the north star, or the south wind, or an April shower, or a January thaw, or the first spider in a new house.

然而在它蔚蓝的水波中，有的不是蓝色的魔鬼，而是蓝色的天使呢。太阳是寂寞的，除非乌云满天，那时候就好像有两个太阳，但其中一个是假的。上帝是孤独的——可是魔鬼就绝不孤独；他看到许多伙伴；他是要结成帮的。我并不比一朵毛蕊花或牧场上的一朵蒲公英寂寞，我不比一片豆叶，一棵酢酱草，或一只马蝇，或一只大黄蜂更孤独。我不比密尔溪，或一只风信鸡，或北极星，或南风更寂寞，我不比四月的雨或正月的溶雪，或新屋中的第一只蜘蛛更孤独。

魅力词汇

wholesome ['həulsəm] *adj.* 有益健康的
dissipate ['disipeit] *v.* 使……消散
intervene [ˌintə'viːn] *v.* 干涉，调停
dervish ['dəːviʃ] *n.* 回教的托钵僧
hoe [həu] *v.* 锄
recreate ['riːkri'eit] *v.* 娱乐，消遣
ennui [ɔn'wiː] *n.* 怠倦，无聊
etiquette [eti'ket] *n.* 礼仪，礼节，成规
stumble over 给……绊倒
suffice [sə'fais] *v.* 足够，使……满足
loon [luːn] *n.* 潜鸟
azure ['æʒə] *n.* 天蓝色，碧空
mullein ['mʌlin] *n.* 毛蕊花属的植物
dandelion ['dændilaiən] *n.* 蒲公英

第七篇

—谦卑的一课—

1 A Real Lesson in Humility 谦卑的一课

难以想象，一位大名鼎鼎的人物会俯下身来帮别人做劈柴的工作，但确有其事，这就是美国著名教育家布克·华盛顿的故事。

文苑漫步

Booker T. Washington, the **renowned** black educator, was an outstanding example of this truth.

Shortly after he took over the presidency of Tuskegee Institute in Alabama, he was walking in an **exclusive** section of town when he was stopped by a wealthy white woman. Not knowing the famous Mr. Washington by sight, she asked if he would like to earn a few dollars by **chopping** wood for her.

Because he had no pressing business at the moment, Professor Washington smiled, rolled up his sleeves, and **proceeded** to do the humble chore she had requested. When he was finished, he carried the logs into the house and **stacked** them by the fireplace.

A little girl recognized him and later **revealed** his **identity** to the lady. The next

译林畅游

布克·华盛顿是著名的黑人教育家。关于谦卑，他是一个典型。

那时，他刚接任阿拉巴马州的杜斯凯吉大学校长一职不久，当他在镇里的高档小区散步时，他被一个富有的白人妇女叫住了。因她从未见过出名的华盛顿先生，她让布克·华盛顿帮她砍柴，并答应付给他几美元。

因为布克·华盛顿那时正好没有紧急的事情，于是他微笑地卷起袖子，做了她要求的卑下的砍柴工作。砍完柴后，他又帮她把柴送进屋里，整齐地在壁炉旁堆好。

一个小女孩认出了布克·华盛顿，她在事后把他的身份告诉了那

morning the embarrassed woman went to see Mr. Washington in his office at the Institute and apologized profusely. "It's perfectly all right, Madam," he replied. "**Occasionally** I enjoy a little manual labor. Besides, it's always a **delight** to do something for a friend."

She shook his hand warmly and **assured** him that his meek and **gracious** attitude had endeared him and his work to her heart. Not long afterward she showed her admiration by persuading some wealthy **acquaintances** to join her in donating thousands of dollars to the Tuskegee Institute.

位妇人。第二天早上，尴尬的妇女来到了华盛顿先生所在的杜斯凯吉大学办公室，非常诚恳地向他道歉。"别放在心上，女士，"他回答道，"有时候我也做些小的体力活。当然，能帮朋友做点事情我很高兴。"

她热情地握着他的手，说他的谦恭亲切的态度让她深深折服。后来，她劝服她富有的熟人加入到捐赠中，为杜斯凯吉大学带来了数千美元的捐款。

魅力词汇

renowned [ri'naund] *adj.* 著名的
exclusive [ik'sklu:siv] *adj.* 高级的
chop [tʃɔp] *v.* 砍，劈，斩
proceed [prə'si:d] *v.* 进行下去
stack [stæk] *v.* 叠成堆，堆放于
reveal [ri'vi:l] *v.* 揭露
identity [ai'dentiti] *n.* 身份
occasionally [ə'keiʒənəli] *adv.* 偶然地
delight [di'lait] *n.* 使人高兴的东西（或人）
assure [ə'ʃuə] *v.* 使确信，使放心
gracious ['greiʃəs] *adj.* 亲切的
acquaintance [ə'kweintəns] *n.* 熟人

温情絮语

From small beginnings come great things.

伟大始于渺小。

2 Hayao Miyazaki 宫崎骏

熟悉日本动画片的读者对宫崎骏这个名字不会感到陌生吧？没错，他是日本的动画大师，制作出了多部高质量的动画故事片。

文苑漫步

Hayao Miyazaki is one of Japan's most popular animators. His **amazing** drawing skills, entertaining plots, and **well-rounded** characters have made timeless masterpieces out of films such as "Princess Mononoke" and "My Neighbor Totoro".

Hayao Miyazaki was born in Tokyo in 1941. His family owned a factory that built airplanes, and he fell in love with planes and flying at an early age. Anyone **familiar** with his films has seen the often breathtaking flying scenes that are his personal trademark.

Miyazaki's career as an animator began in 1963 when he joined Toei Animation to work on a TV series called "Wolf Boy Ken."

At Toei, he also teamed up with Isao Takahata, beginning a partnership that would last many years and lead to some of

译林畅游

宫崎骏是日本最受欢迎的漫画家之一。他令人惊叹的绘画技巧、引人入胜的故事情节和充满活力的人物形象使其多部作品成为影坛上的不朽佳作，如《幽灵公主》和《龙猫》。

宫崎骏1941年出生于日本东京。他的家族拥有一座制造飞机的工厂，他早年也曾醉心于飞机及飞行。熟悉宫崎骏电影的人，都很熟悉他影片中经常出现的常令人叹为观止的飞行场景，那正是宫崎骏动画的一大特色。

宫崎骏于1963年加入东映动画社，开始了他的动漫画家生涯，他参与了电视剧《狼少年》的制作。

在东映工作时，宫崎骏和高畑勋搭档，开始了他们多年的合作关系，也因此创造了日本动画电影史

the great success stories of Japanese animated film.

上数部超级卖座片。

In 1984, Miyazaki **released** a film based on his own manga series, "Nausicaa of the Valley of the Wind". It was a huge success, enabling Miyazaki and Takahata to set up their own company, Studio Ghibli. They were finally free to **concentrate** on doing what they liked best: making high-quality animated feature films.

1984 年，宫崎骏发行了一部根据他自己的漫画集改编而成的电影——《风之谷》。这部影片获得了空前的成功，使宫崎骏与高畑勋得以自行筹组公司——吉卜力工作室。他们终于能够自由地全身心地投入到他们最爱的事业中——制作高质量的动画故事片。

Since it opened in 1985, Studio Ghibli has gone from strength to strength. "Princess Mononoke" is the second-biggest box-office hit in Japanese movie history, and "My Neighbor Totoro," as well as **attracting** huge audiences, was successful in another way. Sales of **stuffed** toys based on its odd central character helped the studio build a sound **financial** base.

自 1985 年开业以来，吉卜力工作室的事业蒸蒸日上。《幽灵公主》高居日本电影史上卖座片的第二名；而《龙猫》不仅吸引了大批观众，而且还在另一个领域取得巨大成功。根据该片主角奇特造型制作的填充玩具的销售额为工作室奠立了稳定的财力基础。

Throughout his career, Miyazaki has traveled widely in search of **inspiration**. Now, he is firmly established as a figure who provides inspiration to others. He has, without a doubt, earned his place in the animators' hall of fame.

在其职业生涯中，宫崎骏曾远赴各地旅行寻找灵感。如今，作为一位启发他人灵感的人，宫崎骏已确立了其不可动摇的地位。毫无疑问，宫崎骏已在漫画家的名人堂中赢得一席之地。

魅力词汇

amazing [ə'meiziŋ]
adj. 惊人的；惊奇的
well-rounded *adj.*（身体，形状等）丰满的，成熟的，全面的
familiar [fə'miliə] *adj.* 熟悉的
release [ri'liːs] *v.* 发布（行）
concentrate ['kɔnsəntreit] *v.* 全神贯注
attract [ə'trækt] *v.* 吸引
stuff [stʌf] *v.* 填满
financial [fai'nænʃəl]
adj. 财政的，金融的
inspiration [ˌinspə'reiʃn] *n.* 灵感

3 Helen Keller 海伦·凯勒

一个双目失明、双耳失聪的人的世界是什么样的？对生活还有希望吗？是一蹶不振还是努力奋发？海伦·凯勒以她的经历告诉了我们答案。

文苑漫步

She fought for women's rights, crusaded for the causes of workers, promoted equality for minorities, and **championed** the **underprivileged** and the oppressed. She also earned several **prestigious** awards from countries as diverse as Japan, Brazil, and Lebanon. An **impressive** list of achievements for any human, all this was accomplished by a woman who was blind and deaf.

Helen Keller was born a healthy child in 1880 in Alabama. Stricken by illness at the tender age of 19 months, Helen lost her ability to see, hear, and speak. Growing up unable to **comprehend** the world around her, Helen became wild and unruly, until her parents found help.

They **contacted** Dr. Alexander Graham Bell, the famous inventor and teacher of the deaf, who introduced them

译林畅游

她为女权而战、投身工人事业、促进弱势团体平等权利、支持受苦和受压迫的人。她还荣获日本、巴西、黎巴嫩等国颁发的几项荣誉奖。对任何人来说，这都是给人印象深刻的成就，然而这是由一位双眼失明双耳失聪的女人取得的。

1880年，海伦·凯勒在美国的阿拉巴马州出生时是个健康的孩子。可在她19个月大时，她得了一场大病，从此失去了视觉、听觉和说话的能力。在成长的过程中，她无法了解周围的一切，变得狂躁而难以管教，最后她的父母只好求助于他人。

他们和著名的发明家、聋哑教师亚力山大·贝尔博士取得联系之后，被介绍到一家位于马萨诸塞州

to an institute for the blind in Boston, Massachusetts. A student there, Annie Sullivan, was asked to help. Annie would later become known as the "Miracle Worker".

波士顿的盲人机构。该机构的学生安妮·苏利文应邀提供帮助。她就是后来那位著名的"奇迹创造者"。

Annie Sullivan taught Helen how to connect objects with letters by spelling words into Helen's hands. Helen's **break-through** came when Annie held her hand under a water pump while spelling "water" into her other hand repeatedly. Helen suddenly understood, and from then on progressed by leaps and bounds.

安妮·苏利文在海伦手上拼字，借此教她如何将物体和字母联系在一起。有一次安妮把海伦的手放在水泵出水口下，并且在她的另一支手上重复拼写"water"的时候，海伦突然明白了，并从那之后在学习上突飞猛进。

Having mastered both the manual and Braille alphabets, Helen became **proficient** in reading and writing, and began learning how to speak in 1890. Helen entered Radcliffe College and, assisted by Annie Sullivan, graduated cum laude in 1904. She was the first blind-deaf person ever to graduate from college.

海伦在学会了手指拼字法和布莱耶盲人点字法后，她的阅读和书写能力变得熟练起来；1890年，她开始学习说话。后来海伦在安妮·苏利文的帮助下，进入拉德克利夫学院就读，1904年以优异的成绩毕业，她成为第一位从大学毕业的盲哑人。

Helen Keller spent the rest of her life as a writer, lecturer, and **advocate** for the deaf and blind and other disadvantaged groups. She traveled to **numerous** countries on behalf of the disabled, and founded the Helen Keller Endowment Fund for the American Foundation for the Blind in 1930. She died on June 1, 1968, an outstanding example of the unconquerable human spirit.

海伦·凯勒的余生都致力于写作和演讲，声援聋哑人、盲人和其他弱势群体。她代表残疾人，足迹踏遍海外各国，并且在1930年为美国盲人基金会创建了海伦·凯勒捐赠基金。海伦·凯勒于1968年6月1日与世长辞，她可以说是人类不屈不挠精神的最佳典范。

魅力词汇

champion ['tʃæmpiən] *v.* 拥护，保卫

underprivileged [ˌʌndə'privilidʒd] *adj.* 贫穷的

prestigious [pre'stidʒəs] *adj.* 有名望的

impressive [im'presiv] *adj.* 给人印象深刻的

comprehend [ˌkɔmpri'hend] *v.* 理解

contact ['kɔntækt] *v.* 联系，接触

breakthrough ['breikθruː] *n.* 突破

proficient [prə'fiʃənt] *adj.* 熟练的

advocate ['ædvəkeit] *n.* 拥护者，提倡者

numerous ['njuːmərəs] *adj.* 众多的

温情絮语

That the best classroom in the world is at the feet of an elderly person.

世界上最好的教室就是老人的脚边。

4 One Success Is Enough 一次成功就够了

有一个人，一生中经历了无数次失败，但他却说："一次成功就够了。"

文苑漫步

There was a man who had **undergone** numerous failures in his life. But he said, "One success is enough for me!"

When he was 5 years old, his father died of illness without leaving him any **property**.

When he was 12, his mother married another man. His step-father treated him strictly and often beat him when his mother was away.

When he was 14, he dropped out from school and began his life of **roving**.

When he was 20, he changed his job from electrician to ferry staff to railway worker. All his jobs were tough for him.

When he was 30, he did a sales work in an insurance company. But before long, he fell out with his boss due to the **bonus** problems.

When he was 31, he learnt law by himself and began working in law with the

译林畅游

有一个人，一生中经历了无数次失败。但他却说："一次成功就够了。"

5岁时，他的父亲突然病逝，没有留下任何财产。

12岁时，母亲改嫁，继父对他十分严厉，常在母亲外出时打他。

14岁时，他辍学离校，开始了流浪生活。

20岁时，他当电工、开轮渡，后来又当铁路工人，没有一样工作顺利。

30岁时，他在保险公司从事推销工作，但不久后因奖金问题与老板闹翻而辞职。

31岁时，他自学法律，并在朋友的鼓励下干起了律师行当。但在

encouragement of his friends. But in a trial, he fought with the litigant on court.

一次审案时，他竟在法庭上与当事人大打出手。

When he was 32, he was out of work and led a tough life.

32岁时，他失业了，生活非常艰难。

When he was 35, he suffered such severe **injuries** in an accident that he could no longer continue his job of promoting tires.

35岁时，他在一次事故中身受重伤，无法再干轮胎推销员的工作。

When he was 66, he made a living by promoting his chicken-fried technics to various restaurants in different places.

66岁时，为了维持生活，他到各地的不同餐馆推销自己掌握的炸鸡技术。

When he was 75, he felt powerless to maintain his company, so he **transferred** his brand and patent to others. The new owner suggested giving him ten thousand stock shares as part of the purchasing price. But he **turned down** the suggestion. Later the price of the stocks of the company soared and he lost the chance of being a billionaire.

75岁时，他对维持公司感到力不从心，因此转让了自己创立的品牌和专利。新主人提议给他1万股作为购买价格的一部分，他拒绝了。后来公司股票大涨，他因此失去了成为亿万富翁的机会。

When he was 83, he opened another fast-food restaurant but fell into a lawsuit due to **trademark** and patent issues.

83岁时，他又开了一家快餐店，却因商标和专利与人打起了官司。

When he was 88, he achieve great success and became well-known to the whole world.

88岁时，他终于大获成功，全世界都知道了他的名字。

He was exactly the founder of Kentucky Fried Chicken, Halunde Sandoz. He often said, "People always complain about the bad weather. Actually the weather is not bad at all. As long as you are optimist and **confident** all the time, you will have a good weather everyday."

他，就是肯德基的创始人——哈兰·山德士。他常说："人们经常抱怨天气不好，实际上并不是天气不好。只要自己有乐观自信的心情，天天都是好天气。"

魅力词汇

undergo [ˌʌndəˈgəu] *v.* 经历，遭受
property [ˈprɔpəti] *n.* 财产，所有权
rove [rəuv] *v.* 流浪，漂泊
bonus [ˈbəunəs] *n.* 奖金，红利
encouragement [inˈkʌridʒmənt] *n.* 鼓励
injury [ˈindʒəri] *n.* 损害，伤害
transfer [trænsˈfəː] *v.* 转让
turn down 拒绝
trademark [ˈtreidmaːk] *n.* 商标，牌号
confident [ˈkɔnfidənt] *adj.* 有信心的

温情絮语

That the easiest way for me to grow as a person is to surround myself with people smarter than I am.

使我成长的捷径就是围绕在比我聪敏的人身旁。

5 Thomas Edison 托马斯·爱迪生

连老师都放弃的一个孩子，却用自己一生诸多的发明，改变了世界，造福了人类。从他身上，我们可以看到什么？

文苑漫步

Born in 1847 in Ohio, Thomas Edison attended school for only three months. After his teacher **claimed** that he could not learn, Edison's mother decided to teach him at home. There he was **allowed** to explore the subjects that most interested him. By age ten, Edison had built a science laboratory in the basement of his family's home and had become an **avid** experimenter.

Edison got his first job at age 12 on the railway selling candy and newspapers. Three years later, he **suffered** an ear injury from a train accident and lost most of his hearing. He could have had an operation, but he refused. He **insisted** that being deaf helped him concentrate on his experiments.

Thomas Edison's first invention was the automatic telegraph repeater. He was already an expert on the telegraph before he came up with a gadget that sent telegraph

译林畅游

1847年托马斯·爱迪生出生于俄亥俄州。他仅仅上了三个月的学。在爱迪生的老师声称他有学习障碍之后，他的母亲决定自己在家教他。在家里，爱迪生可以随心所欲地探索最使他感兴趣的事物。10岁那年，爱迪生在家里的地下室建了一间科学实验室。从此，爱迪生就成了一位孜孜不倦的实验者。

12岁时，爱迪生找到了他的第一份工作——在火车上卖糖果和报纸。三年后，一场火车事故导致他耳朵受伤，几乎完全失聪。他本可以接受手术治疗，但他拒绝了，因为他坚信听觉的丧失可以让他更专心地做实验。

电报自动转发器是托马斯·爱迪生的第一个发明。他发明的这种装置，用于在无人看管的两站之间传输电报信号，在此项发明前，爱

signals between unmanned stations. Thanks to Edison, people were then able to send several telegraph messages **simultaneously**.

迪生就已经是位电报专家了。多亏了爱迪生，我们才能在同一时间传送好几封电报讯息。

Next came the electric vote recorder. It made voting quicker and more **accurate**, yet no one wanted to buy it. Edison then moved on to tackle the stock market ticker, the machine that gave information about stock market prices. Edison improved it, and sold the rights for US$40,000.

接下来的电子记票器让统计票数的速度更快、更准确，但却没有人要买。之后，爱迪生转而进行股票行情收录器的研究，他把收录器作了改进并将该项专利以四万美元卖出。

In his late 30s, Edison built an "invention factory" where he and his business partners could **dedicate** all their time to inventing. After improving upon the telephone, Edison created the phonograph, his favorite and most lucrative invention. Although Edison did not actually invent the light bulb, he did create an electric lighting system which led to its widespread use.

近30岁时，爱迪生盖了一座"发明工厂"，在那里他和他的同事可以全心致力于发明。在改进了电话功能后，爱迪生又发明了留声机，这是他喜爱的而且最能赚钱的一项发明。虽然爱迪生实际上并没有发明灯泡，但他的确发明了电灯照明系统，这促使了灯泡的广泛使用。

A tireless achiever, Edison established the first central electric power station in 1882, **enabling** New York to be the first city in the world to have electric lights. This was the beginning of the modern world in which electricity became a way of life.

1882年，这位孜孜不倦的实践家建成了第一座中央电站，使纽约市成为世界上第一个有电力照明的城市，这就是现代世界的开始，电成为人们的一种生活方式。

Thomas Edison died at the age of 84 in 1931. Three days later, much of America **dimmed** its lights in honor of the inventor — man who had more **impact** on the development of present-day civilization than anyone else in history.

托马斯·爱迪生于1931年去世，享年84岁。在他去世三天后，美国大部分地区以关灯来纪念这位在历史上对现代文明发展最具影响力的发明家。

魅力词汇

claim [kleim] *v.* 声称
allow [ə'lau] *v.* 允许
avid ['ævid] *adj.* 渴望的
suffer ['sʌfə] *v.* 遭受；容忍
insist [in'sist] *v.* 坚持，强调
simultaneously [ˌsiməl'teiniəsli] *adv.* 同时，一起
accurate ['ækjurət] *adj.* 准确的
dedicate ['dedikeit] *v.* (to) 把……献给
enable [i'neibəl] *v.* 使能够
dim [dim] *v.* 使暗淡，使失去光泽
impact ['impækt] *n.* 影响，作用

温情絮语

If we blame the spokesman too much over a minor mistake, they will become overcautious and lose their function as a communication channel.

如果稍有错误就对发言人进行批评，会让他们变得谨小慎微，失去其作为沟通桥梁的作用。

6 James Watt and the Teakettle 詹姆斯·瓦特和水壶

这是一个人们耳熟能详的故事，这也是一个每次看都会有更新的启示的故事，在水壶的背后有蒸汽机的发明，那么在我们的日常用品背后呢？大自然总是这么奇妙，但这奥秘的大自然只向有心人开启。

文苑漫步

A little Scotch boy was sitting in his grandmother's kitchen. He was watching the red flames in the wide open fireplace and quietly **wondering** about the causes of things. Indeed, he was always wondering and always wanting to know.

"Grandma," he presently asked, "what makes the fire burn?"

This was not the first time he had puzzled his grandmother with questions that she could not answer. So she went on with her preparations for supper and paid no **heed** to his query.

Above the fire an old-fashioned **teakettle** was hanging. The water within it was beginning to **bubble**. A thin cloud of steam was rising from the spout. Soon the lid began to **rattle** and shake. The hot **vapor** puffed out at a furious rate.

译林畅游

一个苏格兰小男孩坐在祖母的厨房里。他望着大壁炉里通红的火焰，默默地思索着事物发生的缘由。确实，他总是产生疑惑，总是想要知道究竟。

“奶奶，是什么东西使炉火燃烧的？”一会儿他问道。

奶奶被他所提出的问题难倒已经不是第一次了。所以她继续做她的晚餐，不理会他的疑问。

在炉子上悬吊了一只老式水壶，那里面的水开始沸腾，壶嘴冒出淡淡的云雾般的蒸气。不一会儿，壶盖儿开始掀动，发出咯咯的响声。接着，热气猛烈地喷出来。可是，孩子仔细窥看壶盖下面，却什么也

Yet when the lad **peeped** under the lid he could see nothing.

"Grandma, what is in the teakettle?" he asked.

"Water, my child—nothing but water."

"But I know there is something else. There is something in there that lifts the lid and makes it rattle."

The grandmother laughed. "Oh, that is only steam," she said. "You can see it coming out of the **spout** and puffing up under the lid."

"But you said there was nothing but water in the **kettle**. How did the steam get under the lid?"

"Why, my dear, it comes out of the hot water. The hot water makes it." The grandmother was beginning to feel puzzled.

The lad lifted the lid and peeped inside again. He could see nothing but the bubbling water. The steam was not visible until after it was fairly out of the kettle.

"How queer!" he said. "The steam must be very strong to lift the heavy iron lid. Grandma, how much water did you put into the kettle?"

"About a **quart**, Jamie."

"Well, if the steam from so little water is so strong, why would not the steam from a great deal of water be a great deal stronger? Why couldn't it be made to lift a much greater weight? Why couldn't it be made

没看见。

"奶奶，壶里装的是什么呀？"他问道。

"水呀，孩子，就是水。"

"但是我知道还有别的东西，里面有东西在把壶盖顶起来，而且使壶盖咯咯响。"

奶奶笑了起来，说："啊，那是蒸气。你可以看见蒸气从壶口冒出来，还在壶盖底下噗吱噗吱着。"

"但你刚才说壶里只有水，没有别的东西。那么壶盖底下的蒸气又是打哪儿来的呢？"

"暧，亲爱的，它是从热水里出来的。热水产生蒸气。"奶奶开始感到说不清楚了。

孩子拎起壶盖，再一次向壶里窥探，只见壶里的水在噗噗地冒着气泡，其他可什么也没发现。蒸气只有在完全离开水壶以后才看得见。

"太奇怪了！"他说。"蒸气要顶起这样重的铁盖子，力量一定很不小。奶奶，你在壶里装了多少水呢？"

"大约一夸脱，杰米。"

"噢，如果这么一点点水产生的蒸气力量有那么大，那么大量的水产生的蒸气力量不就大得多了吗？为什么不可以使蒸气顶起比这重得多的东西呢？为什么不可以使

to turn wheels?"

The grandmother made no reply. These questions of Jamie's were more puzzling than **profitable**, she thought. She went about her work silently, and Jamie sat still in his place and studied the tea-kettle.

蒸气转动轮子呢？"

奶奶没有回答。她想：杰米的这些问题没有什么用处，却难以回答。她默默地继续干她的活，而杰米仍一动不动地坐在老地方研究着这把水壶。

魅力词汇

wonder ['wʌndə] *v.* 惊奇，想知道，怀疑
heed [hiːd] *n.* 注意，留心
teakettle ['tiːˌketl] *n.* 茶壶，烧水壶
bubble ['bʌbl] *v.* 冒气泡
rattle ['rætl] *v.* 嘎嘎作响
vapor ['veipə] *n.*（蒸）汽
peep [piːp] *v.* 偷看；隐现
spout [spaut] *v.* 喷出
kettle ['ketl] *n.* 水壶，坑穴
quart [kwɔːt] *n.* 夸脱（容量单位）
profitable ['prɔfitəbl] *adj.* 有益的，有利可图的

温情絮语

Knowing something of everything and everything of something.

通百艺而专一长。

7 Florence Nightingale, Pioneer of Modern Hospital Nursing
弗洛伦斯·南丁格尔——现代医疗护理的先驱

在很早以前就看过南丁格尔的传记，她自比为一朵旷野的小花，所做的一切不足为奇。当我看到这些的时候，我想其实我们所做的相比于上帝所创造的这一切真的太卑微了。与其把南丁格尔看做是一个名人，我更愿意说她是上帝所差来的使者，透过她，上帝把自己对人类的爱播撒了出来。

文苑漫步

In the early nineteenth century, hospitals were not as good as they are now, and nurses were careless and poor in knowledge. A great many soldiers died of **wounds** and **fever** because the doctors were not skillful enough to cure them.

When Miss Nightingale was a little girl, she used to like playing with her dolls and **pretending** to nurse them. When she grew up, she used to visit the poor people near her house and look after them when they were ill. She wanted to be a nurse, but her father said, "Look at the woman who do nursing in the hospital. I don't want you to be like that!" He had plenty of money and let Florence travel to many other countries. Wherever she went she visited hospitals and worked in them herself. Then she was

译林畅游

在19世纪早期，医院并不像现在这么好，护士们粗心大意而且知识贫乏。很多士兵死于创伤和发烧，因为医生没有足够专业的技能来医治他们。

当南丁格尔女士还是个小女孩的时候，她常常喜欢和她的玩具一起玩耍，假装照顾它们。当她长大了，她常探望她家附近的穷人，在他们生病时照顾他们。她想要成为一名护士，但是她的父亲说："看看那些在医院里做护士的女人，我不想让你像她们一样！"父亲拥有很多钱，让弗洛伦斯去很多其他国家旅行。无论她去哪里，她都要去参观医院，并且自己去那里工作一段时间。之后，她负责管理一家小医

placed in charge of a small hospital. Later, she went to learn nursing in Germany and France.

Miss Nightingale worked all day to see that the wounded soldiers were well looked after and properly nursed. Every night she walked around the hospital with a small lamp, visiting the **patients**. The soldiers were pleased to see her. They gave her the name of "The Lady of the Lamp". She and her nurses saved hundreds of lives and she stayed at the hospital until the war was over.

After the war she returned to England and was honored for her services by Queen Victoria. But Florence said that her work had just begun. She raised money to build the Nightingale Home for Nurses in London. She started to train nurses in hospitals. Soon all the big hospitals in England had their own training schools for nurses. Hospitals became clean and **cheerful** places and nurses were much more skillful. She also wrote a book on public health, which was printed in several countries. Today, nurses all over the world remember "The Lady of the Lamp".

Florence died at the age of 90, still trying to serve others through her work as a nurse. **Indeed**, it is because of her that we honor nurses today.

院。再后来，她去德国和法国学习护理。

南丁格尔女士整日工作来保证受伤的士兵能够得到很好的照料和恰当的护理。每天晚上她都提着一盏小灯在医院里四处走动，探访病人们。士兵们很高兴看见她。他们称她为“提灯女神”。她和她的护士们拯救了数以百计的生命，她一直待在医院里直到战争结束。

战争结束后她回到了英国并且得到维多利亚女王的嘉奖。但是弗洛伦斯说她的工作只是刚刚开始。她筹集资金在伦敦为护士们建立了“南丁格尔之家”。她开始培训医院的护士。很快英国所有的大医院都有了他们自己专门的护士训练学校。医院成为一个干净而且令人感到愉快的地方，护士们也更加专业了。她还写了一本关于公共卫生的书在若干个国家印刷发行。今天，全世界的护士都记得“提灯女神”。

弗洛伦斯寿终于 90 岁，仍然试图以护士的身份来服务于他人。事实上，正是因为她我们今天才这么尊敬护士。

魅力词汇

wound [wuːnd] *n.* 创伤，伤口
fever ['fiːvə] *n.* 发烧，发热
pretend [pri'tend] *v.* 假装，装作
patient ['peiʃənt] *n.* 病人
cheerful ['tʃiəfəl] *adj.* 高兴的，快乐的
indeed [in'diːd] *adv.* 真正地，的确

温情絮语

That it is best to give advice in only two circumstances; when it is requested and when it is a life threatening situation.

发表建议最好在以下两个场合：别人发出请求，和生命受到威胁的时候。

8 Beethoven and His *Moonlight Sonata*
贝多芬和他的《月光奏鸣曲》

偶然间的不期而遇孕育了流芳百世的名曲。如果贝多芬不曾为一首钢琴曲驻足？或即使驻足了，他不愿去为这对贫穷的兄妹弹奏一曲呢？即或去弹了，但没有留意周围的景致呢？若非这诸多看似的“巧合”，这首曲子就不会如此唯美地展现，那么我们的生活中，是否也错失了许许多多的美好，只因我们太过忙碌而忘却了周围的景致，抑或失去了停下来满足别人的小小心愿的怜悯之心呢？

文苑漫步

One moonlight evening Beethoven was walking in a street when he suddenly stopped outside a little house. “What is that? It is from my **Sonata** in F. How well it is played!”

Following a sudden break came the voice of **sobbing**. “I can’t play any more. This piece of music is so difficult to play. How I wish I could hear Beethoven himself play it!”

“Ah, my sister, but we are so poor,” said a young man. “And the ticket to the concert is too **expensive**.”

“Don’t be sad, brother,” said the girl. “I just said that for fun.”

Hearing this, Beethoven knocked at the door, and it opened. In the **dim** light of

译林畅游

在一个有月光的晚上，贝多芬正在街上行走，忽然他在一间小房子外面停了下来。“那是什么？这是我的F大调奏鸣曲中的一段。弹得很动听啊！”

音乐突然停了下来，随即传来了一阵啜泣声。“我不想再弹了。这首曲子太难了。多希望能够听听贝多芬本人是怎么弹的啊！”

“哎，但是姐姐，我们太穷了，音乐会的门票太贵了。”一个年轻人说道。

“弟弟，不要伤心，我只是开个玩笑罢了。”女孩说道。

听到这些，贝多芬敲了敲门，门开了。在微弱的烛光中，一个女

a candle a young girl was sitting before a piano and a young man was making shoes by a table.

孩坐在一架钢琴前，一个男孩坐在桌子旁做鞋子。

"Pardon me," said Beethoven, "but I heard the music. You wish to hear..." He paused. To his surprise he found the girl was blind. "Excuse me. Then you play by ear? But where did you hear the music?"

"不好意思，"贝多芬说道，"我听到了钢琴声。你希望听……"他停顿了一下。他惊讶地发现这个女孩是一个盲人。"打扰了。你是凭听觉记忆弹奏的么？那么你是从哪里听到的这首曲子呢？"

"I used to hear a woman practicing pieces in the opposite house. Her windows were open and I walked outside to listen to her."

"我经常听一个女士在对面的房间里演奏曲目。她的窗户开着，我就走到外面听她演奏。"

Beethoven said no more. He sat down before the piano. The moon shone brightly in through the window. He looked up thoughtfully to the sky and stars. He said to himself, "I will **improvise** a Sonata to the Moonlight!" Then his hands dropped on the keys and began to play.

贝多芬没再说什么。他坐到钢琴前面。月亮透过窗户明亮地照了进来。他若有所思地看了看夜空和星辰。对自己说："我将为月光即兴创作一首奏鸣曲！"之后他的手落到琴键上开始弹奏。

Listening silently, the young man laid away his work. The girl, with her head bent slightly forward, and her hands pressed tightly over her **breast**, sat silently near the piano, lost in thought...

年轻人放开自己手中的工作安静地聆听。这个女孩安静地坐在钢琴旁边，头部轻微向前伸，手紧紧地按在胸口，沉思着……

The brother and sister were fully **attracted** by the music. They both lost themselves in it.

这对姐弟完全被音乐吸引了。他们都沉浸在音乐中。

Beethoven rushed to the place where he was staying and spent a whole night writing down the piece of music he had played at the blind girl's house. That was the **origin** of *The Moonlight Sonata*.

贝多芬狂奔回他住的地方，花了一晚上的时间把他在盲女家弹奏的这首曲子写了下来。这就是《月光奏鸣曲》的来源。

魅力词汇

sonata [sə'nɑːtə] *n.* 奏鸣曲
sob [sɔb] *v.* 抽泣，呜咽
expensive [ik'spensiv] *adj.* 昂贵的
dim [dim] *adj.* 昏暗的
improvise ['imprəvaiz] *vt.* 即兴创作
breast [brest] *n.* 胸
attract [ə'trækt] *vt.* 吸引
origin ['ɔridʒin] *n.* 起源

温情絮语

That I can't choose how I feel, but I can choose what I do about it.

我不能改变我的感受，但是我可以改变我的做法。

9 Build Me a Son 塑造我的儿子

当一个人开始承担起为人父母的职责时，他 / 她就需要考虑他 / 她希望他 / 她的孩子成为一个怎样的人。

本文是麦克阿瑟将军为他儿子所做的祷告词。愿我们能从这篇祷告词中看到一个父亲谦卑的心和对儿子的爱。

文苑漫步

Build me a son, O Lord, who will be strong enough to know when he is weak, and brave enough to face himself when he is afraid; one who will be proud and **unbending** in honest defeat, and **humble** and gentle in victory.

Build me a son whose wishes will not take the place of deeds; a son who will know thee... and that to know himself is the foundation stone of knowledge.

Lead him, I pray, not in the path of ease and comfort, but under the stress and **spur** of difficulties and challenge. Here, let him learn to stand up in the storm; here let him learn **compassion** for those that fail.

Build me a son, whose heart will be clear, whose goal will be high, a son who

译林畅游

主啊！求你塑造我的儿子，使他在软弱时，能够坚强不屈；在惧怕时能够勇敢自持；在失败时，能够毫不气馁；在胜利时，仍能保持谦逊温和。

恳求你塑造我的儿子，不致空有幻想而缺乏行动；引领他认识你，同时让他知道，认识自己，才是一切知识的基石。

我祈求你，不要使他走上安逸、舒适之途，求你将他置于困难和挑战的磨练和激励中，求你引领他，使他学习在风暴中挺身站立，并学会怜悯那些在重压之下失败跌倒的人。

求你塑造我的儿子，求你让他有一颗纯洁的心，并有远大的目标；

will master himself before he seeks to master other men; one who will reach into the future, yet never forget the past.

使他在能指挥别人之前，先懂得驾驭自己；当迈入未来之际，永不忘记过去的教训。

And after all these things are his, add, I pray, enough of a sense of humor, so that he may always be serious, yet never take himself too seriously.

在他有了这些美德之后，我还要祈求你赐给他足够的幽默感，以免他过于严肃，还苛求自己。

Give him **humility**, so that he may always remember the **simplicity** of true greatness, the open mind of true wisdom and the **meekness** of true strength.

恳求你赐给他谦卑的心，使他永远记得，真正的伟大是单纯，真正的智慧是坦率，真正的力量是温和。

Then, I, his father, will dare to **whisper**, "I have not lived in vain."

如此，我这做父亲的，才敢低声说："我没有虚度此生。"

魅力词汇

unbending [ʌn'bendiŋ] *adj.* 不屈的
humble ['hʌmbl] *adj.* 谦逊的，谦虚的
spur [spəː] *n.* 激励因素
compassion [kəm'pæʃn] *n.* 怜悯，同情
humility [hju'militi] *n.* 谦逊，谦恭
simplicity [sim'plisiti] *n.* 简单，朴素
meekness ['miːknis] *n.* 温顺，柔和
whisper ['wispə] *v.* 低声说，耳语

温情絮语

That one should keep his words both soft and tender, because tomorrow he may have to eat them.

一个人应该谦卑柔和地遵守诺言，因为明天他可能就食言了。

10 Direct from Dell 来自戴尔的建议

我们每个人都曾怀有独自创业的宏伟梦想，而有的人成功了，有的人却只能将它当作一辈子的梦想。让我们看看戴尔总裁迈克·戴尔的建议。其实创业并不难，难的是能否抓住机遇和是否有一颗坚定不移的心。

文苑漫步

What I saw was a great opportunity to provide computing technology in a much more efficient way. That was the core idea of what became Dell Computer Corporation, and it's one that we've stuck with ever since.

I started the business with a simple question: How can we make the process of buying a computer better? The answer was: Sell computers directly to the end customer. Eliminate the reseller's **markup** and pass those savings on to the customer.

It hadn't occurred to me that others hadn't figured this out. I thought it was pretty obvious. I'm sure if I had taken the time to ask, plenty of people would have told me that my idea wouldn't work — I've heard that a lot in the fifteen years since starting the business.

译林畅游

当时我看到一个很好的机遇，就是以更有效的方式提供计算机技术。那就是后来成立戴尔公司的核心理念，自那以后我们便一直坚持不懈地执行这一理念。

我是从一个简单的问题开始创业的：我们如何使购买电脑的过程变得更方便？答案是：直接把电脑卖给终端用户。去除转销商增加的钱，并把省下的钱还给用户。

当时我并不知道其他人没有意识到这一点。在我看来，那是相当明显的。我确信当时如果我花点时间询问别人的意见的话，会有很多人说我的想法行不通——创业后十五年内我听过许多这样的话。

Sometimes it's better not to ask — or to listen — when people tell you something can't be done. I didn't ask for permission or approval. I just went ahead and did it.

有时不问不听是最好的办法——当别人告诉你行不通的时候。我就没有去征询别人的许可和赞同。我只是一往直前地去做了。

On January 2, 1984, I went back to Austin earlier than I would have to attend classes, and I did all the things you need to do to set up a business. I registered the company with the State of Texas as "PC's Limited". I placed ads in the classified section of our local newspaper.

1984年1月2日，我比开学时间略早一点回到了奥斯汀，我做了成立新公司需要做的一切准备。我注册了个德州公司，名为“个人电脑有限公司”。我在当地报纸的分类广告上登了广告。

Through my previous contacts with customers and the small ad I placed in the paper, I was already getting a lot of business. I was selling between $50,000 to $80,000 a month of upgraded PCs, upgrade kits, and add-on **components** to people in the Austin area. Not too long after starting school, I was able to move from a **stuffy** dorm that I shared with a roommate to a **condominium** with high ceilings and two bedrooms. (I didn't, however, tell my parents for a few months that I had moved.)

通过我与客户的早期接触以及在报纸上的广告，当时我已经接到了很多业务。我在奥斯汀地区出售升级电脑，升级工具，附加零件，每月的销售额在5万到8万美元之间。开学后不久我便从和室友共住的闷热宿舍搬出来，住进了有高高的天花板和两个卧室的公寓套间。（然而，我是在好几个月后才把搬家的事情告诉父母的。）

In early May, about a week before I took my final exams to complete my freshman year, I incorporated the company as "Dell Computer Corporation", doing business as "PC's Limited". We moved the business from my condo to a 1,000-square-foot office space in a small business center

五月初，大约是我一年级期末考试前一周，我将公司改组为“戴尔电脑公司”，业务和原先一样。办公地址也从我的公寓搬到了奥斯汀北部一个一千多平方英尺的小商业中心的写字楼里面。我雇了些人接电话订单，还有一些人负责填单。

in North Austin. I hired a few people to take orders over the telephone and a few more to fulfill them. Manufacturing consisted of three guys with **screwdrivers** sitting at six-foot tables upgrading machines. Business continued to grow, and I began to think hard about what the potential could be if I could devote myself to the **venture**, full-time.

生产部有三个人，拿着螺丝起子坐在六英尺的桌子旁升级电脑。业务逐渐扩大，我也开始考虑如果我全身心的投入到事业上，公司是否还有潜力。

Where I come from, not going to college is not an acceptable option. Convincing my parents to allow me to leave school would have been impossible. So I just went ahead and did it, whatever the consequences. I finished my freshman year, and left.

不上大学在我的家乡是难以被接受的，要说服父母同意我辍学几乎是不可能的。因此我不管结果如何，坚持我行我素。念完大学一年级以后，我便离开了学校。

After a while, my parents forgave me. And a little bit after that, I forgave them, too.

后来，我父母原谅了我。再后来，我也原谅了他们。

People ask me now, “Were you scared?” Sure.

人们现在问我：“你当时害怕吗？”当然害怕。

But it turned out, the timing for PC’s Limited couldn’t have been better.

而结果证明，那个时候成立个人电脑公司是再好不过的了。

魅力词汇

markup ['mɑːkʌp] *n.* 涨价
component [kəm'pəunənt] *n.* 元件，组件
stuffy ['stʌfi] *adj.* 闷热的，窒息的
condominium [ˌkɔndə'miniəm] *n.* 公寓
screwdriver ['skruˌdraivə] *n.* 螺丝起子
venture ['ventʃə] *n.*（有风险的）事业

第八篇

—水仙花法则—

1 The Daffodil Principle 水仙花法则

"如果35年前或者40年前，我也想到一个绝妙的计划，这些年来'一次一株'地努力，我可能做成什么事情呢。想一想，我会取得多大的成就啊。"这句话和"勿因善小而不为"有异曲同工之妙。一个小小的行为并不值得感叹，但是如果可以一直坚持几十年，那么这个行为的影响会是巨大的。所以如果你有什么好的习惯，一定要坚持下去，以后一定会有意想不到的收获。

文苑漫步

Several times my daughter had telephoned to say, "Mother, you must come see the daffodils before they are over."

I wanted to go, but it was a two-hour drive from Laguna to Lake Arrowhead. "I will come next Tuesday," I promised, a little reluctantly, on her third call.

Next Tuesday dawned cold and rainy. Still, I had promised, and so I drove there. When I finally walked into Carolyn's house and **hugged** and greeted my grandchildren, I said, "Forget the daffodils, Carolyn! The road is invisible in the clouds and fog, and there is nothing in the world except you and these children that I want to see bad enough to drive another inch!"

My daughter smiled calmly and said, "We drive in this all the time, Mother."

译林畅游

女儿打了好几次电话说："妈妈，水仙花凋谢之前，你一定得来看看。"

我想去，但是从拉古纳到箭头湖需要两小时的车程。在女儿第三次来电时，我勉强答应说："我下星期二过去。"

星期二一大早就开始下雨，而且还很冷。但是因为我答应了女儿，所以就开车去了。我终于踏进了卡洛琳的家门，在与外孙拥抱问候之后，我对女儿说："卡洛琳，忘掉水仙花吧！外面阴云密布，又下起了雾，根本看不清楚路。在这个世界上，要不是为了看你和这几个孩子，我才不会开车过来。"

女儿淡然一笑说道："妈妈，我们可是经常在这种天气里开车。"

"Well, you won't get me back on the road until it clears, and then I'm heading for home!" I assured her.

"I was hoping you'd take me over to the **garage** to pick up my car."

"How far will we have to drive?"

"Just a few **blocks**," Carolyn said. "I'll drive. I'm used to this."

After several minutes, I had to ask, "Where are we going? This isn't the way to the garage!"

"We're going to my garage the long way," Carolyn smiled, "by way of the daffodils."

"Carolyn," I said sternly, "please turn around."

"It's all right, Mother, I promise. You will never forgive yourself if you miss this experience."

After about twenty minutes, we turned onto a small **gravel** road and I saw a small church. On the far side of the church, I saw a hand-lettered sign that said, "Daffodil Garden".

We got out of the car and each took a child's hand, and I followed Carolyn down the path. Then, we turned a corner of the path, and I looked up and **gasped**. Before me lay the most glorious sight. It looked as though someone had taken a great vat of gold and poured it down over the mountain peak and slopes. The flowers were planted in majestic, **swirling** patterns — great ribbons and **swaths** of deep orange,

"好啦，除非天气转晴，否则你别想让我开车上路。天一晴我就回家。"我郑重其事地跟她说道。

"妈妈，我想让你带我去汽车修理厂把我的车开回来。"

"要开多远？"

"离这只有几条街，"卡洛琳回答道，"我来开车，我习惯了。"

几分钟后，我忍不住问："我们去哪啊？这不是去汽车修理场的路。"

"我们绕道去汽修场，"卡洛琳笑着说，"顺便去看一看水仙花。"

"卡洛琳，"我厉声说道，"请你调头。"

"好啦，妈妈，我敢保证，如果错过这个机会，你会后悔的。"

差不多二十分钟后，我们拐上了一条石子铺的路，我看到一座小教堂。在教堂的对面，有一个手写的标牌："水仙花园。"

下了车，我和女儿一人拉着一个孩子。我跟着女儿沿着这条小路走去。转一个弯后，我举目望去，不由大吃一惊。在我面前呈现的是最灿烂的景色。就好像是有人拿了大桶大桶的金子撒在了山顶上，山坡上。这些花朵被种成了壮丽的漩涡状——深橙色，白色，柠檬黄，橙红色，金黄色和棕黄色的水仙或排成带状，或排成一列一列的。颜色

white, lemon yellow, salmon pink, saffron, and butter yellow. Each different-colored variety was planted as a group so that it swirled and flowed like its own river with its own unique **hue**. There were five acres of flowers.

"But who has done this?" I asked Carolyn.

"It's just one woman," Carolyn answered. "She lives on the property. That's her home."

Carolyn pointed to a well kept A-frame house that looked small and modest in the midst of all that glory. We walked up to the house. On the **patio**, we saw a poster. "Answers to the Questions I Know You Are Asking" was the headline.

The first answer was a simple one. "50,000 bulbs," it read. The second answer was, "One at a time, by one woman. Two hands, two feet, and very little brain." The third answer was, "Began in 1958."

There it was, The Daffodil Principle. For me, that moment was a life-changing experience.

I thought of this woman whom I had never met, who, more than forty years before, had begun — one bulb at a time — to bring her vision of beauty and joy to an obscure mountain top. Still, just planting one bulb at a time, year after year, had changed the world. This unknown woman had forever changed the world in which she lived. She had created something of

各异的水仙形成了一片片鲜艳独特的花海。这里有五英亩的水仙花。

"这些水仙都是谁种的？"我问卡洛琳。

"只是一个女人。"卡洛琳答道，"她就住在这儿，那是她的房子。"

卡洛琳指向一座A字构架的屋子，在周围壮观的景象之下，这座房子显得矮小而又简陋。我们朝那间屋子走去，在门前的露台上看到一张海报，标题是：我知道你们要问什么，这就是答案。

第一个答案比较简单："5万株。"第二个答案是："一次栽一株，一个女人所植，用两只手，两条腿，一点儿智慧。"第三个答案是："开始于1958年。"

这就是水仙花法则，对我来说，这次经历改变了我的一生。

我想，这位素昧平生的女人，早在四十多年前就——一次一株水仙——把自己对于美和快乐的理解带给了这座无名小山的山顶。每次仅仅栽种一株，年复一年，却改变了世界。这位我们并不知其姓名的女人永远改变了她所居住的世界。她做的事情雄伟壮观，美妙绝伦，而又鼓舞人心。

ineffable magnificence, beauty, and inspiration.

The principle her daffodil garden taught is one of the greatest principles of celebration. That is, learning to move toward our goals and desires one step at a time — often just one baby-step at a time — and learning to love the doing, learning to use the accumulation of time. When we multiply tiny pieces of time with small **increments** of daily effort, we too will find we can accomplish **magnificent** things. We can change the world.

水仙花园给我们揭示了一条伟大的礼赞法则。那就是学会朝着目标努力，每次只要求一步——哪怕是婴儿的步伐——一步接一步这样做——并且学会乐在其中，学会利用点滴积累的时间。当我们利用琐碎的时间，每天都努力一点，那么我们会发现自己也可以完成大事。我们可以改变世界。

"It makes me sad in a way," I admitted to Carolyn. "What might I have accomplished if I had thought of a wonderful goal thirty-five or forty years ago and had worked away at it 'one bulb at a time' through all those years. Just think what I might have been able to achieve!"

"这多少让我有点难过。"我向卡洛琳坦言，"如果三十五年前或者四十年前，我也想到一个绝妙的计划，这些年来'一次一株'地努力，我可能做成什么事情呢。想一想，我会取得多大的成就啊。"

My daughter summed up the message of the day in her usual direct way. "Start tomorrow," she said.

女儿以她一贯直率的方式总结今天所得的经验说："那就从明天开始吧。"

魅力词汇

hug [hʌg] *v.* 拥抱，抱住
garage ['gærɑːʒ] *n.* 汽车修理站
block [blɔk] *n.* 街区
gravel ['grævl] *n.* 沙砾，砾石
gasp [gɑːsp] *v.* 喘气
swirling ['swəːliŋ] *n.* 漩涡
swath [swɔθ] *n.* 长而宽的地带
hue [hjuː] *n.* 颜色
patio ['pætiəu] *n.* 露台，平台
increment ['iŋkrəmənt] *n.* 增量
magnificent [mæg'nifisnt] *adj.* 伟大的；壮丽的

2 If the Dream Is Big Enough 为了心中的梦想

"爸爸告诉我，如果梦想足够远大，那么现实的好坏不算什么。"有了这样的信念，那么任何困难或者挫折便不再那么可怕。有的时候并不是我们不能做到，而是我们不能坚持下去，不能正视现实，是我们自己缩小了自己的能力。如果你有梦想，那么不要想着做不到，而要向着梦想一步步扎实地努力。

文苑漫步

I used to watch her from my kitchen window and she seemed so small as she **muscled** her way through the crowd of boys on the playground. The school was across the street from our home and I would often watch the kids as they played during **recess**. A sea of children, and yet to me, she stood out from them all.

I remember the first day I saw her playing basketball. I watched in wonder as she ran circles around the other kids. She managed to shoot jump shots just over their heads and into the net. The boys always tried to stop her but no one could.

I began to notice her at other times, basketball in hand, playing alone. She would practice **dribbling** and shooting

译林畅游

我以前总是通过厨房的窗口看她。当她从一群男生中硬挤着穿过操场时，她看上去是那么瘦小。学校就在我家对面的那条街，我常看到孩子们在课间玩耍。然而对我来说，在如潮水般的孩子里，她是那么显眼。

我记得第一次看到她打篮球的那天。我，惊讶地看着她在其他孩子间穿梭。她跳起，投篮。球越过孩子们的头顶进入篮筐。男孩们总是尽力拦截她，但是无人成功。

我开始在别的时候关注她，她持球，独自练习。她一次又一次地练习运球和投篮，有时会练习到天

over and over again, sometimes until dark. One day I asked her why she practiced so much. She looked directly in my eyes and without a moment of hesitation she said, "I want to go to college. The only way I can go is if I get a **scholarship**. I like basketball. I decided that if I were good enough, I would get a scholarship. I am going to play college basketball. I want to be the best. My Daddy told me if the dream is big enough, the facts don't count." Then she smiled and ran towards the **court** to **recap** the routine I had seen over and over again.

黑。有一天我问她为什么要拼命练习。她直视着我，毫不犹豫地说："我想读大学，对我来说只有拿到奖学金才能上。我喜欢篮球，我觉得如果我打得够好，就能拿到奖学金了。我也可以参加大学联赛了。我想做最棒的那个。爸爸告诉我，如果梦想足够远大，那么现实的好坏不算什么。"接着她微笑着跑去球场，不断重复那些我看了一遍又一遍的动作。

Well, I had to give it to her — she was determined. I watched her through those junior high years and into high school. Every week, she led her **varsity** team to victory.

好吧，只能这么说，她真的很努力。我看着她读完了初中，上了高中。每周，她带领的校队总能获得胜利。

One day in her senior year, I saw her sitting in the grass, head **cradled** in her arms. I walked across the street and sat down in the cool grass beside her. Quietly I asked what was wrong.

在她高三的一天，我见她坐在草坪上，双手托腮。我穿过街，坐在她旁边凉凉的草地上。我轻声问她怎么了。

"Oh, nothing," came a soft reply. "I'm just too short." The coach told her that at "5'5" she would probably never get to play for a top ranked team — much less offered a scholarship — so she should stop dreaming about college.

"没什么，"她柔柔地回答，"我就是太矮了。"教练对她说，5尺5寸的身高几乎永远无法在顶级球队打球——奖学金自然就少了很多——所以她应该别做大学梦了。

She was heartbroken and I felt my own throat tighten as I sensed her disappointment. I asked her if she had

她心碎了，我也嗓子干得说不出话来，因为我能体会她的失落。我问她有没有和她爸爸讲过。她抬

talked to her dad about it yet. She lifted her head from her hands and told me that her father said those coaches were wrong. They just didn't understand the power of a dream. He told her that if she really wanted to play for a good college, if she truly wanted a scholarship, nothing could stop her except one thing — her own attitude. He told her again, "If the dream is big enough, the facts don't count."

头告诉我，她爸爸说那些教练纯属瞎说，他们只是不明白梦想的力量罢了。父亲告诉她，如果她真的想为进一个好学校而打球，想拿奖学金，那么除了一件事——她自己的态度——之外什么也不能阻止她。父亲还说"如果梦想足够远大，那么现实的好坏不算什么。"

The next year, as she and her team went to the Northern California Championship game, she was seen by a college **recruiter**. She was indeed offered a scholarship, a full ride, to a Division I, NCAA women's basketball team. She was going to get the college education that she had dreamed of and worked toward for all those years.

第二年，她和她的大学生球队打入了北加州的冠军赛。她被一个大学球探看中，马上就被授予了一级全程奖学金并编入NCAA女篮队。她渴望了多年并且为之奋斗的大学梦成真了。

It's true: if the dream is big enough, the facts don't count.

千真万确的一句话：如果梦想足够远大，那么现实的好坏不算什么。

魅力词汇

muscle ['mʌsl] *v.* 硬挤
recess [ri'ses] *n.* 中止或暂停期间
dribble ['dribəl] *v.*（足球及其他一些体育运动）运球，带球
scholarship ['skɔləʃip] *n.* 奖学金
court [kɔːt] *n.* 球场
recap [ri'kæp] *v.* 重述，概括（文中指的是重复）
varsity ['vaːsiti] *n.*（学校的）代表队
cradle ['kreidl] *v.* 将……置于摇篮中
recruiter [ri'kruːtə] *n.* 招聘人员

3 Follow Your Dream — the Monty Roberts' Story
为梦想而坚持的罗伯兹

每个人都有自己的梦想，但并不是人人都能坚持自己的梦想。在梦想的道路上，相信自己最重要。

文苑漫步

I have a friend named Monty Roberts who owns a horse ranch in San Ysidro. He has let me use his house to put on fund-raising events to raise money for youth programs.

The last time I was there he introduced me by saying, "I want to tell you why I let Jack use my house. It all goes back to a story about a young man who was the son of an **itinerant** horse trainer who would go from stable to **stable**, race track to race track, farm to farm and **ranch** to ranch, training horses. As a result, the boy's high school career was continually interrupted. When he was a senior, he was asked to write a paper about what he wanted to be and do when he grew up.

That night he wrote a seven-page paper describing his goal of someday owning a horse ranch. He wrote about his

译林畅游

我有个朋友叫蒙提·罗伯兹，他在圣思多罗有座牧马场。我常借用他宽敞的住宅举办筹款活动，以便为青少年活动项目筹备基金。

上次活动，他在介绍我时提到："我让杰克借用住宅是有原因的。这故事跟一个小男孩有关，他是一位驯马师的儿子，他的父亲经常奔波于各个马厩、赛马场、农场和牧场之间去训练马匹。因此，小男孩的高中生活总是被打断。高中时，有一次老师让同学们写篇作文，主题是自己长大后想成为怎样的人以及想做什么。

那晚他写了一篇七页纸的文章，描述他的伟大志愿，那就是拥有一座属于自己的牧场，他仔细地

dream in great detail and he even drew a diagram of a 200-acre ranch, showing the location of all the buildings, the stables and the track. Then he drew a detailed floor plan for a 4,000-square-foot house that would sit on a 200-acre dream ranch.

描述了自己的梦想，甚至还画了一张 200 亩牧场的设计图，上面标有马厩、跑道等的位置，接着在这个 200 亩的梦想牧场中，他还画了一栋占地 4000 平方英尺的巨宅。

He put a great deal of his heart into the project and the next day he handed it in to his teacher. Two days later he received his paper back. On the front page was a large red F with a note that read, "See me after class."

他花了好大心血把作文完成，第二天交给了老师。两天后他拿回了作文，第一页上打了一个又红又大的 F，旁边还写了一行字："下课后来见我。"

The boy with the dream went to see the teacher after class and asked, "Why did I receive an F?"

这位梦想拥有者下课后带着作文去找老师："为什么给我不及格？"

The teacher said, "This is an unrealistic dream for a young boy like you. You have no money. You come from an itinerant family. You have no resources. Owning a horse ranch requires a lot of money. You have to buy the land. You have to pay for the original **breeding stock** and later you'll have to pay large **stud fees**. There's no way you could ever do it." Then the teacher added, "If you will rewrite this paper with a more realistic goal, I will reconsider your grade."

老师说道："这个梦想对于你这样的年轻人来说是不切实际的。你没钱，没家庭背景，什么资源都没有。盖牧场要花很多钱；你需要买地、需要买最初的种畜、接下来还需要付一大笔种畜交配费。这些是你绝对做不到的。"他补充道："如果你肯重写一个比较不离谱的愿望，我会重新考虑你的分数。"

The boy went home and thought about it long and hard. He asked his father what he should do. His father said, "Look, son, you have to make up your own mind on this. However, I think it is a very im-

这男孩回家后反复思索，然后征询父亲的意见。父亲只是告诉他："儿子，你必须自己拿主意。但我想这对你来说是一个很重要的决定。"

portant decision for you."

Finally, after sitting with it for a week, the boy turned in the same paper, making no changes at all. He stated, "You can keep the F and I'll keep my dream."

Monty then turned to the assembled group and said, "I tell you this story because you are sitting in my 4,000-square-foot house in the middle of my 200-acre horse ranch. I still have that school paper framed over the fireplace." He added, "The best part of the story is that two summers ago that same schoolteacher brought 30 kids to **camp out** on my ranch for a week." When the teacher was leaving, he said, 'Look, Monty, I can tell you this now. When I was your teacher, I was something of a dream **stealer**. During those years I stole a lot of kids' dreams. Fortunately you had enough **gumption** not to give up on yours.'"

Don't let anyone steal your dreams. Follow your heart, no matter what.

最后，经过一周的考虑，他决定原稿交回，一个字不改。他声明："你可以给我不及格，但是我不会放弃梦想。"

蒙提此时转向众人："我提起这故事，是因为各位现在就坐在我的位于200亩农场内、占地4000平方英尺的住宅里。高中时写的那篇作文我把它裱在壁炉的上方，至今还在。"他又补充说："最有趣的是，两年前的夏天，那位老师带了30个学生来我的牧场野营了一星期。离开之前，他对我说：'蒙提，说来有些惭愧。曾经作为你的老师，我多多少少是个偷梦者。那些年来，我偷走了很多孩子的梦想。幸亏你有足够的胆识没有放弃。'"

不要让任何人偷走你的梦想。无论遇到什么，跟从自己的内心。

魅力词汇

itinerant [ai'tinərənt]
adj.（尤指因工作而）四处奔波的
stable ['steibl] *n.* 马厩
ranch [rɑːntʃ] *n.*（大）牧场
breeding stock 种畜
stud fees（配种后所付的）种畜交配费
camp out 野营
stealer ['stiːlə] *n.* 偷窃者
gumption ['gʌmpʃn] *n.* 胆识

4 Dream Will Come True 梦想终有成真时

这一生我们尽可能不要留有遗憾。老年人通常不会为做过的事遗憾，而是为还没有做过的事情感到遗憾。只有那些有遗憾的人才会怕死。

文苑漫步

The first day of school our professor introduced a little old lady to us.

"Why are you in college at such a young age?" I asked later. She jokingly replied, I'm here to meet a rich husband, get married, have a couple of children, and then retire and travel."

"No, seriously," I asked. I was curious what may have **motivated** her to be taking on this challenge at her age. "I always dreamed of having a college education and now I'm getting one!" she told me.

We became instant friends. Every day for the next three months we would leave class together and talked nonstop. I was always listening to this "time machine" as she shared her wisdom and experience with me.

At the end of the **semester** we invited Rose to make a speech to our football team. I'll never forget what she taught

译林畅游

开学第一天，教授把一位小个子老太太介绍给了我们。

随后我问道："你为什么这么'年轻'就来读大学？"她开玩笑地回答："我来这儿是为了认识一个有钱的丈夫，结婚，生几个孩子，然后退休去旅行。"

"不，认真点儿。"我请求道。我很好奇，到底是激发她在这个年纪还要接受这样一个挑战。"我一直梦想着上大学，现在我就在读大学！"她告诉我。

我们马上成了朋友。在随后的三个月里，我们每天一起离开教室，不停地交谈。我总是听历经了岁月沧桑的她分享她的智慧和经验。

期末的时候，我们邀请罗斯给我们的橄榄球队讲话。我永远都不会忘记她教给我们的东西。就在

us. As she began to deliver her prepared speech, she dropped her note card on the floor. A little **embarrassed** she simply said, "I'm sorry. This whiskey is killing me! I'll never get my speech back in order so let me just tell you what I know." As we laughed she cleared her **throat** and began: "We do not stop playing because we are old; we grow old because we stop playing. There are only four secrets to staying young, being happy, and achieving success. You have to laugh and find humor every day. You've got to have a dream. When you lose your dreams, you die. We have so many people walking around who are dead and don't even know it! There is a huge difference between growing older and growing up. If you are 19 years old and lie in bed for one full year and don't do one **productive** thing, you will turn 20 years old. Anybody can grow older. That doesn't take any talent or ability. The idea is to grow up by always finding the opportunity in change.

Have no regrets. The elderly usually don't have regrets for what we did, but rather for things we did not do. The only people who fear death are those with regrets."

At the year's end Rose finished the college degree. One week after graduation, Rose died peacefully in her sleep. Over two thousand college students attended her

她要开始进行她事先准备好的演讲时，她把写了要点的卡片掉在了地上。她有点儿尴尬，但只是说道："对不起。这酒可真要命！我没办法再进行有次序的演讲了，就让我把我知道的东西都告诉你们吧。"我们笑了起来，她清了清嗓子，开始演讲："我们并不是因为年老就不再娱乐；我们变老是因为我们不再娱乐。只有四个秘密可以让你保持年轻、快乐并且获得成功。你必须每天都开怀大笑，寻找幽默。你必须有一个梦想。失去了梦想，你就会虽生犹死。我们周围有很多人，他们已经'死了'，自己却不知道。长大和成长之间有着巨大的差距。如果你现在19岁，躺在床上整整一年没有做一件有益的事，你也还会变成20岁。每一个人都会长大，这不需要任何天赋和能力。我们的目标是不断地在变化中寻找机遇成长。

不要留有遗憾。老年人通常不会为做过的事懊悔，而是为那些没有做过的事情感到遗憾。只有那些有遗憾的人才会害怕死亡。"

年底的时候，罗斯获得了大学学位。毕业一星期后，她在梦中安详地离开了人世。两千多名大学生参加了她的葬礼，来纪念这位通过自己

funeral to honor the wonderful woman who taught by example that it's never too late to be all you can possibly be.

的亲身经历来告诉我们永远都可以成就自己的理想的了不起的老人。

魅力词汇

motivate ['məutiveit] *v.* 给予动机，刺激
semester [si'mestə] *n.* 学期
embarrassed [im'bærəst] *adj.* 尴尬的，窘迫的
throat [θrəut] *n.* 喉咙
productive [prə'dʌktiv] *adj.* 富有成效的
funeral ['fjuːnərəl] *n.* 葬礼

温情絮语

Nothing is impossible for a willing heart.

心之所愿，无所不成。

Life is a pure flame, and we live by an invisible sun within us.

生命是一束纯净的火焰，我们依靠自己内心看不见的太阳而存在。

5 What You See Is What You Get
你得到的就是你想到的

“如果你觉得自己不会成功，那你就真的不会成功。”总有人会抱怨自己怀才不遇，慨叹自己没有伯乐来发掘培养，殊不知每个人都是自己命运的主宰。只要敢想，并且坚定地向着梦想努力，那么没有什么是不可能的。如果你处境不佳，那么何不动动脑筋，想想自己想要什么？又该如何得到呢？

文苑漫步

You've probably heard the expression, "What you see is what you get." My grandfather used to say: "If you looked at a tree long enough, it will move." We see what we want to see. **Psychologists** tell us that nothing controls our life more than our self-imagination. We live like the person we see in the mirror. We are what we think we are. If you don't think you'll be successful, you won't. You can't be it if you can't see it. Your life is limited to your vision. If you want to change your life, you must change your vision of your life.

Arnold Schwarzenegger was not that famous in 1976 when he met with a newspaper reporter. The reporter asked Schwarzenegger: "Now that you've retired from bodybuilding, what do you plan to do next?" Schwarzenegger answered

译林畅游

“你得到的就是你想到的”这种说法你一定听过吧。我爷爷以前常说：“如果你看着一棵树足够长的时间，它就会动起来。”我们看到的就是我们想看到的东西。心理学家说，没有什么比自我的想象力更能控制我们的生活。我们就像镜子中看见的那个人那样生活。我们自认为怎样，实际上就会怎样。如果你觉得自己不会成功，那你就真的不会成功。如果你想不到，那你也做不到。你的生活受你视野的限制。如果你想改变自己的生活，你就必须改变自己对生活的看法。

1976年，阿诺·施瓦辛格还没有那么有名，那时他接受一名记者的来访，记者问他：“现在，您退出了健美行业，下一步计划做什么呢？”他镇定自若地说：“我要成

very calmly and confidently: "I'm going to become the No.1 movie star in Hollywood." The reporter was shocked and amused at Schwarzenegger's plan. At that time, it was very hard to imagine how this **muscle-bound bodybuilder**, who was not a professional actor and who spoke poor English with a strong Austrian accent, could ever hope to be Hollywood's No.1 movie star!

为好莱坞头号影星。"那位记者非常惊讶于施瓦辛格的计划，并且感到可笑。那个时候，很难想象一个像他那样肌肉发达的健美运动员怎么能成为好莱坞的一流演员，要知道他不仅不是专业演员，而且还说一口具有强烈奥地利口音的英语。

So the reporter asked Schwarzenegger how he planned to make his dream come true, Schwarzenegger said: "I'll do it the same way I became the No. 1 bodybuilder in the world. What I do is to create a vision of who I want to be, and then I start living like that person in my mind as if it were already true." Sounds almost **childishly** simple, doesn't it? But it worked! Remember: "If you can see it, you can be it."

所以这个记者问他打算怎样实现梦想，施瓦辛格答道："和我成为世界一流健美运动员的方法一样。我会按照自己的理想，先创造一个形象，然后，开始像理想中的那个人一样去生活，仿佛那就是真的一样。"听起来很幼稚，不是吗？但是这方法很有效！记住："如果你能想到，你就能做到。"

A successful businessman I know wears a shirt with these words on it: "Don't just pursue your dreams. Chase them down and tackle them!" You only get one life to live, so why not live the best life possible? So you can be fully satisfied at what you see and get. Just think a minute.

我认识的一位成功的商人穿着一件印有这些话的T恤："不要只追逐你的梦想！要抓住它！征服它！"生命只有一次，那么，为什么不尽可能地使它精彩绽放呢？那样你就会为自己想到的和得到的感到心满意足。想想吧。

魅力词汇

psychologist [sai'kɔlədʒist] *n.* 心理学家

muscle-bound ['mʌsəl,baund] *adj.*（由于运动过度造成的）肌肉僵硬的，失去弹性的

bodybuilder ['bɔdibildə] *n.* 健身者

childishly ['tʃaildiʃli] *adv.* 幼稚地

6 Freedom Parrot 呼喊自由的鹦鹉

这只每天呼喊自由的鹦鹉，当它真的有机会去得到自由时，却仍紧紧地抓住铁杠，它其实并不懂得它每天所喊的“自由”到底是什么意思，所以当它真正得到它所呼喊的东西时，它却并不知道那就是。

文苑漫步

A man, a great man, a fighter for freedom was traveling in the mountains. He stayed in a **caravan** for the night. He was amazed that in the caravan there was a beautiful parrot in a golden cage, **continually** repeating “Freedom! Freedom!”. And it was such a place that when the parrot repeated the word “Freedom!” it would go on echoing in the valleys, in the mountains.

The man thought: “I have seen many parrots, and I have thought they must want to be free from those cages... but I have never seen such a parrot whose whole day, from the morning to the evening when he goes to sleep, is spent in calling out for freedom.” He had an idea. In the middle of the night, when the owner was fast asleep, he got up and opened the door of the cage.

译林畅游

一个人，一个了不起的人，一个为了自由而战的斗士，正在山峦间穿行。他晚上在一个活动住房里过夜。旅店里有一个金鸟笼，里面有一只漂亮的鹦鹉在不停地反复呼喊着“自由！自由”，这让他很震惊。而且在那里，当这只鹦鹉不断地反复呼喊“自由”的时候，这个词便会在山峦间、在深谷中久久回荡。

这个人想：“我看到过很多鹦鹉，也曾想过他们一定想从这些笼子里飞出去获得自由……但是，我从没有见过这样的鹦鹉，从早到晚，直到入睡，一整天都在呼喊着自由。”他有了一个想法。午夜，当店主熟睡的时候，他悄悄起身，打开了鸟笼门，小声地对鹦鹉说：“现在，出去吧。”

He **whispered** to the parrot: "Now get out."

But he was very surprised that the parrot was clinging to the bars of the cage. He said to him again and again: "Have you forgotten about freedom? Just get out! The door is open and the owner is fast asleep; nobody will ever know. You just fly into the sky; the whole sky is yours."

But the parrot was clinging so deeply, so hard, that the man said: "What is the matter? Are you mad?" He tried to take the parrot out with his own hands, but the parrot started **pecking** at him, and at the same time he was shouting, "Freedom! Freedom!" The valleys in the night echoed and re-echoed, but the man was also **stubborn**; he was a freedom fighter.

He pulled the parrot out and threw him into the sky; and he was very satisfied, although his hand was hurt. The parrot had attacked him as forcefully as he could, but the man was **immensely** satisfied that he had made a soul free. He went to sleep.

In the morning, as the man was waking up, he heard the parrot shouting, "Freedom! Freedom!" He thought perhaps the parrot must be sitting on a tree or on a rock. But when he came out, the parrot was sitting in the cage. The door was open.

但是令他吃惊的是这只鹦鹉竟抓着鸟笼的铁杠不放。他对它一遍又一遍地说："你忘了自由了吗？快出去！门开着，店主熟睡着，没有人会看到。你只要飞向天空，整片天空就是你的了。"

但是鹦鹉仍然牢牢地用力抓着铁杠，于是他问："怎么了？你疯了吗？"他试图用手把鹦鹉弄出来，但是鹦鹉却开始啄他，同时大喊："自由！自由！"深夜的山谷里荡起了一声又一声的回音，可是这个人也一样地顽固，谁让他是个自由之士呢。

他把鹦鹉拽出来，扔向空中。他很满意，尽管他的手受伤了。虽然鹦鹉全力地攻击他，但是他却心满意足，因为他使得一个灵魂得到了自由。然后他便回去继续睡他的觉。

早上，他睡醒了，听见鹦鹉正在大喊："自由！自由！"他想也许鹦鹉正落在一棵树上或一块石头上呢。但当他出来的时候，鹦鹉正在笼子里，笼门还开着。

魅力词汇

caravan ['kærəvæn]
n. 活动住房：用汽车拖拽的住所
continually [kən'tinjuəli] *adv.* 不断地
whisper ['wispə] *v.* 低语，耳语
peck [pek] *v.* 啄
stubborn ['stʌbən] *adj.* 顽固的，固执的
immensely [i'mensli] *adv.* 极大地

温情絮语

Great hopes make great man.

伟大的理想造就伟大的人。

Hold fast to dreams, for if dreams die, life is a broken-winged bird, that can never fly.

紧紧抓住梦想，梦想若是消亡，生命就像鸟儿折了翅膀，再也不能飞翔。

7 Digging a Way Out 挖一条出路

当我们被囚禁于不自由的牢笼中时，我们需要挖一条出路，但这并不是那么容易，它是充满艰难的，容易的地方往往没有出口。成功与否，旨在于我们的内心是否真地想要出去得自由！

文苑漫步

There's a man who has been by himself in a prison cell with a dirt floor, **crude** stone walls, and there are two windows, one of which looks out towards the ocean. All of the sudden, he hears a scratching noise, and he looks down at the ground that is furthest away from the window facing the ocean. He sees the ground moving, and he starts to think he's losing his mind. But soon the ground breaks, and up pops a head with long hair and a beard… it's a prisoner.

And the prisoner says: "Sssh. Listen. A group of us have been **tunneling** for about six years, and we've finally reached your cell. We have ways to cover up my **entrance** into this, but now it's all on your shoulders, man. All you have to do," he said while pointing out the window

译林畅游

一个人独自关在一间牢房里，牢房的地面脏兮兮的，石头墙壁很粗糙，有两扇窗户，其中一扇面向着大海。突然，这个人听到了噼噼啪啪的声音，他望过去，发现离对着大海的那扇窗户的最远的地面竟然在动，他开始以为自己疯了。但是不久之后地面裂开了，突然冒出来一个脑袋，长着长长的头发和胡子……是一个囚犯。

这个囚犯说："嘘！听着，我们一群人一直在挖这个地道，差不多六年了，终于挖到了你的牢房。我们自有办法掩盖通往这里的入口，但是现在看你的了，老兄。你所要做的是，"他指着面朝大海的那扇窗户说，"你只要从这里开始向下

towards the ocean, "you just start digging here and go down about six feet and about seventy-five feet in that direction and there is freedom, and we're out of here!" "Oh, I love that! That's great; I want to be free!" "Okay, I'll check back with you in a few weeks."

挖六英尺，朝那个方向大约七十五英尺，那里就是自由，我们就能从这里出去了！"“哦，我喜欢！那太棒了，我要自由！"“好的，几周之后我会过来看看。"

Two weeks later, he pops back in to check on his friend's progress, and his friend nods back with great **affirmation**. "Yeah, I've done it." So the man who was providing the instructions pops down the hole, and two seconds later pops right back up and says: "What have you done?!" "Huh?" "I told you to dig in the direction towards the OCEAN! This tunnel that you dug goes back under the wall and into the prison yard." "Well, the digging was easier in the other direction…"

两周之后，这个囚犯回来检查他这位朋友的进程，他的朋友很肯定地向他点点头："耶，我完成了。"于是，提供指示的这个人迅速跳进洞里，两秒后又突然伸出了脑袋："你都干了什么？！"“嗯？"“我让你朝着大海的方向挖！而你挖的这条地道从墙下穿过又回到了监狱的院子里。"“哦，朝着另一个方向挖起来比较容易……"

魅力词汇

crude [kruːd] *adj.* 粗糙的
tunnel ['tʌnl] *v.* 挖地道，开隧道
entrance ['entrəns] *n.* 入口
affirmation [ˌæfə'meiʃn] *n.* 肯定

8 A Ball to Roll Around 滚球

"这并不是说我宁愿成为盲人，只是失去视力让我更加珍惜自己其他方面的能力。"人们总是习惯在失去以后才懂得珍惜。但是失去之后我们并不应该自怨自艾，而是应该着眼于其他方面，用自己的努力来弥补或者是开拓出一片新的天地。这或许就是人生的缺憾美吧。

文苑漫步

I lost my sight when I was 4 years old by falling off a box car in a **freight** yard in Atlantic City and landing on my head. Now I am 32. I can vaguely remember the brightness of sunshine and what color red is. It would be wonderful to see again, but a **calamity** can do strange things to people. It occurred to me the other day that I might not have come to love life as I do if I hadn't been blind. I believe in life now. I am not so sure that I would have believed it so deeply, otherwise. I don't mean that I would prefer to go without my eyes. I simply mean that the loss of them made me appreciate more what I had left.

Life, I believe, asks a **continuous** series of **adjustments** to reality. The more **readily** a person is able to make these ad-

译林畅游

4岁那年在大西洋城，我从货场的一辆棚车上摔下来，头先着地，于是双目失明。现在我已经32岁了。我还模糊地记得阳光的灿烂和红色的鲜艳。能恢复视觉固然好，但灾难也能对人产生奇妙的作用。有一天我突然想到，倘若我不是盲人，我或许不会变得像现在这样热爱生活。现在我相信生活，但我不能肯定如果我没有失明，自己会不会像现在这样深深地相信生活。这并不是说我宁愿成为盲人，只是失去视力让我更加珍惜自己其他方面的能力。

我认为，生活要求人不断地自我调整以适应现实。人越能及时地进行调整，他的个人世界就越有意

justments, the more meaningful his own private world becomes. The adjustment is never easy. I was **bewildered** and afraid. But I was lucky. My parents and my teachers saw something in me — a potential to live, you might call it — which I didn't see, and they made me want to fight it out with blindness.

义。调整绝非易事。我曾感到茫然害怕，但我很幸运。父母和老师们在我身上发现了某种东西——你可以称之为一种活下去的潜力——而我自己却没有发现。他们激励我与失明拼搏到底。

The hardest lesson I had to learn was to believe in myself. That was basic. If I hadn't been able to do that, I would have collapsed and become a chair rocker on the front **porch** for the rest of my life. When I say belief in myself I am not talking about simply the kind of self-confidence that helps me down an unfamiliar **staircase** alone. That is part of it. But I mean something bigger than that: an assurance that I am, despite imperfections, a real, positive person; that somewhere in the **sweeping**, **intricate** pattern of people there is a special place where I can make myself fit.

我必须学会的最艰难的一课就是相信自己，这是基本条件。如果我没有做到这一点，那我早已经崩溃，只能坐在前门廊的摇椅中度过余生。我说的相信自己并不仅仅指独自走下陌生楼梯的那种自信，那只是其中一部分。我指的范围更大：它是一种相信自己虽然有生理缺陷，却是一个真实的、有进取心的人的信念；一种相信在形形色色的世人中间，我可以找到适合自己的特殊位置的信念。

It took my years to discover and strengthen this assurance. It had to start with the most elementary things. Once a man gave me an indoor baseball. I thought he was **mocking** me and I was hurt. "I can't use this," I said. "Take it with you," he urged me, "and roll it around". The words stuck in my head. "Roll it around!" By rolling the ball I could hear where it went. This

我花了数年才树立并不断加强这一信念。这要从最简单的事做起。有一次，一个人给我一个室内玩的棒球，我以为他在嘲笑我，感觉很受伤。“我玩不了。”我说。“你拿着，”他竭力劝我，“在地上滚。”他的话在我脑子里生了根。“在地上滚！”滚球可以使我听见它朝哪儿滚动。这让我马上想到一

gave me an idea how to achieve a goal I had thought impossible: playing baseball. At Philadelphia's Overbrook School for the Blind I invented a successful variation of baseball. We call it ground ball.

个我曾认为不可能达到的目标：打棒球。在费城奥弗布鲁克盲人学校，我发明了一种很受人欢迎的棒球游戏，我们称它为“地面球”。

All my life I have set ahead of me a series of goals and then tried to reach them, one at a time. I had to learn my limitations. It was no good to try for something I knew at the start was wildly out of reach because that only invited the bitterness of failure. I would fail sometimes anyway but on the average I made progress.

这一辈子我已经树立了一系列目标，然后努力去达到，一次一个。当然我必须知道自己能力有限。因为如果一开始就知道某事根本不能实现却硬要去尝试，那只会带来失败的苦果，不会有任何好处。虽然有时我也会失败，但总的来说我一直在进步。

魅力词汇

freight [freit] *n.* 货物
calamity [kə'læmiti] *n.* 灾难
continuous [kən'tinjuəs] *adj.* 连续的
adjustment [ə'dʒʌstmənt] *n.* 调节，调整
readily ['redili] *adv.* 敏捷地
bewildered [bi'wildəd] *adj.* 困惑的
porch [pɔːtʃ] *n.* 门廊
staircase ['steəkeis] *n.* 楼梯
sweeping ['swiːpiŋ] *adj.* 包罗万象的
intricate ['intrikət] *adj.* 错综复杂的
mock [mɔk] *v.* 嘲弄，愚弄

温情絮语

In doing we learn.

实践长才干。

9 Attitude Is Everything
态度决定一切

生活就像一面镜子，你对它笑，它就对你笑；你对它皱眉，它也对你皱眉。所以，自己生活得幸福与否，关键是看自己的生活态度积极与否。

文苑漫步

Jerry was the kind of guy you love to hate. He was the type of person who was always in a good mood, always up, always had something positive to say. When someone would ask him how he was doing, he would reply, "If I were any better, I would be twins!"

I met Jerry when I was a young manager in the restaurant industry. He was a unique manager because he had several waiters who had followed him around from restaurant to restaurant. The reason the waiters followed Jerry was because of his attitude. He was a natural motivator. If an employee was having a bad day, Jerry was there telling the employee how to look on the positive side of the situation.

Seeing this style really made me curious, so one day I went up to Jerry and asked him, "I don't get it! You can't be a

译林畅游

Jerry真是个让人又爱又恨的家伙。他总是心情愉悦、情绪高涨，总能说出一些积极向上的话来。当人们问他最近如何时，他就回答："如果再好一点的话我就成了双胞胎了！"

在我年轻的时候，我就认识Jerry了，那时，我是一家餐馆的经理。而他则是个很特别的经理，因为他有几个服侍生跟着他从一家餐馆到另一家餐馆。服务员跟着Jerry的原因正是由于他的态度。他天生善于鼓励人。如果哪个雇员哪天倒了霉，Jerry就会去告诉他如何往事情好的一面看。

看到他如此作风我甚感好奇，于是一天我走到Jerry跟前问他："我不明白！你不可能一直保持积

positive up person all the time. How do you do it?"

Jerry replied, "Each morning I wake up and say to myself, 'Jerry, you have two choices today. You can choose to be in a good mood or you can choose to be in a bad mood.' I choose to be in a good mood. Each time something bad happens, I can choose to be a **victim** or I can choose to learn from it. I choose to learn from it. Every time someone comes to me complaining, I can choose to accept their complaining or I can point out the positive side of life. I choose the positive side of life. Life is all about choices."

I thought about what Jerry said. Soon, I left the restaurant business to pursue my own business. We lost touch, but I often thought about him when I made a choice about life instead of reacting to life.

Several years later, I heard that Jerry had done something you are never supposed to do in the restaurant business: he had left the back door open one morning and three armed robbers walked in, and held him up at gunpoint. While trying to open the safe, he got nervous and his hand slipped off the **combination lock**. The robbers got nervous and blew a hole through his hand and then three right through the middle of his abdomen. He lay there on the floor dying as the **paramedics**

极乐观吧。你是怎么做的呢？"

Jerry 回答说："每天早上醒来后我就跟自己说：'Jerry，今天你有两个选择。你可以选择一个好心情，也可以选择一个坏心情。'我选择了好心情。每次坏事发生时，我可以选择成为受害者，也可以选择从中吸取教训。我选择了从中吸取教训。每当有人向我抱怨时，我可以选择听他们抱怨，或者给他们指出生活中积极的一面。我选择了指出生活中积极的一面。生活就是由许多选择组成的。"

我仔细思考着 Jerry 的话。没过多久，我离开了那家餐馆去干自己的事业。虽然我们失去了联系，但是每当我对生活做抉择而非对生活作出反应的时候，我就会想起他。

几年之后，我听说 Jerry 做了件在餐馆里绝不应该做的事情：一天早晨，他没关后门，三个持枪匪徒走进来，拿枪指着他。开保险箱的时候，他由于紧张，手从保险锁上滑下来。匪徒紧张之下开枪打穿了他的手，接着又有三枚子弹正中他的腹部。别人打电话叫医生的时候，他躺在地板上奄奄一息。他们赶紧把他送到当地的伤疗中心，经过 18 个小时的手术和几个星期的悉心护理，一个月后，他终于出院

were called. They rushed him to the local **trauma** center and he was in surgery for 18 hours and intensive cares for weeks, and finally emerged from the hospital a month later with **fragments** of the bullets still in his body.

了，而体内还残留着子弹的碎片。

I saw Jerry about six months later. When I asked him how he was, he replied, "If I were any better, I'd be twins. Wanna see my scars?" I **declined** to see his wounds, but I did ask him what had gone through his mind when the robbery was happening.

六个月后我见到了Jerry。我问他怎样了，他答道："如果再好一些的话，我就是双胞胎了。想不想看看我的伤疤？"我没看他的伤疤，但我问他在抢劫案发生的时候，他脑子里在想些什么。

"The first thing that went through my mind," Jerry replied, "was that I should have locked the back door. Then, as I was lying on the floor, I was thinking that I had two choices: I could choose to live, or I could choose to die. I was choosing to live."

"我首先想到的，"Jerry回答，"是我本应该把后门锁上的。接着，在我躺在地板上的时候，我想到自己有两个选择：我可以选择生，也可以选择死。我选择了生。"

"Weren't you ever scared? Did you lose consciousness?" I asked.

"你难道一点也不怕吗？你失去知觉了吗？"我问。

Jerry continued the story, "The paramedics were great. They kept telling me I was going to be fine. But when they wheeled me into the emergency room, I got really scared when I saw the expressions on the doctors and nurses' faces. They all looked like I was a dead man. I knew I needed to take action."

Jerry继续说："护理人员很厉害。他们不停地告诉我我会好起来的。但当他们推我进急救室的时候，我看到医生和护士们脸上的表情，我确实吓了一跳。他们看起来就像是我已经死了。我知道我需要采取些行动。"

"What did you do?" I asked.

"你做了什么？"我问。

"Well, there was a big, **burly** nurse

"这个，有个高高大大的护士

shouting at me, 'Jerry, are you **allergic** to anything?' 'Yes,' I shouted back. 'What?' she asked. The doctors and nurses stopped and waited for my reply. I took a deep breath and yelled, 'Bullets!' They all started laughing, and I told them, 'Look, I am choosing to live. Operate on me as if I am a living man, not a dead man.'"

Jerry lived in part because of his doctors, but in large part because of his **indomitable** attitude.

朝我喊：'Jerry，你有对什么东西过敏吗？''有，'我喊道。'是什么？'她问。医生和护士们停下来等我的回答。我深深吸了口气，喊道：'子弹！'他们全笑起来，接着我对他们说：'瞧，我选择要活下来。给我动手术，把我当成个活人而不是死人。'"

Jerry 活了下来，部分原因是他的医生医术高明，但更主要是因为他那坚韧不拔的态度。

魅力词汇

victim ['viktim] *n.* 受害者
combination ['kɔmbi'neiʃn] lock 保险锁
paramedic [ˌpærə'medik] *n.* 护理人员
trauma ['trɔːmə] *n.* 外伤（身体的严重损伤或刺激，常由暴力或事故造成）
fragment ['frægmənt] *n.* 碎片，碎块
decline [di'klain] *v.* 谢绝
burly ['bəːli] *adj.* 结实的，健壮的
allergic [ə'ləːdʒik] *adj.* 过敏的
indomitable [in'dɔmitəbl] *adj.* 不屈不挠的

温情絮语

Constant dropping wears the stone.

滴水穿石。

Always will I take another step. If that is of no avail, I will take another, and yet another. In truth, one step at a time is not too difficult.

我总是会再前进一步，如果没有用，就再向前一步，而后再向前一步。事实上，每次进步一点点并不太难。

10 How Can I Love the Job I Have
调整心态热爱你的工作

愉快只是幸福的伴随现象，愉快如果不伴随以劳动，那么它不仅会迅速地失去价值，而且也会迅速地使人们的心灵堕落下来。——乌申斯基

文苑漫步

Every day we hear about people making radical career changes. The opportunities exist, but will all these changes make us any happier once we get there? Maybe the question is not "How can I get the job I love?", but "How can I love the job I have?" Following are four practical steps towards coming to terms with why you do what you're doing. Take some time to think about it, and you might be surprised by what you find.

1. Realize that your job does not define you, but how you do it does. There's a lot to be said for attitude, more than if fit here. Any job can be done well, done with compassion, done with care. Your attitude at work and the way you treat people—even your mood—do not go unnoticed. They have a **profound** influence on the people you work with. There are times

译林畅游

每天我们都听说有人跳槽了。机会确实存在，但一旦跳槽我们真的更快乐吗？可能问题不在于“如何才能找到我喜欢的工作”，而在于“我如何喜欢上我现在的工作”。下面四个可行的步骤就能解释为什么你在做目前的工作。花些时间思考一下，你可能会为你的发现而感到惊讶。

1. 要明白限定你的不是工作本身，而是你的工作方式。很多时候都是态度问题，而不是适不适合这里。干任何工作只要带着热情和细心，都能干好。你对待工作的态度和为人处事的方式——甚至你的情绪——不是没人注意。这些都会给你的同事带来很大的影响。有时你无法控制你的境遇，但是你总能选

when you can't control your situation, but you can always choose how you live in it.

2. Stop focusing on the money. Money will never be enough, so stop using it (or the lack of it) as an excuse. Whatever you are bringing home on the 15th and 30th, there are always going to be things you could do or would do if you had more. Try taking tracking every penny you spend in a week. Seeing where your money is really going can help you to refocus your spending towards the things you really want. Getting paid is only one small part of what you do, your work has to be more than just a **paycheck** to be fulfilled.

3. Find the significance in what you do. This may require you to think big, but it can be done. Take some time to really think about what you do. Do you provide an **essential** service? Do you get to see the finished product? Do you give direction that gets things done? Then ask yourself "how is this job done differently because I am doing it?" **Perspective** plays a huge role in personal satisfaction and sense of well-being. Try to remember why you took the job in the first place. If it was only going to be "for now", are you actively looking for other work?

4. Dare to ask yourself if it's worth it. If you can't find the part of your job that you like, or if you can see yourself turning

择如何在这种处境中生活。

2.不要总是盯着金钱。金钱永远都不会够的，因此不要再把钱（或者缺钱）作为一个借口。无论在每月15号或30号带什么回家，如果你有更多的钱，也总会有更多的事情可以去做或者想要去做。试着记录下来一周内你花的每一分钱。看看你把钱都花在哪儿了，这能帮你重新确定把钱花在你真正需要的东西上。取得报酬只是你工作的一小部分，工作的成就感不应仅仅是一份工资就可以满足的。

3. 发现你工作的重要意义。这可能需要雄心壮志，但这是可以做到的。花些时间认真考虑一下你的工作，你有没有提供最基本的服务？你有没有看到过成品？你有没有对某件事进行过指导？然后自问一下“若是我做这项工作的话，结果会有何不同？”独特的视角对提升自我满足感和幸福感起着很大的作用。努力回忆一下当初你为何选择这份工作，如果仅仅是为了“暂时”的权宜之计，那么你还在积极寻找其他的工作吗？

4. 敢于问自己是否值得。如果在工作中你不能找到自己感兴趣的部分，或者你发现自己正在转变

into the person you said you would never be, consider the reasons. It may not be a new job that you need, just a new direction. Do you like the person you are doing this job? If not, are there changes you can make to the way you do your job or is the job itself the problem? Do you need to be doing a different position within the same company? Are additional responsibilities taking you away from the work you were hired to do? Maybe all that's needed is some refocusing. Learn to say "no". As much as you can choose the things you spend your time on, don't attend events or meetings only because everyone expects it.

成你永远都不想成为的那种人，那么思考一下原因吧。你需要的可能不是一份新工作，而是一个新的方向。你喜欢工作时的那个自己吗？如果不喜欢，你能否改变一下自己的工作方法，还是工作本身存在问题？你是否需要在这个公司调换一下岗位？是否因为承担额外的责任而脱离了本职工作？或许所需要的就是重新聚焦。学会说“不”。尽量选择做那些你需要投资时间去做的工作，而不要仅仅因为所有人都期待你那样做而去参加一些活动或会议。

Asking yourself why you do your job doesn't mean you're dissatisfied, just **self-aware**. This awareness can lead to greater job satisfaction, increased sense of well-being and a little more control over what you do, rather than just "going along for the ride". For some, it may be time for a change — if so, don't be afraid of it. Change isn't necessarily bad, it's just different. For the rest of us, take a look around, you may find you've got a great view.

问问自己为何做这项工作并不意味着你对它不满意，而是一种自省。这种认知可以使你获得更高的工作满意度，增加幸福感，能更好地把握自己的工作，而不仅仅是“随波逐流”。对有些人来说，可能是到了应该改变的时候了——如果是这样，不要害怕。改变不一定是坏事，只是变得不同而已。而对于其他人，环顾四周，你会发现风景这边独好。

Take a look at your life. How would you describe it? Contented? Rushed? Exciting? Stressful? Moving forward? Holding back? For many of us it's all of the above at times. There are things we dream

审视一下自己的生活。你怎么描述它呢？满足？匆忙？刺激？紧迫？前进？退缩？对许多人来说，有时以上都有。有些事情我们梦想着有一天可以去做，而有些事情我

of doing one day, there are things we wish we could forget. In the Bible, it says that Jesus came to make all things new. What would your life look like if you could start over with a **clean slate**?

们希望可以忘却。圣经上说，耶稣使一切焕然一新。如果你能重新开始，你的生活会是怎样的呢？

魅力词汇

profound [prə'faund] *adj.* 极大的
paycheck ['peitʃek] *n.* 薪水支票，工资
essential [i'senʃl] *adj.* 基本的
perspective [pə'spektiv] *n.* 视角
self-aware [selfə'weə] *adj.* 自知的，有自知之明的
clean slate 无过错记录，清白的历史

温情絮语

Nothing great was ever achieved without enthusiasm.

无热情成就不了伟业。

The prizes of life are at the end of each journey, not near the beginning.

生命的奖赏远在旅途终点，而非起点附近。

11 To Love Life Through Labour 因工作而热爱生活

“唯有劳作不息，你们才能真正活在爱的生命里。因劳动而热爱生命，才能彻悟生命至深的奥秘。”一切乐境，都可由劳动得来，一切苦境，都可由劳动解脱。工作让我们的生活变得充实、有意义，让我们更加热爱生活。

文苑漫步

Then a **ploughman** said: “Speak to us of work.”

And he answered, saying:

“You work that you may keep pace with the earth and the soul of the earth.

For to be idle is to become a stranger **unto** the seasons, and to step out of life’s procession, that marches in **majesty** and proud **submission** towards the infinite.

When you work you are a **flute** through whose heart the whispering of the hours turns to music.

Which of you would be a reed, dumb and silent, when all else sing together in **unison**?

Always you have been told that work is a curse and labour a misfortune.

But I say to you that when you work you fulfil a part of earth’s furthest dream,

译林畅游

接着，一位农夫说：“跟我们说说工作吧。”

他回答：

“人们工作，是为了可以紧跟天地万物的步伐。

“因为蹉跎岁月会让你们成为四季的陌客，让你们离散于生命队伍之外，而这队伍正以庄重而自豪的谦恭走向永生。

“工作时的你们，便如那长笛，浅吟低唱的光阴自你们心底流溢，化作曼妙乐曲。

“你们中有谁愿意做一茎芦苇，当众生齐声歌唱的时候，独你沉默无语？

“你们常听人说，工作是祸，劳动是灾。

“但是我告诉你们，工作时，你们完成了大地之梦的部分悠远乐

assigned to you when that dream was born.

And in keeping yourself with labour you are in truth loving life.

And to love life through labour is to be **intimate** with life's inmost secret."

章，那梦想自诞生之初，便已注定由你们完成。

“唯有劳作不息，你们才能真正活在爱的生命里。

“因劳动而热爱生命，才能彻悟生命至深的奥秘。”

魅力词汇

ploughman ['plaumən] *n.* 农夫
unto ['ʌntə] *prep.* 对，对于
majesty ['mædʒisti] *n.* 威严，庄严
submission [səb'miʃn] *n.* 服从
flute [fluːt] *n.* 长笛
unison ['juːnisn] *n.* 和谐
intimate ['intimət] *adj.* 亲密的

温情絮语

A bold attempt is half success.

勇敢的尝试是成功的一半。

The greatest test of courage on earth is to bear defeat without losing heart.

世界上对勇气的最大考验是忍受失败而不丧失信心。

12 How to Be True to Yourself 怎样做个表里如一的人

德塞曾说过："诚实是人生的命脉，是一切价值的根基。"诚实是一种发自内心、不加任何伪饰的态度，诚实待人才是最完美、最轻松、最圆融的处世之道。可见，诚信于人价值不菲：一诺千金！

文苑漫步

My grandparents believed you were either honest or you weren't. There was no in between. They had a simple **motto** hanging on their living-room wall: "Life is like a field of newly fallen snow; where I choose to walk every step will show." They didn't have to talk about it — they demonstrated the motto by the way they lived.

They understood **instinctively** that **integrity** means having a personal standard of morality and ethics that does not sell out to **expediency** and that is not relative to the situation at hand. Integrity is an inner standard for judging your behavior. Unfortunately, integrity is in short supply today and getting scarcer. But it is the real bottom line in every area of society. And it is something we must demand of ourselves.

A good test for this value is to look at

译林畅游

我的祖父母认为，你要么是诚实的，要么是不诚实的。不可能介于两者之间。他们在起居室的墙上挂着一幅简短的座右铭："生活就像一片刚落满白雪的土地；无论走到哪里，我的脚印都会出现在那里。"他们无需就此加以评说——他们是以身体力行的方式来实践这幅座右铭的。

他们本能的理解是，诚实意味着要具备自己的一套伦理道德标准，既不见风使舵，也不趋炎附势。诚实是判断你行为举止的内在标准。遗憾的是，当今社会，诚信缺失且呈越来越稀少的趋势。然而，它却是社会每一个领域的真正底线，也是我们必须严格要求自己做到的。

检验这种价值标准的一个有效

what I call the Integrity Trial, which consists of three key principles:

1. Stand firmly for your convictions in the face of personal pressure. There's a story told about a **surgical** nurse's first day on the medical team at a well-known hospital. She was responsible for ensuring that all instruments and materials are accounted for during an **abdominal** operation. The nurse said to the surgeon, "you've only removed 11 **sponges**, and we used 12. We need to find the last one."

"I removed them all," the doctor declared, "we'll close now."

"You can't do that, sir," objected the **rookie** nurse, "Think of the patient." Smiling, the surgeon lifted his foot and showed the nurse the 12th sponge. "You'll do just fine in this or any other hospital," he told her.

2. Always give others credit that is rightfully theirs. Don't be afraid of those who might have a better idea or who might even be smarter than you are.

David Ogilvy, founder of the advertising firm Ogilvy & Mather, made this point clear to his newly appointed office heads by sending each a **Russian nesting doll** with five progressively smaller figures inside. His message was contained in the smallest doll:

"If each of us hires people who are smaller than we are, we shall become a

方法是，参考我所谓的诚实检验，其中包括三条核心原则：

1. 面对个人压力，要坚定信念。有这样一个故事：在一所有名的医院，一位外科护士第一天到医疗组去上班。在一个腹部手术中，她负责清点所有使用的器材。这位护士对外科医生说："我们用了 12 块药棉，您却只取出了 11 块。我们必须找到最后那一块。"

"我全都取出来了，"医生肯定地说，"我们现在缝合刀口吧。"

"先生，您不能那么做，"这位新来的护士反驳道，"想想这位病人吧。"外科医生一边微笑，一边抬起脚，给护士看第 12 块药棉。"不管是在这所医院，还是在其他任何医院，你都会干得非常出色，"他称赞这位护士说。

2. 要经常赞扬那些值得肯定的人。切莫害怕那些比你有见解或者比你更聪明的人。

奥美公司的创建人戴维·奥格尔维就很清楚这一点，他给新上任的部门经理每人送一套俄罗斯嵌套娃娃，里面共有五个依次变小的玩具娃娃。在最小的玩具娃娃里面，有戴维的留言：

"如果我们雇佣的每个人都比我们矮小，我们的公司就会变成侏

company of **dwarfs**. But if each of us hires people who are bigger than we are, Ogilvy & Mather will become a company of giants." And that is precisely what the company became — one of the largest and most respected advertising organizations in the world.

儒公司。反之，如果我们每个人所雇佣的人比我们高大，那么，奥美将会成为一个巨人公司。"正是这样，后来，它终于成为世界上最大、最有声望的广告公司之一。

3. Be honest and open about who you really are. People who lack genuine core values rely on external factors — their looks or status — in order to feel good about themselves. **Inevitably** they will do everything they can to preserve this **facade**, but they will do very little to develop their inner value and personal growth.

3. 真诚、坦率地展示真实的自己。只有那些缺乏核心价值观念的人，为了使自我感觉良好，才会依靠外在因素——相貌或社会地位。他们势必尽一切可能来保全这种表面形象，却很少会去培养自己内在的价值，也不注重个人的成长。

So be yourself. Don't engage in a personal cover up of areas that are unpleasing in your life. When it's tough, do it tough. In other words, face reality and be adult in your responses to life's challenges.

因此，要展示真实的自己。不要设法掩盖生活中令人不快的方方面面。要坚强地面对生活中的困难时刻。换言之，要面对现实。要成熟地应对生活中的种种挑战。

Self-respect and a clear conscience are powerful components of integrity and are the basis for enriching your relationships with others. Integrity means you do what you do because it's right and not just fashionable or politically correct. A life of principle, of not **succumbing** to the **seductive sirens** of an easy morality, will always win the day. It will take you forward into the 21st century without having to check your tracks in a **rearview** mirror. My grandparents taught me that.

自尊和问心无愧是构成诚实的强有力的成分，是丰富你与他人关系的基础。诚实意味着，你之所以做你所做的事是因为你做的是对的，而不是因为你的行为很时髦或在政治上是正确的。坚持自己的准则，不屈从于充满诱惑的追求安逸的道德观，这样的人生才能获得成功。这种生活将带你迈进21世纪，而你无需从后视镜里检查你留下的轨迹。这是我爷爷和奶奶给我的教导。

魅力词汇

motto ['mɔtəu] *n.* 座右铭，箴言
instinctively [in'stiŋktivli] *adv.*（出于）本能地
integrity [in'tegriti] *n.* 诚实，正直
expediency [iks'pi:diənsi] *n.* 权宜之计，私利
surgical ['sə:dʒikl] *adj.* 外科的
abdominal [æb'dɔminəl] *adj.* 腹部的
sponge [spʌndʒ] *n.* 药棉，消毒纱布
rookie ['ruki] *n.* 新手
Russian nesting doll 俄罗斯嵌套娃娃
dwarf [dwɔ:f] *n.* 侏儒，矮子
inevitably [in'evitəbli] *adv.* 不可避免地
facade [fə'sɑ:d] *n.* 外表（犹指虚伪的）
succumb [sə'kʌm] *v.* 屈从
seductive [si'dʌktiv] *adj.* 诱惑的
siren ['sairən] *n.* 娇艳而危险的女人
rearview ['riəvju:] *n.*（车辆上的）后视镜

温情絮语

Everyone wants to live on top of the mountain, but all the happiness and growth occurs while you're climbing it.

所有的人都想停留在山顶，但所有的乐趣和成长发生在攀爬的过程里。

Only they who fulfill their duties in everyday matters will fulfill them on great occasions.

只有在日常生活中尽责的人才会在重大时刻尽责。

13 Excellence Is Not an Act, but a Habit
优秀不是行动，而是一种习惯

习惯就是习惯，谁也不能将其扔出窗外，只能一步一步地引下楼。

——马克·吐温

文苑漫步

Our character, basically, is a composite of our habits. "Sow a thought, reap an action; sow an action, reap a habit; sow a habit, reap a character; sow a character, reap a destiny," **the maxim goes**.

Habits are powerful factors in our lives. Because they are consistent, often unconscious patterns, they constantly, daily, express our character and produce our effectiveness or ineffectiveness.

As Horace Mann, the great educator, once said: "Habits are like a cable. We weave a **strand** of it everyday and soon it cannot be broken." I personally do not agree with the last part of his expression. I know habits can be learned and unlearned. But I also know it isn't a quick fix. It involves a process and a **tremendous** commitment.

Those of us who watched the lunar

译林畅游

人的品德基本上是由习惯组成的。俗语说：播种思想，收获行为；播种行为，收获习惯；播种习惯，收获性格；播种性格，收获人生。

习惯对我们的生活有很大的影响，因为它们是连贯一致的，在不知不觉中，经年累月影响着我们的品德，暴露出我们的本性，左右着我们的成效。

美国著名教育家贺拉斯·曼恩曾说："习惯就仿佛是一条缆绳，我们每天编织一股，用不了多久就会变得牢不可破。"这句话的后半句我不敢苟同，我相信习惯可以养成，也可以打破，但绝不是一蹴而就，而是需要长期的努力和极大的毅力。

宇航员搭乘阿波罗 11 号太空

voyage of Apollo 11 were **transfixed** as we saw the first men walk on the moon and return to the earth. But to get there, those astronauts **literally** had to **break out of** the tremendous **gravity pull of the earth**. More energy was spent in the first few minutes of lift-off, in the first few miles of travel, than was used over the next several days to travel half a million miles.

船，首次登陆月球在月球上行走，并返回地球，的确令人叹为观止。但宇航员得先摆脱地球强大的引力，才能飞往月球。在刚发射的几分钟，也就是整个任务一开始的几英里之内，是最耗费能量的，往往超过往后几天内飞行的几十万英里。

Habits, too, have tremendous gravity pull — more than most people realize or would admit. Breaking deeply **imbedded** habitual tendencies such as **procrastination**, impatience, **criticalness**, or selfishness that violate basic principles of human effectiveness involves more than a little **willpower** and a few minor changes in our lives. "Lift off" takes a tremendous effort, but once we break out of the gravity pull, our freedom takes on a whole new dimension.

习惯也是一样，它具有极大的引力——只是大多数人没有意识到或不肯承认。拖拖拉拉、缺乏耐心、吹毛求疵或自私自利这些不良习性违反了我们要取得成功所需秉持的基本原则。想要革除这些根深蒂固的不良习惯，一点点的毅力和生活中的微小改变就可以达到的。“起飞”需要极大的努力，然而一旦脱离了重力的牵绊，我们便可享受前所未有的自由。

Like any natural force, gravity pull can work with us or against us. The gravity pull of some of our habits may currently be keeping us from going where we want to go. But it is also gravity pull that keeps our world together, that **keeps** the planets in their orbits and our universe **in order**. It is a powerful force, and if we use it effectively, we can use the gravity pull of habit to create the **cohesiveness** and order necessary to establish effectiveness in our lives.

习惯的引力就如同自然界所有的力量一般，既可以为我们所用，也可能给我们带来危害。有些习惯或许一时有碍于我们达到目标。但是，宇宙万物作为一个整体，各循轨道运行，彼此保持一定的秩序，毕竟也都有赖于引力的作用。所以只要我们善于利用习惯的庞大引力，就能使生活有重心、有秩序，从而获得成功。

魅力词汇

the maxim goes 俗话说
strand [strænd] *n.* (线等的)股
tremendous [tri'mendəs] *adj.* 极大的
transfix [træs'fiks] *v.* 使呆住
literally ['litərəli] *adv.* 实在地
break out of 摆脱，突破
gravity pull of the earth 地球引力
imbed [im'bed] *v.* 放入，嵌进
procrastination [prə'kræsti'neiʃn] *n.* 延迟，耽搁
criticalness ['kritikəlnis] *n.* 批判性
willpower ['wilˌpauə] *n.* 意志力
keep... in order 保持秩序
cohesiveness [kəu'hiːsivnis] *n.* 凝聚性

温情絮语

While I breathe, I hope.

我们心怀希望，只要一息尚存。

A man's best friends are his ten fingers.

人最好的朋友是自己的十个手指。

14 Strength in Surrender
顺服中的力量

总会有那么一个时期，仿佛生命中的一切都是那么糟糕，而我们也是那么不堪一击；总会有那么一个时期，我们需要承认自己的无力，面对自己的软弱；总会有那么一个时期，我们发现我们是如此地需要他人的帮助。这才让我们更加感恩和谦卑。

文苑漫步

The day my fiancé fell to his death, it started to snow, just like any November day, just like the bottom hadn't fallen out of my world when he freefell off the roof. His body, when I found it, was lightly covered with snow. It snowed almost every day for the next four months, while I sat on the couch and watched it pile up.

One morning, I **shuffled** downstairs and was startled to see a snowplow clearing my driveway and the bent back of a woman shoveling my walk. I dropped to my knees, crawled through the living room, and back upstairs so those good Samaritans would not see me. I was **mortified**. My first thought was, how would I ever repay them? I didn't have the strength to brush my hair let alone shovel someone's walk.

译林畅游

我未婚夫去世那日，天开始下雪，就仿佛是十一月里某个普通的一天，就仿佛当他从房顶上跌下时，我的世界并没有垮塌。当我发现他时，他的身体上已经覆盖了一层薄薄的雪花。之后的四个月，差不多每天都在下雪，而我就坐在沙发上，看着雪一点点堆积起来。

一天早上，我拖着沉重的脚步下楼，却惊奇地发现一台扫雪机正在清扫我的车道，还有一个女人正弯腰铲去走道上的雪。我感到十分羞愧。为了不让外面的好心人看到我，我跪在地上，爬着穿过客厅，回到楼上。我首先想到的就是，怎样才能回报他们？我情绪低落得连梳头的力气都没有，更别说帮别人铲雪了。

Before Jon's death, I took pride in the fact that I rarely asked for help or favors. I defined myself by my **competence** and independence. So who was I if I was no longer capable and busy? How could I respect myself if all I did was sit on the couch everyday and watch the snow fall?

Learning how to receive the love and support that came my way wasn't easy. Friends cooked for me and I cried because I couldn't even help them set the table. "I'm not usually this lazy," I **wailed**. Finally, my friend Kathy sat down with me and said, "Mary, cooking for you is not a **chore**. I love you and I want to do it. It makes me feel good to be able to do something for you."

Over and over, I heard similar sentiments from the people who supported me during those dark days. One very wise man told me, "You are not doing nothing. Being fully open to your **grief** may be the hardest work you will ever do."

I am not the person I once was, but in many ways I have changed for the better. The fabric of my life is now woven with **gratitude** and **humility**. I have been surprised to learn that there is incredible freedom that comes from facing one's worst fear and walking away whole. I believe there is strength in **surrender**.

Jon去世之前，我把自己定位为一个独立的、能干的人，我因为很少请求别人的帮助和关心而自豪。如果我不再能干，不再忙碌，那么我是谁？如果我整天只蜷在沙发上看着窗外飘落的雪花而什么都不去做，我拿什么获得自尊？

学习怎样接受别人给予我的爱和帮助并不简单。朋友们为我做饭，我哭了，因为我甚至不能帮他们摆餐具。"我通常不是这样懒惰的"，我哀泣道。后来，我朋友Kathy坐在我旁边，安慰我说："Mary，为你做饭并不是个负担。我爱你，我很愿意为你做饭，能够帮上忙让我感觉很好。"

一次又一次，那些帮助我度过人生中黑暗时刻的人们，用相似的充满感情的话来安慰我。一个很睿智的人告诉我："你现在并不是什么都没做。完全地无保留地直面痛苦，可能是最困难的事。"

我已经不是以前的我，但是在很多方面我已经变得更好。现在，我生命的锦缎是由感恩和谦恭织成的。我很惊奇地了解到，在面对了自己最痛苦的、最可怕的经历并且毫发无伤地走过来后，你会得到难以置信的解脱。我相信顺服可以带来力量。

魅力词汇

shuffle ['ʃʌfl] *v.* 拖着脚步走
mortified ['mɔːtifaid] *adj.* 羞愧的
competence ['kɔmpitəns] *n.* 胜任
wail [weil] *v.* 悲叹，嚎啕
chore [tʃɔː] *n.* 令人厌烦的工作
grief [griːf] *n.* 悲痛，悲伤
gratitude ['grætitjuːd] *n.* 感恩，感谢
humility [hjuː'militi] *n.* 谦逊，谦卑
surrender [sə'rendə] *n.* 投降，屈服

温情絮语

Our attitude toward life determines life's attitude towards us.

我们对生活的态度决定了生活对我们的态度。

One never loses anything by politeness.

讲礼貌不吃亏。

15 Cooperate with the Inevitable
接受不可避免的事实

在荷兰阿姆斯特丹有一座十五世纪的教堂遗迹，上面留有一段题词警策人心："事必如此，别无选择。"当一切成为既定事实，逃避、委顿、怯懦都无济于事，莫不如挺起胸膛乐观地去面对。要乐观地接受必然发生的情况。能够接受所发生的事实是克服随之而来的任何不幸的第一步。

文苑漫步

The late Booth Tarkington always said: "I could take anything that life could force upon me except one thing: blindness. I could never endure that."

Then one day, when he was along in his sixties, Tarkington glanced down at the carpet on the floor. The colors were **blurred**. He couldn't see the pattern. He went to a specialist. He learned the tragic truth: he was losing his sight. One eye was nearly blind; the other would follow. That which he had feared most had come upon him.

And how did Tarkington react to this "worst of all disasters"? Did he feel "This is it! This is the end of my life"? No, to his amazement, he felt quite gay. He even called upon his humor. Floating "**specks**"

译林畅游

已故的布思·塔尔金顿常说："人生加之于我的任何苦难我都能够承受，但除了一样——失明。那是我根本无法承受的。"

然而，就在他六十几岁的时候，有一天，当他低头看地上的地毯时，发现呈现在他眼前的色彩开始变得模糊不清，他无法看清花纹的样式。他当即去找了一位眼科专家，最终却证实了那个不幸的事实：他的视力正在渐渐衰退，有一只眼几乎完全失明，而另一只也即将面临同样的状况。他此生最担心的一件事终究还是降临在他身上了。

塔尔金顿对这个"灾难性的打击"做何反应呢？他是不是认为"就这样了，我的一生就这么毁了"呢？不，连他自己都未曾想过他还

annoyed him; they would swim across his eyes and cut off his vision. Yet when the largest of these specks would swim across his sight, he would say: "Hello! There's Grandfather again! Wonder where he's going on this fine morning!"

How could fate ever conquer a spirit like that? The answer is it couldn't. When total blindness closed in, Tarkington said: "I found I could take the loss of my eyesight, just as a man can take anything else. If I lost all five of my senses, I know I could live on inside my mind. For it is in the mind we see, and in the mind we live, whether we know it or not.

In the hope of **restoring** his eyesight, Tarkington had to go through more than twelve operations, within one year. With local **anesthetic**! Did he rail against this? He knew it had to be done. He knew he couldn't escape it, so the only way to lessen his suffering was to take it with grace. He refused a private room at the hospital and went into a ward, where he could be with other people who had troubles, too. He tried to cheer them up. And when he had to **submit to** repeated operations — fully conscious of what was being done to his eyes — he tried to remember how fortunate he was. "How wonderful!" he said. "How wonderful, that science now has the skill to operate on anything as delicate as

能够感到开心，甚至不失幽默。以前，那些常常浮动在他眼前的“黑斑”令他非常苦恼，正是这些“黑斑”使他无法看清眼前的东西。可是现在，即便那些最大的黑斑在他眼前浮过的时候，他都会幽默地说：“你好啊！黑斑爷爷又来了！不知道今天这么好的天气它想到哪里去！”

命运怎么能够打败这样的精神呢？回答是：不能！当塔尔金顿完全失明之后，他说：“我发现自己能够接受这一事实，就像别人能够承受其他事情一样。哪怕我的五种感官都已丧失功能，我知道我还可以靠着我的内心而生活。因为我们是通过思想而看，也是通过思想而生活，不论我们是否清楚这一点。”

为了恢复视力，塔尔金顿在一年之内共接受了十二次以上的手术。使用的是局部麻醉剂！他有没有为此而抱怨呢？没有，因为他知道这些都是他必须经历的，他没有办法逃避，唯一能够减轻痛苦的方法就是带着感恩的心来接受它。他拒绝使用医院里的私人病房，而是住在大病房里，与其他病友住在一起。他用尽一切办法鼓励病友们。而当他必须接受反复的手术时——非常清楚地知道要对他的眼睛做什么——他仍尽力去想自己有多么幸运。他说：“实在太神奇了！现在的科学已经发展到可以为人类的眼

the human eye!"

The average man would have been a nervous **wreck** if he had had to endure more than twelve operations and blindness. Yet Tarkington said: "I would not exchange this experience for a happier one." It taught him acceptance. It taught him that nothing life could bring him was beyond his strength to endure. It taught him, as John Milton discovered, that: "It is not miserable to be blind, it is only miserable not to be able to endure blindness."

If we rail and kick against it and grow bitter, we won't change the inevitable; but we will change ourselves. I know. I have tried it.

I once refused to accept an inevitable situation with which I was confronted. I played the fool and railed against it, and **rebelled**. I turned my nights into hells of **insomnia**. I brought upon myself everything I didn't want. Finally, after a year of self-torture, I had to accept what I knew **from the outset** I couldn't possibly alter.

I should have cried out years ago with old Walt Whitman:

Oh, to confront night, storms, hunger, **ridicule**, accident, **rebuff**, as the trees and animals do.

睛这么脆弱的东西做手术了！”

一般人如果经历了十二次以上的手术并且不得不在黑暗中生活，恐怕会精神崩溃。可是塔尔金顿却说："我可不愿意把这样的经历拿去换一个更开心一点儿的。"正是这次特殊的经历教会他如何去接受无法改变的一切。他懂得了，生活带给他的一切没有一样是他无法承受的。这件事同时使他领悟了约翰•弥尔顿所说的："失明并不可怕，可怕的是你无法承受失明。"

如果我们因此而感到无比愤慨，或牢骚满腹，我们也无法改变那些无可逃避的事实。可是，我们可以改变自己。我知道这一点，因为我曾亲身尝试过。

一次，我拒绝接受一件我必须面对的无法避免的事情。我做了一件傻事，我反抗它，抱怨它。结果，我陷入了失眠的深渊中。我给自己招来了所有不想要的事情。经过一整年的自虐，我终于接受了那个我从一开始就知道我终归无法拒绝的事实。

我应该在几年前就大声朗读出沃尔特·惠特曼的诗句：

啊，去面对黑夜、暴风雨、饥饿、愚弄、意外和挫折吧！就像树木和动物所做的那样。

魅力词汇

blurred [bləd] *adj.* 模糊不清的
speck [spek] *n.* 斑点
restore [ri'stɔ] *vt.* 恢复，使复原
anesthetic [ˌænəs'θetik] *n.* 麻醉剂，麻药
submit to 屈服，屈从于
wreck [rek] *n.* 破坏，毁灭
rebel [ri'bel] *v.* 反抗
insomnia [in'sɔmniə] *n.* 失眠（症）
from the outset 开始
ridicule ['ridikjuːl] *n.* 嘲笑，愚弄
rebuff [ri'bʌf] *n.* 断然拒绝

温情絮语

The shortest way to do many things is to only do one thing at a time.

做许多事情的捷径就是一次只做一件事。

One song can spark a moment, one flower can wake a dream.

一首歌能点燃岁月的激情，一朵花能唤醒一个梦想。

16 Ten Reasons Why You Failed
你失败的10个原因

我们在追求成功的同时，免不了会遇到许多的挫折和失败，人生有如一块用成与败的丝线织成的布，我们的成功必须受失败的鞭挞，而失败却又依赖成功来弥补。失败是上帝赐予的礼物，每次遇到失败，把它消化后，我们就会变得比以前更强大，把每一次失败都当成人生的一次涅槃，爬起来检查一下新的收获，我们将勇往直前。

文苑漫步

A couple of months ago, I asked you not to fear failure, saying that embracing failure—or at least the possibility of failure—was essential to success. But, of course, in the end the goal is to succeed, and fear of failing isn't the only thing that keeps us from succeeding.

I speak from experience here. Six or seven years ago, I was the picture of success—a straight-A graduate student, top of my class, a job I loved, a relationship that I was happy in, **the whole enchilada**. And then, those successes started slipping away. Nothing obvious at first, but gradually I found myself stuck in a **rut** academically, my relationship **dissolved**, things just weren't going my way. I wasn't

译林畅游

几个月前，我让你不要害怕失败，告诉你要拥抱失败——或者至少拥抱可能的失败——对成功来说，这是必要的。但是，当然了，我们最终的目标是要取得成功，而害怕失败也不是阻止我们成功的唯一障碍。

现在我来说说自己的经历。大概六七年前，我是很成功的——我是全优毕业生，在班级里名列前茅，有一份自己喜欢的工作，有一段令人愉悦的爱情，所有的事情都很成功。然后，所有这些成功开始开溜。最初一切并不明显，但我渐渐发现自己在学术上停滞不前，我的亲密关系破裂，所有的事情都脱离了我的掌控。就其本身而言，我并不是

failing, **per se**, just losing my **grip** on the successes I had won.

In the last couple of years, I've been reassessing some aspects of my life, trying to figure out what had happened so I could rebuild. To some extent this has worked well—I have a job I love (although I need to develop it into a career, not just a job), I have a book coming out in my academic field, I'm writing quite a bit, and most importantly I have a new relationship that is going strong. To get here, I've had to figure out what I was doing wrong in the years in between, where I had lost my footing, and I think I've figured out a thing or two in doing so.

If you're not reaching the kind of success you imagine in the areas that are important to you, one or more of the following things might well be true of you, too:

1. You don't have a goal. A lot of time we find ourselves "**spinning our wheels**", struggling through a day-to-day **routine** that isn't getting us anywhere because we don't know where we want to go. Sometimes we had goals when we set ourselves on a particular path, but we've changed along the way and those goals are no longer that important. Sometimes we simply did what was expected of us without ever stopping to think about what we eventually wanted to accomplish for ourselves.

失败了，只是在已拥有的成功上失去了掌控权。

在过去几年中，我一直在反思自己生活的方方面面，试着找出是哪里出了问题好让自己能重整旗鼓。从某种程度上来说，这很有效——我拥有一份自己喜欢的工作（虽然我得把它发展成为一份事业，而不仅仅是一份工作），我即将出版一本自己学术领域的书，已经写了不少了，最重要的是我又有了一份趋于稳定的感情。说到这儿，我得指出自己在那段时间中做错的事，那使我失去了成功地位，我想我已经提到过了其中的一两件了。

如果你还没有在你认为重要的领域中取得你想象的成功，那么你至少符合下面的一种情况：

1. 你没有一个目标。很多时候，我们发现自己在“原地踏步”，终日和时间赛跑，却没有取得任何成就，这是因为我们不知道自己的目标是什么。有时候，我们已经在前进的道路上设立了特定的目标，但一旦我们改变了自己的方向，那些目标就不再重要了。有时候，我们只是简单地去做那些别人期望我们去做的事，却没有停下来想想自己最终想要做的是什么。不论在哪种情况下，想想你的目标是什么以及

Whatever the case, figuring out what your goals are and, just as importantly, whether your current actions are helping to achieve them, is important.

你现在的行动对实现目标是否起作用，它们同样重要。

2. You don't have a vision. Setting goals is important but isn't enough to drive you to the finish line; it's important, too, to be able to imagine yourself as the achiever of your goals. How will you feel? What's the **payoff**? Why is it worthwhile to follow these goals and not some other ones? If goals are the end result of a journey, your vision is the fuel to get you there.

2. 你没有一个远见。设定目标是很重要，但这还不足以促使你去达到它。设想你自己已经实现目标也很重要。你会如何感觉？收获了什么？为什么是这些目标值得追随，而不是其他目标？如果目标是一场旅行的最终目的地，你的远见就是让你到达那里的燃料。

3. You don't have a plan. If goals are your destination and a vision is your fuel, your plan is the map to get you there; without a plan, you have no idea what immediate steps to take to achieve your goals. Planning means taking stock of the resources you have, the resources you need, and the steps you have to take to put those resources into action. The world is full of people with goals they have never accomplished because they didn't have a plan—don't you be one of them.

3. 你没有一个计划。如果目标是你的终点，远见是你的燃料，你的计划就是让你到达那里的地图。没有计划，你就不知道眼下要做什么去达到你的目标。计划意味着估量你所拥有的和所需要的资源，以及那些把这些资源转化为行动的步骤。这个世上有太多的人拥有目标却从未实现，这是因为他们不曾有一个计划——别让你自己成为他们中的一员。

4. You're too certain. Too much certainty creates **inflexibility**. If you're sure that your plan is correct, and refuse to accept the possibility of error, you may well find yourself stuck when an unexpected change comes about, or when your plan takes you in an unexpected direction.

4. 你过于肯定。太多的肯定会造成僵化。如果你确定你的计划是正确的，并且拒绝承认出现错误的可能性，当预期以外的情况发生时，或当你的计划往一个你预料之外的方向发展时，你会发现自己陷入了困境。不论你的计划多么周详，也

However strong your plan is and however sure you are of your goals, make room for periodic **reassessment**.

不论你对自己的目标有多么肯定，都要为定期重新评估留有余地。

5. You're not certain enough. At the same time, too little certainty will **paralyze** you. If you refuse to take a step because you aren't positive it will move you towards success, you won't make any better progress than if you had no goals at all. Keep your eyes open and be willing to change, but have faith in yourself, too.

5. 你不够肯定。同样的，不够肯定会让你气馁。如果你因为不确定是否能迈向成功就拒绝向前迈一步，那你就不会比完全没有目标更有进展。保持开阔的眼界，并且愿意改变，但也要对自己有信心。

6. You don't learn from your mistakes. A lot of people take their mistakes as signs of their unworthiness. They take setbacks as proof that they were never meant to achieve anything in the first place, and that they were stupid to even try. Mistakes are crucial to success—if we take the time to analyze them and learn from them. Even when they bar us **irrevocably** from attaining a goal, the lessons we learn from our mistakes help us to make new and better goals.

6. 你没有从错误中吸取教训。许多人都将自己所犯的错误视为他们毫无价值的标志。他们将挫折视为自己一开始就不打算取得成功并且愚蠢到要去尝试的证明。错误是成功的关键——如果我们花些时间去分析它们并从中学习的话。即便是错误不可避免地阻挠了我们达成目标，我们从错误中吸取的教训也能帮助我们设定新的、更好的目标。

7. You reject outside influences. A lot of people see the influence of others as a weakness, or worse, a restriction or even "pollution" of their **innate** creativity. This is, in a word, **hogwash**. We are first and foremost social beings, none of whom has ever accomplished anything without the help of others. Welcome and accept other perspectives on your strengths and weak-

7. 你拒绝外部的影响。许多人把他人的影响看作是一个弱点，更糟的是，看作是一种限制，甚至是一种对他们与生俱来的创造力的一种“污染”。总之就是一派胡言。我们首先是社会人，没有一个人可以完全不需要他人的帮助就能获得成功。欢迎并接受他人对你的优缺点和成败的评述。优雅地接受他人

nesses, your successes and failures. Accept help **graciously** when it's offered. This doesn't mean you should take every piece of advice offered you, but you should listen seriously and openly and weigh carefully the input of others. And learn from their mistakes, when you can.

的意见。这并不代表你要接受所有的建议，但是你要认真而坦率地倾听，并仔细斟酌。可以的话，从他人的错误中汲取教训。

8. You worry about being copied. Often we close ourselves off from other people not because we're afraid that they will influence us but that we will influence them, that our brilliant ideas will be taken up by someone else and no longer be solely ours. So we avoid sharing our passions, and spend our energy jealously guarding our "secret" rather than simply moving forward. In the end, we turn our passions into burdens that become difficult to carry instead of a joy.

8. 你担心被模仿。经常，我们会让自己和他人保持距离，并不是因为担心他人会影响自己，而是担心自己会影响他人。我们害怕自己出色的点子被他人占有，不再仅仅属于我们。因此，我们避免与人分享自己的激情，并且花精力谨慎地保守我们的"秘密"，而不是往前走。最后，我们把自己的激情变成一种很难承担起的负担，而不是快乐。

9. You **use up** your reserves. When I've found myself at my lowest points, it's always been for lack of a reserve — whether of money, of time, or most crucially of energy. In part this was the fault of inadequate planning and over-certainty — I should have reassessed my situation more realistically before exhausting my resources — but whatever the cause, it's a dangerous place to be. A mistake that could be easily recovered from under normal circumstances becomes overwhelming when you're too broken or too exhausted

9. 你耗尽了储备。当我发现自己处在最低谷时，也总是缺乏储备——无论是金钱还是时间，或者是最为关键的活力。在某种程度上来说，这是计划不足和过度肯定带来的后果——在耗尽我的储备之前，我本应该对现状重新做一次更实际的评估，但是我却没有——无论如何，这都是危险的情况。一个在正常情况下可以很容易被纠正的错误会在你精疲力尽不能对它作出适当反应的时候变得势不可挡。在你觉得情况太坏而不能继续以前，要在

to respond adequately. Keep track of where you are financially, materially, and emotionally before you find yourself too worn down to continue.

经济上、物质上和情感上跟上进展。

10. You fear success. Forget fear of failure, it's fear of success that kicks us the hardest. It's the **darnedest** thing, too — the kind of thing that you don't imagine possible, until one day you realize that you really don't know what to do with yourself if you ever accomplish your goals. On the other side of success is the unknown, and believe it or not, the unknown is often scarier than the known world of struggle and unfulfillment of success. When I realized this, one night as I drifted unhappily to sleep, it jerked me straight up in my bed!

10. 你害怕成功。忘记对失败的恐惧之后，对成功的恐惧最使我们受伤。这也是最有可能的。你不太可能会想到这类事，直到有一天，你真正意识到，如果你达到了所有设立的目标，你将无事可做。成功的另一面是未知的，不管你相信与否，未知都比现实世界中已知的斗争和未实现的成功更可怕。一天晚上，当我不开心地渐渐入睡时，一想到这些，我就猛地从床上坐了起来！

My father, an **avid** collector of seemingly random quotes, is fond of saying that **insanity** is doing the same thing over and over and expecting different results. (I've never had the heart to ask him why he keeps saying this...) At some point, you have to stop doing whatever you're doing and figure out why you're doing it, especially if it doesn't seem to be getting you where you want to be. When you do, I think you'll find that at least one of the above applies to you. Whatever your reasons, though, the important thing is to realize that it's in your nature neither to be a

我的父亲喜欢收集一些看似很随意的格言。他喜欢说的一句话就是，愚蠢就是总是重复做相同的事却期望有不同的结果。（我从没有用心问过他为什么老是这么说……）在有些时候，无论你在做什么，你都要停下来，想一想你为什么要这样做，特别是在你做的事并没有让你达到你想要的目标的时候。一旦你这样做了，我想你将会找出至少一条上面说的情况与你相符。不论你的理由是什么，最重要的是你要明白，你的本质并不是要成为一个失败者或成功者，成功是

failure, nor to be a success, that success is something we make rather than something that happens to us — and when you realize that, you can start to make the changes that move you from "insanity" to success.

要争取的，它不会自动发生在我们身上。一旦你意识到这点，你就能开始做出改变，这将会促使你从"愚蠢"走向成功。

魅力词汇

the whole enchilada [ˌentʃə'ladə] 一切，所有的事情
rut [rʌt] *n.* 陈旧不变的一套，陈规
dissolve [di'zɔlv] *v.* 结束，终止
per se [ˌpə 'sei] 本身，本质上
grip [grip] *n.* 掌握，控制
spin one's wheels 浪费时间
routine [ruː'tiːn] *n.* 例行公事，常规
payoff ['peiɔf] *n.* 回报
inflexibility [inˌfleksə'biliti] *n.* 僵化
reassessment [ˌriːə'sesmənt] *n.* 重新评估
paralyze ['pærəlaiz] *v.* 使气馁
irrevocably [i'revəkəbli] *adv.* 不可改变地
innate [i'neit] *adj.* 先天的，天生的
hogwash ['hɔgwɔʃ] *n.* 废话
graciously ['greiʃəsli] *adv.* 优雅地
use up 用完，耗尽
darnedest [daːndist] *adj.* 最有可能的
avid ['ævid] *adj.* 热切的，渴望的
insanity [in'sæniti] *n.* 愚蠢

温情絮语

There's only one corner of the universe you can be sure of improving, and that's your own self.

这个宇宙只有一个角落你肯定可以改进，那就是你自己。

17 Do You Act or React? 主动还是被动？

"不要被动地去回应这个世界，用冷漠回应冷漠，用傲慢回应傲慢，我们应主动将自身的善意、修养和人格的光辉奉献给世界。"给自己一个鼓励，也许自己做事的方式过于被动了，该主动起来了，鼓励自己积极面对生活。

文苑漫步

I walked with my friend, a Quaker, to the newsstand the other night, and he bought a paper, thanking the newspaper seller politely. The newspaper seller didn't even acknowledge it.

"A **sullen** fellow, isn't he?" I asked.

"Oh, he's that way every night," shrugged my friend.

"Then why do you continue to be so polite to him?" I asked.

"Why not?" inquired my friend. "Why should I let him decide how I'm going to act?"

As I thought about this incident later, it occurred to me that the important word was "act". My friend acts towards people; most of us react toward them.

He has a sense of inner balance which

译林畅游

有天晚上，我和朋友——一个贵格会教徒，一起散步，走到一个报摊前，朋友买了一份报纸，很有礼貌地跟那位报摊贩道谢，但是，那报贩却毫不在意。

"这家伙太沉闷，不是吗？"我问道。

我朋友耸耸肩说，"噢，每天晚上他都这样。"

"那你为什么还对他这么有礼貌呢？"我问道。

"为什么不呢？"朋友反问道，"我为什么要让他决定我怎么做呢？"

我后来又仔细思考这件事，终于悟出了重要的一点，即"主动去做"。我的朋友主动地对待人，而我们大多数都是被动地回应。

他拥有内心的平衡感，而这种

is lacking in most of us — he knows who he is, what he stands for, how he should behave. He refuses to return **incivility**, because then he would no longer be **in command of** his own conduct.

平衡感却是我们大多数人很缺乏的——他知道自己是什么样的人，代表什么样的立场，应该如何处事。他拒绝无理地回复别人，如果那样做的话，他将不再是自己行为的主宰。

When we are **enjoined** in *the Bible* to return good for evil, we look upon this as a moral **injunction** — which it is. But it is also a psychological **prescription** for our emotional health.

我们尊奉《圣经》以德报怨的训诫时，我们视其为一种道德准则——它的确如此。但同时，它也是情绪健康的一剂良药。

Nobody is unhappier than the **perpetual** reactor. His center of emotional gravity is not rooted within himself, where it belongs, but in the world outside him. His spiritual temperature is always being raised or lowered by the social climate around him, and he is a mere creature at the mercy of these elements.

总是被动回应的人最不容易快乐，他的情感的重心并非根植于自己的内心世界，而是随外界而转移的；他的情绪总是随着周围的社会风尚而改变，成了受这些因素摆布的可怜虫。

Praises give him a feeling of **euphoria**, which is false, because it does not last and it does not come from self-approval. Criticism depresses him more than it should, because it confirms his own secretly shaky opinion of himself. Snubs hurt him, and the merest suspicion of unpopularity in any quarter rouses him to bitterness.

称赞给他带来一阵幸福愉快感，但是，那种快感却是虚假的。因为，它不会持续很久，也并非来自自我的认可；批评会使他过度悲伤，因为他内心深处的不自信再一次得到确认，冷落会使他伤痛，在任何一处感受到的极为轻微的一丝冷落也会让他痛苦不堪。

A **serenity** of spirit cannot be achieved until we become the masters of our own action and attitudes. To let

我们要想得到心灵的平静，就必须成为自己的行为和态度的主宰。如果我们的举止是粗鲁或优雅，是欢

another determine whether we shall be rude or gracious, **elated** or depressed, is to **relinquish** control over our own personalities, which is ultimately all we possess. The only true possession is self-possession.

欣或沮丧，要由他人来决定的话，就是放弃对自我的主宰，而对自我的主宰才是我们真正拥有的东西。我们唯一真正拥有的就是自我控制。

魅力词汇

sullen ['sʌlən] *adj.* 闷闷不乐的
incivility ['insi'viliti] *n.* 无礼，粗鲁
in command of 指挥
enjoin [in'dʒɔin] *v.* 命令，吩咐
injunction [in'dʒʌŋkʃn] *n.* 命令
prescription [pri'skripʃn] *n.* 处（药）方
perpetual [pə'petʃuəl] *adj.* 永久的
euphoria [juː'fɔːriə] *n.* 幸福愉快感
serenity [si'renəti] *n.* 平静
elated [i'leitid] *adj.* 兴高采烈的
relinquish [ri'liŋkwiʃ] *v.* 放弃

温情絮语

All things are difficult before they are easy.

凡事必先难后易。

18 True Nobility 真正的高贵

悔恨自己的错误，力求不再重蹈覆辙，这才是真正的悔悟。优于别人并不高贵，真正的高贵应该是优于过去的自己。

文苑漫步

In a calm sea every man is a pilot.

But all sunshine without shade, all pleasure without pain, is not life at all. Take the lot of the happiest — it is a tangled **yarn**. **Bereavements** and blessings, one following another, make us sad and blessed by turns. Even death itself makes life more loving. Men come closest to their true selves in the sober moments of life, under the shadows of sorrow and loss.

In the affairs of life or of business, it is not intellect that tells so much as character, not brains so much as heart, not genius so much as self-control, patience, and discipline, **regulated** by judgment.

I have always believed that the man who has begun to live more seriously within begins to live more simply without. In an age of **extravagance** and waste, I wish I could show to the world how few the real

译林畅游

风平浪静的大海上，每个人都是领航员。

但是，只见阳光而无阴霾，只闻欢笑而未感伤痛，那都全然不是人生。拿最幸福的人来说——他们的生活也像是一团纠缠在一起的纱线。丧亲之痛和神恩赐福交互而至，让我们悲喜交替。甚至连死亡本身也使生命更加珍贵。在生命的庄严时刻，在哀伤和丧亲的阴影之下，人们最接近真实的自我。

在生活或事业中，性格比才智更能指导我们，心灵比头脑更能引导我们，经过判断而采取的自制、忍耐和自律比天资更能让我们受益。

我一向认为，人若内思严谨，于外则必显朴实。在物欲横流的年代，但愿我能向世人表明：人类真正需要的东西是少之又少的。

wants of humanity are.

To regret one's errors to the point of not repeating them is true **repentance**. There is nothing noble in being superior to some other man. The true nobility is in being superior to your previous self.

反思自己的过错，力求不再重蹈覆辙，这才是真正的悔悟。胜人一筹并没有什么值得夸耀的。真正的高贵是超越过去的自己。

魅力词汇

yarn [jaːn] *n.* 纱线

bereavement [bi'riː vmənt] *n.* 丧友，丧亲

regulate ['regjuleit] *v.* 调节

extravagance [ik'strævəgəns] *n.* 奢侈

repentance [ri'pentəns] *n.* 悔改

温情絮语

Storms make trees take deeper roots.

风暴使树木深深扎根。

Suffering is the most powerful teacher of life.

苦难是人生最伟大的老师。

19 The World as I See It
我的世界观

我们这些总有一死的人的命运是多么奇特！我们只是一个生命历程中匆匆的过客，我们因何而来，为何而去？其实生命的意义似乎是个没有答案的课题，我们只需懂得如下的道理似乎就足够：人是为别人而生存的，首先是为那样一些人，我们的幸福全依赖于他们的喜悦和健康；其次是为了许多我们不认识的人，他们的命运通过同情的纽带与我们密切结合在一起。

文苑漫步

How strange is the lot of us mortals! Each of us is here for a brief **sojourn**; for what purpose he knows not, though he sometimes thinks he senses it. But without deeper reflection one knows from daily life that one exists for other people — first of all, for those upon whose smiles and well-being our own happiness is wholly dependent, and then for the many, unknown to us, to whose destinies we are bound by the ties of sympathy.

A hundred times every day I remind myself that my inner and outer life are based on the labors of other men, living and dead, and that I must **exert** myself in order to give in the same measure as I

译林畅游

我们这些总有一死的人的命运是多么奇特！我们每个人在这个世界上都只作一个短暂的逗留；目的何在，却无从知道，尽管有时自以为对此若有所感。但是，不必深思，只要从日常生活就可以明白：人是为别人而活着的——首先是为那样一些人，我们的幸福全部依赖于他们的喜悦和健康；其次是为许多我们所不认识的人，他们的命运通过同情的纽带与我们密切结合在一起。

我每天上百次地提醒自己：我的精神生活和物质生活都是以别人（包括生者和逝者）的劳动为基础的，我必须尽力以同样的方式来报偿我所领受了的和至今还在领受

have received and am still receiving. I am strongly drawn to a **frugal** life and am often oppressively aware that I am **engrossing** an undue amount of the labor of my fellow-men. I regard class **distinctions** as unjustified and, in the last resort, based on force. I also believe that a simple and **unassuming** life is good for everybody, physically and mentally.

着的东西。我强烈地向往着俭朴的生活，我经常不安地发现自己占用了同胞们过多的劳动成果。我认为阶级的区分是不合理的，它最后所凭借的是基于强制手段的。我也相信，简单淳朴的生活，无论在身体上还是在精神上，对每个人都是有益的。

My passionate sense of social justice and social responsibility has always contrasted oddly with my **pronounced** lack of need for direct contact with other human beings and human communities. I am truly a "lone traveler" and have never belonged to my country, my home, my friend, or even my immediate family, with my whole heart; in the face of all these ties, I have never lost a sense of distance and a need for solitude—feelings which increased with the years. One becomes sharply aware, but without regret of the limits of mutual understanding and **consonance** with other people. No doubt, such a person loses some of his innocence and unconcern; on the other hand, he is largely independent, of the opinions, habits, and judgments of his fellows and avoids the temptation to build his inner **equilibrium** upon such insecure foundations.

我有强烈的社会正义感和社会责任感，但我又明显地缺乏与别人和社会直接接触的要求，这两者总是形成古怪的对照。我实在是一个“孤独的旅客”，我未曾全心全意地属于我的国家、我的家庭、我的朋友，甚至我最为亲近的家人；在所有这些关系面前，我总是感觉到一丝距离而且需要保持孤独——而这种感觉一年比一年强烈。人们会清楚地发觉，同别人的相互了解和协调一致是有限度的，但这不值得惋惜。无疑，这样的人在某种程度上会失去他的天真无邪和无忧无虑的心境；但另一方面，他却能够在很大程度上不为别人的意见、习惯和判断所左右，并且能够避免那种把他的内心平衡建立在这样一些不可靠的基础之上的诱惑。

魅力词汇

sojourn ['sɔˌdʒən] *n.* 停留，旅居
exert [ig'zəːt] *v.* 用（力），尽（力）
frugal ['fruːgl] *adj.* 节省的，节俭的
engross [in'grəus] *v.* 占用
distinction [dis'tiŋkʃn] *n.* 区别
unassuming [ˌʌnə'sjuːmiŋ] *adj.* 谦逊的
pronounced [prə'naunst] *adj.* 明显的
consonance ['kɔnsənəns] *n.* 和谐，协调
equilibrium [ˌiːkwi'libriəm] *n.* 平衡

温情絮语

While there is life, there is hope.

有生命就有希望 / 留得青山在，不怕没柴烧。

Death comes to all, but great achievements raise a monument which shall endure until the sun grows old.

死亡无人能免，但非凡的成就会树起一座纪念碑，它将一直屹立直到太阳冷却之时。

20 On Resignation 论放弃

放弃源于不可征服的希望。无论我付出怎样的努力，我都可能被死亡或某种疾病击败；我可能被敌人打倒；我可能发现自己走上了一条不能成功的蠢路。在百转千回之中，纯属个人希望的破灭也许不可避免，但若个人的目标已成为人类的大希望的一部分，那么当失败到来时，就不至于被彻底击倒了。

文苑漫步

Resignation is of two sorts, one rooted in despair, the other in unconquerable hope. The man who has suffered such fundamental defeat that he has given up hope of serious achievement may learn the resignation of despair, and if he does, he will abandon all serious activity. He may **camouflage** his despair by religious phrases, or by the **doctrine** that **contemplation** is the true end of man, but whatever disguise he may adopt to conceal his **inward** defeat, he will remain essentially useless and fundamentally unhappy. The man whose resignation is based on unconquerable hope acts in quite a different way. Hope which is to be unconquerable

译林畅游

放弃有两种，一种源于绝望，一种源于不可征服的希望。一个人遭到重创以致对重大的成就不抱希望时，也许会走向绝望的放弃，果真如此，他将中止一切重要的活动；他也许会用宗教上的词句或者沉思默想才是人类的真正目标的说教来掩饰他的绝望。但是无论他使用何种托辞来遮掩他内心的失败，他本质上将是一个无用的和不快乐的人。把放弃建立在不可征服的希望之上的人，行动则截然不同。不可征服的希望必定是很大的而且是非个人性质的。无论我付出怎样的努力，我都可能被死亡或某种疾病击败；我可能被敌人打倒；我可能

must be large and impersonal. Whatever my personal activities, I may be defeated by death, or by certain kinds of diseases; I may be overcome by my enemies; I may find that I have **embarked** upon an unwise course which cannot lead to success. In a thousand ways the failure of purely personal hopes may be unavoidable, but if personal aims have been part of larger hopes for humanity, there is not the same utter defeat when failure comes.

发现自己走上了一条不能成功的蠢路。在百转千回之中，纯属个人希望的破灭也许不可避免，但若个人的目标已成为人类的大希望中的一部分，那么当失败到来时，就不至于被彻底击倒了。

魅力词汇

camouflage ['kæməflaːʒ] *v.* 掩盖
doctrine ['dɔktrin] *n.* 教条，教义
contemplation ['kɔntempleiʃn] *n.* 冥想
inward ['inwəd] *adj.* 内心的
embark [im'baːk] *v.* 开始从事，着手

温情絮语

Success comes from doing what you really love and what you are really good at. If you really love something, and if you are really good at it, you are less inclined to give up.

成功来自于做你真正喜欢的事，做你真正擅长的事。如果你真的很喜欢做某件事，并且真的很擅长它，你就不会轻易放弃。

第九篇

—冬日的温暖—

1 The Warmth in Winter 冬日的温暖

冬有情思盼春到，窗上冰凌莲花俏，夜半开放清晨落，哪如花开春季好。

文苑漫步

Winter gives us the opportunity to stay inside and look outside, as we're not called outdoors to enjoy the warmth and sunshine. **Snuggle** up in the sofa, put a blanket over you, have a cup of hot cocoa, and enjoy the observations on this precious season…

Winter is the time for comfort, for good food and warmth, for the touch of a friendly hand and for a talk beside the fire: It is the time for home.

During the winter I am **content**, or try to think I am. There is a wonderful joy in leaving behind the noisy city streets and starting out along the white road that leads across the hills. With each breath of the sharp, reviving air one seems to **inhale** new life. A peace as evident as the sunshine on the fields takes possession of one's inner being. The **trivial** cares are driven away by the first **sweep** of wind

译林畅游

当我们没有出外享受温暖和阳光时，冬季为人们创造了一个待在室内，观察室外的机会。铺条毯子在身上，蜷曲在沙发上，喝着一杯热可可，享受着观察这个美丽季节的快乐……

冬季是一个享受舒适、美食与温馨的季节。冬季也是传递友谊的季节，冬季还是围坐在火炉旁谈天说地的季节。冬季是享受家之温暖的季节。

在冬季，我很满足，或自认为满足。把喧闹的城市街区抛在身后，沿着白皑皑的公路前往山冈。随着每一次呼吸凛冽的，令人振奋的空气，整个人也好像注入了新生。照射在田野上的宁静的阳光同时也感染了我们的内心世界。从山冈上径直吹来的第一丝风也将心中琐碎的烦恼一并吹走。白雪覆盖着的大地显得分外寂静，这是一份来自大自

that comes straight from the mountains. The intense silence that **broods** over the snow-bound land is a conscious blessing from the nature.

然的祝福。

Sometimes our fate **resembles** a fruit tree in winter: Who would think that those branches would turn green again and blossom, but we hope it, we know it.

有时我们的命运就像冬天里的一棵果树：当时，谁会去想这棵果树的枝叶会再次变绿，开花，但我们一直怀有希望，并坚定着信念。

魅力词汇

snuggle ['snʌgl] *v.* 舒服地蜷伏
content ['kɔntent] *adj.* 满意的
inhale [in'heil] *v.* 吸入
trivial ['triviəl] *adj.* 琐碎的
sweep [swi:p] *n.* 打扫，扫除
brood [bru:d] *v.* 笼罩
resemble [ri'zembl] *v.* 类似，像

温情絮语

Stray birds of summer come to my window to sing and fly away.

And yellow leaves of autumn, which have no songs, flutter and fall there with a sign.

夏天的飞鸟，飞到我的窗前唱歌，又飞去了。

秋天的黄叶，它们没有什么可唱，只叹息一声，飞落在那里。

2 Summer 夏日

本文出自英国女诗人艾丽斯·梅内尔之手，文笔细腻而且饱含感情。让我们一起来领略一下女诗人笔下的夏日吧。

文苑漫步

One has the leisure of July for perceiving all the differences of the green of leaves. It is no longer a difference in degrees of maturity, for all the trees have darkened to their final tone, and stand in their differences of character and not of mere date. Almost all the green is grave, not sad and not dull. It has a darkened and a daily color, in majestic but not obvious harmony with dark grey skies, and might look, to **inconstant** eyes, as **prosaic** after spring as 11:00 looks after the dawn.

Gravity is the world — not **solemnity** as towards evening, nor **menace** as at night. The daylight trees of July are signs of common beauty, common freshness, and a mystery familiar and **abiding** as night and day. In childhood we all have

译林畅游

七月间，人们有余暇观察树叶绿翠的千差万别。这不再是成熟程度上的差异，因为所有的树木，或转苍翠，或呈墨绿，色调均已固着定格，从而展现出来的，并非时节上的不同，而是各自特性上的差异。几乎各种绿色，品味凝重，既不流于悒郁，也不失之沉闷，它具有一种深沉、日常的色泽，与灰暗的苍穹浑然一体，构成庄重却非一眼可见的和谐，故而在游览扫掠的目光看来，可能会有阳春繁景过后的平淡之感。一如黎明之后 11 点的光景。

凝重，才是世界本来的样子——凝重并非时近黄昏的阴沉，亦非黑夜之中的森然。七月白昼的葱郁树木，体现出普通的美，常见的清新，是一种如同黑夜白昼般惯常而又永恒不变的不解之谜。童年

a more exalted sense of dawn and summer sunrise than we ever fully retain or quite recover; and also a far higher sensibility for April and April evenings — a heartache for them, which in riper years is gradually and **irretrievably** consoled.

The poetry of mere day and of late summer becomes perceptive to mature eyes that have long ceased to be sated, have taken leave of weariness, and cannot now find anything in nature too familiar; eyes which have, indeed, lost sight of the further awe of midsummer day break, and no longer see so much of the past in April twilight as they saw when they had no past; but which look freshly at the dailiness of green summer, of early afternoon, of every sky of any form that comes to pass, and of the darkened **elms**.

时代，我们看到黎明和夏天日出盛景，会油然生出一股日后无法充分保留，也难以完全恢复的奋激狂喜；同时，对四月和四月的日暮黄昏，还产生一种陶然忘情的欣赏共鸣——一种为之怦然心动的神驰向往，进入壮年之后，又无可挽回地逐渐淡化平息。

只有阅历丰富的慧眼，才能感受到白昼本身的夏末时令固有的诗意——这双慧眼已久未获满足矣，同时也摆脱了厌倦感，此刻发现在自然界，即使最常见的景物也另有一番情趣；诚然，面对仲夏红日的喷薄欲出，已不再萌发敬畏之情；凝望四月的苍茫暮色，也不会比一无阅历的童年，引发更多的联想；然而，对司空见惯的日常景象——树木葱茏的盛夏，日过中天的午后，来而复去、变幻不定的每一片云天，还有幽暗的榆树——反倒会投以新的目光。

魅力词汇

inconstant [in'kɔnstənt] *adj.* 多变的
prosaic [prəu'zeiik] *adj.* 单调的，无趣的
solemnity [sə'lemnəti] *n.* 严肃
menace ['menəs] *n.* 威胁，胁迫
abiding [ə'baidiŋ] *adj.* 永久的
irretrievably [ˌiri'tri:vəbli] *adv.* 不可挽回地
elm [elm] *n.* 榆树

3 The Patch of Life
人生的补丁

“事事不可能都完美。补丁无法避免，人的生命也一样有缺憾，生命中会出现伤害、残疾和疾病。”这句话道出了真正的人生。世界上并没有完美，缺憾是不可避免的。但是我们应该正确对待生活的“瑕疵”，凭借我们的努力和创造，我们还是可以享受不完美的完美生活。

文苑漫步

Not long ago, my daughter’s frosting shoes were **scratched** by someone’s knife. She burst into tears. I took the shoes to the shoemaker to get them repaired.

The young **apprentice** glanced at the opening and said, “There is nothing I can do but to replace the upper.”

His master looked at them and said to me, “If you trust me, I will add more scratches on both of the shoes.”

I was confused and asked why.

He explained, “As if the opening was made on purpose for the sake of special style and reuse.”

I didn’t fully understand him, but I decided to leave the shoes.

译林畅游

不久前，女儿的磨砂鞋被人用刀子划了几道，她失声痛哭。我把鞋子拿给鞋匠去修。

年轻的学徒看了一眼上面划的口子，说：“除了换鞋帮，我无能为力。”

他的师父看了看鞋子，对我说：“你要是相信我，我就在两只鞋上再划几道口子。”

我被搞糊涂了，问师傅为什么。

他解释说：“这样看起来这些口子就好像为了突出风格故意弄的，还能再穿。”

虽然我还是没有完全明白，但是我决定把鞋子留下。

Two days later I dropped by from work to fetch the shoes. At the first sight I found they were indeed five or six scratches on each shoe, but all the openings were **patched** by soft leather in **rust** red with edges **sewed** by thick **hemp thread**; the stitches were **twisted** with the appearance of roughness and plainness which was in accordance with the quality of frosting leather, more unique and interesting than ever. I couldn't help making compliments on the master's **craftsmanship**.

两天后，我下班后直接去取鞋。我一眼就发现那两只鞋上果然又划了五六道口子，只是所有的口子都用铁锈红的软皮缝补，四周用粗麻线缝合，针脚歪歪扭扭，显得朴素粗犷，和磨砂皮的质地一致，只是比原来更与众不同、更有趣了。我禁不住称赞师傅的独具匠心。

Another time, my wife's sister's white blouse was torn a large opening on the back. My wife took it over and checked carefully, and then said, "Let me take it home and mend it."

还有一次，我妻子的妹妹的白衬衣后背处被挂了一个大口子。妻子接过来，仔细地看了看，说："我拿回去给你补补吧。"

Three days later, seeing the blouse again, I was shocked: all the **cracks** and openings were sewed up by thin and white thread and they took on a look of branches, like the **ice crystal** on winter's branches in the north. In order to **intensify** the effect, she attached a fatty snowman and a cabin made of flowery cotton **rags** on the shirt. I sighed with praise, "It's just as beautiful as a piece of art."

三天后，再见到那件衬衣时，我大吃一惊，只见所有的裂痕和口子都用细白线缝合，看上去如同树枝，仿佛北方冬天树枝上的冰花。为了增强这种效果，她还用棉质花布拼了一个胖乎乎的雪人和一座小木屋。我赞叹道："这就像一件艺术品一样漂亮。"

"I was **inspired** by the craftsman.

"我是受了那个补鞋匠的启发。

Patches are supposed to be a regret, but a skillful craftsman can make it take on a look of perfection," replied my wife.

Her words inspired me even more: perfection is impossible to achieve in everything; patches are unavoidable, so is human's life, which will appear in the form of injury, disability or disease. Since you can't change the existence of wound, you should not expect people's sympathy by the wound, which reveals nothing meaningful. All you can do and have to do is to **suture** the wound by patches and try your best to bloom a most beautiful flower on the wound, and that is the significance of life.

尽管补丁原本是一种缺憾，但能工巧匠却能让他们呈现出一种完美。"妻子回答道。

她的话给了我更大的启发：事事不可能都完美。补丁无法避免，人的生命也一样有缺憾，生命中会出现伤害、残疾和疾病。既然你无法改变伤口的存在，就不要因为受伤而期盼同情，那没有任何意义。你能做的和必须做的就是用补丁缝合伤口，尽力在伤口上开出最美丽的花朵，而这正是人生的意义。

魅力词汇

scratch [skrætʃ] *v.* 刮，划
apprentice [ə'prentis] *n.* 学徒
patch [pætʃ] *v.* 补
rust [rʌst] *n.* 铁锈
sew [səu] *v.* 缝
hemp [hemp] thread 麻线
twist [twist] *v.* 扭曲
craftsmanship ['kraːftsmənʃip] *n.* 技能，技术
crack [kræk] *n.* 裂缝
ice crystal ['kristəl] 冰花
intensify [in'tensifai] *v.* （使）增强
rag [ræg] *n.* 破布，碎布
inspire [in'spaiə] *v.* 赋予某人灵感，启迪
suture ['suːtʃə] *v.* 缝合伤口

4 Struggle 奋斗

“如果自然允许我们一帆风顺地度过一生，那我们就会变得软弱甚至残疾。”虽然我们都希望生活可以一帆风顺，可是如果理智地想想，我们会发现，正是因为有了不同的经历，生活才变得丰富多彩。一成不变的生活，再幸福也只是一潭死水。有了失败的苦，才衬托出成功的甜。

文苑漫步

A man found a **cocoon** of a butterfly. One day, a small opening appeared; he sat and watched the cocoon for several hours as it struggled to force its body through that little hole. But it seemed to stop making any progress. It appeared as if it had gotten as far as it could, and it could go no further.

Then the man decided to help the butterfly, so he took a pair of scissors and **snipped** off the remaining bit of the cocoon. The butterfly then emerged easily. But it had a **swollen** body and small, **shriveled** wings.

The man continued to watch the butterfly because he expected that at any moment the wings would enlarge and ex-

译林畅游

一个人捡到一个蝴蝶茧。一天，茧上出现了一个小孔；他坐下观察了这茧几个小时。茧内的蝴蝶努力挣扎着让身体通过小小的茧孔。但是，看起来没有什么进展。茧里的蝴蝶似乎已经使尽了全部力气，再也钻不动了。

于是这个人决定帮助这只蝴蝶，他拿剪刀剪掉了茧的剩余部分。蝴蝶很容易就出来了。但是它的身体很臃肿，翅膀也萎缩着。

这个人继续观察着蝴蝶，他期望有那么一刻蝴蝶的翅膀会变大，张开支撑住身体，臃肿的身体也会

pand to be able to support the body, which would **contract** in time.

及时缩小。

Neither happened! In fact, the butterfly spent the rest of its life **crawling** around with a swollen body and shriveled wings. It was never able to fly.

然而，什么都没有发生！事实上这只蝴蝶只能拖着臃肿的身体和萎缩的翅膀度过余生了。它再也飞不起来了。

What the man in his kindness and fast action didn't understand was that the restricting cocoon and the struggle required for the butterfly to get through the tiny opening were nature's way of forcing **fluid** from the body of the butterfly into its wings so that it would be ready for flight once it achieved freedom from the cocoon.

这个好心而性急的人没有明白的是，茧的束缚和蝴蝶通过小孔的努力是把体内的液体挤压到翅膀的自然方式，这样它破茧而出的时候就可以展翅而飞了。

Sometimes struggles are exactly what we need in our lives. If nature allowed us to go through our lives without any difficulties, it would weaken or even disable us. We would not be as strong as what we could have been and we could never fly.

有时候奋斗恰恰是我们生活中需要的。如果大自然允许我们一帆风顺地度过一生，那我们就会变得软弱甚至残疾。如果那样，我们就不会像我们原本可以变成的那样强大，我们也永远不能飞翔。

魅力词汇

cocoon [kə'kuːn] *n.* 茧，蚕茧
snip [snip] *v.* 剪
swollen ['swəulən] *adj.* 肿胀的，浮肿的
shriveled ['ʃrivld] *adj.* 皱缩的
contract [kən'trækt] *v.* 缩小，紧缩
crawl [krɔːl] *v.* 爬，爬行
fluid ['fluːid] *n.* 液体，流体

5 Turn Your Face to the Sun 面朝太阳

看到这首诗的标题，耳边响起了海子的那首诗：

"从明天起，做一个幸福的人

喂马，劈柴，周游世界

从明天起，关心粮食和蔬菜

我有一所房子，面朝大海，春暖花开……"

很美好很温暖的诗。他告诉我们，只要我们心中充满阳光，充满爱，我们就会看到生活积极的一面。

文苑漫步

Beloved,

There are days when nothing seems right.

When every shell you pick up on the winding shore is broken,

When the **silken** treasure slips through your fingers too quickly,

When comforts are empty,

And the world is noisy.

On those **jagged** edged days,

When the wind is **screaming** for a reason only she understands,

And you find yourself all alone.

Turn your face to the sun.

There is goodness in the world that

译林畅游

亲爱的：

生活总有不如意的时候。

当你在蜿蜒迂回的沙滩上捡起的每一个贝壳都是残缺的，

当丝绸锦缎从你的指尖飞快溜走，

当别人的安慰都是徒劳，

整个世界喧嚣无比。

在这些诸事不顺的日子里，

当风儿莫名其妙地呼啸不止，

当你发现自己孤单一人时，

面朝太阳吧。

世界总有善和美，即便是泪水

even the river of tears cannot erase.

There is love in the world that the **numbed** armies of fear cannot destroy.

Sometimes that goodness is everywhere apparent.

It pours from the heart of every moment,

From the light of every smile.

On those soft days,

Love hides in the **caves** to drop like sweet honey on your forehead,

And sings her **lilting lullabies** in the arms of the winds.

But on some days, beloved.

On days like today...

We need to look, to see.

So turn your face to the sun.

Even when she is nowhere to be seen.

Go inside yourself. Find a **speck**, a **splinter** of beauty to be grateful for.

"Yes," the day has worn you. And "yes" our mistakes have been so many.

But say "thank you" anyway.

Take account of all that is in your possession.

A mind. A heart. A body.

A life that breathes, even if for just one more day.

Now count the eyes that have smiled at you on your wild journey,

The hands that have held you tenderly,

之河也无法将其冲掉。

世界总有关爱，即便是无情的恐惧也无法将其摧毁。

有时，那种美好随处可见，清晰明朗。

它来自每时每刻跳动的心，

来自每一个微笑。

在那些温和的日子里，

甜蜜的真爱由天而降，如蜂蜜落在你的额头上一样，

在和风的怀抱中唱着轻快的摇篮曲。

但是亲爱的，在有些日子里，

就像今天……

我们要放眼远望，仔细观察。

所以，面朝太阳吧。

即使太阳无处可寻。

走进自己的内心。寻找一处可以让你感激的点点美丽吧。

“是的”，生活让你精疲力竭。“是的”，我们犯下许多错误。

但不管怎样，请说声“谢谢”。

理清自己所拥有的一切：

思想，心灵，还有躯体。

还有一个会呼吸的生命，即便只剩一天。

现在数一数在你流浪的旅途中，曾经对你微笑过的眼睛，

曾经温柔地握着你的手，

The ears that have listened,
The prayers that have been made on your behalf.
And whisper your "thank you" again.

Count the sky that has watched you grow with his painted eyes,
The **heaving** waves that find their echo in the tides of your breathing,
The little birds that have sung you their songs,
The stars which have been a lamp to your path,
They are your rightful inheritance.
Count unexpected laughter,
Count undeserved grace,
Count passion and dreams yet to be born,
And bow your head and say "thank you",

Now count the lives who still need your light,
The hungry, the sick, the helpless,
Count the children who will die today,
And imagine if with the breath of your body,
You could help just one.
Turn your face to the sun,
And know yourself as a child of the light.
You are the goodness that cannot be

曾经倾听过你心声的耳朵，
曾经为你祈祷的声音，
然后，再次轻轻地说声"谢谢"吧。

数一数那用五彩斑斓的眼睛注视你成长的蓝天，
随着你呼吸的节奏而回响的起伏的波浪，
那些为你歌唱的鸟儿，
那些为你充当指路明灯的繁星，
它们皆是你应得的上天赠礼。
数一数突如其来的欢笑，
数一数不期而遇的恩惠，
数一数即将萌发的热情和梦想，
然后，低下头，道一声"谢谢"吧。

现在，数一数仍需要你照亮的生命，
那些饥饿的人，那些生病的人，那些无助的人，
数一数今天将要夭折的孩子，
试想假若你一息尚存，
你就能拯救他们，哪怕就一个。
面朝太阳吧，
你要清楚自己就如同光明之子。
你就是那不会消失的善良，

extinguished,

The love that burns through the darkest night.

是在最黑暗的夜晚燃起的真爱。

And perhaps,

In turning,

You will see what I have seen,

That this day where everything seemed wrong,

Was not your curse.

It was your gift,

Your chance...

To find inside yourself a forgotten "thank you",

To smile in the face of the **grim suppressors**,

To stand in the heart of the **glowering** darkness,

And turn your face to the sun.

也许，

在转身那一瞬，

你会明白我已经明白的，

看起来诸事不顺的一天，

并非是对你的诅咒。

而是生活给你的馈赠，

给你的一个机会……

在你的内心寻找那一句被遗忘的"谢谢"，

在充满挫折的生活面前微笑，

在弥漫的黑暗中站立起来，

面朝太阳吧。

魅力词汇

silken ['silkən] *adj.* 柔软光滑的

jagged ['dʒægid] *adj.* 锯齿状的，参差不齐的

scream [skriːm] *v.* 尖叫

erase [i'reiz] *v.* 除去，擦掉

numb [nʌm] *v.* 使……麻木，无动于衷

cave [keiv] *n.* 洞穴

lilting [liltiŋ] *adj.* 轻快的

lullaby ['lʌləbai] *n.* 摇篮曲

speck [spek] *n.* 小点；少量

splinter ['splintə] *n.* 尖片，碎片

heaving [hiːviŋ] *adj.* 起伏的

extinguish [ik'stiŋgwiʃ] *v.* 熄灭，使消亡，使破灭

grim [grim] *adj.* 无情的

suppressor [sə'presə] *n.* 镇压者

glowering ['glauəriŋ] *adj.* 阴森森的，恐怖的

6 Life Is Like a Coffee 生活是杯咖啡

生活像一杯浓咖啡，如果怀着囫囵吞枣的心态去对待它，只能尝到苦的滋味；如果用心细细品尝，则会是另一种味道：香甜，仿佛杯中盛着满满的一杯温情，使人品后更觉温暖。

文苑漫步

A group of **alumni**, highly established in their careers, got together to visit their old university professor. The conversation soon turned into complaints about stress in work and in life. Offering his guests coffee, the professor went to the kitchen and returned with a large pot of coffee and **an assortment of** cups — **porcelain**, plastic, glass, crystal, some plain-looking, some expensive, some **exquisite** — telling them to help themselves to the coffee.

When all the students had a cup of coffee in hand, the professor said:

"If you noticed, all the nice-looking expensive cups were taken up, leaving behind the plain and cheap ones. While

译林畅游

一群毕业生，各自在事业上都已有所建树，相约一起去看望他们年老的大学教授。谈话没过一会儿就变成了各自对工作和生活压力的抱怨。在用咖啡招待这些客人时，教授去厨房端来一大壶咖啡，并拿出各式各样的咖啡杯——陶瓷的、塑料的、玻璃的、水晶的，有看上去普通的、有价值不菲的、有做工精细的——让他们自己倒咖啡喝。

当所有学生手中都端了一杯咖啡后，教授发话了：

“如果你们注意一下，就会发现所有好看的昂贵的杯子都被挑走了，剩下的只是那些普通的和便宜

it is normal for you to want only the best for yourselves, that is the source of your problems and stress."

"What all of you really wanted was coffee, not the cup, but you consciously went for the best cups and were eyeing each other's cups."

"Now consider this: Life is the coffee and the jobs, money and position in society are the cups. They are just tools to hold and contain life, and do not change the quality of life. Sometimes, by **concentrating** only on the cup, we fail to enjoy the coffee God has provided. So, don't let the cups drive you... enjoy the coffee instead."

的。当然，每个人都只想拥有最好的，这很正常，但这也正是你们的问题和压力的根源所在。"

"其实你们真正想要的是咖啡，而不是杯子，但你们却又都下意识地去挑选最好的杯子，并观察别人拿到的杯子。"

"现在设想一下：如果生活是杯中的咖啡和工作，那么财富和社会地位就是那些杯子。它们只是维持生活的工具而已，并不改变生活的质量。有时候，我们在过于关注杯子的同时却忘了去品味上帝赐予的咖啡。所以，不要成为杯子的奴隶……好好品味杯中的咖啡。"

魅力词汇

alumnus [ə'lʌmnəs]
n. 男校友，男毕业生（复数形式 alumni）
an assortment [ə'sɔːtmənt] of
各种各样的

porcelain ['pɔːsəlin] *n.* 瓷
exquisite ['ekskwizit] *adj.* 精致的
concentrate ['kɔnsntreit]
v. 集中，全神贯注于

7 What's Love? 什么是爱?

要去喜爱面貌姣好或谈吐风趣的人很容易，但是要喜欢那些造成我们不便和不快的人却太难了。值得感激的是，不管我们变得多么糟糕，我们身边总有人会无条件地爱着我们。但是你的爱是无条件的吗？还是有条件的？

文苑漫步

A story is told about a soldier who was finally coming home from the war. He called his parents from San Francisco.

"Mom and Dad, I'm coming home, but I've a favor to ask. I have a friend I'd like to bring home with me."

"Sure!" they replied, "We'd love to meet him."

"There's something you should know," the son continued, "he was hurt pretty badly in the fighting. He stepped on a land mine and lost an arm and a leg. He has nowhere else to go, and I want him to come live with us."

"I'm sorry to hear that, son. Maybe we can help him find somewhere to live."

"No, Mom and Dad, I want him to

译林畅游

这是一个终于从战场归来的士兵的故事。他从旧金山打电话给他的父母：

“爸爸妈妈，我要回家了，可是我有个请求。我想带一个朋友和我一起回家。”

“当然好啊！”他们回答，“我们会很高兴见到他的。”

“有些事情你们应该了解，”儿子又继续说道，“他在战场上受了重伤。由于踩到了地雷，他失去了一只胳膊和一条腿，他现在无处可去，我想让他和我们一起生活。”

“儿子，听到那个我很难过，或许我们可以帮他找个安身之处。”

“不行，爸爸妈妈，我想让他和

live with us."

"Son," said the father, "you don't know what you're asking. Someone with such a **handicap** would be a terrible burden on us. We have our own lives to live, and we can't let something like this **interfere** with our lives. I think you should just come home and forget about this guy. He'll find a way to live on his own."

At that point, the son hung up the phone. The parents heard nothing more from him.

A few days later, however, they received a call from the San Francisco police. Their son had died after falling from a building, they were told. The police believed it was **suicide**. The **grief-stricken** parents flew to San Francisco and were taken to the city **morgue** to identify the body of their son.

They recognized him, but to their horror they had also discovered something they didn't know, their son had only one arm and one leg.

我们一起生活。"

"儿子，"父亲说，"你不知道自己在说些什么。像他这样的残疾人会对我们的生活造成很大的负担。我们还要过自己的生活，不能让这样的事情干扰我们的生活。我认为你应该先回家然后忘了他，他会找到自己的生活方式的。"

就在此时儿子挂断了电话，他的父母再也没有得到他的消息。

然而几天后，他们接到了旧金山的警察打来的电话，被告知他们的儿子已经坠楼身亡了。警方认为这是一起自杀案件。于是这对伤心欲绝的父母飞往旧金山，被带到停尸间去辨认儿子的遗体。

他们认出了他，但令他们感到惊骇的是，他们发现了之前不知道的一些事情：他们的儿子居然只有一只胳臂和一条腿。

魅力词汇

handicap ['hændikæp] *n.* 残疾
interfere [ˌintə'fiə] *v.* 干涉
suicide ['suːisaid] *n.* 自杀
grief-stricken ['griːfˌstrikən] *adj.* 极度悲伤的
morgue [mɔːg] *n.* 陈尸所

温情絮语

It is the tears of the earth that keep her smiles in bloom.

大地的泪珠使她的微笑保持着青春不谢。

A creek twines the vast green field just like the blue color satin ribbon, a distant place, modelling is being plain, color harmonious hut, a school of beantiful moving rural scenery!

一条条小河宛如蓝色的缎带缠绕着一望无际的绿色田野，远处是一座座造型古朴、色彩和谐的小屋，一派美丽动人的田园风光！

8 Four Seasons of Life
人生四季

人生路上既有寒冬的萧条，也有暖春的生机，既有秋的收获，也有夏的繁华。可是，一些人一遇到寒冬就沮丧了，放弃了，就算有再多的机会，也不敢去尝试，其实就放弃了所有的机会。生活中难免荆棘丛生，没必要为一时的失利而痛苦，所以请记住：不要为一时痛苦而放弃其他快乐。

文苑漫步

There was a man who had four sons. He wanted his sons to learn not to judge things too quickly. So he sent them each on a **quest**, in turn, to go and look at a pear tree that was a great distance away. The first son went in the winter, the second in the spring, the third in the summer, and the youngest son in the fall.

When they had all gone and come back, he called them together to describe what they had seen. The first son said that the tree was ugly, **bent**, and twisted. The second son said no — it was covered with green **buds** and full of promise. The third son disagreed. He said it **was laden with** blossoms that smelled so sweet and looked

译林畅游

从前有一个人，他有四个儿子。他希望儿子们能学会不急于对事物下结论，于是依次派四个儿子出去，让他们去很远的地方看一棵梨树。大儿子冬天前往，二儿子春天启程，三儿子夏天出发，而小儿子则是在秋天动身。

等他们都去过回来之后，这位父亲把他们叫到一起，让他们描述各自的所见。大儿子说梨树很难看，被压得很弯，枝干扭曲。二儿子却说并非如此——梨树绿芽初发，生机勃勃。三儿子不同意他们的看法，他说那棵梨树花苞满树，芬芳扑鼻，赏心悦目，是他见过的最美丽的东

so beautiful, and it was the most graceful thing he had ever seen. The last son disagreed with all of them; he said it was ripe and **drooping** with fruit, full of life and **fulfillment**.

西。小儿子的意见跟他们都不一样，他说那棵树果实累累，成熟在望，充满了生机和收获。

The man then explained to his sons that they were all right, because they had each seen but one season in the tree's life. He told them that they cannot judge a tree, or a person, by only one season, and that the **essence** of who they are — and the pleasure, joy, and love that come from that life — can only be measured at the end, when all the seasons are up.

这位父亲说他们答得都对，因为他们都只看到了梨树生命中的一个季节。他告诉他们：不应仅凭一个季节来判断一棵树，一段时间来看一个人的本质；最后，到所有的季节都已终结时，才能衡量一个人的本质——以及他生命中的快乐、喜悦和爱。

If you give up when it's winter, you will miss the promise of your spring, the beauty of your summer, fulfillment of your fall. Don't let the pain of one season destroy the joy of all the rest. Don't judge a life by one difficult season.

如果你在寒冬时放弃，你将错过春之希望，夏之灿烂，秋之收获。所以，不要让一时的痛苦毁弃所有其他的快乐。不要用一段艰难的时光来判定人生。

魅力词汇

quest [kwest] *n.* 追求，寻找
bent [bent] *adj.* 弯曲的
bud [bʌd] *n.* 芽
be laden with 充满，载满
drooping ['dru:piŋ] *adj.* 下垂的
fulfillment [ful'filmənt] *n.* 实现，完成
essence ['esəns] *n.* 本质，实质

9 A Moment of Joy 片刻的欢乐

人们可能不会完全记住你所做的事，或者你所说的话……但他们却会永远记住你带给他们的感觉。老妇人记得那片刻的欢愉，这趟旅程便足够了。

文苑漫步

Twenty years ago, I drove a **cab** for a living. It was a cowboy's life, a life for someone who wanted no boss.

What I didn't realize was that it was also a ministry. Because I drove the night **shift**, my cab became a moving **confessional**. Passengers climbed in, sat behind me in total **anonymity**, and told me about their lives. I encountered people whose lives amazed me, **ennobled** me, made me laugh and weep, but none touched me more than a woman I picked up late one August night.

I was responding to a call from a small brick **fourplex** in a quiet part of town. I assumed I was being sent to pick up some people who had been partying, or someone who had just had a fight with a lover, or a worker heading to an early shift

译林畅游

二十年前，我以开出租车为生。这是一种富有冒险精神的生活，适合那些不想受老板管制的人。

开始我没有意识到它也是一种牧师职业。由于上夜班，我的出租车就成为一个流动的忏悔室。素不相识的乘客们爬进车里，坐在我后面，然后给我讲述他们的生活。我遇到过很多人，有些人的生活让我感到惊奇，有些人的生活让我肃然起敬，有些人带给我欢笑，有些人让我哭泣。然而最使我感动的，是在八月的一个晚上乘车的一位老妇人。

我接到从一座砖造四套公寓住宅小楼打来的电话。我想可能是让我去那里接一个参加舞会的人，或者刚与爱人打过架的人，或者要去城镇工业区的某个工厂赶早班的

at some factory for the industrial part of town.

When I arrived at 2:30 a.m., the building was dark except for a single light in a ground floor window. Under these circumstances, many drivers would just **honk** once or twice, wait a minute, then drive away. But I had seen too many **impoverished** people who depended on taxis as their only means of transportation. Unless a situation smelled of danger, I always went to the door. The passenger might be someone who needs my assistance, I reasoned to myself. So I walked to the door and knocked.

"Just a minute," answered a **frail**, elderly voice. I could hear something being dragged across the floor. After a long pause, the door opened. A small woman in her 80s stood before me. She was wearing a **print** dress and a **pillbox** hat with a veil pinned on it, like somebody out of a 1940's movie. By her side was a small nylon suitcase.

The apartment looked as if no one had lived in it for years. All the furniture was covered with **sheets**. There were no clocks on the walls, no **knickknacks** or **utensils** on the counters. In the corner was a cardboard box filled with photos and **glassware**.

工人。

凌晨两点半我赶到的时候，楼里除了第一层窗户那儿亮着一盏孤灯外，漆黑一片。在这种情况下，很多司机都是按一两下喇叭，等一会儿，然而就开车离开了。但我见过太多穷困的人们，他们把出租车作为唯一的交通工具。除非嗅到危险的气氛，我总是会走到门前。这位乘客也许需要我的帮助，我为自己找理由。于是我走到门前，敲门。

"请等一下，"一个虚弱而苍老的声音答道。我能听到在地板上拖东西的声音，过了好一会儿，门开了。一位 80 多岁的弱小老妇人站在我面前。她穿着印花外套，戴着别有面纱的筒状女帽，就像从 20 世纪 40 年代的电影里走出来的人。她身旁是一个小型的尼龙手提箱。

这座公寓看上去好像很多年没人住过了，所有的家具都用帆布蒙着，墙上没有挂钟，柜台上也没有任何装饰物或家用器具。墙角放着一个纸箱，里面堆满了照片和玻璃器皿。

"Would you carry my bag out to the car?" she said.

"你能帮我把包拿到车上吗？"她说。

I took the suitcase to the cab, then returned to assist the woman. She took my arm and we walked slowly toward the cab. She kept thanking me for my kindness.

我把箱子放到车上，又回来搀扶老妇人。她挽住我的胳膊，我们慢慢走到车旁。她不停地感谢我的好心。

"It's nothing," I told her. "I just try to treat my passengers the way I would want my mother treated."

"没什么，"我对她说，"我只是在用我期望我的母亲被对待的方式来对待我的乘客。"

"Oh, you're such a good boy," she said.

"哦，你真是个好孩子。"她说。

When she got in the cab, she gave me an address, then asked, "Could you drive through downtown?"

她上车后递给我一个地址，然后又问道："你能从城镇中心穿过去吗？"

"It's not the shortest way," I answered quickly.

"那不是最近的路。"我很快回答。

"Oh, I don't mind," she said. "I'm in no hurry. I'm on my way to a **hospice**."

"哦，没关系，"她说，"我不急着赶路，我就要去临终关怀医院了。"

I looked in the **rearview** mirror. Her eyes were **glistening**. "I don't have any family left," she continued. "The doctor says I don't have…"

我从后视镜看了看，她的眼睛闪着光。她继续说着："我没有任何家人了，医生说我没有……"

I quietly reached over and shut off the meter.

我轻轻地伸手关掉了计量表。

"What route would you like me to take?" I asked.

"您想让我走哪条路线？"我问。

For the next two hours, we drove through the city. She showed me the building where she had once worked as an elevator operator. We drove through the

接下来的两个小时，我们开车穿过了整个城市。她指给我看当年她做电梯操作员的那座大厦，她和她的丈夫当年新婚时生活过的小

neighborhood where she and her husband had lived when they were **newlyweds**. She had me pull up in front of a furniture warehouse that had once been a ballroom where she had gone dancing as a girl.

区，她让我在一家家具商店前面停车，那儿以前是个舞厅，她还是个小姑娘时常去那儿跳舞。

Sometimes she'd ask me to slow in front of a particular building or corner and would sit staring into the darkness, saying nothing.

有时经过一个特殊的大楼或角落时她会让我放慢车速，她会坐在那里注视着夜空，默默无语。

As the first **hint** of sun was ceasing on the horizon, she suddenly said, "I'm tired. Let's go now."

当第一缕阳光打破了地平线，她突然说："我累了，咱们现在就走吧。"

We drove in silence to the address she had given me. It was a low building, like a small **convalescent** home, with a driveway that passed under a **portico**.

我们默默地驱车向她给我的那个地址驶去。那是一座低矮的楼房，就像一个小疗养院，在门廊的下面有一条车道。

Two **orderlies** came out to the cab as soon as we pulled up. They were **solicitous** and **intent**, watching her every move. They must have been expecting her. I opened the **trunk** and took the small suitcase to the door. The woman was already seated in a wheelchair.

我们刚停车，就有两个护理员向我们走来。她们关切而热心地注视着她的一举一动，看样子一定是在等着她的到来。我打开车尾的行李箱，把她的小型手提箱提到门口。老妇人已经坐进一个轮椅里了。

"How much do I owe you?" she asked, reaching into her purse.

"我该给你多少钱？"她边说边把手伸进钱包。

"Nothing," I said.

"不用了。"我说。

"You have to make a living," she answered.

"你得谋生呢，"她说。

"There are other passengers," I responded.

"还有其他的乘客。"我回答。

Almost without thinking, I bent and gave her a hug. She held onto me tightly.

"You gave an old woman a little moment of joy," she said. "Thank you."

I **squeezed** her hand, then walked into the dim morning light. Behind me, a door shut. It was the sound of the closing of a life.

I didn't pick up any more passengers that shift. I drove aimlessly, lost in thought. For the rest of that day, I could hardly talk. What if that woman had gotten an angry driver, or one who was impatient at the end of his shift? What if I had refused to take the run, or had honked once, then driven away? On a quick review, I don't think that I have done anything more important in my life.

We **are conditioned to** think that our lives **revolve** around great moments. But great moments often catch us unaware — beautifully wrapped in what others may consider a small one. People may not remember exactly what you did, or what you said, but they will always remember how you made them feel.

Take a moment to stop and appreciate the memories you have made, the memory making opportunities around you and make someone feel special today.

几乎想也没想，我弯下腰拥抱了她一下。她也紧紧地抱着我。

"你给了一个老妇人片刻的欢乐，"她说，"谢谢你。"

我紧紧地握了握她的手，便走进了微弱的晨光中。我身后的门关上了。这也是生命结束的声音。

那晚我没有再拉其他的乘客。我漫无方向地开着车，陷入沉思中。那天剩余的时间，我几乎说不出话。如果那位老妇人碰到一位狂暴的司机，或者急着结束晚班的司机，会发生什么呢？如果我拒绝跑这趟车，或者只是按一声喇叭，便开车离开，会发生什么呢？匆忙回顾了一下，我认为我做了一件生命中再重要不过的事情。

我们习惯性地认为我们的生命围绕着一些重大的时刻旋转，然而重大的时刻往往在不经意时降临到我们身上——带着别人看起来是小事的美丽妆扮。人们可能不会完全记住你所做的事，或者你所说的话……但他们却会永远记住你带给他们的感觉。

花上片刻的时间，停下脚步欣赏一下你的回忆，那些为周围的人创造了机会的回忆，那些使他人今天感觉很特别的回忆。

魅力词汇

cab [kæb] *n.* 出租汽车
shift [ʃift] *n.* 轮班
confessional [kən'feʃənəl] *n.* 忏悔室，告解室
anonymity [ænə'nimәti] *n.* 匿名者
ennoble [i'nəubl] *v.* 增加对……的尊敬
fourplex ['fɔːpleks] *n.* [美] 四套公寓住宅楼
honk [hɔŋk] *v.* 按汽车喇叭
impoverished [im'pɔvəriʃt] *adj.* 穷困的
frail [freil] *adj.* 虚弱的
print [print] *n.* 印花布
pillbox ['pilbɔks] *n.* 矮圆筒形女帽
sheet [ʃiːt] *n.* 帆布；床单
knickknack ['niknæk] *n.* 小摆设，小装饰物
utensil [juː'tensəl] *n.* 用具，器皿
glassware ['glɑːsweə] *n.* 玻璃器皿
hospice ['hɔspis] *n.* 安乐护理医院，临终关怀医院
rearview ['riəvjuː] *n.* 后视镜
glisten ['gliːsn] *v.* 闪耀，发光
newlywed ['njuːliwed] *n.* 新婚者
hint [hint] *n.* 细微的迹象
convalescent [kɔnvə'lesənt] *adj.* 康复的
portico ['pɔːtikəu] *n.* [建] 门廊
orderly ['ɔːdəli] *n.* 护理员
solicitous [sə'lisitəs] *adj.* 热心的
intent [in'tent] *adj.* 专心的；热切的
trunk [trʌŋk] *n.* 汽车车尾的行李箱
squeeze [skwiːz] *v.* 紧握
be conditioned to 习惯于
revolve [ri'vɔlv] *v.* 旋转，绕转

温情絮语

The sands in your way beg for your song and your movement, dancing water, will you carry the burden of their lameness?

舞动的流水呀，你途中所遇的泥沙，请求听你的歌声，随着你流动，你肯挟瘸足的泥沙而俱下吗？

White clouds flow in the blue sky like quiet fish swimming in broad ocean.

白云朵朵飘在蓝天中，就像静静的鱼儿在广阔的海洋中畅游。

10 Chief Seattle's Thoughts 西雅图宣言

每个人来到这个世界上，都会发出一种追问，何处是自己生命的原点？读《西雅图宣言》，你的心灵会受到极大震撼，原来生命的原点就是你的自身，就在你的身边，空气、山峦、河流、草木、太阳和星光，它们与你的生命息息相关，缕缕相连，互为一体。读《西雅图宣言》，你会热泪纵横，思绪潮涌……西雅图酋长，人类环保的先声；他的宣言，是一部人与自然的永恒启示录。在现代人患上了形形色色的都市病之时，人们重新思考每一片绿叶的价值，重聚自然界绿色力量的今天，请再读一读《西雅图宣言》吧，让人类幽暗的心灵里多几缕明丽的阳光……

文苑漫步

How can you buy or sell the sky, the warmth of the land? The idea is strange to us. If we do not own the freshness of the air and the sparkle of the water, how can you buy them?

Every part of the Earth is **sacred** to my people. Every shining pine needle, every sandy shore, every mist in the dark woods, every clear and **humming** insect is holy in the memory and experience of my people. The **sap** which courses through the trees carries the memories of the red man.

The white man's dead forget the country of their birth when they go to walk

译林畅游

你怎能把天空、大地的温馨买下？我们不懂。若空气失去了新鲜，流水失去了晶莹，你怎能把它们买下？

每一方土地对我们红人来说都是圣洁的。在我们的记忆里，我们的经历中，每一根晶亮的松针，每一片沙滩，每一撮深林里的气息，每一种引人自省、鸣叫的昆虫都是神圣的。树液的芳香在林中穿越，也渗透了红人自亘古以来的记忆。

白人死后漫游星际之时，早忘了生他的大地。红人死后永不忘我

among the stars. Our dead never forget this beautiful Earth, for it is the mother of the red man. We are part of the Earth and it is part of us. The **perfumed** flowers are our sisters, the deer, the horse, the great eagle, these are our brothers. The rocky **crests**, the juices in the **meadows**, the body heat of the pony, and the man, all belong to the same family.

们美丽的出生地。因为，大地是我们的母亲，母子连心，为一体。芬芳的花朵是我们的姐妹，鹿、马、雄鹰都是我们的兄弟。山岩峭壁、草原上的露水、人和马身上所散发出的体热，都属于同一个家园。

So, when the Great Chief in Washington sends word that he wishes to buy our land, he asks much of us. The Great White Chief sends word he will reserve us a place so that we can live comfortably to ourselves. He will be our father and we will be his children. So we will consider your offer to buy land. But it will not be easy. For this land is sacred to us.

因此当华盛顿的大总统传话来说要买我们的土地时，也询问了很多关于我们的事情。白人大统领说，会留下一块保护地，留给我们过安逸的日子。这么一来，大统领成了我们的父亲，我们成了他的子女。因此，我们会考虑你想要买地的提议，但这买卖不是那么容易，因为这块土地对我们来说是圣洁的。

This shining water that moves in streams and rivers is not just water but the blood of our ancestors. If we sell you land, you must remember that it is sacred blood of our ancestors. If we sell you land, you must remember that it is sacred, and you must teach your children that it is sacred and that each ghostly reflection in the clear water of the lakes tells of events in the life of my people. The waters murmur is the voice of my father's father.

小溪和河流里的晶晶流水不仅是水，更是我们世代祖先的血液。如若卖地给你，务请牢记，这块土地流淌着我们时代祖先圣洁的血液。如若卖地给你，务请牢记，这地是圣洁的，务请教导你的子子孙孙，这地是圣洁的。湖中清水里的每一种映像，都代表一种灵，诉说着我们的生活事迹。流水的低语声是我们祖先的声音。

The rivers of our brothers they **quench** our thirst. The rivers carry our canoes and feed our children. If we sell

河流是我们的兄弟，它为我们解渴，运送我们的独木舟，养育我们的子女。若要卖地给你，务请记

you our land, you must remember to teach your children that the rivers are our brothers, and yours, and you must **henceforth** give the rivers the kindness that you would give my brother. We know that the white man does not understand our ways. One **portion** of land is the same to him as the next, for he is a stranger who comes in the night and takes from the land whatever he needs. The Earth is not his brother, but his enemy and when he has conquered it, he moves on.

得，务请教导你的子女，河流是我们的兄弟，也是你们的兄弟。自此以后，你们要仁慈地对待它，就像对待我的兄弟一样。我们知道，白人不能体会我们的想法。在白人眼里，哪一块地都一样，因为他是趁夜打劫的陌生人，他从这块土地上索取他所需要的一切。对白人来说，大地不是他的兄弟，而是他的仇敌，他要一一征服。

He leaves his father's graves behind, and he does not care. He **kidnaps** the Earth from his children, and he does not care. His father's grave, and his children's birthright are forgotten. He treats his mother, the Earth, and his brother, the same, as things to be bought, **plundered**, sold like sheep or bright beads. His appetite will **devour** the Earth and leave behind only a desert.

白人弃父亲的墓地于不顾，从子子孙孙那里攫取土地，也一点不在乎。父亲的安息之地，儿女的权利，他可以不放在心上。在他看来，他的大地母亲以及他的兄弟都像物品一样可以随意买下、掠夺，或像羊群或明亮的珠子一样卖出。他贪得无厌，大口大口吞食土地之后，任由大地成为片片荒漠。

I do not know. Our ways are different from your ways. The sight of your cities pains the eyes of the red man. But perhaps it is because the red man is a **savage** and does not understand.

我不懂。你我的生活方式完全不同。红人的眼睛只要一看见你们的城市就觉得疼痛。或许是因为红人还尚未开化，不能理解吧。

There is no quiet place in the white man's cities. No place to hear the **unfurling** of leaves in spring, or the **rustle** of an insect's wings. But perhaps it is because I am a savage and do not understand. The

白人的城市里没有安静之地，没地方可以听到春天里树叶临风招展的声音，也听不见昆虫振翅作乐的声音。或许是因为我还尚未开化，不能理解吧。城市的噪音侵犯了我

clatter only seems to insult the ears. And what is there to life if a man cannot hear the lonely cry of a **whippoorwill** or the arguments of the frogs around a pond at night.

们的双耳。如果一个人在夜间听不到池塘边青蛙在争论，也听不见北美夜鹰的孤独的鸣叫，这种生活，算是活着？

I am a red man and do not understand. The Indian prefers the soft sound of the wind **darting** over the face of the pond, the smell of the wind itself, **cleansed** by a midday rain, or scented with the **pinon** pine.

我是红人，我不懂。清风的声音轻轻扫过池塘的水面，清风的芳香，是经午后雨露洗涤或浸过松香的，这才是红人所愿听愿闻的。

The air is precious to the red man, for all things share the same breath — the beast, the tree, the man, they all share the same breath. The white man does not seem to notice the air he breathes. Like a man dying for many days, he is numb to the **stench**. But if we sell you our land, you must remember that the air is precious to us, that the air shares its spirit with all the life it supports.

红人珍爱大气，所有一切都共享一种气息——野兽、树木还有人类都分享着同一种气息。白人似乎不会注意他要靠空气才能存活，像一个死去多日的人，对恶臭已经麻木。但若卖地给你，务请牢记，我们珍爱大气，空气养育着所有的生命，它的灵力，人人有份。

The wind that gave our grandfather his first breath also receives his last **sigh**. If we sell you our land, you must keep it apart and sacred, as a place where even the white man can go to taste the wind that is sweetened by the meadow's flowers.

风，迎着我祖父出生时的第一口气，也送走它最后一声的叹息。如若卖地给你，务请将它划为圣地，使白人也能闻到风中来自牧草地上的花香。

So we will consider your offer to buy our land. If we decide to accept, I will make one condition — the white man must treat the beasts of this land as his brothers.

因此，我们将考虑你们要购买我们的土地的提议。如果我们决定接受，我会有一个条件——白人必须像对待兄弟一样对待这块土地上的野兽。

I am a savage and do not understand

我是个尚未开化的人，不明白

any other way. I have seen a thousand rotting **buffaloes** on the **prairie**, left by the white man who shot them from a passing train. I am a savage and do not understand how the smoking iron horse can be made more important than the buffalo that we kill only to stay alive.

其他任何方式。我看到白人在行进的火车上射杀的数千头野牛在大草原上腐烂。我是个尚未开化的人，我无法理解那冒烟的“铁皮大马”怎么就会比我们用来维持生存才宰杀的野牛更重要。

What is man without the beasts? If all the beasts were gone, man would die from a great loneliness of the spirit. For whatever happens to the beasts, soon happens to man. All things are connected.

人在没有了野兽之后会变得怎样呢？如果所有的野兽都消失了，那么人类也会在灵魂深处的巨大寂寞中死去。因为任何发生在野兽身上的也会发生在人身上。万事万物都是息息相关的。

You must teach your children that the ground beneath their feet is the ashes of our grandfathers. So that they will respect the land, tell your children that the Earth is rich with the lives of our **kin**. Teach your children what we have taught our children, that the Earth is our mother. Whatever **befalls** the Earth befalls the sons of the Earth. If men spit upon the ground, they spit upon themselves.

务请教导你们的子女，他们脚下的土地埋着我们祖先的骨骸；告诉你们的子女，大地因我们亲族的生命而滋润，以便他们能够尊崇大地；请教给你们的子女我们所教给子女的：大地是我们的母亲。大地的命运，就是人类的命运，人若唾弃大地，就是在唾弃自己。

This we know — the Earth does not belong to man — man belongs to the Earth. This we know. All things are connected like the blood which unites one family. All things are connected.

我们确知一事——大地并不属于人类——人类，属于大地。这是我们知道的。世界万物皆相连，如血缘团结一家亲。万事万物都是息息相关的。

Whatever befalls the Earth — befalls the sons of the Earth. Man did not **weave** the web of life — he is merely a **strand** in it. Whatever he does to the web, he does to himself.

大地的命运，就是人类的命运。人类并不是编织生命之网的主宰，他只不过是其中一根丝线而已。无论人类对这个网做了什么，都会回应到自己身上。

Even the white man, whose God walks and talks with him as friend to friend, cannot be exempt from the common destiny. We may be brothers after all. We shall see. One thing we know, which the white man may one day discover — Our God is the same God. You may think now that you own Him as you wish to own our land, but you cannot. He is the God of man, and His compassion is equal for red man and the white. The Earth is precious to Him, and to harm the Earth is to **heap contempt** on its creator. The whites too shall pass, perhaps sooner than all other tribes.

虽然白人的上帝与他并肩齐步，和他交谈犹如朋友，但白人也无法豁免于同样的命运。也许，你我都是兄弟。等着看，我们知道，也许有一天白人会发现：他们所信的上帝，与我们所信的神，是同一位神。或许，你以为可以拥有上帝，像你想要拥有我们的土地一样。其实你办不到，上帝，是全人类的神，上帝对人类怜恤平等，不分红人与白人。上帝视大地为至宝，伤害大地就是亵渎大地的创造者。白人也终将消失，说不定比其他种族消失得更快。

But in your perishing you will shine brightly, fired by the strength of the God who brought you to this land for some special purpose, gave you dominion over this land and over the red man. That destiny is a mystery to us, for we do not understand when the buffalo are **slaughtered**, the wild horses **tamed**, the secret corners of the forest heavy with scent of many men, and the view of the ripe hills **blotted** by talking wires.

但即使你们死了，也会靠着上帝给你们的力量在世上灿烂发光，祂因着一些特别的目的而引领你们来到这片土地，赐予你们统治这片土地和红人的权利。这种命运让我们费解，因为我们不懂，为什么野牛会被杀戮，野马会被驯服，森林的秘密角落里布满了人群的异味，优美的山景，全被电话线玷污。

Where is the **thicket**? Gone.

Where is the eagle? Gone.

The end of living and the beginning of survival.

丛林在哪里？没了。

雄鹰在哪里？不见了。

生命的尽头，幸存者的开始。

魅力词汇

sacred ['seikrid] *adj.* 神圣的
hum ['hʌm] *v.* 发嗡嗡声
sap [sæp] *n.* 树液
perfumed [pə'fju:md] *adj.* 芳香的，香味的
crest [krest] *n.* 坡顶，山顶
meadow ['medəu] *n.* 草地
quench [kwentʃ] *v.* 解（渴）
henceforth [ˌhens'fɔ:θ] *adv.* 今后，自此以后
portion ['pɔ:ʃn] *n.* 部分，一份
kidnap ['kidnæp] *v.* 绑架，劫持
plunder ['plʌndə] *v.* 掠夺，抢劫，侵吞
devour [di'vauə] *v.* 吞食
savage ['sævidʒ] *n.* 未开化的人，野蛮人
unfurl [ˌʌn'fə:l] *v.* 使……临风招展
rustle ['rʌsl] *n.* 沙沙声，窸窣声
clatter ['klætə] *n.* 噪声，喧哗声
whippoorwill ['wipəwil] *n.*［鸟］北美夜鹰
dart [dɑ:t] *v.* 猛冲
cleanse [klenz] *v.* 使……纯净
pinon ['pinjən] *n.*［植］矮松
stench [stentʃ] *n.* 恶臭，臭气
sigh [sai] *v.* 叹息，叹气
buffalo ['bʌfələu] *n.* 水牛，野牛
prairie ['preəri] *n.* 大草原
kin [kin] *n.* 亲戚，家族，同族
befall [bi'fɔ:l] *v.* 降临，发生
weave [wi:v] *v.* 编织
strand [strænd] *n.* 线
heap [hi:p] *v.* 堆积
contempt [kən'tempt] *n.* 轻视，蔑视
slaughter ['slɔ:tə] *v.* 屠宰，屠杀
tame [teim] *v.* 驯养
blot [blɔt] *v.* 涂污，弄脏
thicket ['θikit] *n.* 灌木丛，丛林

温情絮语

Rivers Know this: there is no hurry, we shall get there some day.

河流懂得一个道理：无需匆忙，该到的地方终有一天会到达。

A right color bright, fine gorgeous, is drafting the happy love sabot likely! Also has that magnificent tulip to fall the season which innumerable sweetheart...

一对对色彩鲜艳、精致绚丽，象征着甜蜜爱情的木鞋！还有那华丽的郁金香倾倒无数情人……